1804

DISRAELI

ON

WHIGS AND WHIGGISM

Disraeli the Younger,
from a dry point etching by
James McBey

WHIGS AND WHIGGISM

POLITICAL WRITINGS

BY BENJAMIN DISRAELI

EDITED, WITH AN INTRODUCTION, BY
WILLIAM HUTCHEON

WITH ILLUSTRATIONS

SIR ADAM FERGUSON: But, Sir, in the British Constitution it is surely of importance to keep up a spirit in the people, so as to preserve a balance against the Crown.

DR. JOHNSON: Sir, I perceive you are a vile Whig.

BOSWELL : *Life of Johnson.*

NEW YORK
THE MACMILLAN COMPANY
1914

PREFATORY NOTE

THE suggestion for the preparation of a volume of by-products of Disraeli's pen came from Mr. John Murray; for the selection and treatment I alone am responsible. I have to acknowledge Mr. Murray's helpful counsel and encouragement, and I have also to express my thanks to Mr. Coningsby Disraeli for advice willingly rendered; to the proprietors of the *Morning Post* for special facilities for the identification of Disraeli's contributions to that journal; to Mr. T. E. Kebbel; to Sir James Murray; to Messrs. Maggs Brothers for permission to reproduce the Disraeli letters in facsimile from the originals in their possession; and to Mr. B. L. O'Malley for his criticisms and suggestions. Lastly, I cannot but make grateful acknowledgment of my wife's co-operation, which has made the work a pleasure.

It should be noted that the frontispiece, from a dry-point by my friend, Mr. James McBey, does not profess to be an actual portrait. It is rather an endeavour to realise the Young Disraeli from the published descriptions of the period, with the well-known portrait by A. E. Chalon, R.A., in the possession of Mr. Coningsby Disraeli, as a basis.

W. H.

v

CONTENTS

[Those of Disraeli's political writings which are now reprinted for the first time are indicated by an asterisk; that portion which has been previously republished in book form, but which is not now readily accessible, is indicated by a dagger.]

ILLUSTRATIONS

DISRAELI ON WHIGS AND WHIGGISM

INTRODUCTION

I

THE contents of this volume call for no elaborate introduction. Some of them are familiar to close students of
the life and works of Disraeli, and by reputation to a
wider circle. The rest are here republished for the first
time. The early life of Disraeli is a mine in which many
men have quarried. Every known biographical vein has
been exhausted, and the output has been turned over,
sifted, and analysed by hundreds of hands. The book-
shelves of the British Museum indeed bear notable
evidence of the monumental industry of Disraeli's anno-
tators, both at home and abroad. But it fell to the lot
of the late Mr. Monypenny, through the private papers
placed at his disposal, to indicate the existence of unsus-
pected seams in which new material might be found.
These have now been systematically explored, and that
portion which has been considered of permanent value
has been brought to the surface, and is here made available to the public. Disraeli contributed freely to the
Press in the thirties, at a time when he was struggling to
obtain a foothold in politics. Those contributions varied
in quality and interest. Not all were worthy of being
rescued from the dusty files in which they were embedded.
The others, however, will probably be welcomed by those
—and the number is steadily growing—who follow with
interest the various phases of the career of that marvel-

1

lously diversified personality. It has been thought well
to go outside the period so far covered by the authoritative "Life" now in process of publication, and to open
for a moment the pages of a later chapter, when, after a
lapse of over ten years, Disraeli renewed his connection
with journalism. That chapter has yet to be written
from inside knowledge, and very absorbing it should prove.
For present purposes, however, two extracts only are
given from his anonymous contributions to his own
periodical, *The Press*, which was founded in 1853.   To
facilitate comparison and research, and to complete
the record of Disraeli's political writings of the period,
there are included the "Vindication," the Runnymede
Letters, and other known works. Readers will thus be
enabled to trace for themselves at first-hand, in a setting
deliberately kept free from party bias, the gradual evolution of a career that in its opening stages offered so many
enigmas to the historian, and has been so diversely inter-
preted.

The period of Disraeli's greatest journalistic activity
was that between the passing of the Reform Act in 1832
and the breaking of the Whig power in 1841. It marked
a stage of much importance in the political development
of the young statesman. Through all those writings the
insistent note is that of fierce and uncompromising hostility to Whigs and Whiggism, and to Lord Melbourne as
their official exponent. It makes itself heard in the first
sentence of "What is He?" (1833)—a tiny and much
canvassed pamphlet which, though written in advocacy
of the formation of a national party, is quoted by his
critics and enemies as showing that he was at the time
at heart a Radical. It becomes more pronounced in
"The Crisis Examined" (1834), the manifesto which
marked his definite alliance with the Conservative party.
The note becomes vehement in his articles in the *Morning
Post* in the summer of 1835, and still more vehement in
the Letters of Runnymede and other subsequent contributions to the columns of the *Times*. In the more

matured letters "To the Whigs" in *The Press* of 1853,
there is a searching and acute analysis of the causes of
their decay as a political factor. Whatever taunts may
be levelled at Disraeli's inconsistency, he was at least
unchanging in his whole - hearted hatred of Whig
rule.

During the earlier of those busy years the dominant
influence was that of Lord Lyndhurst. In "Vivian
Grey" (1826) Disraeli foreshadowed the future with
prophetic accuracy. "At this moment," exclaims the
hero, "how many a powerful noble wants only wit to
be a Minister; and what wants Vivian Grey to attain the
same end? That noble's influence. When two persons
can so materially assist each other, why are they not
brought together? Shall I, because my birth baulks my
fancy, shall I pass my life a moping misanthrope in an
old château?" Assuredly there was little of the "moping
misanthrope" about Disraeli. Into the years between
1831, when he returned from a prolonged tour in the
East, and 1837, when he entered Parliament as Member
for Maidstone, he crowded much varied life. He had the
qualities necessary to ensure success in politics—youth,
an acute intellect, a mind broadened by travel and reading, a brilliant pen, and, like Vivian Grey, he "could
perform right skilfully upon the most splendid of musical
instruments, the human voice." He had a genius for
political missionary work, and an extraordinary acquaintance with men and things. He combined with these
advantages a force and dash that were ruthless where a
political end was to be gained. A man of such varied
parts, endowed by Nature with a striking personality
accentuated by an extreme coxcombry of dress, was
bound to be buzzed about in society, and his growing
fame in politics was aided by his growing fame in literature.

The meeting with his patron in July, 1834, was marked
by instant and mutual confidence. Lyndhurst had ambitions, and needed Disraeli's pen; Disraeli had ambitions,

and needed Lyndhurst's influence. Probably one of the
first results of the alliance was the publication a few
months later of "The Crisis Examined." Politics at the
moment were full of interest. Disraeli was entering on
his third unsuccessful contest for High Wycombe; his
future rival, Gladstone, was already Member for Newark.
Indeed, on the very day (December 16) that Disraeli,
addressing the Wycombe electors, was taking his fateful
political plunge, there was in the post the letter from Peel,
the Tory Prime Minister, that led to Gladstone's first
brief tenure of office. For the Government in which Melbourne had succeeded Grey as Prime Minister had been
summarily dismissed by the King in November. There
had been numerous changes in its personnel, and the
King had become disgusted. As Disraeli put it in his
familiar simile, the six horses on which Ducrow had undertaken to ride round the arena had been replaced by
donkeys. But the Peel Ministry, in which Lyndhurst
took the Great Seal, lived but a few months, and with
the defeat of Disraeli for Wycombe, the return of Melbourne for the second time as the Minister "not of the
King's choice, but of the King's necessity," and the rele-
gation of Lyndhurst once more to Opposition, crumbled
glorious dreams.

II

Lyndhurst was what in latter-day politics would be
termed a "Diehard," and in Disraeli he saw the eager
dare-devilry of a master-controversialist. The opportunity for united action was not long delayed. During
Lyndhurst's brief Chancellorship he gave a dinner-party
which is historic as being that at which Gladstone and
Disraeli, the great protagonists of the Victorian era,
first met round the same table. To this dinner may,
perhaps, be traced the series of articles which Disraeli
contributed to the *Morning Post* in the summer of the
same year (1835). Another of the guests was Winthrop
Mackworth Praed, at the moment terminating his asso-

ciation with the *Morning Post* as a contributor of graceful prose and verse in order to take a place in Peel's Ministry ; and so, when opposition to the Municipal Corporations Bill was being organised by the "Diehards," what more natural than that, through Lyndhurst's influence, Disraeli should be the chosen writer, and that, through Praed's influence, the *Morning Post* should be the chosen journal, to voice the views of the leaders of the campaign ?

The origin of the articles may be stated in a few sentences. Melbourne, on his return to office, had set himself the task of reforming the Municipal Corporations of the country. The Commission which had been appointed in 1833 to inquire into municipal abuses had issued its report, and on June 5, 1835, Lord John Russell, as leader of the House of Commons, introduced the Municipal Corporations Bill. It was read a second time on June 15, was in Committee for about a month, and was sent to the House of Lords, without material change, on July 21. Here there was mustered a strong majority opposed to reform. Lyndhurst took the direction of affairs in his own hands, and under his masterful leadership the Tory peers decided to fight the Bill inch by inch. They introduced and carried amendments which had been rejected in the Commons, and there was soon much talk of the inevitability of a "collision" between the Peers and the People. For a time the position was threatening, but the progress of the Bill was delayed for only a few weeks. The House of Commons refused to accept the more drastic alterations, Peel discountenanced Lyndhurst's extreme methods, Wellington advised compromise, and in the end the House of Lords, while holding its own on some points, gave way on others, and the "crisis" passed.

Disraeli's authorship of the *Morning Post* articles was revealed by the following entry in his diary for September, 1835:

"Wrote the 'M.P.' during the English Municipal Bill for L—— three leading articles a day for nearly a month."

These articles, and many further contributions to the *Times* in subsequent years, were written for political and not pecuniary reward. Disraeli was never a "hired scribbler of the Press "; he has himself recorded that his sole object in writing for the newspapers at the time was to connect himself with a man who had already been a Minister, and who was destined to take a conspicuous part in public affairs, and to establish a claim upon him which might some day be useful. His connection with the *Post* was kept a profound secret. Even to his sister Sarah, throughout her life the repository of his secrets, he wrote mysteriously on August 20 about a great unknown whose exploits in the *Post* formed almost the sole staple of conversation. "All attempts at discovering the writer," he added, "have been baffled, and the mystery adds to the keen interest which the articles excite."

The contributions of that week contained really little that was distinctive or that would merit reproduction; but in the following week, when the Bill reached Committee in the Lords, and Lord Lyndhurst was overwhelming it with drastic amendments, there was ferment everywhere. Disraeli, who pooh-poohed the outcry as manufactured clamour, was in his element. From August 22 onward there appeared a series of articles the brilliance, pungency, and vigour of which may well have set political London talking. The invective was unsparing, rough, and occasionally even coarse, but the literary power was marked. That able journalist, the late W. T. Arnold, used to trace a relation between the pace at which a thing was read and that at which it was written, and one of the means by which he thought a sympathetic relation between reader and writer might be attained was an extreme rapidity in writing; that those who run might read, it was best to write running.[1] No better illustration of Arnold's theory could be found. Disraeli's articles

[1] "Studies of Roman Imperialism," by W. T. Arnold, with memoir of the author, by Mrs. Humphry Ward and C. E. Montague.

for the *Post* were written running. They have no flavour
of the study and the reference book; some of them have,
indeed, the ring of the platform. Swift, unhesitating,
mocking, his written word was as typical as his speech;
he talked, it was said, like a racehorse approaching the
winning-post, every muscle in action. He loved the
rapier, but he did not disdain to use the bludgeon.

At the present day few such articles could be published
without spelling financial ruin to a paper. Each day's
" airy flank of the thong " would invariably produce its
concomitant flow of writs. Barnes of the *Times* com-
mented on Disraeli's surprising disdain for the law of
libel. Nowadays the Press is much restricted by the
libel law; even a casual slip of the pen may cost thousands
of pounds. But most journalists would prefer the restrictions and reticence of to-day to the licence of yesterday.
Throughout the House of Lords crisis of 1910–11 the
relations between Sovereign and Minister were delicately
handled by almost every writer in the Press, not through
fear of libel law or Court displeasure, but because of the
prevalence of a healthier tone and of a stronger sense of
responsibility. It was not so in Disraeli's day. It was,
of course, matter of current gossip that Melbourne and
his colleagues were no favourites of the King. " I would
rather see the Devil than any one of them in my House,"
was His Majesty's bitter observation. Disraeli made
frequent and daring use of the estrangement between
King and Premier. Time and again he returned to the
attack on Melbourne, and the assault was carried through
with a vigour of invective to which the present generation
is, fortunately, unaccustomed.

Personalities apart, however, there is much in these
articles that is worthy of preservation. It was here that
Disraeli first put forward the Constitutional theories that
were afterwards more fully developed and identified with
his name. It is sufficient testimony to their quality that,
written for the day and fragmentary as they were bound
to be, they yet have in them, three-quarters of a century

later, so very much that will secure the approval of the Conservative politician of the twentieth century.

With the passing of the Corporations Bill, Disraeli's active association with the *Post* ceased, although he remained for many years in friendly communication with it. He entered upon that association to "establish a claim" upon Lord Lyndhurst, and he succeeded. The Bill passed on September 7; on September 10 he wrote to his mother a joyful letter respecting the promise of a seat in Parliament. To his sister, recording an invitation to dine with Lord Lyndhurst and meet certain important political personages, he wrote: "I do not know what you think of the *Morning Post*, but Fitzgerald says they drank my health in a bumper at Sir H. Hardinge's on Saturday, and said 'He is the man.'"[1]

III

In December, 1835, Disraeli published as a political tract his well-known "Vindication of the English Constitution." It took the form of a letter to Lord Lyndhurst, and is an elaborate and learned disquisition on constitutional history. The case for the Peers in their recurrent collisions with the People is set out with a fulness and subtlety that drew encomiums from Sir Robert Peel. At this time of day there is no need to do more than refer to its publication, which, according to Mr. Monypenny, gave Disraeli what his fugitive efforts could never have given him—a recognised position as a political writer and thinker. A keen judge of his own work, Disraeli liked it better than anything he had written.[2]

The publication of the "Vindication" gave rise to a bitter attack on Disraeli in the *Globe*. Disraeli's reply appeared in the *Times*, and the controversy was carried on with great freedom of language on both sides. It would

[1] See facsimile letter, p. 41.
[2] See facsimile letter, p. 112.

serve no good purpose to republish this correspondence; its ashes have been raked over often enough. What is of interest is that from now Disraeli went over bag and baggage to the *Times*. Here again Lyndhurst was doubtless the moving influence, and there can be little question that Barnes, the editor, had noted the effect of Disraeli's anonymous work on the reputation of the rival paper, and was willing to encourage as Edward Sterling's colleague and co-swashbuckler so able a controversialist. The full extent of Disraeli's work for the *Times* will probably never be known. Only a very few of the contributions have been acknowledged, but buried in the files of that journal for the next few years are leading articles which proclaim themselves to one familiar with his style as unquestionably his.

Of his now acknowledged contributions to the *Times* the most important were his famous Letters of Runnymede, nineteen in number. Throughout his life Disraeli did not publicly accept their authorship, but it was never seriously in doubt. They were republished anonymously in July, 1836, incorporated with them being a tract entitled "The Spirit of Whiggism." The letters rank in the public estimation second only to the Letters of Junius; yet they are little read, and, so far as we know, they have only once been republished. We are able to reprint in this volume two further letters by "Runnymede," which were published in the *Times* of the following year, and have not since seen the light. They are in the same vein as their forerunners. Melbourne, as always, comes under the lash. "It has sometimes been my humble but salutary office," writes "Runnymede," "to attend your triumph and remind you in a whisper that you are mortal. Amid the blaze of glory that at present surrounds you, it may be advisable for me to resume this wholesome function, lest in the intoxication of success your Lordship may for a moment forget that, although still a Minister, you are yet only a man."

It seems difficult now to understand why the common

2

origin of the *Morning Post* articles, "The Vindication," and "Runnymede," should not at the time have been definitely established, and why it should have been left to the twentieth century to discover what ought to have been palpable to the nineteenth. The parallelism in argument was convincing. In the *Post* he began to lay down his theory of the constitutional position; and as Disraeli the younger and as "Runnymede" within the space of a few short months he re-expounded his views. And later, in a speech in the House of Commons on household suffrage (March 21, 1839), he propounded the same arguments in similar language. Disraeli was indeed a confirmed self-plagiarist. One instance may be quoted; readers will discover many others for themselves. In "The Crisis Examined" (1834), Disraeli the younger writes of Lord John Russell as one

> "who, on the same principle that bad wine produces good vinegar, has somehow turned from a tenth-rate author into a first-rate politician."

In the *Morning Post* of September 4, 1835, we find another reference to Lord John as one who

> "has written a book upon the English Constitution, and who, on the same principle that bad wine makes very good vinegar, has somehow or other been metamorphosed from a tenth-rate author into a first-class statesman."

We turn to the *Times* of January, 1836 (Runnymede Letters), to find that

> "the seals of the principal office of the State are entrusted to an individual who, on the principle that good vinegar is the corruption of bad wine, has been metamorphosed from an incapable author into an eminent politician."

It is this characteristic of Disraeli's that emboldens me to put forward the view, in a subsequent section, that he was the author of at least three of the biographical sketches in *Fraser* (subsequently reprinted in the "Maclise

Portrait Gallery ") which up to the present have been attributed to Dr. Maginn.

On December 13, 1836, Disraeli began in the *Times* a series of political allegories entitled " A New Voyage of Sindbad the Sailor, recently discovered." This was, perhaps, the least happy of his journalistic efforts; it was laboured and obscure, and its publication dragged over a considerable period. Between the publication of the eleventh and twelfth chapters nearly a month elapsed, and, though the series was evidently unfinished, Barnes appeared to have had enough, and it ended there. More happy was the touch in the " Old England " series of papers (January, 1838), written in unfamiliar vein, and in parts in obvious imitation of Carlyle. It was a vigorous attempt by the new Member for Maidstone to wake up John Bull to a sense that a real " Crisis " in the Queen's Government had at last been reached. The articles ran through ten issues of the *Times*, and there is contemporary evidence that they were not without effect on the public mind.

So far as is known, that was Disraeli's last contribution of any length to the *Times*. In the previous year he had tried his hand at satirical verse, of which several samples, now reprinted for the first time, appeared in the month of March; but here again Barnes was not sympathetic. Disraeli wrote four open letters—one to Lord John Russell, one to the Queen, one to Melbourne, and the last (in 1841) to the Duke of Wellington—each with a distinct point of interest. In the following year Barnes died, and was succeeded by Delane. The Melbourne Ministry came to an end, and was followed by Sir Robert Peel's administration, in which, again outdistanced by Gladstone, Disraeli to his "intolerable humiliation " found no place.

" I am not going to trouble you," he wrote to Peel, " with claims similar to those with which you must be wearied. I will not say that I have fought since 1834 four contests for your party, that I have expended great sums, have exerted my intelligence to the utmost for the propagation of your policy, and have that position in life which can command a costly seat. But there is one peculiarity on which I cannot be silent. I have had to struggle against a storm of political hate and malice which few men ever experienced, from the moment when, at the instigation of a member of your Cabinet, I enrolled myself under your banner, and I have only been sustained under those trials by the conviction that the day would come when the foremost man of this country would publicly testify that he had some respect for my ability and character."

Peel's reply, however, was cold and formal. With the *Times* under new control, the Whigs out, and a Tory Ministry, from which he had been excluded, in power, Disraeli's incentive to journalistic effort had gone.

IV

It is a long jump from 1841 to 1853, when Disraeli's active association with journalism was renewed. In those twelve years much had happened. In literature, as in politics, he had amply fulfilled his earlier promise. The dramatic breach between Peel and Disraeli in 1846 was followed by the overthrow, and finally by the death, in 1850, of the Tory leader. Disraeli's political star rose as Peel's fell. He succeeded to the leadership of the party in the House of Commons, became Chancellor of the Exchequer in Lord Derby's Ministry for a few brief months in 1852, and then was sent back once more to Opposition. To strengthen his hands in fighting the Coalition Government under Lord Aberdeen, Disraeli founded *The Press*, a political weekly. During its early years it was ably conducted, and several of its contributors afterwards attained celebrity in literature. After the accession of the Conservatives to office in March, 1858, the paper changed hands, and it died in 1862. The full extent of Disraeli's connection with *The*

Press will doubtless be revealed by Mr. Buckle, when the Beaconsfield papers for the period have been thoroughly examined. For much of the information that follows the writer is indebted to the kindness of Mr. T. E. Kebbel, whose active connection with the paper began in 1855. Mr. Kebbel is now a veteran of over fourscore years. Most of the staff and contributors at the time were his seniors, and he alone survives. We have his authority for stating that the leading article on "Coalition" in the first number of *The Press* was by Disraeli, but Mr. Walter Sichel is the only writer who has positively identified as Disraeli's the masterly series of letters "To the Whigs," which ran through the early numbers—an identification confirmed by the internal evidence. Samuel Lucas, the versatile journalist and critic, was the first editor. He resigned the position in 1855, though he continued to write for the paper afterwards. He was succeeded in 1855 by Mr. David T. Coulton, who conducted the paper till his death, two years later, and who always wrote the first leader. Coulton used to go to the House of Commons on Friday nights, and return to the office later laden with notes taken down from Disraeli's dictation which he had to reduce into leading article form; and very cleverly, says Mr. Kebbel, he used to do it. Among the earlier contributors were Lord Stanley (afterwards fifteenth Earl of Derby); Shirley Brooks (the novelist and dramatist, better remembered as editor of *Punch*); and George Sydney Smythe (afterwards Lord Strangford). Then there were Madden, who, like Brooks and Lucas, came from the *Morning Chronicle*, and John Holt Hutton, editor of the *Economist*, who was responsible for the financial articles. Subsequent contributors were John Robert Seeley, author of "Ecce Homo," and subsequently Professor of Modern History at Cambridge; F. W. Haydon (son and biographer of Benjamin Robert Haydon, the painter), who was sub-editor till 1858, when Disraeli made him an Inspector of Factories. A still later editor was Patterson, under whom Mortimer Collins, novelist and poet, and Edward Pember, the distinguished Parliamentary counsel, were contributors. Mr. Kebbel, during his seven years' connection with the staff, contributed leaders and reviews, and helped to "make up" the paper on Friday nights. Mr. T. H. Sweet Escott, in his "Masters of Journalism," says the management of *The Press* was vested in a committee, whose meetings Disraeli regularly attended; and he records impressively an occasion when the article of the week was considered inadequate, and was replaced in an hour by another of Disraeli's composition. Having regard to the known rapidity of his pen and the extent of his journalistic experience, there was nothing in that feat to cause surprise.

A word or two in conclusion on Disraeli's choice of pseudonyms, which was influenced by his classical reading. Apart from "Runnymede," a happy inspiration suggested by his immersion at the period in the history of the Constitution, there are five which make their appearance in this volume — "Manilius," "Lælius," "Atticus," "Cœur de Lion," and "Skelton Junior." Of the choice of "Manilius" he writes: "The name I have assumed is so far appropriate that it is obscure to those who may yet well remember the more prominent disputants in the grand arena of old Roman politics; it is a name incidentally cited by Cicero as that of one, amongst others, who had studied the customs of his country, and might therefore be competent to suggest an occasional counsel to his fellow-citizens." "Lælius" was regarded by Cicero as a second Socrates, and figures in "De Amicitia," "De Senectute," and "De Republica." "Atticus"—a *nom de guerre* also used by Sir Philip Francis, in whose footsteps as a writer for the Press Disraeli clearly followed—was the name given to Titus Pomponius, Cicero's second self, and editor of his letters. "Skelton Junior" had a nodding acquaintance with Cicero, for, curiously enough, it is said that the first work of John Skelton the poet (1460–1529), was a translation of Cicero's letters, of which no copy is extant. He was

the inventor of Skeltonian metre. Here there may be
mentioned an added "Curiosity of Literature." The
only other John Skelton who left behind him a notable
record was Sir John (1831–1897), an author who was
appointed by Disraeli to an official position in Scotland
in 1868, the choice, it is said, having been due to
Disraeli's admiration of his literary style. In the following year he published a sympathetic sketch entitled
"Benjamin Disraeli: The Past and the Future." It
would be interesting to learn whether "Skelton Junior's"
interest in Sir John was first aroused by his recollection
of his own earlier usurpation of the name.

W. H.

August 30th, 1913.

WHAT IS HE ?

By the Author of "Vivian Grey"

"I hear that . . . . is again in the field; I hardly know whether we ought to wish him success. ' What is He ?' "—*Extract from a Letter of an Eminent Personage.*

["What is He ?" was published in 1833. Disraeli, who in 1832 had made two unsuccessful efforts to enter the House of Commons for High Wycombe, opened his candidature for Marylebone in the following year, but a vacancy did not arise. He seized the opportunity, however, to set forth his political views, then in process of evolution, in a little pamphlet which purported to be a reply to a question in a letter by Lord Grey. In all probability the quotation was merely a literary device to attract attention. The views propounded gave rise to the impression, never since wholly effaced, that Disraeli was then a Radical. His consistency must not be too rigidly insisted upon, but at the time he was really unlabelled. "Toryism," he had written of an earlier candidature, "is worn out, and I cannot condescend to be a Whig." Hence his appeal for the formation of a National party. Even when Chancellor of the Exchequer in 1852, he returned to the idea of a Radical-Tory coalition; witness his midnight interview with Mr. Bright on December 14, and his suggestion of a future Cabinet with Cobden and Bright as his co-members.]

I

The Tories have announced that they could not carry on the Government of this country with the present State machinery; every day the nation is more sensible that

the Whigs cannot. A third party has arisen who propose
certain additions and alterations in this State machinery,
by the aid of which, they believe, the Government of the
country might be conducted.

II

The first object of a statesman is a strong Government,
without which there can be no security. Of all countries
in the world England most requires one, since the prosperity of no society so much depends upon public confidence as that of the British nation.

Our Government, before the recent change,[1] was based
upon an aristocratic principle, and as the principle was
decided, the practice was vigorous. By the recent change
we have deserted the old principle of Government without
adopting a new one. As the Government has no im-
pelling principle, the Government cannot of course act.
Hence a session of Parliament, from which so much was
expected by the thoughtless, spent only in barren discussion, in the proposition of abortive measures, or the hasty
adoption of temporary and provisional enactments.

III

It is evident that public confidence must decrease in
exact proportion to the increasing weakness of a Government. Unless means therefore be discovered by which
the Government in this country can be rendered strong,
by which it may be enabled to act, a public convulsion
must soon occur. At present Property is only threatened; in a few months it will be a question as to the preservation of Order; another year, and we must struggle
for Civilisation.

IV

By what means, then, are we to obtain a strong Government ? We must discover some principle on which it
can be founded. We must either revert to the *aristocratic*
principle, or we must advance to the *democratic*.

[1] The Reform Act of 1832.

V

The Tories announce by their leaders that to govern the country with the present State machinery is impossible. Unless, therefore, they believe that it is possible to restore the old principle of Government, or unless they have embraced a martyrdom of political insignificance, they must advance to the new. Do they believe that they can restore the old principle? Not merely to expedite the argument, I will believe that they do not.

I, for one, believe it utterly impossible to revert to the aristocratic principle, for reasons which I shall adduce in a subsequent section. Believing so, however, and being convinced that, unless the Government of the country be founded upon some decided principle, the country must fall, I feel it absolutely necessary to advance to the new or the democratic principle.

VI

In the House of Commons, as at present constituted, neither of the principles predominates. Essentially the aristocratic is much the strongest, but as the aristocratic party is divided into two rival sections, which can seldom coalesce, the democratic contrives nearly to balance the antagonist principle. Superficial observers cannot understand how a measure which is so essentially aristocratic as the Reform Act has produced such threatening consequences to the aristocratic principle of government. They say, and they say truly, the Reform Act was a law, not to destroy close government, but to destroy Toryism. The Boroughs of the Tories were invariably sacrificed, and those of the Whigs, in many instances, essentially preserved. Everywhere the power of Whig nomination was favoured. "We have only changed masters," continue these observers. "We are governed by an aristocratic party, and that party how strong! Mark their vast majorities! Observe the numerous scions of noble

houses lounging behind the Treasury Bench. Talk of
Revolution indeed—there never was such an aristocratic
House of Commons as the present !" Doubtless it was
impressed with these ideas that the Whigs were induced
to introduce their famous Reform Bill. But if they have
not already discovered, it is time that they should dis-
cover, a great truth—THE ARISTOCRATIC PRINCIPLE HAS
BEEN DESTROYED IN THIS COUNTRY, NOT BY THE REFORM
ACT, BUT BY THE MEANS BY WHICH THE REFORM ACT
WAS PASSED.

VII

The Whigs, who, with a Sovereign and a House of
Commons alike pledged to their purpose, were nevertheless so incapable that they could not contrive to carry a
substantive measure of Reform through the unpledged,
yet weakest, Estate of the Realm, excited a deadly struggle
between the House of Lords and the Political Unions.
The House of Lords was vanquished, and the moment
that they passed the Reform Act that assembly was as
completely abrogated and extinguished as if its Members
had torn off their robes and coronets, and flung them
into the river, and, stalking in silence to their palaces,
had never returned to that Chamber, which every Peer
must now enter with a blush or with a pang.

The moment the Lords passed the Reform Bill, from
menace[1] instead of conviction, the aristocratic principle
of government in this country, in my opinion, expired
for ever. From that moment it became the duty of
every person of property, talents, and education, unconnected with the unhappy party at present in power, to
use his utmost exertions to advance the democratic principle in order that the country should not fall into that
situation in which, if I mistake not, it will speedily find
itself—absolutely without any Government whatever. A
Tory and a Radical, I understand; a Whig—a democratic
aristocrat, I cannot comprehend. If the Tories indeed
despair of restoring the aristocratic principle, and are

[1] The threat to create new Peers.

sincere in their avowal that the State cannot be governed
with the present machinery, it is their duty to coalesce
with the Radicals, and permit both political nicknames
to merge in the common, the intelligible, and the dignified
title of a National Party.   He is a mean-spirited wretch
who is restrained from doing his duty by the fear of being
held up as insincere and inconsistent by those who are
incapable of forming an opinion on public affairs; and who,
were it not for the individual " inconsistency " which
they brand, would often become the victims of their own
incapacity and ignorance.   A great mind that thinks and
feels is never inconsistent, and never insincere.   He who
will not profess opinions without first examining them is
ever considered insincere by the mass who adopt doctrines without thought, and retain them with the ob-
stinacy which ignorance can alone inspire.   He who will
not act without a reason will always be considered inconsistent by the irrational.   The insincere and the inconsistent are the stupid and the vile.   Insincerity is the vice
of a fool, and inconsistency the blunder of a knave.

VIII

It is possible that the Tories may imagine that there
are two modes by which the aristocratic principle may be
restored—firstly, by Force; secondly, by a coalition
between the two aristocratic parties.

Firstly, by Force.   It seems to me impossible for a
military leader to practise upon the passions of an insular
people, to whom he can promise no conquests.   If it be
urged that a military despotism has already been erected
in this country, I remind the respondent of the different
state of society in England at present to what it was in
the time of Cromwell.   It appears to me that the manufacturing districts alone, which, in a moment, would
supply masses of population and abundance of arms,
are a sufficient security against the imposition of a
military despotism.

Secondly, by a coalition between the aristocratic parties.

Such a combination might, unquestionably, retard the advance of the democratic principle, and raise, as it were, for an instant, a ghost of the departed aristocratic. But its ultimate tendency would only be to place the House of Commons again at variance with the people, and again to develop the triumphant organisation of popular self-government. But a coalition between the aristocratic parties would be attended with so many difficulties that it is almost impossible to conceive its formation.

IX

Believing, then, that it is utterly impossible to restore the aristocratic principle, and believing that unless some principle of action be infused into the Government a convulsion must ensue, what are the easiest and most obvious methods by which the democratic party may be made predominant ? It would appear that the easiest and the most obvious methods are the instant repeal of the Septennial Act and the institution of Election by Ballot, and the immediate dissolution of Parliament.[1] There is reason to believe that the consequence of this policy would be the election of a House of Commons a great majority of which would be influenced by the same wishes, and, consequently, the machine of the State would be able to proceed. I shall not here enter into the discussion of the nature of the measures which are likely to be adopted by a Parliament so constituted. This is not a party Pamphlet, and appeals to the passions of no order of the State: I record here my solemn conviction, and the result of my own unprejudiced meditation. The sole object of these pages is to show that we are in a situation in which it is necessary either to recede or to advance; that it is not probable that the present state of affairs can subsist six months; and that it becomes all men who are sincere well-wishers to their country, and

---

[1] On October 1, 1832, in his second Wycombe election address, he announced that he was prepared to support the ballot, and was desirous of returning to triennial Parliaments.

who are really independent—that is to say, who are not
pledged to the unhappy party in power—to combine
together for the institution of a strong Government.

X

In conclusion, I must observe that there is yet a reason
which induces me to believe that the restoration of the
aristocratic principle in the Government of this country
is utterly impracticable. Without being a system-monger,
I cannot but perceive, in studying the history of the past,
that Europe for the last three centuries has been more or
less in a state of transition from Feudal to Federal principles of government. If these contending principles of
government have not originated all the struggles that
have occurred, they have, at least, in the progress of
those struggles, in some degree blended with them. The
revolt of the Netherlands against Spain impelled, if it did
not produce, the Revolution in England under Charles
the First. The revolt of the Anglo-American Colonies
against Great Britain impelled, if it did not produce, the
revolution in France under Louis the Sixteenth. It is
unnecessary to touch upon later events. It is wise to be
sanguine in public as well as in private life; yet the
sagacious Statesman must view the present portents with
anxiety, if not with terror. It would sometimes appear
that the loss of our great Colonial Empire must be the
necessary consequence of our prolonged domestic dissensions. Hope, however, lingers to the last. In the sedate
but vigorous character of the British nation we may
place great confidence. Let us not forget also an influence too much underrated in this age of bustling mediocrity—the influence of individual character. Great
spirits may yet arise to guide the groaning helm through
the world of troubled waters—spirits whose proud destiny
it may still be at the same time to maintain the glory of
the Empire, and to secure the happiness of the People.[1]

[1] "Who will be the proud spirit ?" asked his father, Isaac
D'Israeli.   c

THE CRISIS EXAMINED

By Disraeli the Younger

["THE CRISIS EXAMINED" (1834) marks the beginning of Disraeli's definite alliance with the Tory party. It was published with the following advertisement:

> "The following pages form a genuine report of an address to the Electors of High Wycombe, delivered in their Town Hall, Dec. 16th. As its subject is one of general importance, and as it was then considered that a question of great public interest was placed in a proper position and a just light, it has been published."

Melbourne's Ministry had been dismissed by the King, Peel had taken office, and a General Election was in prospect. In November, Disraeli was inviting Lord Durham's influence in his projected candidature as a Radical for Aylesbury; in the following month his patron, Lord Lyndhurst, was striving to secure his selection as Conservative candidate for Lynn—a "mighty impartial personage," was Greville's comment. In the end it was Wycombe again, on the basis once more of a Radical-Tory alliance. A few weeks later Disraeli was nominated for the Carlton Club, and finally assumed the Tory label. The pamphlet, which has never been republished, contains many passages of permanent interest.]

GENTLEMEN,—A considerable period has elapsed since I last had the honour of addressing you within these walls; and in that interval great revolutions have occurred—revolutions of government and revolutions of opinion;

I can, however, assure you that I remain unchanged. I appear before you this day influenced by the same sentiments that I have ever professed, and actuated by the same principles I have ever advocated. There are some among my supporters who have deprecated this meeting; who have believed that I stood in so favourable a position as regarded the final result of this contest that to move might perhaps endanger it; who, observing that I was supported by individuals of different opinions and hitherto of different parties, were fearful that, in hazarding explanation, I might hazard discomfiture. But, Gentlemen, unless I enter Parliament with a clear explanation of my views, there is little chance of my acting with profit to you or with credit to myself. I cannot condescend to obtain even that distinguished honour by jesuitical intrigue or casuistical cajolery; I cannot condescend, at the same time, to be supported by the Tories because they deem me a Tory, and by the Liberals because they hold me a Liberal; I cannot stoop to deception, or submit to delusion.

It is the fashion to style the present moment an extraordinary Crisis. I will not quarrel with the phrase. The times are, indeed, remarkable: we have a new Administration just formed; a new Parliament immediately threatened. It is therefore incumbent on the constituent body throughout the Empire to prepare, and to resolve upon the course expedient to pursue. Hoping, even believing, that I shall be your representative,[1] I will venture to offer to your consideration the course of policy which, under existing circumstances, I think it the duty of an Administration to pursue. And, in the first place, I think that Administration should be based upon a determination to reduce the burthens, to redress the grievances, and to maintain the rights of the people. I will not, however, and certainly I do not wish them to shield themselves under a declaration so vague. Let us, therefore, be

[1] His third contest at Wycombe ended in defeat. The figures (January 7, 1835) were—Smith, 289; Grey, 147; Disraeli, 128.

definite. I think the necessary measures may be classed
under four heads: Financial Relief, Ecclesiastical Reform,
Sectarian Reform, and Corporate Reform. I will consider the Irish Question as collateral to the general one
of Ecclesiastical Reform.

As to Financial Relief, I am of opinion that the agricultural interest at the present moment is more entitled
than any other class to whatever boon the Minister may
spare. All who hear me know, and most who hear me
feel, that that interest is fearfully depressed. We may
hope, therefore, that the Exchequer may grant them at
least the partial relief of the malt tax, although I recommend them to petition for the whole.[1] I would not at
the same time make a request and intimate a compromise.
As for any further relief that may be conceded us, I am
always an advocate, in spite of political economists, for
the abolition of direct taxes. I hope, therefore, the
window tax will soon disappear; it is a tax the most
onerous and the most unjust.[2] Further relief we cannot
certainly now anticipate.

I approach now the solemn subject of Ecclesiastical
Reform. Church Reform, Gentlemen, is the popular cry
of the country: and when I recall the desperate professions that have been made, and the abortive measures
that have been prepared upon this subject, I confess I
recoil from a cant phrase which only reminds me of the
intrigues of ignorant faction, or the wily projects of the
protectors of vested interests. I hope the time approaches
when we may hear less of Church reform, and more of
Church improvement. I deem it absolutely necessary
that pluralities should be abolished,[3] and that the great
and consequent evil of non-residence should be terminated
for ever. It is, perhaps, unnecessary for me to observe
that I cannot conceive that this all-important object can
be obtained without increasing the value of the lesser

[1] This was dealt with in Disraeli's first Budget.
[2] Repealed in July, 1851.
[3] Legislation dealing with this subject was passed in 1838.

livings, and the incomes in general of the inferior clergy. Ecclesiastical Reform naturally and necessarily draws our attention to Ireland, a name fatal to so many Governments.

I deem it absolutely necessary, even for the existence of the Protestant Establishment itself, that the question of the Irish Church should be forthwith grappled with; that it should be the object of a measure in its nature as final, in its operation as conclusive, as human wit can devise. It is now impossible to avoid and too late to postpone it; it must be met immediately—the question is how it may be met efficiently. Twelve months, therefore, must not pass over without the very name of tithes in that country being abolished for ever; nor do I deem it less urgent that the Protestant Establishment in that country should be at once proportioned to the population which it serves. But, Gentlemen, I for one will never consent that the surplus revenues of that branch of our Establishment shall ever be appropriated to any other object save the interests of the Church of England, because experience has taught me that an establishment is never despoiled except to benefit an aristocracy. It is the interest of the people to support the Church, for the Church is their patrimony, their only hereditary property; it is their portal to power, their avenue to learning, to distinction, and to honour. I see no reason why the surplus revenues of the Church of England in Ireland should not be placed in trust of the Prelates of that land, and of lay trustees, for the purpose of advancing the propagation of the Protestant faith in Ireland by all salutary and sacred means. We may fail, Gentlemen, in this great end, but failure under such circumstances is preferable in my mind to seeing this property, hallowed by its original consecration to the purposes of religion, of learning, and of charity, in the ruthless and rapacious grasp of some bold absentee Baron. I know the love that great Lords, and especially Whig Lords, have for abbey lands and great tithes, but I remember Woburn, and I profit by the reminiscence. As I am upon the subject of Ireland, I will at once declare that I see no chance of tranquillity and welfare for that impoverished and long-distracted land until the Irish people enjoy the right to which the people of all countries are entitled— namely, to be maintained by the soil that they cultivate by their labour. I cannot find terms to express my sense of the injustice and the impolicy, the folly and the wickedness, of any longer denying to Ireland the consolation and the blessing of a well-regulated system of poor-laws. But not, Gentlemen, that system which has recently made all England thrill with feelings of horror and indignation as they wept over the simple, though harrowing, tale of the sufferings of our unhappy neighbours at Bledlow.

Under the head of Sectarian Reform I approach the delicate subject of the claims of the Dissenters. In my opinion these are claims which must not be eluded by any Government that wishes to stand. I would grant every claim of this great body that the spirit of the most comprehensive toleration required, consistent with the established constitution of the country. Therefore I think that the Registration and the Marriage claims should be conceded. As for the question of the Church rate, it is impossible that we can endure that every time one is levied a town should present the scene of a contested election. The rights of the Establishment must be respected, but for the sake of the Establishment itself that flagrant scandal must be removed. These are concessions which, I think, are due to a numerous and powerful portion of our fellow-subjects; due, I repeat, to their numbers, their intelligence, and their property, and consistent, in my opinion, with the maintenance of an Established Church—a blessing with which I am not prepared to part, and which I am resolved to uphold, because I consider it a guarantee of civilisation and a barrier against bigotry.

I now arrive at the fourth head under which I classed the measures, in my opinion, necessary to be adopted by the Government, Corporate Reform—a subject, I believe, very interesting to those I am now addressing.[1] I am of opinion that a municipality should be formed upon the model of that mixed constitution which experience has proved to be at the same time so efficient and so beneficial. I am desirous that the burgesses should be elected by the general body of inhabitants of a town, subject, of course, to certain limitations and restrictions; that the Aldermen should be elected by the burgesses, and serve the office of Mayor in rotation; for I never will consent that the Mayors and returning officers of boroughs shall be appointed by the Crown. This is part and parcel of the Whig system of centralisation, fatal to rural prosperity and provincial independence—one of those Gallic imitations of which they are so fond, but which, I hope, the sense and spirit and love of freedom of Englishmen will always resist. Paris decides upon the fate of France, but I hope we may continue to receive our morning papers by the Oxford coach without acknowledging a ukase in every leading article and recognising a revolution in every riot.

Gentlemen, I need not, I am sure, remind you that peace and economy are two things without which no Government could now exist four-and-twenty hours. The question for you to decide this day is whether, if a Government be prepared to adopt and carry measures similar to those I have detailed, and are determined to support, with their utmost energy and resolution, everything which may tend to the improvement and amelioration of the society of this realm—whether, under these circumstances, your representative in Parliament is to support such a Government ?

I am glad to hear that cheer. You are not ignorant that a contrary axiom is now laboriously propagated. I am for measures, Gentlemen, and not men, and for this simple reason, that for four years we have had men and not measures, and I am wearied of them. But we

---

[1] In 1835 Disraeli strongly opposed in the *Morning Post* the Municipal Corporations Bill.

are told we ought not to accept any measures, however
desirable, from the hands of those who opposed the
Reform Bill. This is a proposition which it becomes us
to examine with an unimpassioned spirit and a severe
scrutiny, for it is a very important one. The country is
now divided into two parties, headed by different sections of the aristocracy: those who introduced, and those
who opposed, the Reform Bill. Admit the proposition
of men and not measures, and the party that introduced
that Bill are our masters for life. Are you prepared for
this ? Is your confidence in the Whigs so implicit, so
illimitable, that you will agree to the perpetual banishment of their political rivals from power ? Are you
prepared to leave the Whigs without opposition, without
emulation, without check ? I think it very dangerous;
I think it very unconstitutional.

But let us examine this famous proposition a little
more severely. All of you have heard of the Duke of
Wellington's declaration against reform. God knows it
is very famous.[1] One would almost fancy that the
people of England had listened to a declaration against
reform from a Prime Minister for the first time in their
lives. And yet but a few years before, a very few brief
years, and they had listened to another declaration
against reform not less decided, not less vehement, not
less vindictive—ay ! and uttered, too, in the House of
Commons, and not in the House of Lords—uttered, too,
by a Prime Minister the head of a Government of which
all the individuals composing the recent Cabinet were
either members or supporters. I allude to the declaration of Mr. Canning—a declaration that compromised
Lord Lansdowne and Lord Melbourne, and, indeed, every
member of their party, who are now so loud in their

---

[1] " I am not only not prepared to bring in any measure of the
description alluded to by the noble lord " (Lord Grey), " but I
will at once declare that, as far as I am concerned, as long as I
hold any station in the Government of the country, I shall always
feel it my duty to resist such measures when proposed by others."—
The Duke of Wellington in the House of Lords, November 2, 1830.

anathemas against apostacy, and their personal horror of renegadoes. One solitary Whig alone stood aloof from Mr. Canning, and that was Lord Grey. Will the late Cabinet screen themselves under the shadow of his mantle ? Lord Grey did not leave it behind; he did not leave them with his blessing, or the odour of his sanctity. Gentlemen, what strange changes have we not lived to witness ! You all remember when my gallant opponent, for whom I entertain sincere respect, first appeared among us ? You remember it was the most sudden thing in the world ? We did not know where he came from; we thought he had dropped from the skies. You remember that Mr. Ellice, the Right Hon. Mr. Ellice,[1] called upon us to elect the Colonel,[2] although a stranger, out of "*gratitude*" to Lord Grey. Gratitude to Lord Grey ! I suppose, when he makes his appearance among us again, we shall be summoned to elect him out of "*ingratitude*" to Lord Grey, for that seems more the fashion now. Yes, Gentlemen ! Lord Grey refusing the Privy Seal, and Lord Brougham soliciting the Chief Barony, are two epigrammatic episodes in the history of reform that can never be forgotten.

But, Gentlemen, fancy Mr. Spring Rice cheering Mr. Canning in his anti-reform tirade, and Mr. Ellice, the Right Hon. Mr. Ellice, who was so good as to send us down a member, crying " hear, hear," and Sir John Hobhouse,[3] who, from his conservatory of consistency, throws stones at the Duke of Wellington—Sir John Hobhouse, the supporter of Mr. Canning, who sailed into public life on the popular wings of Annual Parliaments and Universal Suffrage, and afterwards

" Got pelted for his pains."

---

[1] Edward Ellice, Member for Coventry, and brother-in-law of Earl Grey.

[2] Colonel (afterwards General) Grey, son of the Prime Minister, better known subsequently as private secretary to Queen Victoria. "That most true-hearted man " (*Mr. Gladstone in a letter to General Ponsonby, March 5, 1894*).

[3] Afterwards Lord Broughton.

Oh! rare Sir John Hobhouse! Are we to be told that men like these, who backed and supported Mr. Canning under such circumstances, because they afterwards introduced and supported the Reform Bill, possess an exclusive right of calling every man an apostate who sees, in the altered condition of affairs, a ground for applying to a totally different set of circumstances a class of measures essentially new? What an exquisite pretence to consistency there is in saying, " So pure is the love we bear it, that we will sacrifice for its sake every chance of freedom—that we will endure the worst tyranny, rather than accept the greatest blessings that Reform may shower down upon us from the hands of renegadoes?" When the Whigs came forward with their Reform Bill, did the country twit them with their inconsistencies, gross as they might be? Did anyone, adopting the principles now so much in vogue among their party, dub them renegadoes? Did anyone chalk " apostate " on the back of Lord Palmerston, or outrage the nerves of those delicate tergiversators, the Messrs. Grant,[1] by squibbing them in the streets for their change of opinion? On the contrary, a remarkable abstinence from such crimination prevailed, as, I think, Gentlemen, it prevails at this present moment. The people were content to accept the Reform Bill as a great remedial measure which they had often demanded, and which had been always denied, and they did not choose to scan too severely the previous conduct of those who conceded it to them. They did not go about saying, We must have reform, but we will not have it from Lord Palmerston, because he is the child of corruption, born of Downing Street, and engendered in the Treasury, a second-rate official for twenty years under a succession of Tory Governments, but a Secretary of State under the Whigs. Not they, indeed! The people returned Lord Palmerston in triumph for Hampshire, and pennies were subscribed to present him with

[1] Charles (afterwards Lord Glenelg), and Robert (afterwards Sir Robert), appointed Governor of Bombay in 1834.

testimonials of popular applause. The people then took reform as some other people take stolen goods, "and no questions asked." The Cabinet of Lord Grey was not ungenerously twitted with the abandonment of principles which the country had given up, and to which no man could adhere who entertained the slightest hope of rendering himself an effective public servant.

The truth is, Gentlemen, a statesman is the creature of his age, the child of circumstance, the creation of his times. A statesman is essentially a practical character ; and when he is called upon to take office, he is not to inquire what his opinions might or might not have been upon this or that subject—he is only to ascertain the needful and the beneficial, and the most feasible manner in which affairs are to be carried on. The fact is, the conduct and opinions of public men at different periods of their career must not be too curiously contrasted in a free and aspiring country. The people have their passions, and it is even the duty of public men occasionally to adopt sentiments with which they do not sympathise, because the people must have leaders. Then the opinions and the prejudices of the Crown must necessarily influence a rising statesman. I say nothing of the weight which great establishments and corporations, and the necessity of their support and patronage, must also possess with an ambitious politician. All this, however, produces ultimate benefit; all these influences tend to form that eminently practical character for which our countrymen are celebrated. I laugh, therefore, at the objections against a man that at a former period of his career he advocated a policy different to his present one: all I seek to ascertain is whether his present policy be just, necessary, expedient; whether, at the present moment, he is prepared to serve the country according to its present necessities ? Besides, Gentlemen, remember our Reform Bill—remember that Ministers now have but a Ministerial duty to perform. The representatives of the people have now, we hope, a due share of power in their

hands: they should be able to compel any Administration
to observe the strict line of its duty, and doubtless would
make it clearly understand that the tenure of office must
depend upon an accommodation of its measures to the
existing wants of the community. No, Gentlemen, these
are not times when men look complacently on the Phari-
saical Whig reproaching the Tory for a publican and
sinner.[1]

But, Gentlemen, upon the authority of the Whigs themselves, I am justified in believing that nothing can be more
noble, at the same time more wise and more magnanimous,
than a bold adaptation of policy to the demands of public
opinion. What is the change now anticipated compared
with that prodigious alteration which led to the Reform
Bill itself, and for acquiescing in which Sir Robert Peel
was so loudly and vehemently applauded by the Whigs
themselves, they being then out of office—I mean the
carrying of Catholic Emancipation ? Even Dr. Lushing-
ton himself was among the loudest and most extravagant
eulogists of the Right Honourable Baronet for proposing
this measure, and professed himself unable to find language to do justice to the superlative greatness of mind
which led Sir Robert Peel to become the proposer of that
momentous change, which throughout his life he had
always ardently opposed.

So much for the factious cry of apostacy. Let us now
endeavour to ascertain what the Whigs did, when in
power, to entitle them to the extraordinary confidence
to which they lay claim. They opened business with
three favourite articles: Peace, Reform, and Retrenchment. I say at once their Peace consisted of blockades,
their Reform of the creation of commissionerships, and
their Retrenchment of the cutting down of clerks. But
they say they have taken off taxes. Could they avoid
doing so ? No Minister could go on a session without
taking off taxes long before the Reform Bill. Have they

---

[1] A much-quoted passage on Consistency.

exceeded the other party in their ratio of progressive relief ? I say, no ! I was sure you would respond. The Whigs plunged you into a revolution. For what ? To take the duty off stone bottles ? Or, if we are indeed to " wake a louder and a loftier strain," is your consolation for four years of misery to be found in the Irish Coercion Bill, or the English Poor Law Bill, their increase of the army, or their defence of the Pension List ? I will grant that they have undertaken some great questions ; but have they disposed of any ? A practical statesman would have settled them in a session; but, for the Whigs, their philosophy ends in a report, and their patriotism in a job.

Such are the claims to public confidence which may be put forth on behalf of the Whigs; but if, instead of being so miserably slender, they were indeed substantial and important, I would say that no claims can entitle them to become the masters for life of the British people; and, for my own part, I have no doubt, and I have ever thought, that they intended to become our masters for life; and decidedly they would have gained their object had they succeeded in swamping the House of Peers as well as packing the House of Commons. One of the most distinguished writers of the day, and a member of the extreme Liberal party in the House of Commons, has recorded, in a work which many of you have read, his regret that he ever was a supporter of the Whigs in their threatened attempt to overpower the House of Lords, and his self-congratulation that the attempt failed. Had it, however, succeeded, Gentlemen, it well fits us to con- sider what would have then become of the liberties of England. I do assure you that, in drawing your atten- tion to this important topic, I am not influenced by any party, any electioneering views. The remarks which I shall venture to make upon it have pressed upon my mind in the calmness and solitude of study. I will allow for the freedom of the Press; I will allow for the spirit of the age; I will allow for the march of intellect; but I

cannot force from my mind the conviction that a House
of Commons, concentrating in itself the whole power of
the State, might—I should rather say, would—notwithstanding the great antagonist forces to which I have
alluded, establish in this country a despotism of the most
formidable and dangerous character.   Gentlemen, I repeat, I cannot resist the conviction, because I cannot
shut my eyes to the historical truth.   Let us look to the
reign of Charles the First—a period as eventful, ay !
infinitely more so, than any that has since occurred in
this country.   Believe me, Gentlemen, we err when we
take it for granted that this present age in England is
peculiarly distinguished from preceding ones by the
general diffusion of public knowledge and public spirit.
Two great revolutions immediately preceded the events
of the reign to which I have alluded, revolutions productive of as much excitement and as much effect on the
public mind of Europe as the great French Revolution,
the Protestant Reformation, and the establishment of a
Republic in the Netherlands.   There was about this time,
too, doubtless in some degree impelled by these great and
strange events, a springtide in the intellect of England.
What marvellous men then met in the walls of Parliament.   The indefatigable Pym, the inscrutable Hampden,
the passionate Eliot, the austere genius of Strafford !
Worthy companions of these were St. John, Hollis, Vane ;
nor should we forget a Digby and a Capel, the chivalric
Falkland, and the sagacious Clarendon.   Why, Gentlemen, these were names that imparted to the deliberations
of your Parliament an intellectual lustre not surpassed,
perhaps not equalled, even in the brightest days of Pitt,
and Fox, and Burke, and Sheridan.   There was the same
feeling abroad in favour of freedom, and the same enthusiasm for the rights of the subject.   There was also,
although it is not generally supposed, the same omnipotent influence operating in favour of this cause, which we
now hug ourselves in believing to be an invincible bulwark
of our liberties.   Yes, Gentlemen, I am induced to believe

that the English Press exercised at that moment a power
not inferior to the authority it wields at the present day.
Every street had its journal, every alley its ballad; and
besides these great methods of communication, public
Opinion, that vaunted public Opinion which we would
fain believe to be the offspring of the present hour, appealed to the people in favour of the people by an oracle
that for political purposes is now happily silent: I mean
the pulpit.

Yet, Gentlemen, notwithstanding all these checks, and
all these guarantees—checks and guarantees for your
rights and liberties, I maintain, as powerful as any that
exist at the present day—what was the result ? Your
House of Commons, in which you are now called upon to
place implicit confidence, your boasted House of Commons which I for one will no more trust than any other
human institution—your omnipotent House of Commons,
after having pulled down the throne and decapitated the
monarch, after having expelled the Bishops from the
House of Peers, and then abrogated the peerage, set you
at defiance—they concentrated in themselves all the
powers of the State, and then voted their sittings perpetual—they began by quarrelling with the King about
one hundred thousand pounds, and ended, in the short
space of five years, in imposing upon the people burdens
to the amount of forty millions sterling; confiscated the
estates of a large portion of their fellow-subjects, divided
themselves into separate committees, and monopolised in
their own persons all the functions of the State, and,
finally, on one morning, divided among themselves three
hundred thousand pounds of the public money. Did I
say *finally?* Can we forget that this same House of
Commons, when their rapacity had dried up all other
sources of spoliation, invented the tax, most odious to
Englishmen, the Excise, and which they laid, too, not
merely upon the luxuries, but the very necessaries of
existence ?

Looking then, Gentlemen, at such consequences of an

implicit confidence in the House of Commons, I confess myself reluctant to quit the vantage ground on which the constitution of the country is now felicitously placed. Looking at such consequences, I think we may feel that we have some interest in maintaining the prerogative of the Crown and the privileges of the Peers. I, for one, shall ever view with a jealous eye the proceedings of any House of Commons, however freely chosen. Nor have I marked in the conduct of the reformed House of Commons anything, I confess, to lull me into over-confidence or security. I think I perceive even thus early in their career some symptoms of jobbing which would not have disgraced the Long Parliament itself; and some instances of servility which perhaps we must go to the reign of Charles the Second to rival.

So much for the Reformed Parliament, Gentlemen; and now for the Reform Ministry !

One would think from the cry that is now raised by the partisans of these persons that they were a band of patriots, who had never been animated by any other sentiment than the welfare of their country, and had never, by any chance, quarrelled among themselves. The Reform Ministry ! Where is it ? Let us calmly trace the history of this " united Cabinet."

Very soon after its formation, Lord Durham withdrew from the royal councils—the only man, it would appear. of any decision of character among its members. Still it was a most " united " Cabinet. Lord Durham only withdrew on account of his ill-health. The friends of this nobleman represent him as now ready to seize the helm of the State; a few months back, it would appear, his frame was too feeble to bear even the weight of the Privy Seal. Lord Durham retired on account of ill-health; he generously conceded this plea in charity to the colleagues he despised. Lord Durham quitted the " united Cabinet," and very shortly afterwards its two most able members in the House of Commons, and two of their most influential colleagues in the House of Lords,

suddenly secede.[1]   What a rent !   But then it was about
a trifle.   In all other respects the Cabinet was most
" united."   Five leading members of the Reform Ministry
have departed; yet the venerable reputation of Lord Grey,
and the fair name of Lord Althorp, still keep them together, and still command the respect, if not the confidence, of the nation.   But marvel of marvels !   Lord
Grey and Lord Althorp both retire in a morning, and in
—disgust !   Lord Grey is suddenly discovered to be
behind his time, and his secession is even intimated to be
a subject of national congratulation—Lord Althorp joins
the crew again, and the Cabinet is again " *united.*"   Delightful union !   Then commenced a series of scenes
unparalleled in the history of the Administrations of any
country—scenes which would have disgraced individuals
in private life, and violated the decorum of domestic
order.   The Lord Chancellor[2] dangling about the Great
Seal in postchaises, spouting in pot-houses, and vowing
that he would write to the Sovereign by the post; while
Cabinet Ministers exchanged menacing looks at public
dinners, and querulously contradicted each other before
the eyes of an admiring nation.   Good God, Gentlemen !
could this go on ?   Why, even Mr. Ellice—the Right Hon.
Mr. Ellice—who was so good as to send us down a Member
of Parliament, he could no longer submit to nestle in this
falling House, and he, too, quitted the " united " Cabinet,
because he had—what, for a ducat ?—a sore throat !

Why, they ridicule themselves !   And yet the tale is
not all told.   There is really too much humour in the
entertainment.   They make us laugh too much—the fun
is overdone.   It is like going to those minor theatres
where we see Liston[3] in four successive farces.   Lord
Melbourne, whose claim to being Prime Minister of
England, according to the Whigs, is that he is " a gentleman," Lord Melbourne flies to the King, and informs him

[1] Mr. Stanley, Colonial Secretary, and Sir James Graham, First
Lord of the Admiralty, resigned in 1834 on the Irish Church
question, and were followed by Lord Ripon, Privy Seal, and the
Duke of Richmond, Postmaster-General.
[2] Lord Brougham.   [3] John Liston, the comedian.

that a plan of " Church Reform " has been proposed in
the " united " Cabinet, and that Lord Lansdowne and
Mr. Spring Rice, the only remaining Ministers in the
slightest degree entitled, I will not say to the confidence,
but the consideration of the country, have in consequence
menaced him with their resignations.

I doubt not, Gentlemen, that this plan of " Church
Reform " was only some violent measure to revive the
agitation of the country, and resuscitate the popularity
of the Whigs, a measure which they never meant, and
never desired, to pass. Perhaps, feeling that it was all
over with them, it was a wretched *ruse*, apparently to go
out upon a *popular* measure. However, Lord Melbourne,
with as serious a face as he could command, informed
His Majesty that the remains of the " united " Cabinet,
Sir John Hobhouse and Lord John Russell, were still as
"united " as ever, and he ended by proposing that the
House of Commons should be led by his Lordship, who,
on the same principle that bad wine produces good
vinegar, has somehow turned from a tenth-rate author
into a first-rate politician.[1] And then Lord Melbourne
says that the King turned them out. Turned them out,
Gentlemen; why, His Majesty laughed them out ! The
truth is that this famous Reform Ministry, this great
" united " Cabinet, had degenerated into a grotesque and
Hudibrastic faction, the very lees of Ministerial existence,
the offal of official life. They were a ragged regiment
compared with which Falstaff's crew was a band of
regulars. The King would not march through Coventry
with them—that was flat. The Reform Ministry indeed !
why, scarcely an original member of that celebrated
Cabinet remained. You remember, Gentlemen, the story
of Sir John Cutler's silk hose.[2] These famous stockings
remind me of this famous Ministry; for, really, between
Hobhouse darns and Ellice botching, I hardly can decide

[1] See Introduction, p. 10.
[2] The London miser merchant, of whom Arbuthnot recorded that
he had a pair of black worsted stockings which his maid darned
so often with silk that they became at last a pair of silk stockings.

whether the hose are silk or worsted. *The* Reform
Ministry. I dare say, now, some of you have heard of
Mr. Ducrow, that celebrated gentleman who rides upon
six horses. What a prodigious achievement! It seems
impossible, but you have confidence in Ducrow! You
fly to witness it; unfortunately, one of the horses is ill, and
a donkey is substituted in its place. But Ducrow is still
admirable; there he is, bounding along in a spangled
jacket and cork slippers! The whole town is mad to
see Ducrow riding at the same time on six horses; but
now two more of the steeds are seized with the staggers,
and, lo! three jackasses in their stead! Still Ducrow
persists, and still announces to the public that he will
ride round his circus every night on his six steeds. At
last all the horses are knocked up, and now there are
half a dozen donkeys. What a change! Behold the
hero in the amphitheatre, the spangled jacket thrown
on one side, the cork slippers on the other! Puffing,
panting, and perspiring, he pokes one sullen brute, thwacks
another, cuffs a third, and curses a fourth, while one brays
to the audience, and another rolls in the sawdust. Behold
the late Prime Minister and the Reform Ministry! The
spirited and snow-white steeds have gradually changed
into an equal number of sullen and obstinate donkeys.
While Mr. Merryman, who, like the Lord Chancellor,
was once the very life of the ring, now lies his despairing
length in the middle of the stage, with his jokes exhausted
and his bottle empty!

Enough, Gentlemen, of the Reform Ministry and the
Reformed Parliament. Let us hope that the time has
arrived when we may be favoured with a National
Administration and a Patriotic House of Commons. Let
us hope that by their salutary influence the peace of
Europe and the honour of England may be alike maintained; the great interests of the country fostered and
protected; and those considerable changes firmly, but
cautiously, prosecuted in our social system, which the spirit
of the age demands and the necessities of the times require.

DISRAELI TO HIS SISTER ON THE "MORNING POST" ARTICLES.

(From the original in the possession of Messrs. Maggs Brothers.)

PEERS AND PEOPLE

[IN the vigorous leading articles contributed to the
Morning Post in August and September, 1835, and now
republished under the title "PEERS AND PEOPLE," Disraeli
strongly supported the action of the House of Lords in
amending the Municipal Corporations Bill. They were
written at the request of Lord Lyndhurst, the prime
mover in the agitation against the Bill, and their authorship remained a secret until revealed seventy-five years
later by an entry in Disraeli's diary. They mark the
beginning of his connection with the Press as a political
writer; but Disraeli, though he claimed to be a journalist,
constantly gibed against the "hired scribbler," and took
pains to point out that he never received payment—his
price was power—for his anonymous contributions to
political journalism. Only a selection has been given;
the earlier articles, written before the contending parties
had got to grips, were irregular in appearance, and lacked
the fire and continuity of the later contributions. In this
series Disraeli first outlines his views on Constitutional
questions, subsequently to be developed more fully in
"The Vindication," the "Runnymede Letters," the
"Spirit of Whiggism," and his public speeches.]

CHAPTER I

Lord Melbourne—His political profligacy—Indolence and inefficiency—O'Connell's Prime Minister, not the King's—The
Lords and the "People"—The coming "collision"—Principles of the Corporation Bills—Lord Lyndhurst's qualification—The Commissioners.

Saturday, August 22.

THE miserable Lord Melbourne, for shame and misery are
stamped upon his suffering countenance, rose on Thursday
night in the House of Lords to propose the second reading
of the Irish Church Spoliation Bill.

The annals of political profligacy do not contain an instance of more barefaced apostasy than is exhibited by the career of this unhappy leader of the Whigs.

Always a notorious place-hunter, Mr. William Lamb veered for a long time between the two aristocratic parties into which the State was then divided, and for a considerable period enjoyed the enviable reputation of being considered a man ready to sell himself under the somewhat disagreeable circumstances of not being able to command a market. At length, by dexterously coming forward when Lord Castlereagh was rather pushed, and defending the Manchester Magistrates, and making a somewhat ingenious and very uncompromising speech against Parliamentary Reform, the trading trimmer succeeded in becoming a recognised Tory.

Lord Castlereagh despised him, Mr. Canning distrusted him, and Lord Grey did both. And now this most indolent and inefficient of official men—this Lord Melbourne—Manchester-massacre Melbourne—is the revolutionary Prime Minister of England, by the grace, or disgrace, of Daniel O'Connell, with whom Lord Melbourne, in his coteries, affects to have no connection. If he be not Mr. O'Connell's Prime Minister, his lordship is not the King's, our Gracious Sovereign's, whom Lord Melbourne's paid servants and instructed toad-eaters load with every species of seditious abuse in the solitary organ of the Government. There never yet was a public man so completely ignorant of public business as this egregious nobleman.

He has read the *Edinburgh Review* and Horace. This is the extent of his studies. His mind is impregnated with a sort of bastard French philosophy, filtered through the pages of blue and yellow, and relieved with an occasional gay or poignant reminiscence of an ode, or epistle, of the Roman epicurean. It is observable in all debates how studiously Lord Melbourne avoids details, and the moment he is pressed with an awkward argument, or an inconvenient fact, how speedily he takes refuge in some vague generalities about the spirit of the age, the progress of philosophy, and the rights of the people. Except Palmerston, he is the veriest and most thorough political hack going; but his career until the Reform Bill was so obscure that the mass of the public are quite ignorant of his proverbial jobbing and his pitiful tergiversation.

Yesterday his Lordship dined with his Royal Master. Rare occurrence ! Some whisper 'tis the first time during his notable Premiership; there is no doubt 'tis for the last.

*   *   *   *   *

The baffled and craven Whigs, *trembling at what is about to happen*, talk daily of " the Lords opposing themselves to the wishes of THE PEOPLE." We wish we could induce these gentry to define what they mean by this favourite phrase of theirs—THE PEOPLE.

The King of England is the avowed leader of the Conservative party—according to the Whigs, who raise seditious cries in consequence. We have upon our side also the Peers of England; we have upon our side the Gentlemen of England; we have upon our side the yeomanry of England; we have upon our side their armed and gallant brethren ; we have upon our side the universal peasantry of England; we have upon our side the army and navy, the Church, the learned professions to a man, the Universities, the Judges, the Magistrates, the merchants, the corporate bodies of all descriptions, and a large party in every town, agricultural, commercial, even manufacturing. What constitutes a people if these do not afford the elements of a great and glorious nation ? Why—to say nothing of rank, of property, honour, intelligence, experience—in numbers, in sheer and very numbers we beat these brawling braggarts.

Yet the Whig-Radicals talk not only of the indignation and resolution, but even of the meetings of THE PEOPLE in their favour.

Where do they meet ? " *Yesterday Birmingham met —to-day Westminster.*" To tell the truth, when Lord

Ellenborough proposed, and passed, his clause for entrusting the division of the boroughs into wards to the
Gentlemen of England, and *Pis-aller* Parkes[1] lost his
job, we were quite prepared for a *Birmingham* meeting,
and meet it certainly did. A precious meeting of THE
PEOPLE! The rump of the Political Union, the débris of
that " aristocracy of blackguards " listening to the brainless brayings of that melancholy ass Attwood[2] over
Cossacks and currency. But, for Westminster! Why,
we live in Westminster; we ourselves are part and parcel
of *the people* of Westminster. And who doth the gentle
public suppose was the great lion at the Westminster
meeting of THE PEOPLE? Why, one Juggins, who
described himself as a member of " the Annoyance Jury."
Shade of Dogberry! Spirit of Verges! Ye are at length
outdone. What are ye to Master Juggins of the Annoyance Jury? Oh, William Shakspeare! and, oh, Walter
Scott! the most ideal creations of your choice humour
must yield to this grotesque existence. And Juggins is
a leader of THE PEOPLE! And Juggins wishes to know
what is the use of the Lords?

If this be " THE PEOPLE " with whom the threatened
collision is to take place, we think the fray may fairly be
left to the new police—and with whom else it is to take
place? What do the Whig-Radicals mean by this word
" collision "? Do they mean civil war? If so, we
deprecate, but we are prepared for it. Fancy John
Russell in a civil war! Our English Don Carlos[3] would
scarcely gain as many laurels as his namesake in Navarre.
Fancy Spring Rice[4] waving a shillelagh, or Palmerston[5]
tilting with a lady's fan. Civil war, indeed! Why, when
the last civil war took place it commenced by Hampden's

[1] Joseph Parkes, secretary and solicitor to the Corporations
Commission.
[2] Thomas Attwood, Member for Birmingham, and father of
the Political Unions; Cobbett's " King Tom."
[3] Lord John Russell wrote " Don Carlos," a tragedy, 1822.
[4] Chancellor of the Exchequer.
[5] Foreign Secretary.

green horsemen riding up from Buckinghamshire, and
alone overawing the King and Court. Let William the
Fourth now raise his standard in that very county, ay,
the birthplace of Hampden, and the whole male population to a man would rally round the Throne. The counties
within a day's journey of London would furnish His
Majesty within a week with fifty thousand Cavalry, a great
portion of them already armed and trained, and led by
skilful and experienced Officers.

But the Whigs and the Whig-Radicals do not mean
a civil war by their word *collision*. Oh no, they mean a
row, a riot, a short revolution, a Metropolitan bang-up,
paving stones, White Conduit House,[1] broken windows,
a fire or two, Cheapside and Regent Street plundered,
and the prisons thrown open. This is what the King's
Ministers want. They want three days, three glorious
days, three glorious and beautiful days, as their prescient
flashman Macaulay styled the bloody riot that was the
fitting precursor of the iron despotism of Louis Philippe.
The Whig Ministers want a revolutionary riot to consolidate their power—the power which they have now failed
in establishing, although they carried the Reform Act,
and attempted the Corporation Bill.

But it won't do. We tell these Gallomaniac apes of
everything that is detestable in the French character
that these things will ever be " managed better in France
than in England." Let the " collision " be tried, and as
soon as they please. They shall have row enough !

*   *   *   *   *

We hope, and we believe, that the Lords will not bate
a jot of their amendments of the Whig Corporations Bill.
Never were amendments in a projected law more just,

[1] A famous Islington tea-house in bygone days. A mass
meeting of working men was summoned by manifesto to assemble
there on November 7, 1831, to ratify a new Bill of Rights. Melbourne declared that the meeting would certainly be seditious,
and perhaps treasonable in law, and it was abandoned. Shortly
afterwards a royal proclamation was issued declaring organised
political associations, assuming powers independent of the civil
magistrate, to be " unconstitutional and illegal."

more salutary, and more statesmanlike. The majority of them are merely, to use the coal-heaving jargon of the Radical Press, a *carrying out* of the principles of the Bill.

By fully developing the principles of the Bill, the Conservatives have simultaneously eradicated the *party virus* of the measure. Thus it is in the clauses in which they have baffled the conspiracy to plunder the freemen of England, and to deprive them of the political rights so recently and so solemnly guaranteed to them by the Whigs themselves in their famous final measure; thus it is in the Conservative qualification clause, in which the Opposition have applied to the town council the test which the Government itself have applied to the electors of that town council. Nothing is more ludicrous than the howlings of the beggarly Radicals at this most discreet regulation.

Property not a qualification, forsooth! What other general qualification is there? That some wealthy blockheads may be elected on the town council is possible, but rich blockheads are at any rate more trustworthy than poor ones—ay, more trustworthy than insolent knaves.

The solitary organ of the unhappy Government, in the last gasp of its frantic insolence, inquires whether the qualification of the Noble Mover of the Amendment for a seat in the Upper House is *property?* Why, if his Lordship were as rich as the Duke of Bedford himself— if he had been the fortunate descendant of some favoured minion of an unprincipled tyrant, and the possessor of the plunder of the Church—they know that *property* would not be Lord Lyndhurst's qualification for his seat. His genius, his learning, his public services, form his qualification. These placed him in the House of Peers. But if his Lordship were not as independent in his fortune as two-thirds of the present Cabinet—which we rejoice he is—are men of Lord Lyndhurst's calibre of such common occurrence that we are to legislate upon the obvious exception to a plain rule?

How rare such a character must ever be in public life is proved by the simple circumstance that the rapacious Whigs themselves, eager as they ever are to gorge their creatures with the public money, have not yet been able to find a single individual in their whole faction competent to discharge the onerous duties and to clutch the rich remuneration of the office of Lord Chancellor.

Then for the clause which divides the towns into wards. Here again the Conservatives have only adopted and developed the principle of the Whig Measure; but then they have entrusted its execution to the Gentlemen of England, and not to notorious and convicted jobbers. Ay, there's the rub !

It is true that the Peers, in a wise sympathy with ancient associations and time-honoured forms, existing authority and vested rights, have retained the titles and offices, the powers and privileges, of Aldermen. To be sure. Are the institutions of Alfred to be kicked into a ditch for the sake of *Pis-aller* Parkes and roaring Rushton and the sober Drinkwater, and the immaculate Cockburn, and that provincial oracle, the thrice-unheard-of Wilkinson, and Dwarris — our friend "Horrors-and-Hell" Dwarris ?[1] By-the-by, we owe an apology to this gentleman. We understand his dramatic effusion was never performed at Sadler's Wells: it was refused.[2] Fortunatus Dwarris (Phœbus, what a name !)[3] lithographs his letters : as long as he does not *print* his tragedies we care not what he does.

To-day it is proposed that Aldermen should be abro-

[1] Edward Rushton (nicknamed " Roaring " Rushton by Cobbett), John Elliott Drinkwater, Alexander James Edmund Cockburn (afterwards Lord Chief Justice of England), G. H. Wilkinson, and Fortunatus William Lilley Dwarris (afterwards Sir F. W. L. Dwarris), members of the Corporations Commission. Joseph Parkes, in addition to being Secretary of the Commission, was the chief Parliamentary agent of the Whig party.

[2] " We advise him to revise his tragedy of ' Horrors and Hell,' and get it again performed at Sadler's Wells."—Disraeli in *Morning Post*, August 21.

[3] "O Amos Cottle ! Phœbus, what a name !" (Byron, "English Bards and Scotch Reviewers ").

gated—to-morrow the constable and the tithing-man will
be attacked. The militia is already doomed. The
Whigs have previously carved up the old English Counties,
and now they are going to Radicalise the old English
towns. It is their evident determination to assimilate
the institutions of this country to those of France—free
and favoured France. Instead of the county and the
borough we shall soon have the *arrondissement* and the
commune. The préfet and the gendarmerie follow, of
course. Alas, Old England !

CHAPTER II

The friends of the " People "—Popish rebels—Mr. Hume and his
allies—Their illiteracy—A comparison—O'Connell—Patriots
and conspirators.

Monday, August 24.

WHILE the Peers of England have been making a triumphant stand for the rights and liberties of their countrymen, a knot of individuals, by courtesy styled the House
of Commons, have been as actively engaged in wagering
a furious war against all those constitutional securities
which hitherto, as freeborn men, we have been taught to
value.

Some sixty or seventy persons, by courtesy styled the
House of Commons, all of the same hue and kidney,
liberals, friends of THE PEOPLE, unchecked by the
presence of any Members of the Opposition, and utterly
disregarding the faint remonstrances of the unhappy
members of the Government who are at their mercy, and
whom they can place in a minority at a moment's notice,
have during the last week revived *general warrants*,
issued *lettres de cachet*, inferentially recommended the
rack, declared that their *pleasure* is above the *law*, and
consistently in the same breath that they denounce what
they term the *irresponsible* power of the Peers have
declared their own power *despotic*.

And of whom is this knot of tyrants formed ? First
and foremost, of course, of the Popish rebels. The other
moiety is led by Mr. Hume and his Utilitarian or rather
Brutilitarian allies. They altogether form a company
utterly contemptible in point of number, intelligence,
and influence in the country. Besides the Popish rebels,
we repeat, there is Hume, and Warburton, of course;
one Tooke, a Socinian attorney; a brother quill-driver,
Mr. Wilks, the godly father of the Moorfields Tabernacle;
Roebuck, the Bath delegate, whose bray was once mistaken
for a roar, but who of late has shed his lion's skin, and
most elaborately " written himself down an ass "; a
pedantic schoolboy, by name Buller; that melancholy
young man, who must for a few weeks longer misrepresent
West Somerset, young Mr. Tynte, whom, to distinguish
from his Parliamentary father, we must in future recognise
as *Tyntoretto*. Ranting Attwood must not be forgotten,
worthy of some theatre " over the water." Wason,
Whalley, and Wakley complete the crew.[1] Hudibrastic
triad ! Why, if they could only induce Mr. Abercromby
to resign the chair, and contrive to smuggle Juggins into
his seat, we should have a Praise God Barebones Parliament again and the Rump to the very life.

The vast majority of these men, who are thus disposing
of the lives and fortunes of their fellow-countrymen, are
illiterate persons. Hume, for instance, can neither speak
nor write English; his caligraphy reminds one of a
chandler's shop, and his letters resemble a butterman's
bill. Warburton is, if possible, more ignorant even
than Hume, but more discreet and consequently less
loquacious. Both these men have some property, a rare
occurrence in the party; and all the petty plunderers,
would-be Commissioners, and other small toad-eaters, for

[1] A group of Liberal Members of Parliament: Joseph Hume
(Middlesex), Henry Warburton (Bridport), William Tooke (Truro),
John Wilks (Boston), J. A. Roebuck (Bath), Charles Buller
(Liskeard), C. J. K. Tynte (West Somerset), Thomas Attwood
(Birmingham), Rigby Wason (Ipswich), Sir Samuel Whalley
(Marylebone), and Thomas Wakley (Finsbury), founder of the
Lancet.

the sake of a positive dinner and a possible job, laud
them with great praise. But the ignorance of Warburton
rather staggers even these parasites. As a sort of extenuating compensation for the Cimmerian gloom of his
unlettered mind, they assure us he is a man of *science*,[1] a
great chemist. A fine qualification this for the part he
is playing ! We believe he has an air-pump in his house.
Wakley is of a lighter order of mind than the preceding
worthies. There is a vulgar vivacity about him which is
not unamusing. He would make an admirable cad[2] or a
first-rate conductor of an omnibus.

Wakley is a great leader of THE PEOPLE, and almost
as inquisitive an inquirer as to the use of the Lords as
Juggins himself. No one, indeed, denounces the Peers
with greater fervour; his anathema of the Duke of Newcastle set all Finsbury in a roar of indignation. It is
very evident what Mr. Wakley's definition of THE PEOPLE
means. It means those electors of Finsbury who honoured him with their suffrage. Now, with due deference
to the Editor of the *Lancet*, we are disposed to believe
that the Duke of Newcastle is as much one of THE PEOPLE
as the Honourable Member for Finsbury himself. Some
heretics may be disposed to hold that His Grace is even a
more valuable and a more estimable member of that great
society.

Comparisons are so proverbially odious, and often so
very inconvenient, that we are not inclined to push this
parallel between His Grace and Mr. Wakley any further—
the more so, as we might find some difficulty in ascertaining the points they hold in common. They both certainly
have shared one common misfortune—*they have both had
their houses burnt down*.[3]

[1] At Cambridge, according to Grote, Warburton obtained distinction as " a scholar and man of science."

[2] *Penny Magazine*, March 31, 1837: " He who hangs behind
—who opens the door and receives the money—is conductor, or,
in the vulgar tongue, cad."

[3] Wakley's house was burned to the ground on August 20, 1820,
by Thistlewood's gang; Nottingham Castle was burned down on
October 10, 1831, during the Reform Riots.

And these are our patriots. Different men, certainly, to those who headed the Movement of the Seventeenth Century. For Hampden we have Hume, and Warburton for Pym. Sir Samuel Whalley for Sir John Eliot, and, instead of Sir Edward Coke, Sir Monsey Rolfe![1] O'Connell, indeed, might find a more fitting representative in that age. He is doubtless prepared most efficiently to perform the part of Sir Phelim O'Neale,[2] his rival in savage treachery, but scarcely in savage courage!

And these, we repeat, are our patriots. Why, compared with the heroes of our earlier movement, they are as the tallow candles of the Marylebone Vestry in relation to the glorious firmament. These are not the men to upset an ancient realm, whatever may be their will. Such awful exploits require spirits of a different order. Such sublime conspirators are found among men who, with all their errors and all their fond ambition, are of a heroic mould of mind, great scholars, learned in human nature and human history, of a commanding eloquence, of a marvellous subtilty, and an undaunted courage.

But if these men were by some ludicrous destiny to succeed, what then? If they were less ignorant, they would know that all they are attempting has been already achieved. We have " relieved " the Bishops from their legislative functions, we have voted the " inutility " of the House of Lords, we have rooted up the Throne, and what was the result? The leaders of the present movement may be too ignorant to know; but the people of England, the real people of England, have not forgotten.

[1] Mr. R. Monsey Rolfe was appointed Solicitor-General in April, 1835, and was knighted. Afterwards, as Lord Cranworth, he became Lord Chancellor.

[2] Sir Phelim O'Neill (or O'Neale), an Irish rebel, was executed on March 10, 1653.

CHAPTER III

The " Rump " and the Supplies—A " Praise God Barebones "
crew—Single Chamber government—And Cromwell—Airy
flanks of the Disraelian thong—Small deer and their masters
—The *Globe* and Scipio Africanus.

Tuesday, August 25.

So the Rump will stop the Supplies,[1] will they ? Ay,
and embezzle them too if they can. Pretty pickings—
the revenues of England—for the shirtless Tail and the
starving Brutilitarians.

We do not know whether the people of England will in
consequence be tempted to do what the Right Hon. Sir
John Cam Hobhouse, one of His Majesty's Ministers, once
recommended them to do, namely, " throw the House
of Commons into the Thames." [2] But we should not be
surprised.

What ! are not general warrants and *lettres de cachet*,
and the recommendation of the rack, and the setting up
of their pleasure above the law, and the declaration
that their power is irresponsible—are not these enough ;
but, forsooth, our dividends are also to be unpaid, our
judges and public officers, our sailors and soldiers, to be
starved ? The conduct of the Ministers on this occasion
is the most pitiful on record.

" Willing to wound, and yet afraid to strike,"

stood the Chancellor of the Exchequer, while Lord John
Russell menaced the Peers, and was the next morning
obliged to eat his words and recant his threat. His
threat ! In fact, the Ministers are well aware that the
collision is a failure, and ranting Attwood was obliged
to acknowledge in the House on Saturday that even the

[1] A threat by Mr. Spring Rice, defended by Lord John Russell.
[2] Hobhouse, in his Radical days, was committed to Newgate by
the House of Commons for breach of privilege. In an anonymous
pamphlet (1819) he had asked : " What prevents the people
from walking to the House, and pulling out the members by the
ears, locking up their doors, and flinging the key into the Thames?"

Birmingham Union could not be revived. According to his statement, Attwood had recommended that the Union should not be revived, and Lord John Russell praised Attwood for his wisdom and moderation. Can anything be more supremely farcical ?

The long and the short of the affair is this, that the present leaders of " The People " have just begun their collision, or civil war, the wrong way. They have reversed the order of revolution—they have begun with the Rump —they have commenced by the ridiculous, and want to get on to the sublime.

If these fellows were not so absurd, we would gravely argue the desirableness of this country being governed by the House of Commons alone; but it is profaning history to appeal to it in order to illustrate the sayings and doings of such a Praise God Barebones crew. Yet we may as well remember how the House of Commons conducted itself when it monopolised for a season the whole power of the State. In the course of five years that House of Commons levied taxes to the amount of forty millions, a sum at that period unprecedented, and nevertheless they were loaded with debts and encumbrances which the writers of to-day declare to be "prodigious." Moreover, one agreeable morning (how Wakley's mouth will water !), the House of Commons openly took the sum of £300,000 and divided it among themselves. Then their Committees, to whom the management of the different branches of revenue was entrusted, never brought in their accounts, and had unlimited power of secreting whatever funds they pleased from the public treasure. These branches were needlessly multiplied, in order to render the revenue more intricate, to share the advantages among greater numbers, and to conceal the frauds of which they were universally suspected. But this is nothing. The House of Commons sequestered nearly one half, not only of the lands, rents, and revenues of the Kingdom, but nearly one half of the goods and chattels of all Englishmen. Finally, when all

other sources of plunder were exhausted, these leaders of
"The People," the House of Commons, invented the
Excise, the most odious of taxes, and extended it even to
provisions and the common necessaries of life. All who
appealed against these fiscal or other arrangements of the
House of Commons were sequestered, fined, imprisoned,
and corporally punished, without law or remedy. Who
can wonder that the English nation submitted without
a murmur to Cromwell ?

      *   *   *   *   *

What ! There is yelping and whining in the kennel,
is there, eh ? And miserable moans from our slight
lashing. These are the bold spirits who menace our
gracious Sovereign and insult his Royal consort—these
are the men who want to know what is the use of the
Lords, who sneer at the Church, and brand the Corporations—these are the men who call each morning for a
"collision."

Mark how pale they grow in an instant, how they
tremble when they are told the bitter truth by concealing
which they can alone live. They announce an Honourable
Gentleman as the writer of this journal, and grossly insult
him, and complain in the same breath of our personalities.

Personalities, indeed ! Why, if we wished to be personal, do they flatter themselves we don't know them ?
Do they fancy they are "unseen" ? If a single airy
flank of our thong has created such a pother, what will
it be if it please our humour to lay it on in good earnest ?
Lord have mercy upon them !

Personal, indeed ! If we had wished to be personal—
if we chose now to follow their example of this morning
and arraign the confederate scribblers by name—do they
flatter themselves it is not in our power ? Do they hug
themselves in the fond belief that we could not summon
before us the old hack who is their nominal chief ; and the
bankrupt attorney who has turned agitator by trade ;
and the editor of a more reputable journal who fights in
a visor to conceal his blushes at the ragged ranks in which

he is enlisted; and the pursers[1] and steamboat stewards, grotesquely metamorphosed in this age of marvels into private secretaries and confidential agents of Peers and Ministers; and the "rich banker" of whom they boast, and whose opulence is probably as actual as that of Laffitte and Ternaux,[2] once equally appealed to for proof of the possible combination of liberalism and property before the three glorious days revealed the bankrupt bank of one, and exposed the mortgaged manufactory of the other.

We wish not to combat with these small deer; our business is with their masters. But there are many arrows in our quiver, and, if they seek a fray, we are ready, to use their jargon, for the "collision."

So they complain of personality—and on the same morning publish a lying biography of one of the most illustrious men in England,[3] full of base sneers at his family, and blackguard stories of his early fortunes, and lying reports of his table conversations, styled by these eavesdroppers his "opinions."

Personality, indeed! Why this very Journal, this *Morning Chronicle*, some little time back sullied even its columns with foul and cowardly insinuations against a virtuous and accomplished lady who had never stepped for a moment out of the decorous privacy of her life. And the craven and malignant sneer is actually repeated this morning. Is this the spirit in which war is to be carried on? Well—let it be so. And let their arch-apostate leader, who for a few more hours may be Prime Minister of England, look to his character and conduct. Are they so pure and immaculate?

*   *   *   *   *

The *Globe* of last night "meant to have taken some notice of the peculiar virulence of the *Morning Post* of

---

[1] Mr. Tom Young ("Ubiquity" Young), Melbourne's private secretary, was originally a purser in the navy.
[2] Jacques Laffitte, the French financier and politician (1767-1844), and Baron Ternaux, French manufacturer and representative (1763-1833).   [3] Lord Lyndhurst.

Saturday and yesterday, but," adds our considerate contemporary, "we don't see why we should." It is a
doubtful matter, then. The silly *Globe*, trying to be
supercilious, can be only simpering. 'Tis most amusing;
writing a long belaboured article, intended to be an attack
upon us, and then suddenly losing courage at the striking
point. Why, the writer in the *Globe* knoweth full well that
he had been concocting an attack upon the *Morning Post*
the whole day, yet after all this preliminary bluster he
suddenly loses heart—he tucks up his sleeves and even
squares his elbows, but then his stomach fails him, and
he determines to keep the King's peace. The writer in
the *Globe* must be more courageous; this is not the way
great men get out of scrapes. He should take a lesson
from Scipio Africanus.

CHAPTER IV

Protestants and Papists—House of Commons not representative
    of the People—The "constituency"—A tryannical and
    vexatious oligarchy.
                                   Wednesday, August 26.

THE division in the House of Lords on Monday night
realised our proudest anticipations! We said that on
that night the Protestant Peers of England were about
to struggle with Papacy; and their Lordships were conscious of the awful character of the contest. They may
rest assured that the eyes of all Europe were upon them.

The speech of the Lord Bishop of London in particular
was worthy of his high theme, worthy of the august
assembly to which it was addressed, worthy of the
reverend and lettered bench of which he is one of the
most pious and distinguished ornaments. It was earnest,
it was eloquent, it was argumentative and convincing in
the highest degree. In fact, it exhausted the subject,
and the thrilling peroration not only struck to the hearts,
and was echoed by the voices, of all present, but we feel

5

confident has stirred the spirit, and been responded to by the sympathy of every Protestant in the United Kingdom.

Nothing can exceed the factious conduct of the Premier, if Premier he still be, on this great question. Two Measures which had no necessary connection with each other, but which are avowedly incorporated with each other for party purposes of a discreditable character, are submitted to the consideration of the House of Commons. By a very small majority, confessedly on all hands obtained by the mere suffrages of the Popish members, the Siamese Act passes the Lower House, and is sent to the Peers. The Peers, to prove the sincerity of their wishes to advance all measures for the benefit of the State, and of Ireland especially, allow the Bill to be read a second time, pass unanimously in Committee every clause which relates to the relief of the practical evils complained of, and strike out the clauses referring only to an abstract principle of the assertion of which nearly half the House of Commons had previously disapproved.

The Prime Minister hereupon turns round, and coolly declares that he will not take upon himself the responsibility of carrying on the measure any further. Could anything be more barefaced, more unjust, more wicked ?

Insolent, audacious man ! Or, rather, should we pity him ? The loud clamour of his braggadocio failed of its purpose. In the midst of it we still heard the clank of his fetter. The Slave of O'Connell ! Those who remember Lord Melbourne in his calmer and happier hours must indeed be thunderstruck.

Now mark—mark the dilemma of this unhappy Minister. The Catholic Peers of England, inspired by the remembrance of their heroic ancestors, decline voting on this occasion *in deference to their oath*. What a brand for O'Connell. Now the Bill has past the Commons only by the votes of perjured Papists. So Lord Melbourne announces that his consideration for these false slaves outweighs his respect for the Peers of England ! We leave him in this melancholy position.

*   *   *   *   *

If at this moment Lord Melbourne be Prime Minister
of England, or is not on the eve of resigning the trust
which he has abused, then he has virtually announced that
the Government of this country is in future to be carried
on by the House of Commons alone. We yield our
adhesion, of course, to the new order without a murmur,
knowing full well that if this be the case the career of
independent journalists is over, and that the year will not
elapse without some severe ukase being promulgated which
will efficiently prevent any criticism of the Press upon the
conduct and " pleasure " of our new lords and masters.
Yet, while there is time, even if it be the last exercise of
our right, and the last fruitless fulfilment of our duty, in
the discharge of the noble function of upholding truth and
diffusing knowledge, we will attempt to assist our countrymen in clearly understanding what this hitherto third
estate of the realm styled the House of Commons really
is; and what has formerly been the Government of this
country when carried on by the House of Commons alone.

The House of Commons affects to be the representative
of The People. 'Tis no such thing. It never was, it
never will, it never can be. It is the representative of a
section, and a limited and varying section of the people,
called THE CONSTITUENCY—a body certainly more
numerous, but as conventional, as privileged, and as
irresponsible as the House of Lords itself. The vast
majority of the people is unrepresented, and must ever
be unrepresented. No Government of any form or frame
can last without the existence of some irresponsible power
in its structure, and if the House of Lords were rendered
elective to-morrow, what is to check, what is to guard the
people of England against the irresponsibility of the
constituency and the Representatives of that constituency
styled the House of Commons ?

The constituency of to-day is different, very different,
from the constituency of five years back, and five years
hence it may be found to vary still more widely from its
present character. Only a few days since the King's

Minister proposed a measure to Parliament which would
at one blow have cut off and disfranchised eighty thousand
members of the constituency. Had the proposition been
successful, would these men, therefore, have ceased to be
of the people ? The freemen of England, that is, a portion of the constituency of England, whose rights were
menaced by a more powerful portion of the same body,
acting through their Representatives, fled to the Peers of
England for succour; and the Peers saved them ; and
herein was seen, and in this just and courageous conduct
might have been detected, the strong claim which those
" pillars of the State " [1] have upon the trust and affection
of the nation; herein might have been discovered the
reason why, when the constituency of England in the
seventeenth century had succeeded in abolishing the
Upper House of Parliament, and in establishing a tyranny
of the constituency over the people, why the same people,
harassed and plundered, rose at length against this
despotic and cruel constituency, called back their banished Sovereign and natural leader, and re-established the
abolished House of Peers, in whom they recognised
their legal and Constitutional champions against the
inroads and assaults of a favoured and privileged section
of their number, namely, that portion of them who are
entrusted with the right of electing Representatives in the
House of Commons, and thus have a Chamber set apart for
the advocacy of their rights and interests, and are
established into a third estate of the realm—an institution, we repeat, as purely conventional as the institution
of the limited Monarchy and the hereditary Peerage.

Now, the constituency of England, as distinguished from
the people of England, are, as appears by the divisions in
their peculiar Chamber, equally divided in opinion. It is
probable that the majority of the constituency are indeed
Conservative, for the Conservative Representatives of
the constituency have in general been elected by large

---

[1] Shakespeare, 2 *Henry VI.*, I., i. 74 ; see also *The Contention*, I.,
i. 75, " Braue Peeres of England, pillers of the State."

majorities, and the Destructive Representatives of the constituency by very small ones; but this matters little. We have to-day pointed out, for the consideration of our countrymen, an important distinction, over which they will do well to ponder—that there is a vast difference between the people of England and its constituency; that this same constituency is a purely conventional body; that the House of Commons is their peculiar Chamber, and not the Chamber of the people in general; that if the House of Commons alone rules the nation, the nation will not be ruled by itself or its representatives, but by the representatives of a limited section of itself; and that the natural consequences of this arrangement will be, as it has been before—and which we shall take an early opportunity of demonstrating—that the favoured minority who will thus obtain the whole power of the State will establish a tyrannical and vexatious oligarchy, and soon obtain also the whole property of the State.

* * * * *

"Marylebone has met." According to the solitary organ of the Government, there were between three and four thousand persons present. Why, before the fatal competition of the Fantoccini Punch could have assembled half the number.

It was a very characteristic meeting of "The People." But the muse of the immortal Samuel Butler could alone do justice to it. We should like to draw up a catalogue of the orators, like Homer's Ships; Potter, and Kensitt, and Savage,[1] and Sappy. Why was not Juggins present? Why will that illustrious member of the Annoyance Jury, that rival of Dogberry and Verges, devote himself to Westminster? Oh, rare Juggins! Savage, however,

[1] " Mr. (John) Savage, the Radical, very pertinently observed that he knew the faces of the greater number present, and was in the habit of meeting them. When it is considered that Savage addresses a Radical meeting at his public-house in Circus Street every Sunday evening . . . the public voice in Marylebone on this occasion will be justly considered in its proper light."—*Morning Post* report, August 25, 1835.

nearly made up for him, and was as ferocious as his name. "Down with the Lords and their foul influence!" This was the Savage cry, and received, of course, with "tremendous cheering." Another orator declared all the Peers were "bastards," a compliment, we suppose, to Lord Melbourne. The chivalric Whalley was very elaborate on the Qualification Clause, and indignantly asked assembled Marylebone "what property was." Sir Hudibras paused for a reply, and it was not wonderful that no one present could furnish him with a definition. Mr. Henry Bulwer[1] closed the proceedings. "Alas, poor Yorick!" 'Tis lamentable to see one who is at least a Gentleman and a man of letters in such a predicament. 'Tis paying dear for a return even if the expenses of the Parliamentary elected were so slight as they boast. Mr. Henry Bulwer declared that the *Morning Post* had announced that the Royal Standard was about to be raised, and that fifty thousand cavalry would march to London. Lord bless his little soul, we said no such thing. We said that, as far as we could form an opinion, the "collision" might be left to the police. Mr. Henry Bulwer tries to be very violent, while he laughs in his sleeve. He must be coarse, or, he may take our word for it, at the next election he will stand no chance against Juggins.

CHAPTER V

The Constitutional position elaborated—Hereditary election—
Government by the Commons—Whigs and the spirit of the
age—Don Carlos and the Premier—The distracted Cabinet—
A new Commission.

Thursday, August 27.

WE repeat that the House of Commons is not the representative of THE PEOPLE any more than is the House of Lords. The House of Commons is the representative of the Commons. The Commons of England (and the Com-

---

[1] H. Lytton Bulwer (afterwards Lord Dalling) then colleague of Sir S. Whalley in the representation of Marylebone.

mons in the original, genuine, and legal signification of
the term is a title confined to those, and those only, who
have a right to sit, or to vote for representatives, in that
estate of the Realm)—the Commons of England, like the
Peers of England, formed and still form a favoured section
or order of the people enjoying for the advantage of the
nation in general certain powers and privileges of a very
eminent and exalted character.

The number of the Commons, like the number of the
Peers, is purely conventional. The King can increase
the number of the Peers, and the King and the Peers
and the representatives of the Commons can by convention increase the numbers of the Commons. During the
last half-century the number of the Peers has been greatly
increased; yet the Commons, although far outnumbering
the Peers, still bear a very small relative proportion to
the number of the people. Nevertheless the Commons
are so numerous and so scattered that it is not possible
for them to assemble together for the purpose of legislation; therefore they meet in the persons of their representatives. There is no other apparent reason why the
Commons should not in their own persons exercise legislative power. Before the Reform Act they might have
met in Spa Fields, and now they might meet on
Salisbury Plain. It would be possible for all the Commons
of England to encamp within five miles of Stonehenge.

So much for these two sections or bodies of the people,
the Peers and the Commons, alike privileged orders
and alike exercising irresponsible power. And the only
material difference between them is that the qualification
of one is purely hereditary, while in addition to the hereditary qualification which is enjoyed by that portion of
the Commons who are landowners they have also the
advantage of a qualification by tenure.

If the Peers, therefore, in voting for laws, exercise a
power for which they are not responsible, so also do the
Commons in voting for lawmakers; and if it be a blot in
our Constitution that the Peers should be invested with

the function of hereditary legislation, so it must be an
equal blur that the Commons should be invested with the
function of hereditary election. Thus much in answer
to the ignorant fools and superficial knaves who pretend
to write nowadays on political subjects, and criticise,
forsooth, our ancient Constitution, of the principles of
which, as of everything else, they are absolutely and
profoundly ignorant.

The Constitution of England consists of King, Lords,
and Commons, not King, Lords, and People, and the
member of the House of Commons who talks of " the
People's House " is either a gross blockhead or an insolent
usurper.

Now, will the people of England be governed by the
Commons alone ? That is the question which we shall
soon be called upon to decide. Will the people of England
permit the whole power of the State to be monopolised
by one favoured class ? For our part, we will not trust
the Commons of England with despotic power one jot
more than the Peers of England or the Monarch of
England. The Monarch of England has at times exercised
despotic power, and we found it hard enough. The Peers
of England have never exercised despotic power, and we
hope never will. But the Commons of England have
exercised despotic power before this, and compared with
their infamous tyranny the recollection of the rule of the
stoutest tyrant that ever waved in this island a solitary
sceptre is a dream of bliss. Let us not, in God's name,
try them again; but if we are mad enough the Republic
of jobbers will not last long. Some brawny arm will soon
be extended to " take away this bauble."

*   *   *   *   *

The Whigs have given us an eminent specimen this
year of a factious Opposition. It appears they are going
to favour us now with a factious Government. Vast are
the obligations for which England is indebted to the
Whigs.

They govern in " the spirit of the age " forsooth. If

so, 'tis a shabby spirit, a very pitiful spirit, indeed; a most lick-spittle, place-loving, pelf-adoring spirit.

Lord Viscount Melbourne, ever since he assumed office, has been the Minister of the King's necessity, not of the King's choice. Now, it appears, he is going to carry on the Government in spite of the House of Lords. A bold fellow this! If we did not find him crawling in the dust before a Popish rebel, one might suppose that he was animated with some degree of headstrong heroism. But the scene behind the curtain proffers such a humiliating and instructive contrast to the swaggering sulkiness with which the audience is greeted that the charm vanishes in a moment.

Never was a Cabinet in such a condition: all fighting among themselves and contradicting and reproaching each other.

The Premier would retire, but our "Don Carlos,"[1] who is for a "collision," opposes this.

Then Melbourne urges that he has to bear the brunt of the battle, and face each night an overwhelming majority: Carlos replies 'tis only for a short season; and that though he, to be sure, has the majority in the Commons on his side, 'tis a very delicate one, and then his labour should be taken into consideration; some seven months' hard work and O'Connell to aid; "while you," he quaintly observes, "after all, are only badgered for three weeks."

"But the King," replies the Premier. "May be," etc., says Carlos.

All this time Lansdowne looks grave, and already meditates joining an anti-Papal Cabinet. The needy members of the clique, of course, are in convulsions, and the moment the division was announced Lord Auckland flew to his wine-merchant, and bargained that, in case of his appointment[2] being cancelled, the Burgundy was to

[1] Lord John Russell.
[2] To the Governor-Generalship of India, in succession to Lord Heytesbury, who, appointed by Sir Robert Peel, never took up the office.

be taken back, and his Lordship only to pay for the laths and sawdust. 'Tis a right merry crew!

*　　*　　*　　*　　*

On Tuesday night the Marquis of Lansdowne moved the second reading of the Charities Commission Bill. On this Lord Lyndhurst rose and very pertinently exposed the job. Thirty Commissioners appointed to inquire— thirty more Commissioners! An arrangement entailing such heavy expenses on the country could not be assented to without evidence and inquiry.

Lord Lyndhurst opposed the Bill—his recent experience of Commissioners did not authorise him to confide the execution of any trust to such Gentry without the most suspicious inquiry.

Lord Lansdowne, a great patron of Commissions, for he has many protégés, fought hard for his parasites, but even Lord Brougham gave up the affair as a bad job, and supported the motion of Lord Lyndhurst for throwing out the Bill.

What a cut-up for Parkes, whose name has actually become a proverb throughout England for a job—and all the queer gang, roaring Rushton, and sober Drinkwater, and the unknown Wilkinson, and Cockburn the trustworthy, and "Horrors - and - Hell" Dwarris! Great gnashing of teeth, we suspect.

CHAPTER VI

A meeting of the "People"—Defence of Lord Lyndhurst— Mushroom Peers—The Estates of the Realm—Rivalry and its sequel—A Popish conspiracy—Mr. Hume's threat—Lessons from past history—A challenge to the *Courier*.

Friday, August 28.

ST. GILES'S has met. It was a very great meeting of "The People." The rapscallions amounted to some hundreds. Juggins was not there, because Juggins is of Westminster; and Sappy was not there, because Sappy is of Marylebone; and Savage was not there, because Savage is the comrade of Sappy; and Sir Hudibras was not there, because Sir Hudibras[1] is the confederate of Savage.

But although Savage was wanting, there was no lack of unlettered ruffians; and although Sir Hudibras was missed, other parochial Cleons poured forth their plebeian ribaldry. The dogs demanded the "use of the Lords" with a most dinning bow-wow.

The chief orator, one Dr. Epps, after abusing the hereditary legislators, very quaintly and consistently assured "the people" that the old Nobles were on their side, and that they were only opposed by "Lord Lyndhurst and the Duke of Wellington, and the upstart Peers." And then the brute characteristically added, "How Sir John Copley's mother would stare if she could rise from her grave, and find her son a Lord!"

Fortunately, there needs no such miracle for that happy lady, "Sir John Copley's mother, to find her son a Lord." She still lives, in the enjoyment of all her faculties, and she has lived, not merely lived to find her son a Lord, but twice Lord Chancellor of England. We are very much mistaken if, before her venerable eyes be closed, and before her pious voice shall exclaim "Now let Thy servant depart in peace," this proud mother will not have the unprecedented gratification of seeing her offspring Lord Chancellor of England for the third time, ay, for the third time keeper of that Great Seal which he has guarded with such fidelity, and used with so much wisdom and so much honour.

But observe the reasoning of this parish orator—and we only notice his reasoning because it is a fair sample of the political logic of the faction, and only re-echoed from the silly and seditious journals which are the evangelists of the gang—they denounce the principle of hereditary legislation, and in the same breath anathematise what they call upstart Peers—that is, Peers like Lord Lynd-

[1] Sir Samuel Whalley.

hurst and the Duke of Wellington, whom they quote, raised to that distinction by their public services.

Now, let us take the case of Lord Lyndhurst, the very instance they themselves bring forward. Here is a nobleman who has sprung from the Commons, a great statesman, a most accomplished orator, an unrivalled lawyer. He obtains a seat in the upper House of Parliament entirely through the influence of his talents and his public services; and, unfortunately, there is at present no prospect of his honours descending to his posterity.

Why, this is the very ideal of a senator whom the Brutilitarian sages are always bawling about, and this is the very Peer of England whom their St. Giles's disciples denounce as " an upstart." Lyndhurst and Wellington upstarts ! Would there were more such mushrooms !

*　　*　　*　　*　　*

The Constitution of England is a profounder piece of human wit than the Brutilitarian philosophers imagine when they recommend us their new lamps with so much pert conceit, and so much complacent ignorance. The Constitution has endured for centuries, and under it the country has obtained, and enjoyed, a degree of greatness and prosperity which has seldom fallen to the lot of empires. As long as the King and the two privileged orders of the Kingdom—first the Peers and secondly the Commons acting through their Representatives—have drawn together, the polity of Great Britain may be fairly instanced as the one which has the nearest approached the object of all great legislators, namely, the happiness of all the people.

But when the usual and desirable harmony has not subsisted between the King and the estates, and especially when an unwholesome rivalry has sprung up between the estates themselves, and, from some accession of power or other unusual circumstance, one House of Parliament has endeavoured to obtain supremacy over the other, there have ever been in this land great heart-burnings, fatal dissensions, much injury to arts and commerce, infringements of our rights and liberties, a halt in the prosperity of the realm, a defalcation of the imperial revenue, bloodshed and rebellion, and, finally, civil war.

The great accession of strength which that privileged order of the State called the Commons obtained by the Whig Reform Act has filled the imaginations of certain representatives of the Commons, and members of their peculiar House of Parliament, with the bold but ruinous project of destroying the authority of the Upper Chamber, and so monopolising within themselves, or, rather, a petty number of their members, the whole power of the State ; whereby they propose founding, as in times past they have established, a most grinding tyranny, neither respecting the persons nor the properties of the people of this realm. And in the first place these arch-conspirators, finding they could not obtain the co-operation of a majority of the British members of the House of Commons in their wicked device, entered into a most infamous and sacrilegious conspiracy with the Popish rebels of Ireland, by whose aid alone they have already upset the King's Government, and by whose continued assistance they propose abolishing the House of Lords, and rooting up the Throne itself.

These conspirators have already afforded the people of England a specimen of the mode in which they will exercise arbitrary power when they have succeeded in obtaining it, and the House of Lords no longer subsists to keep them in check. They have already revived general warrants and issued *lettres de cachet ;* they have declared their pleasure to be above the law ; and they have announced themselves as irresponsible for the exercise of their power. Moreover, they have inferentially recommended the revival of the rack or other similar torture.

Englishmen will remember the sufferings of their fathers under a similar domination, and will take good counsel in good time.

The House of Commons have before this abolished the Lords and rooted up the Throne, under the pretence of maintaining the liberties of the people. But when one of that people, and not even a Royalist, was summoned before that despotic House of Commons, and refused to answer certain illegal questions, as Colonel Fairman[1] did the other day, that same House of Commons, after adjourning several times in great dilemma, finally ordered a red-hot iron to be bored through the tongue of the man who refused to answer their questions; and the iron was heated, and the tongue was bored accordingly.[2]

Now we understand what Mr. Hume means by " compelling witnesses to answer, whether they will or no." The Hon. Member as yet has only inferentially recommended torture; he has only given it as his abstract opinion that " witnesses whether they will or no shall be compelled to answer the House of Commons "; but the instance of Naylor, which we have quoted above, will afford an instructive commentary to Mr. Hume's threat, and teach the people of England what they have to expect.

They have other things to expect if the past, instead of a dream, be a lesson of practical life and profitable experience. They have to expect that the taxation of this country will be doubled, while its public debt will be simultaneously augmented. They have to expect that the Representatives of the Commons will meet one fine morning, and vote the money of the people to the amount of at least £300,000, or more probably to an amount equal to that sum at this day—a good million— openly among themselves. They have to expect that, in order to carry on their tyranny without the slightest

[1] Colonel Fairman, Grand Secretary and Treasurer of the Orange Lodges, refused to give up to the House a letter-book relating to the correspondence of the Lodges.

[2] The case of James Naylor, a Quaker religious enthusiast, who, on October 24, 1656, made a triumphant entry into Bristol after the manner of Christ's entry into Jerusalem, was arrested and examined by a committee of the House of Commons, and was sentenced by the House to be twice set in the pillory, to be whipped, to be branded, and to have his tongue bored with a hot iron. He was then to be sent to Bristol for a second scourging, and to be imprisoned with hard labour in Bridewell.

check, the majority of the House of Commons—that is
to say, the English Radicals and the Popish repealers or
rebels—will vote that the minority are disqualified from
taking any part in these proceedings; further, the people
of England have to expect that their bodies will be tortured, their properties sequestered, their persons banished,
and their lives forfeited, without the shadow of redress,
or the solace even of a murmur; and that "trial by Jury"
will be voted, as it hath been voted, "a breach of privilege."

The young, the ignorant, the headstrong, who read
this, may read and shudder. It is but a brief and very
hurried sketch of a few of the more marked and salient
features of English revolution. And are all these awful
calamities impending over this country because a weak
faction cannot maintain themselves in power without the
aid of levellers and the co-operation of rebels ?

　　　*　　　*　　　*　　　*　　　*

The *Courier* last night borrowed a little of "Cambyses'
vein" recently recommended by Lord Melbourne, and
we have seen a beggar in a barn who has ranted much in
the same manner.

The *Courier* announces that "Ministers are firm, and
so are the Commons." Thus have we heard exclaim
two drunken dogs, as they have been reeling home at
nights. Yet the morning generally finds them in the
gutter, low and dirty enough, or at the best in the watch-
house where they are immured, or sent to the treadmill.

Follows then much twaddle about "the nation" and
"the people." Define "the nation," Mr. *Courier*, define
"the people," define if you can and dare.

As for coming events, far from thinking it necessary for
the King to raise his standard, or the Yeomanry to rally
round it, it is our firm and fixed opinions that "the crisis"
may be left to the constables, and "the collision" to
the police.

Whether we consider the question in reference to
property, intelligence, or numbers, we are convinced that

the Conservative party has the superiority, and a vast one. But as far as we can deduce a meaning from this ranting rigmarole of our usually calm contemporary, there is no nation, no people of England, at all, for he boldly announces that " the Commons are backed by twenty-seven millions of constituents." Good Mr. *Courier*, is it so ? You indeed ride post-haste. The constituency of England does not amount to the population of a second-rate capital, and more than half of that constituency is Conservative.

" All power," announces the *Courier*, " is now in the hands of the House of Commons." The deuce it is ! Then the sooner we get it out of their hands the better. The people of England know by experience the blessing of the whole power of the country being in the House of Commons. As for that old Brutilitarian charlatan Bentham, we will prove any day the *Courier* likes that " the balance " is not a nursery tale. This trash has been too long current, but it is base for all that.

Good-day, Mr. *Courier*, and we hope you are more sober than you appeared last night. We meant to have said something to the gentle *Globe*, but on reflection, to use its own dainty phrase, " we don't see why we should." The truth is, we do see, but we have not room ; so to-day we will not pluck a laurel from the honoured brow of Scipio Africanus.

CHAPTER VII

The Devil and his bond—Honest Lord Althorp and high-minded
   Lord Melbourne—More about Single Chamber rule—Hazel
   rigg precedent—Lord Lyndhurst and Lord Denman—A
   " violent party man."

Saturday, August 29.

THE solitary organ of the Rump raves and rants with desperate but desponding fury. It feels, like its doomed faction, that the Popish taint has poisoned the fame and influence of the Whig-Radicals in this Protestant country for ever. In its despair and bewildered cowardice it abjures its friends; it utterly renounces O'Connell and his crew; it exclaims, with frantic ejaculation, " Get thee behind me, Satan !"

But those who have sold themselves to the Devil err if they suppose when the dark day of reckoning arrives they can extricate themselves from the awful " crisis," from the terrible " collision " which they have provoked, by taking refuge in this pious retort. The fiend points to his bond, and forthwith pitchforks them into Hades.

The solitary organ asks for evidence of Lord Melbourne's sacrilegious and treasonable connection with O'Connell. We need not go far to find it. Why have Lord Melbourne and his colleagues recanted in the course of six short months all their previous principles and pledges on the sacred subject of the Church of England ? To conciliate O'Connell, and, by bribing him with the plunder of the Establishment in Ireland, compensate themselves with the plunder of the Treasury in England.

Why, there is not a boy who runs through the street on a sixpenny errand who cannot supply the Whigs with an answer, quick on the tongue and engraven on the heart of every Briton and every Protestant.

But Lord Melbourne denies the connection, and Lord Melbourne, according to the solitary organ of the Rump, is " a high-minded Nobleman." We believe Lord Viscount Melbourne to be as much a " high-minded Nobleman " as Lord Viscount Althorp[1] was an " honest " one. Honest Lord Althorp and high-minded Lord Melbourne are fit to run together in the national chariot, and dash the car down the revolutionary precipice with the greatest skill imaginable, while all the time the deluded driver flatters himself that one of his steeds is remarkably steady, and the other marvellously well broken. " Honest " Lord Althorp was no doubt a remarkably honest fellow, for all his friends said so; yet his Lordship continued sometimes to act like a marvellously indifferent knave; and " high-minded " Lord Melbourne is no doubt a very

---

[1] Leader of the House of Commons in Melbourne's first Ministry.

6

noble-spirited Gentleman, for all his friends say so; yet his Lordship, throughout the whole of his trimming and tortuous career, has generally managed to leave the impression behind him that he was but a pitiful jobber.

"High-minded " Lord Melbourne, indeed! What! William Lamb "high-minded "? William Lamb, the *pis-aller* of Castlereagh, whose best speeches have been in defiance of what the Radicals call "the Manchester massacre " and in favour of the repeal of the Habeas Corpus! William Lamb, who was always brought forward by the old Tories to oppose Parliamentary reform, and who was the champion of the Indemnity Bill. The Arch-apostate!

Never mind; he has been used by Castlereagh, abused by Canning, drilled by Wellington; he has intrigued with Huskisson against Wellington; he has betrayed Lord Grey; and he has deserted Lord Brougham ; and now he is at his old tricks with O'Connell, and we mistake the Popish rebel much if he be circumvented by this old hack—this most unprincipled of public men, even of Whigs.

"And then, he looks so modest all the while."

*   *   *   *   *

When people wake in the morning, and remember that the King's Minister is pursuing a system which must ultimately place their lives and properties at the disposal of Wakley and Silk Buckingham,[1] they wake in terror.

The same feeling pervades Society as influences a crowded assembly when there is a sudden cry of "Fire !" or "Take care of your pockets!" Everyone is alarmed and on his guard.

The Whigs publicly boast now that the House of Commons possesses the whole power of the country. If this dreadful allegation be true, the sooner we take measures to clip their high-flying wings the better for all those who value liberty, property, and life, the fruits

---

[1] James Silk Buckingham, Liberal Member for Sheffield, founder of the *Athenæum*.

of their industry, and the enjoyment of their freedom.
Never let us forget what the rule of the House of Commons
was when they before possessed the whole power of the
country. Never let us forget that the House of Commons,
when they had got rid of the House of Lords, voted " trial
by Jury " a breach of privilege; that they doubled the
taxes of this country, and loaded it at the same time with
enormous debts; that they divided the public money
openly among themselves; bored men's tongues with
red-hot irons who refused to answer their questions; and
sequestered the property and imprisoned the persons of
all whom they styled, or chose to consider, malignants.

If the Whig-Radicals, by the aid and co-operation of
the Popish rebels, could re-establish this old despotism
of the House of Commons to-morrow, as they are trying
to do, every Conservative would immediately be treated
as a malignant, and any Parliamentary member of the
Movement would enjoy the high privilege of seizing any
of our estates or properties to-morrow, without any chance
on our side of redress, or even a Court of Justice to which
we could appeal.

Hazelrigg, as impudent a fellow as Hume, and as great
" a Church Reformer," practically exemplified what
" Church Reform " meant by seizing hold of great portions
of the Bishops' lands, and sacking them, during one year
only, to the amount of £60,000; a good booty at all times,
and equal then to £180,000 of our present money. Em-
boldened by his impunity, and following the examples
of his colleagues, who had voted the Conservative minority
out of the House, Hazelrigg commenced seizing private
estates, and when the plea of malignancy was exhausted
he and his friends seized those of their own party.

Thus this same impudent adventurer, who was the
Hume of those days, laid violent hands on a profitable
colliery in the North to which he had taken a fancy, and
which belonged to the famous Lilburne, a stout fellow
and " a true reformer " for he stood up right manfully
against the Star Chamber in the old days of its tyranny,

now so mild in comparison to the free rule of the House of Commons. Lilburne petitioned the House. The House appointed a Committee on the subject, who, without even receiving the evidence proffered in favour of this injured man and this "tried Reformer," decided that the petitioner, in accusing any Member of the House of Commons of forcibly dispossessing him of his estate, was guilty of a high contempt and gross libel, and that Lilburne and his fellow-petitioner should consequently pay £3,000 to the House of Commons each, and £500 each to be divided among the Members of the Committee itself.

There, "Reformers of England," you see how your friends will treat you. It is evident that a Wakley and a Buckingham must have been on the Committee.

*   *   *   *   *

The overwhelming defeat which the base Whigs experienced in the House of Lords on the Corporation job, as flagrant a job, by-the-by, as their India Bill, and concocted in the same party and anti-national spirit, has enraged them beyond measure with the distinguished leader of the Conservative party in the Upper House. The only way in which they hoped to neutralise the irresistible exposure they received from Lord Lyndhurst was very Whiggish indeed; they had recourse to a lie, and they boldly announced that his Lordship had been originally a Radical, or, to use his milder language, "a Whig and something more."

Lord Lyndhurst met the insinuation with a firm, a manly, an uncompromising, and an unequivocal denial. Lord Melbourne and poor Lord Lansdowne, who were the tools and champions of their protégés and parasites, the Commissioners, ate their words, of course, and there the matter, so far as authority was concerned, ended; and only the confederate scribblers who concoct that queer journal which is the solitary organ of the Rump repeated the base and recanted imputation.

But still there were dark whispers about. It was very

true that Lord Melbourne had recalled his words; "he could do no more and he could say no less"; and all that gaberdash with which cowardly slanderers conceal their flinching scandal and detected calumny. But when Lord Denman came to town he would say "such things." Lord Denman knew all about it. He was the authority —old Nero Denman[1]—Denman who called His Gracious Majesty a slanderer—old Nero Denman was to do the deed, and "settle" the affair for ever.

And this was uttered with an air of triumph, and a base interchange of smiles, among the initiated, congratulatory of complacent and coming victory.

Dogs! and viler far than dogs! Denman has come to town, and has found himself called upon, from the spirit of party, to confirm in the most august assembly in the world some of the factious exaggerations of his own factious falsehoods, uttered after the miserable inspiration of some of his own bad wine, at some of his own wretched dinners. Denman has "settled" the question with a vengeance. We shall hear no more of it. It is the only case that Denman ever did satisfactorily settle.

The most that Lord Denman's friends could ever say for him was that, although an ass, his bray was rather melodious; but in his melancholy exhibition in the House of Lords on Thursday night even his voice failed him; even the *vox et preterea* were wanting; *nihil* alone remained.

He made two accusations, one of which he immediately withdrew; the other was destroyed by Lord Lyndhurst amid the enthusiastic cheering of the House before his luckless antagonist could withdraw it.

First, he accused Lord Lyndhurst of owing his introduction to public life to "the Liberals." Lord Lyndhurst replied that he owed his introduction to public life to Lord Liverpool, and previously to entering Parliament had never interfered in political affairs in the slightest degree.

---

[1] Thomas, first Lord Denman, Lord Chief Justice. His supposed comparison of George the Fourth to Nero was the origin of the nickname.

Then Lord Denman, having swallowed his previous charge, equivocated, and declared that he meant the professional life of the Noble Lord. Whereupon Lord Lyndhurst rejoined that the only party business in which he had been professionally employed was in the defence of Watson, a defence which he had undertaken at the request of Sir C. Wetherell, with whom he had co-operated. Finally he called upon Lord Denman to make a specific charge; even to allege a single private conversation which could justify his original imputation, and Denman was silent.

A word or two about this person. Lord Denman may be considered a very fortunate individual, for, of humble origin, he is now a Peer of the Realm, and fills one of the very highest offices in the State. But Lord Denman may also be considered a very remarkable individual, for he has attained this great eminence confessedly by all parties in the total absence of any qualities which could justify his rise and his appointment.

It is a grand characteristic of my Lord Denman that he has failed, and failed decidedly, in everything which he has undertaken. He was called to the Bar, and was soon acknowledged as one of the worst lawyers and one of the clumsiest advocates that ever practised; yet he was not altogether void of employment, because he was a violent party man.

He was brought into Parliament, and cut so melancholy a figure that he himself voluntarily retired from the theatre of his discomfiture. And why was he brought into Parliament? Because he was a violent party man. He was then made Common Sergeant, and might just as well have been made Jack Ketch; but he was appointed Common Sergeant because he was a violent party man.

At length he was metamorphosed into Attorney-General because he was a violent party man; and he was found so clearly incompetent that the Junior Crown Officer was obliged to discharge his duties; but this was winked at because Sir Thomas Denman was a violent party man.

Now behold him for the same reason a Peer and a Chief Justice, a nonentity in the Lords, unfortunately not quite a nonentity on the circuit, only a blunderer; but still his incompetence and his mistakes are alike forgiven, because he is a violent party man.

At last Lord Denman resolves to shiver a lance with Lord Lyndhurst; and the Lord Chief Justice, who has failed in every purpose, of course, as usual, fails in this, and the Lord Chief Justice is now universally acknowledged to be an ass, although he is a violent party man.[1]

CHAPTER VIII

The approaching " crisis "—Principle of the Bill—Whig and Tory policy—Lord Melbourne and the Irish Church Bill—Peers and party menaces—" And now for Lord Melbourne "—Impeachment—The advice of the Press—Scylla and Charybdis—Sir John Campbell—Haggis and cockaleekie.

Monday, August 31.

EIGHT-AND-FORTY hours have elapsed since we last addressed our readers, and the crisis, like the comet,[2] is supposed to be somewhat nearer, though it is not yet visible to the naked eye.

Eight-and-forty hours have elapsed, and Lord Viscount Melbourne is still the Prime Minister of England. He has sneaked through one day and he has shuffled through another, and he is to swindle through a third. By that time the storm or the bubble will have burst, and the crisis, with its fiery tail, will be fairly in sight.

The present position of this eminent Minister and " high-minded " Nobleman is very peculiar. Let us dispassionately review it. The Ministry of which he is the

---

[1] The article relates to a somewhat notable encounter between Denman and Lyndhurst, in which the former was generally acknowledged to have been worsted.

[2] Halley's comet was due to appear about this time.

chief carried through the House of Commons a Bill for the amendment of the municipal corporations of England and Wales. Lord Melbourne introduces his Bill to the House of Lords, and the Peers of England in the most unqualified manner admit its principle—yes, admit its principle—and we call upon any one of the base block-heads who have been for the last three weeks brawling about "the mutilation" of their measure, and insulting the Lords with the valiant blare of their penny trumpet, to deny this if they can.

Let these imbecile scribblers define "The PRINCIPLE" of the Bill. We asked them the other day to define their favourite phrase of "The PEOPLE," but not one has been skilful enough to satisfy our request. They know very well that an analysis of the people would demonstrate that all the elements of a great nation are banded and mar-shalled in the ranks of the Conservatives.

Well, we will define what THE PRINCIPLE of the Cor-poration Amendment Bill is. The principle is that SELF-ELECTION IN MUNICIPAL BODIES SHALL BE TERMIN-ATED BY THE SUBSTITUTION OF A FREE ELECTION BY A POPULAR CONSTITUENCY. There, that is THE PRINCIPLE of the Bill about which we hear so much gaberdash from all the brainless knaves who live by writing "on politics," forsooth, and asking the use of the Lords. That, we repeat, is the principle of the Bill; the principle, the whole principle, and nothing but the principle; and that principle, identically as it is carried into effect by the clauses of the projected law, has been thoroughly, com-pletely, unreservedly, and unequivocally admitted by the Peers. Their Lordships have made many and most valuable alterations in the details of this measure, but with its principle they have never for a moment tampered.

Now, the Whig policy is ever to smuggle in laws for the increase and consolidation of the power of their party under the specious guise of advancing the cause of popular amelioration. The principle of the Corporation Bill

advances the popular cause with which the Tories sympathise; the details of the Corporation Bill only promote
and confirm Whig power, and that the Tories oppose,
because they believe that power by the Whigs will ever
be employed for anti-national purposes.

Toryism is the national spirit exhibiting itself in the
maintenance of the national institutions, and in support
of the national character which those institutions have
formed.

If the Lords bate one jot of their amendments of the
Whig Corporation Bill, they will deserve all their worst
enemies wish them, and they will go far to realise the
ban. Let them bate one jot of those amendments, and
if they do not find a mysterious and simultaneous cloud
steal over the jewels of their coronets, then there is no
magic in the prime tokens of their order.

But will they bate a jot ? Not they. The Radicals
have most indiscreetly chosen to make this a trial of
strength between the two privileged orders of our Constitution—the Peers and the Commons of England.
Whatever they might deem the result, the Peers of
England, we imagine, would be just and fear not. But in
the present instance they may be just without the shadow
of apprehension. The nation is with the Peers, not with
the Popish majority of the Commons; the people will not
back the factious Representatives of a very limited class
in this country, and the individuals who form the Popish
and factious majority are in the main individuals of a
discreditable character.

We could dilate upon this theme, but having despatched
the Corporation Bill we must now proceed to Lord
Melbourne and the Irish Church Bill.

We cannot too clearly comprehend the nature of that
measure by which the Whigs propose to settle the long-
controverted question of the Church establishment in
Ireland. Their Bill combines two propositions which
not only have no natural connection with each other ;
but two propositions which, less than twelve months ago,

the Whigs themselves, at their own instance, declared to have no natural connection with each other.

One is of a real, the other is of an abstract, character; one is of the most urgent nature, the other only concerns the possible and the future.

One is to settle the question of tithes in Ireland, described by the Ministers themselves to be a measure of more pressing importance and immediate interest than any subject which ever engaged the attention of the Legislature; the other is to decide what shall be the object of the surplus of Church property which may possibly accrue after the projected arrangement be completed, and the possible existence of which surplus is denied by many and calculated by the Whigs themselves at a most insignificant amount.

This Bill is introduced to the consideration of the Lords by the Minister, and the Peers, after a most able discussion, have decided exactly as the Whigs did last year; they have decided on the adoption of the Ministerial plan for the settlement of the great, practical and urgent portion of the Measure; and with regard to a few clauses of the Bill which relate to the abstract principle and hypothetical arrangement, they adopt the resolution of the Whigs themselves, entered into only a year ago, and which nearly half of the House of Commons have attempted to establish and guarantee during this very session.

Such is a brief but impartial statement of the conduct of the House of Lords on the two great Measures which the Minister has submitted to their recent consideration. In the first instance they admitted the principle of the measure in the most unqualified manner, and confined their labours entirely to the alteration of its details; in the second instance they adopted, without opposition, the entire Ministerial plan for the settlement of the practical question of urgent interest, and with regard to the abstract principle, the recognition of which could be of no urgency whatever, since it only asserted a dogma

respecting a nonentity, they adopted the opinion which
had been advocated by the Government only during the
last session, and carried, through their influence, by a
great majority in the House of Commons.

Is it possible for the conduct of a legislative assembly
to have been less factious ? Is not the *prima facie* case
in favour of the Peers having exercised their power and
privilege with calmness and conciliatory moderation
absolutely irresistible ?

Doubtless the Peers of England who laugh to scorn the
menaces of their adversaries, and who, as long as they are
just and honest, will never be influenced in their conduct
by the fear of consequences—doubtless the Peers of
England have exercised their power and privileges in these
legislative instances as far as they deemed necessary;
but how much more vehemently in opposition to their
measures could they not have constitutionally conducted
themselves ?   And how much less, in deference to the
high functions which they have to perform, and with
which they are invested, could they have well achieved ?
Why, if they had done less, we might well have asked,
" What is the use of the Lords ?"   But, thank God, the
Peers of England have given a very significant reply to
that once famous query.

*   *   *   *   *

And now for Lord Melbourne—for to his Lordship all
this time we are as surely and as scientifically approaching
as the leaguer makes his way to the citadel.   How has
his Lordship conducted himself towards that august
assembly of which he appears so often of late to have
forgotten that he is a member ?

In return for having unequivocally and cheerfully
admitted the principle of his Corporation Bill, and con-
fining their labours merely to the alteration of some of its
details, Lord Melbourne salutes the Peers of England with
a menace, announces that he cannot be responsible for the
Commons listening to a Bill which, in his opinion, is
destroyed, declares that the Peers of England are suicidal

madmen—that they have torn up its roots by their own
authority, and more than insinuates that a revolution is
consequently inevitable.

In return for having unequivocally adopted his Lordship's measure for the settlement of the tithe question in
Ireland, which he himself describes as the most urgent
and important measure ever submitted to Parliament, and
for having, with respect to the contingency of a future
surplus in correspondence with three hundred Members
of the House of Commons, adopted Lord Melbourne's
opinion of last year in preference to Lord Melbourne's
opinion of the present, the Prime Minister, forsooth, turns
round in a puerile pet, throws up the urgent and important
Bill, pouts forth another menace, and more than insinuates that the Peers will occasion the total destruction of
the Church in Ireland and a dismemberment of the
Empire.

Now, my Lord Melbourne, if, as you assert, a revolution and the destruction of the Church, and the dismemberment of the Empire, will be the consequence of the
Commons not adopting the amendments of the Lords in
the Corporation Bill, and of your not consenting to the
separation of the practical relief and urgent settlement
from the abstract principle and the hypothetical arrangement in the case of the Church in Ireland—why do you
not secure the adoption of the Corporation amendments
by the Commons; why do you not assent to the separation of the practical from the abstract question in the
case of the Irish Church, as the Lords have decided by an
immense majority, of which decision nearly half the
House of Commons have previously approved ? You
know very well that you could carry both points by an
immense majority !

Ah, my Lord Melbourne, we have you on the hip. You
dare not answer these questions. But is there any necessity ? All England, all Europe, can supply us with a
solution.

If you do that which, according to your own statement,

will preserve us from a revolution, will save the Church
of England in Ireland, will prevent a dismemberment of
the Empire—Hume and the English Radicals, O'Connell
and the Popish rebels, desert you, and your Ministry is
lost, though your country is saved.

There is but one way now to manage you, my Lord
Melbourne, there is but one mode to punish a Minister
who, for the sake of power and place, leagues with the
disaffected, and attempts to pass laws which will confessedly occasion a revolution, the destruction of the
Church, and the dismemberment of the Empire. You
have despised the counsel of the English Commons in
favour of the desires of the Popish rebels; you have outraged the Peers of England; you are, as we told you
before, the Minister not of the King's choice, but of the
King's necessity. The cup is full. The indignant and
Protestant people of England will endure your impotent
tyranny no longer; and if we have any knowledge of
human nature or human history, if we have profited by
the study of the annals, or the observation of the living
conduct of our kind, there is an event whose coming
shadow even now obscures your path, and that is your
IMPEACHMENT.

      *   *   *   *   *

Confusion and irresolution reign throughout the Ministerial ranks. More than a week has past since the scope
and tenour of the Lords' amendments of the Corporation
Bill were known, and yet up to the present hour it
remains undecided what course the Cabinet will pursue
relative to those amendments! It will hardly surprise
us if, up to the very moment of Lord John's rising this
afternoon, the Ministerial pack should be left in doubt as
to the cry they are to set up. A similar case, we will
venture to say, is not to be found in the British annals.

Meanwhile this "glorious uncertainty" at head-
quarters produces a most edifying contrariety of opinion
among the Treasury scribes. Nothing can be more
diverting than to see them groping in the dark—no two

agreeing as to the course to be pursued. Take Saturday's columns as an example.

The *Morning Chronicle* is for dying in the breach. All is " Ercles' vein." Ministers must be firm, resolute, and the like. They must "put themselves at the head of the people"; there must be "no flinching, no drawing back," etc.

The *Globe* snatches a momentary courage from an article in the *Times*. This, it considers, shows that the Lords are frightened at their own work, and that it will be quite "practicable" to make them rescind all their own amendments.

The *Courier* is evidently in much lower spirits. Anything, everything, is to be acceded to, so that "the principle of the Bill" be preserved. As if the principle of the Bill, which is undeniably the termination of the close self - elective system, and the establishment of popular elections in its room—as if this had ever been assailed by the Peers !

Catching at a sentence in the *Times,* which suggested a slight modification of the Aldermanic terms of office, the *Courier* eagerly exclaims, "There must be no Aldermen for life." If this be but conceded by the Peers, the Commons may admit all the other amendments !

Supposing that the question were narrowed to this compass, we would ask the *Courier* whether the Commons would do wisely to reject the amended Bill on so trifling a point as whether Aldermen should hold their offices for life or for seven years.

Can it be shown that the average duration of Aldermanic existence is equal to a septennial term ?

However, to come back to the main subject, it is clear that the Ministry are at their wits' ends. (Some may think, perhaps, that it would not take them long to get that length.) In sober sadness, however, their predicament is assuredly anything but pleasant.

Common-sense and reason, supposing them to possess a few grains of either, would naturally suggest that the

alterations made by the Peers in the Corporation Bill
are really amendments, and that, whatever O'Connell and
Hume might say, the correct course would be to adopt
them all. But then comes a serious question, How are
they to get on without O'Connell and Hume ? To keep
on good terms with these two respectable Gentlemen is
clearly essential to their very existence, and none know
this better than the said Gentlemen themselves. What,
then, is to be done ? Scylla is on one side, Charybdis
on the other ?

Imagine the honest course taken—the right of the
Lords to exercise their own judgment admitted—the
correctness of their judgment in this particular case
admitted also—and, finally, the Corporation Bill, with the
Lords' amendments finally passed. But, then, how are
the Movement party to be appeased ? By what means
can the lost affections of the Roebucks and Wakleys
be won back ? Yet if every vote is not preserved, what
chance is there of a week's continuance in office.

Well, then, suppose the *Chronicle's* advice be taken;
the Ministry " puts itself at the head of the people "
(of St. Giles's and Saffron Hill), and the Bill is rejected.
What then ? Is the prospect any better now ? Not a
whit. The result of the whole session will then be—
manifestly set forth in the eyes of all the people—that
the present Cabinet cannot govern the country. The
longest session ever known will then have been passed
through without any result. Nor will there be the slightest
prospect of any more favourable state of things in the
ensuing year. The reason is obvious. The present
Ministry, by the terms of their compact with O'Connell,
are compelled to bring forward none but destructive
measures. The House of Lords, by their duty to the
country, by the first law of Nature, that of self-preserva-
tion, are equally compelled to strip these measures of
their destructive character, and to make them Conservative enactments. Thus " the Tail," with its bare
majority of thirty in the one House, will ever be weaving

webs of iniquity, which the Peers, with a majority of nearly a hundred, will as promptly sweep away.

The sooner this state of things is made apparent to the country the better. The first dissolution of Parliament that occurs will easily rectify this matter. But it is not the wish of the Ministers that the case should be understood. They hope to find a way between Scylla and Charybdis. The Lords are to be got to concede half their amendments, and then the Commons are to agree to the other half. And the Ministry are to claim great credit with each party in turn for having made so good a bargain with the other.

We doubt, however, if the Conservative Peers will submit to be played off in this fashion. We believe they have been in earnest in what they have done, that they have proposed no alteration in lightness or without just grounds, and that it is their deliberate conviction that without the amendments which they have introduced the Bill would be an unsafe measure. We doubt, therefore, if they can be brought to consent to a compromise when they have asked no more than they feel to be right, and when they have the power to insist on all that they ask.

The great object, in fact, of the proposed "mutual concession" is just to relieve Ministers from their unhappy position. But we should like to know what interest the Conservative Peers can feel in any such object ?

*   *   *   *   *

A Radical who fills the office of champion of the King's prerogatives has a difficult part to play ; yet we can assure Sir John Campbell, the King's Jacobin Attorney-General, that there is yet a more difficult character for him to support, and that is the character of a wit. Indeed, there are few things among the petty annoyances of life more excruciating than to witness an attempt at playfulness by this shrewd, coarse, manœuvring Pict.

Fancy an ourang-outang of unusual magnitude dancing under a banana-tree, and licking its hairy chaps, and

winking with exultation its cunning eyes as it beholds
the delicious and impending fruit, and one may form a
tolerable idea of Sir John Campbell's appearance in the
House of Commons on Friday night when he tried to be
jocular about the Imprisonment for Debt Bill,[1] and was
fain to treat the Peers of England and the execution of
their solemn justice with his base and scullion raillery.

Sir John Campbell sneer at the Peers of England! In
God's name, what next?

That the Hudibrastic Hawes[2] should sing a serious
second to the pothouse playfulness of the Attorney-
General is not wonderful, for doubtless his ignoble mind
has its genuine and congenial misgivings as to the " use "
of a nobility.

That Wakley should shake his incendiary arm in flaming
menace at the Peers of England, or O'Connell cock his
red bonnet on his brow with a ferocious grace becoming
that destructive scalp, were no mighty marvel; but that
this baseborn Scotchman, who knows right well that if the
tide were, in his opinion, the other way, he would lick
the very dust a Lord might tread on—that this booing,
fawning, jobbing progeny of haggis and cockaleekie
should dare to sneer at the Peers of England—pah!
vulgar insolence must have run to seed to have produced
this scampish jest.

And look at the facts, too. Here is a Bill which proposes at one fell swoop to change the whole law of debtor
and creditor—a law upon which the whole present system
of credit in this great commercial country has been established and is now based. This law has engaged the attention of the Commons for two sessions; it has been during
their present sittings for two months before the House,
and that House, feeling the importance of the complicated
question with which they were called upon to deal, have
deemed it necessary to submit it to a Committee, who

[1] Campbell, in his "Lives of the Chancellors," records that
Lord Lyndhurst was "much alarmed" by this Bill; hence,
probably, Disraeli's savage attack on the Attorney-General.
[2] Benjamin Hawes, Member for Lambeth.

7

have examined into the details and summoned witnesses on its subject.

All this the Commons have felt it fitting to do, and at the fag end of August they send their Bill to the Lords, their proposition to change one of the most important laws of our code—a proposition, too, of which the great mass of the trading community highly disapprove ; and because the Peers will not legislate blindfold, because they will not pass this most important and interesting Bill without discussing its novel principle, without examining its elaborate and complicated details, and without obtaining evidence on the controverted subject which it presumes to decide, the conduct of the Peers is called in question, their " utility " challenged because they will not consent to be ciphers, and their wise carriage and high authority submitted to the rascal jeering of a clumsy ribald who ought, in consequence, to have been expelled the high office he degrades the very next morning.

CHAPTER IX

The impeachment of Lord Melbourne—His Majesty and the Premier—Playing at statesmen—Reign of Charlatans over.

Tuesday, September 1.

WHETHER the Lords be right or wrong, one thing is certain, that Lord Melbourne cannot carry on the Government of the country, and probably before this article appears he may have retired to Brocket, where the Fauns and wood-nymphs will receive him with a shout of laughter. But if, as we have ever upheld, and, as far as we can form an opinion, as the whole country has decided, the Peers of England, in the course which they have pursued, have only performed their duty to their country, and demonstrated the utility of the high powers and privileges with which they are invested, if in this case Lord Melbourne still retains the reins of power, which he originally obtained by a conspiracy, and which he now holds to the manifold let and flagrant hindrance of all good government, we repeat—we deliberately repeat—that the high constitutional process of an impeachment of this weak and guilty man must be the ultimate recourse of an injured and insulted nation.

Lord Melbourne complains of the coldness of His Majesty, and Lord Melbourne's solitary organ of the Press has squalled out most hideous and seditious cries in consequence. That His Majesty must be disgusted with the insolent presence of a man who, after having forced himself into the Royal councils by one of the most odious conspiracies upon record, is now confessedly incapable of securing the object for which the plot was formed, and the offensive obtrusion was perpetrated, and who, after all his faction and effecting a quasi revolution for six months, cannot carry on the Government, is the most natural circumstance in the world: nor do we require the allegation of the *Morning Chronicle* to assure us that His Majesty is a Conservative, though, to be sure, it is the only assertion of the *Morning Chronicle* that we ever could believe.

But Lord Melbourne not only cannot carry on the Government—he never has carried on the Government. During the whole period of his Downing Street roost, he has done nothing but issue Treasury warrants for his own salary, and approve of the project of laws which he knew never could be passed. We have heard of children playing at soldiers. Lord Melbourne and his fellows have been playing at statesmen, and now that the holidays are over they must go to school again; or, rather, they have been executing that military exploit which consists of an active march over ground from which the battalion never budges an inch, and all that is accomplished, after all their exertions, is only kicking up a dust.

The country is sick of these fellows. It positively nauseates the whole gang of pseudo-Reformers and political economists and inquiring Commissioners and dissenting delegates, and all the other base and unsavoury fungi that have been generated of late years in the hotbed of Whig agitation.

It does not become an ancient nation to be inquiring for ever into the origin and " utility " of every traditionary custom and immemorial institution, like one of the vulgar parvenu societies formed ten years back, and which in half a century will be forgotten. England can no longer submit to be treated like Greece or Guatemala for the sake of serving the purposes of a weak faction and filling the maws and pouches of their rascally retainers.

A free, flourishing, and famous people, who have acquired their liberty, enjoyed their prosperity, and gained their glory, under institutions which have lasted for a thousand years do not want to know the *pourquoi* of all their laws and customs.

The reign of Charlatans is over, and the Minister, their chief, if he wishes to avoid punishment, had better immediately retire to his country-seat.

CHAPTER X

The "collision" and the Comet—The "use" of the Lords—
Limits of concession—Imprisonment for debt—More Com-
missioners—Sir John Campbell's breechless ancestors—The
People's House—Popish rebels—"Thank God there is a
House of Lords!"

Wednesday, September 2.

WELL, the collision has appeared before the Comet ; and
if that fiery meteor do not portend worse consequences
to the Constitution of England than the exhibition in the
House of Commons on Monday night, there is less chance
than some imagine of our imitating the grovelling days

"When Bradshaw bullied in a broad-brim hat." [1]

After all the meetings of THE PEOPLE—after all the
valiant threats and "strong" resolutions—after the
menace of vestries, and the more awful and mysterious
murmurs of the Ministers—after the demand by the
Radicals from the Government that the Supplies should
be at least placed in the power of the Commons, and the
virtual promise of the Government, in answer to the
Radicals, that this great precautionary step should be
taken—what has happened ?

Why, that the same Ministers and the same Radicals
have swallowed every important amendment of the Peers
without a struggle, save in one point—the continuance
of their worships the Aldermen. The political and proprietary rights of the freemen of England, to destroy
which the Ministers twice appealed to the House of
Commons and succeeded in their object, by the votes
of the Irish Papists, are retained ; although Lord Melbourne characterised this constitutional amendment of
the Peers as the most injurious of all their propositions,
and thought it necessary at the very tenth hour in the
House of Lords again to declare his invincible aversion
to its ratification; yet these great and noble efforts of

---

[1] James Bramston in " A Man of Taste."

Lord Lyndhurst and his brother Peers in favour of the rights and liberties and property of a vast portion of their fellow-subjects are now supported and seconded in the House of Commons even without a murmur.

Who shall hereafter ask the " use " of the Lords ?

Again the great principle of qualification so violently repudiated by that party in the Commons who owe their support in so great a degree to the needy and insolvent is recognised and submitted to in the same House of Commons without a division.

And will anyone hereafter ask the " use " of the Lords ?

In short, there appear to us to be only three propositions of the Peers of any magnitude to which the Ministers finally object. The first of these, which relates to the toll-exemption of the freeman, may be easily settled by compensation; the second, relating to the distribution of Church patronage by the Dissenters, will probably be managed in a way not injurious to the Church; against the third, which regards the retention of the Aldermen and Town Clerks for life, the Government is disposed to make a stand, because Sir Robert Peel, the leader of the Conservatives of England, combining the quality of firmness with the desire of conciliation, does not think it necessary to contend for a life tenure of office in the Aldermen, when the humbled Whigs and Radicals offer to give a six years' lease.

* * * * *

Lord Lyndhurst, in the House of Lords on Monday night, felt it his duty to notice the impertinent observations of Sir John Campbell, the King's Attorney-General by the grace of O'Connell, on the reception of the Imprisonment for Debt Bill in their Lordships' House. And the murder was soon out, and all the lamentations of the Learned Gentleman and his desperate ribaldry soon explained, when it turned out that this vaunted Bill, which, by-the-by, was indecently passed in a House of Commons consisting only of forty Members, proposes, besides other

enormous patronage, to establish FIFTY MORE COMMIS-
SIONERS.

Why, if the Whigs go on at this rate, where, in another
year or two, will be the boasted independence of the
British Bar ? Fifty more Commissioners, and all with
heavy salaries, and fifty registrars, and fifty ushers. Why,
'tis as good as plundering a city ; and not one of Sir John's
base and breechless ancestors at a Border fray could
ever have meditated a richer spoil. There was, then, no
trifle at stake when Sir John Campbell rushed down to
the House of Commons the other night to insult the Peers
of England, to the great diversion and edification of the
assembled Brutilitarians who represent "the People"
and ask the "use" of the Lords, and to the disgust of
the Conservative members who were present. Even
Lord Brougham agreed that this Imprisonment for Debt
Bill was "too bad."

The British people will no doubt be of opinion that
their Lordships acted most discreetly in postponing the
consideration of such an important measure for another
session, although the hopes of the crew are again dashed ;
and Parkes, whose name is now a proverb for a job
throughout "the two islands" to the plundered people
of which he so characteristically appeals to abolish the
House of Lords, must rest awhile from his spoil. We
hope that Joseph by this time clearly comprehends what
"the use of the Lords" is. One of the manifold uses of
that august assembly, Joseph, is to quash jobs by whomsoever concocted ; and if your mind be not now fully
enlightened, you may seek further information from the
roaring Rushton and the sober Drinkwater and the
unheard-of Wilkinson, or Cockburn the trustworthy,
and last, but, oh ! not least, "Horror-and-Hell" Dwarris.

*   *   *   *   *

There was great bawling in the House of Commons on
Monday night about "THE PEOPLE" and "the wishes of
the people" and "the power of the people." It was a
field-day for jargon, and the nonsense that Hume, and

O'Connell, and Warburton and Whalley, and that meagre-
minded rebel Roebuck, and that last desperate effort of
masculine organisation which lays claim to the name of
man, Ewart, who looks for all the world like Ralph, Sir
Hudibras's squire—the nonsense, we repeat, that these
fellows talked has seldom been equalled, even by themselves.

What do they mean by their favourite phrase, THE
PEOPLE's House ?   The available constituency of England
amounts to three hundred thousand.   Are these three
hundred thousand men the people of England ?   No,
these three hundred thousand men are the Commons,
not the people of England; and these Commons form a
class in the State, privileged, irresponsible, and hereditary,
like the Peers.   The Commons, on account of their
number, meet by their representatives, and, to say nothing
of a majority of the Commons being opposed to the
Ministerial measure, the question when placed in the
most favourable light for the Government is just simply
this: They have thirty-seven Representatives of the
Popish Commons to place in opposition to one hundred
British Peers.   Now, to say nothing of wealth and stake
in the country, and the usual considerations, it will become us during "the collision" exactly to understand
how these Popish Commons are affected to the Constitution under which we have flourished, and which, in spite
of Brutilitarian nonsense, we are determined to uphold.

These Popish rebels avow their desire to effect a dismemberment of the Empire.   By the aid of the Whigs
and the Brutilitarians they have nearly uprooted the
Protestant Church in Ireland; and their prime leader,
that arch-traitor O'Connell, has seized every opportunity
to declare that it is his wish, and shall be his endeavour,
to destroy the authority and abrogate the existence of
the House of Peers.

To be sure.   Why, it is only the House of Lords
that at this moment maintains the Protestant cause in
this realm.   "Thank God, there is a House of Lords!"

said Cobbett a very short time before he died, and that
grateful ejaculation should be inscribed in letters of gold
on every temple and every dwelling-house in this still
free and still Protestant country.

CHAPTER XI

Nearing a settlement—Mutual concessions—A remedial measure
—The war upon Aldermen—Reform not necessarily revolution—State surgery—" Proceed, Peers of England "—The
flower of the nation.

Thursday, September 3.

THERE seems but one rational and satisfactory standard
by which the estates of the realm can at this moment
guide themselves in the mutual concessions which they
are called upon to make. The House of Commons established a principle as the basis of their Bill for the Amendment of Municipal Corporations, and this principle was
the abolition of close bodies by the substitution of a
popular election.

The House of Lords admitted the principle of the Bill
sent up to them by the Commons, and in reserving to
themselves the right of altering its details established as
the principle of these alterations that they should secure
the improvement without aiming at the reconstruction
of Corporations.

Now it remains for the two Houses, in the points of
controversy at present between them, exactly and consistently to guide themselves by a becoming deference
to the two principles which they have separately established. This is the only mode by which they can escape
a factious imputation. As the Lords neither expect nor
desire that Representatives of the Commons should make
any concession which may affect the principle which
Honourable Members have established, so it is equally
just that the Representatives of the Commons should

neither expect nor desire that the Peers should make
any concession which may affect the principles which
their Lordships have established.

In return for the concessions which the Representatives of the Commons have made upon the political and
proprietary rights of freemen, the principle of qualification, and other very important subjects, the Lords, we
understand, are, with a similar liberality, disposed to
concede to the House of Commons as to the mode by
which that qualification shall be ascertained, as to the
proposed arrangement respecting the ecclesiastical patronage of the Corporations, and the question of tolls, for
·which their Lordships will be satisfied if they obtain for
the freemen a compensation.

When we remember that these further concessions are
offered by an assembly which has already cheerfully and
unreservedly acceded to the propositions of the Commons
for abolishing the system of nomination, for establishing
popular and annual elections, for placing the Corporate
funds under the supervision of the inhabitants, and for
providing for the prompt and efficient administration of
local justice, no impartial person can deny that there is
on the part of the Peers of England a fixed and friendly
determination to improve and ameliorate the institutions
of the Empire.

With regard to the questions of the justices and the
division into wards, and one or two points of minor
interest and importance, the Representatives of the
Commons, in all probability, will not insist upon their
opposition to their Lordships' amendments.

The important clauses retaining Aldermen, acknowledging the authority of the present Aldermen for life,
and continuing the official existence of the present Town
Clerks, remain to be considered. Is a compliance by the
Commons with the amendments of the Lords in this
respect inconsistent with the maintenance of the principle
of the Bill ? In no degree. The most ingenious reasoner
could not for a moment support a contrary reply.

These arrangements are the necessary consequence of respecting at the same time vested interests while you establish popular rights. The Bill is a Bill to amend, not to reconstruct, Corporations. This is now the genuine character and avowed title of the Bill, and this the Lords have established as the principle on which they have founded their amendments.

The Bill is essentially of a remedial nature. The grievances occasioned by the existence of the old Corporations are to be remedied, but the institutions are to be respected. No organic changes are contemplated by the measure, which, we repeat, assumes throughout a remedial, not a destructive or creative, character. It has been determined that the authorities heretofore nominated by themselves shall in future be elected by their fellow-citizens; but the authorities are still to remain. The Alderman in future will be elected by his townsmen; but there is no reason why we should part with a title which, as Earl Fitzwilliam wisely and well observed at the Yorkshire meeting, " sprang from the cradle of our liberties."

But shall an Alderman who now holds his authority under the sanctity of a Royal charter—shall he be punished for possessing so high a title, and be turned adrift as if he had committed a high misdemeanour instead of enjoying a high privilege ? Why this war upon Aldermen ? Why should not the municipal rights of Aldermen be respected as well as the municipal rights of freemen ? The Whigs, who proposed to confiscate the property and privileges of the freemen, were quite consistent in proposing to abolish the dignity and authority of Aldermen; but the House of Lords, who have secured the gratitude of a hundred thousand of the Commons of England by their firm and triumphant vindication of their rights, would only be establishing an anomaly to rescue the freemen and desert their rulers. The same undeniable principle applies to the Town Clerks. Their municipal rights are as sacred as those of the Aldermen and freemen. To

neglect them because they are few in number would be
an act of cowardice of which the Upper House of Parliament could never be guilty.

By establishing at once a popular constituency, and
allowing them to elect their Town Council, and when a
vacancy occurs among the other members of the municipal
bodies to supply the vacant place in the same popular
mode, the Lords and Commons have most liberally and
effectually established a system of free election and
popular control throughout the country. By respecting
the rights of the existing members of the municipal body,
the House of Lords have given another proof that reform
is not necessarily revolution, and that the observance of
the sanctity of vested rights is not incompatible with the
establishment of popular franchises.

We trust the House of Commons will follow their wise
and patriotic example; but if, unhappily, the influence of
a fatal connection force the Ministry to refuse their co-
operation with the Peers in this great behalf, this we do
know, that no consideration in the world will induce the
Peers to depart from their resolution, which will be as
firmly acted upon as it was deliberately taken.

The events of the last few hours have not induced the
Peers to repent the firmness with which they have exercised their privileges.

Where now are the incendiary menaces which were
hurled so liberally but a few days back at this august
assembly. Why are the leading agitators silent ? Are
there no more abortive meetings to be dry-nursed ? The
vestries are as mute as swine that have had their swill.
The Supplies are not stopped.

Yet the "mutilations" have been duly sent to the
House where Hume acutely reasons and Roebuck softly
persuades; and instead of the Lords being arrested under
the "Cutting and Maiming Act," they have suddenly and
universally been recognised as very skilful and approved
State Surgeons.

Proceed, Peers of England.   Proceed in your course—

at once wise and courageous, temperate and dignified. Your authority rests upon the confidence and affection of your fellow - countrymen ; its recent exercise has doubly entitled you to their respect and support. It is not without a struggle that this England, so free, so famous, so abundant in all that maketh the heart glad, shall fall before a base and dastardly faction. You are the chief flower of the nation,

"In peace our ornament, in war our shield ;"

and if the bitter records of the past bear any wisdom, it is not lightly, or with a careless spirit, that the people of England will part with the salutary institution of your high estate.

CHAPTER XII

Reform of the House of Lords—Rebellious nonsense—Ignorance of the Constitution—The estates of the realm—An exposed fallacy—Concerning etiquette.

Friday, September 4.

MR. HUME and his jackal, Mr. Roebuck, and Mr. Rippon, who represents the Commons of Gateshead, opened the Parliamentary campaign on Wednesday night against the House of Lords by detailing their plans and projects for what they called "a reform" of that ancient and august institution.

To carry on a controversy with men so deeply and darkly unlettered is impossible. Appeals to history, of which they are ignorant, cannot, of course, be expected to influence them ; and as for any conclusions which are arrived at by the higher process of abstract disquisition, it is very plain that we might as well address the member for Middlesex in Greek or argue with the Bath delegate in some of the dialects of the Hurons. But the rebellious nonsense which these men utter affords a convenient peg whereon to hang much instruction ; and if we neither hope nor desire to convince them, we may at least attempt to enlighten those whom they endeavour to delude.

And, in the first place, these men are utterly ignorant of the very nature of the English Constitution. Yes, these reformers are most completely in the dark as to the very character of the institutions which they profess their anxiety and intention to alter.

The other night Lord John Russell, who has written a book upon the English Constitution, and who, on the same principle that bad wine makes very good vinegar, has somehow or other contrived to be metamorphosed from a tenth-rate author into a first-rate statesman[1]— the other night Lord John styled the King of England one of the estates of the realm. We should like to know in what authority his Lordship ever found the King of England so styled ? In Coke ? In Selden ? In Blackstone ?

The three estates of the realm are the Lords Spiritual and Temporal, and the Commons ; that is to say, originally the three privileged classes or orders of the Kingdom— the Nobles, the Church, and the Commons. And Lord John Russell, who made this gross mistake, is a Secretary of State, a writer upon our Constitution, and leader of one of the Houses of Parliament.

As little as the KING is an estate of the realm is the PEOPLE. Yet the whole basis on which Mr. Hume and his click found their arguments and attack upon the Upper House of Parliament is the fallacy which we have already exposed, that the COMMONS of England are the PEOPLE of England. The representative of the Commons of Middlesex is not the representative of the People of Middlesex ; he is one of the representatives of a privileged class or order in the State. The Commons of Middlesex, forming a very insignificant fraction of the people of Middlesex, are privileged, irresponsible, and hereditary electors of legislators ; and they hold and exercise their high functions by virtue of the same Convention that the Peers of England, who form the other privileged, irresponsible,

---

[1] See Introduction, p. 10.

and hereditary order of the State, meet and vote in the House of Lords.

Therefore the moment that the rights, powers and privileges of the House of Lords are violated by the Representatives of the Commons the Convention is broken, the social compact abrogated, society itself resolved into its original elements, and the great body of the people called upon to create and sanction some new form of government.

Mr. Hume and his Brutilitarians oppose the Peers because they exercise an "irresponsible" power. As well might the Peers oppose the Commons because they exercise an irresponsible power. Their power to elect law-makers is just as irresponsible as the power of the Peers to make laws.

Is irresponsible power a whit more tolerable because it is participated in by three hundred thousand men, the number of the English Commons who exercised their suffrage at the last election, instead of three hundred. On the contrary, the three hundred are known, and therefore much more under the influence of public opinion than the three hundred thousand who pervade society like a favoured sect, and in some degree, like the Jesuits, form a secret order.

Let Mr. Hume and his school push on their principles, and see to what results they tend. Destroy the existing Constitution of England and establish the principle that no class shall exercise irresponsible power, and universal suffrage follows, of course. Whether a social system under any circumstances could flourish on such a basis is more than doubtful—that it could be established in this ancient realm is morally and physically impossible. Enough for the present of these sciolists. That they are completely ignorant of the nature of the British Constitution in particular and of the nature of human society in general is quite evident. When they meet the Peers of England, Mr. Hume and Mr. Wakley complain that they must stand and doff their beavers while their Lordships are seated with covered heads. Why not ? As far as the *rationale* of etiquette is concerned, it is most fit that precedence and superior honours should be enjoyed by the Peers, in themselves a privileged order, when they meet a deputation of Gentlemen who are only the representatives of a privileged order.

If precedence and etiquette, and those forms and ceremonies which the experience of our ancestors have found convenient and decorous, are to be maintained, and we are not all at once to sink in the degrading slough of a base equality, we are acquainted with no form and ceremony more rational and fitting than the one of which these ignorant men complain.

The order of the Peers is a higher order than that of the Commons. Thus the Constitution has decided. As well might the Peers complain of vailing their coronets before their SOVEREIGN as the Commons or their representatives of uncovering their heads before the Peers, and with the same grace that the Representatives of the Commons maintain their right to equal ceremonies with the Peers might any one of the people summoned to the bar refuse to uncover, and claim a seat.

CHAPTER XIII

Pym and Hampden—A lesson from history—An illegal notice— The law and the Constitution—The Lords Spiritual—A democratic institution.

Saturday, September 5.

ABOUT two centuries back the " prentices of London," at the instigation of a party in the House of Commons, made themselves hoarse with bawling out " Down with the Bishops and the rotten-hearted Lords !" The arts of insurgency were full as well understood in those days as the present; indeed, we suspect that Pym and Hampden were as dexterous hands at getting up a crisis or fostering a collision as any Roundhead of the present Cabinet, or any Rump-agitator in their train.

In consequence of these riots a pretext was obtained for sequestrating the Lords Spiritual from their seats in Parliament; and in due course the Lords Temporal were as successfully attacked, and the House of Peers, to quote the identical language of the resolution, voted " useless." In five years' time the omnipotent House of Commons, that had carried affairs with this high ambition, was itself sequestrated and itself declared " useless," and a military despotism established in our country.

It appears that Mr. Cuthbert Rippon, the Representative of the Commons of Gateshead, has revived the cry of the " prentices of London " ; and probably thinks he is giving utterance to a very bright and original idea. The Lords Spiritual have just as much right to question the propriety of Gateshead sending their Representative to the Lower House as that functionary has to question the right of the Lords Spiritual to seat themselves in the House of Peers. Their title, indeed, to their power and privileges is of a far more ancient date than that of the Commons of Gateshead; nor do we see how, with any respect for the old and still existing Constitution of these realms, such notices as those of Mr. Rippon and Mr. Hume can be publicly given and officially registered in the House of Commons. We hesitate not to say they are illegal, although John Russell may be of a different opinion, and Lord John Russell, as we proved yesterday, is especially distinguished for constitutional lore.

Lord John Russell, who announces the King to be one of the estates of the realm—a fact unknown to Coke, or Selden, or Blackstone—will perhaps inform us whether it would be Parliamentary, constitutional, or legal, to give notice of a motion in the House of Commons to question the hereditary succession of the Throne, or the Royal prerogative to make peace or declare war. Lord John Russell knows that such a motion cannot be made, that Parliamentary usage alone would not permit it to be entered on the journals, and that Parliamentary privilege

8

alone would prevent the mover from being sent to the Tower.

What difference is there in attacking the powers and privileges of what Lord John Russell calls and considers the second estate of the realm from attacking those of the first ?   Such notices are, without doubt, illegal; such irreverend mention of any part or portion, member or branch, of the Constitution is a high misdemeanour, and it was the duty of some Conservative member immediately to prevent the notice of those motions being recorded.

We repeat that the English Constitution is a conventional arrangement, that by virtue of the compact certain classes or orders of the people are privileged, that if the privileges of one order are invaded by the privileges of the other the compact is destroyed, and society is resolved into its original elements.

So much for the law and the Constitution.   Let us now consider the abstract expediency of Mr. Cuthbert Rippon's modest proposition.   The great cry of the levellers of the present day is against the hereditary jurisdiction of the House of Lords.   We have at other times shown that this privilege is not of the peculiar and exclusive character that the superficial imagine, but that it is in harmony with the whole system of our Constitution.   Nevertheless, for the sake of the argument, we will for a moment admit that the privilege is an anomaly, and that the consequences may be that the highest powers may be exercised by those little qualified for the office.

Well, then, here is the estate of the Lords Spiritual, the very Peerage for life, for which the Radicals clamour— an estate, too, of which the members must in general necessarily be more distinguished for their talents, their learning, and their piety, and often spring from the humbler classes of the people.

There is not a more democratic institution in the country than the Church, and this is the institution the Radicals are ever menacing and decrying.

CHAPTER XIV

The Parliamentary Session—Summing up—Triumph of Constitu-
tional principles—" A rascally crew of jobbing sciolists "—
Utilitarian misrepresentations—Lord John Russell's blunder
—The Revolutionary party—Tribute to Sir Robert Peel.

Monday, September 7.

THE Parliamentary session about to terminate will be
memorable for circumstances even more important than
its unprecedented duration and the passing of the Corporation Bill.

The principles of the English Constitution have not
only rallied, but triumphed.[1]   The independent authority
of the Upper House of Parliament, to the exercise and
influence of which we have, in so many periods of our
history, been indebted for the maintenance of our rights
and liberties, has during the present session been asserted
by its native and essential strength alone, and will, we
confidently hope, be this night again virtually and signifi-
cantly acknowledged by the further and judicious compliance of the House of Commons with those salutary
amendments to which the Peers have wisely deemed it
their duty to adhere, and the propriety of which they know
to be sanctioned by the opinion of the people.

It is undeniable that in the later events there is much
to cheer the heart of every lover of his country, and every
admirer of those ancient institutions which have alike
formed and sprung from the national character ; and
which, like all institutions founded on so sound a basis,
are invested with a remarkable and a happy power of
adapting themselves to the wants and wishes of the
society which they regulate and protect.

At present the people of England have a wiser trust in
the practical wisdom of Alfred the Great than in the
verbose and windy theories of Jeremy Bentham and his
Utilitarian disciples ; and as long as this be the case we

[1] See parallel passage in Dedication to the Letters of Runnymede.

shall adhere to our laws, our customs, and our institutions. They have made this realm " the inviolate island of the sage and free," and we should be base fools indeed to desert our Constitution—ay, our still unrivalled Constitution, for such *we* hold it, and to which we are indebted for all our famous liberty, and more than Tyrian wealth, and blaze of intellectual glory.

We are not ashamed in this cold-blooded coxcombical nineteenth century to praise the Constitution of England; and if all dared speak as they deem, the good old times would soon return, when we were grateful to Providence for our free and famous Constitution as for the beauteous and fertile land wherein we dwell.

But a rascally rabble of jobbing sciolists have of late years been distilling their leprous poison into the unguarded ears of our generation. We love our Constitution, we honour it, we cherish it, and we understand it. But as for the Utilitarian sophists who, for the last few years, in public and private, in Press and market-place, senate and saloon, have been gabbling against the institutions and sneering at the wisdom of our ancestors— they know nothing about the Constitution, they are absolutely in the dark respecting the very subject they criticise; every observation they make, when they descant on the English Constitution, would apply as well to the Aulic Council, the Hungarian Diet, or the Divan itself.

We have several times of late taken an opportunity in this journal of exposing the flagrant fallacies which these persons make when they venture on the sacred ground they too often violate, and indulge in their Constitutional comments and criticisms. We have already destroyed the great " discovery " of the Utilitarians—to wit, " the anomalous irresponsibility of the House of Lords," and on which blunder one journal has lived for the last six years, and dinned the noisy nonsense every week into the ears of the lieges. It may truly be said of the Lords that

" Sunday shines no Sabbath-day on them."[1]

---

[1] " Ev'n Sunday shines no Sabbath-day to me " (Pope).

This mighty discovery, we repeat—this pompous axiom, which is regularly enunciated with such practised complacency—we have already proved to be nothing more than a big mare's nest, the Peers of England not being one whit more irresponsible than the Commons of England.

The next mischievous representation that the Utilitarians have taken much pains to pass current is that the House of Commons is "the People's House." But although this statement has passed current, it is nevertheless base, for, as we have before shown, the House of Commons is no more "the People's House" than the House of Lords.

The third artifice of the revolutionary school is their abuse of the word "people" altogether. We have proved that all the elements of a great people are enlisted in the cause of the Constitution, and in analysing the elements of the Conservative party we have demonstrated that, instead of a party, it is in fact a nation.

So much for the Utilitarians; they are miserable successors to the Girondists. But the Utilitarians are deep enough for the Whigs, when the English leader, who has written a book on the English Constitution, describes our Most Gracious Sovereign in the assembled House of Commons as one of the three estates of the realm. We venture to say that, considering the quarter from whence it emanated, this was the greatest blunder ever made in a legislative assembly. But it is a very instructive blunder, people of England—and we do not speak to the Peers and Commons merely, but to the whole people—this, we say, is a very instructive blunder for you; for by Lord John Russell's knowledge of your Constitution you may judge of his ability to amend it. The man who is even now ignorant of what the THREE estates of the realm really are, was five years ago selected by the Whigs to reform ONE of them. We are only surprised that he did not fix upon His Majesty by mistake.

But to-day we are disposed to treat the Whigs with

lightness. Lord John Russell, it appears, has not forgotten that his father is Duke of Bedford.

The judicious and well-timed notices of Mr. Hume and Mr. Rippon and Mr. Roebuck have reminded the Whigs of what they sometimes would willingly forget.

The essential strength of the Revolutionary party in the House of Commons is much overrated. Five-sixths of the present members of the Lower House are personally interested in the preservation of the House of Lords and the maintenance of its authority. Five-sixths, and more than five-sixths, of the people sympathise with them.

The Whigs and the House of Commons have acted wisely; they have done well—very well indeed. They have not suffered themselves to be misled by the rant and riot of a party insignificant in point of number—more insignificant in point of influence and talent.

The House of Commons will, we doubt not, accept this evening all the important amendments of the House of Lords save one, and one only, to the modification of which the Lords have consented in deference, not to the Government, but to the wisdom, experience, and moderation of the eminent leader of the Conservatives of England, Sir Robert Peel.

VINDICATION OF THE ENGLISH CONSTITUTION

IN A LETTER TO A NOBLE AND LEARNED LORD

By DISRAELI THE YOUNGER

["THE VINDICATION OF THE ENGLISH CONSTITUTION" appeared in December, 1835. It took the form of a "letter to a noble and learned lord." This was Lord Lyndhurst, with whom during the year the young politician had become closely connected. The tract is described by Mr. Monypenny as "the most important of Disraeli's early political writings," and as giving him "what his fugitive efforts could never have given him— a recognised position as a political writer and thinker." It has twice been republished, but the reprints are almost as scarce as the original. Its reappearance will be welcomed by those who desire to have by them for reference the fullest authoritative exposition of Disraeli's views on the Constitution.]

CHAPTER I

Of Writers on the English Constitution.

YOUR Lordship has honoured me by a wish that some observations which I have made in conversation on the character of our Constitution might be expressed in a more formal and more public manner. When I transmit you this long letter I fear you may repent your friendly suggestion; but the subject has given rise to so many reflections that I did not anticipate that what I originally intended for a pamphlet has, I fear, expanded almost into a volume.

The polity of England, which has established the most flourishing society of modern ages, and regulated the destinies of a nation which for many centuries has made

LETTER FROM DISRAELI TO HIS SISTER (DECEMBER 5, 1835) CONCERNING THE "VINDICATION."

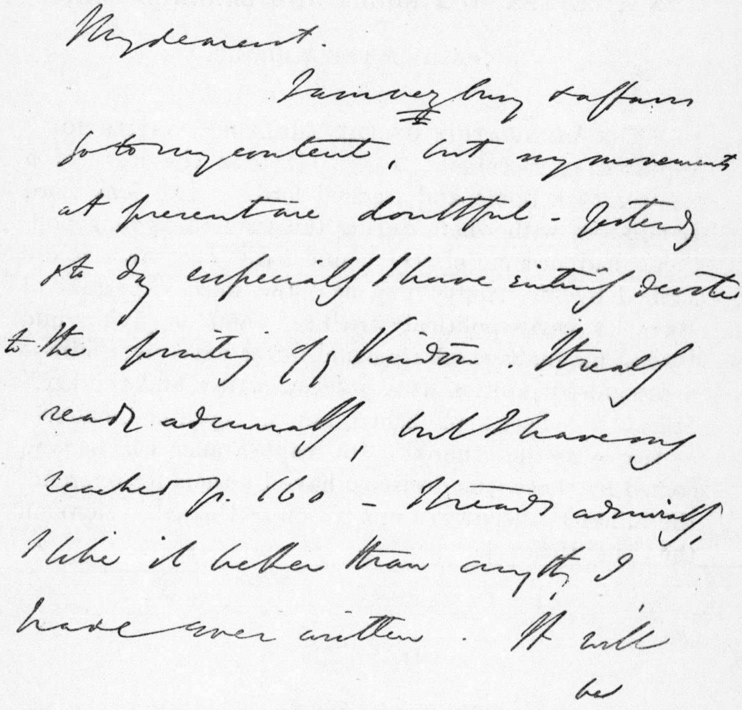
My dearest.

I am very busy & affairs go to my content, but my movements at present are doubtful – Yesterday & to day especially I have entirely devoted to the finishing of Vindication. It really reads admirably, but I have only reached p. 160 – It reads admirably; I like it better than anything I have ever written. It will be

The letter continues: "It will be out next week, but not, I fear, in the early part."

(By permission of Messrs. Maggs Brothers, from the original in their possession.)

a progressive advance in the acquisition of freedom, wealth, and glory, undoubtedly presents one of the most interesting subjects of speculation in political philosophy. Nor is it one that has been neglected; and illustrious foreigners have emulated our native authors in their treatises of the English Constitution. Our own constitutional writers may, in general, be divided into two classes: firstly, the mere antiquaries, whose labours, however, are inestimable; and, secondly, that order of political writers who have endeavoured, in an examination of what they style the theory of the Constitution, to promulgate the opinions and maintain the interests of the party in the State in whose ranks they have been enrolled: the dissertations upon our Constitution have therefore been either archæological treatises or party manifestoes.

Yet for many years the general result of these writings, whichever might be the quarter whence they emanated, was, as far as their subject was concerned, one of unqualified panegyric. However the excesses of factions might be deplored, or the misrepresentations of factious writers exposed and stigmatised, the English Constitution was universally recognised as an august and admirable fabric, and counted among the choicest inventions of public intellect on record. That a very different tone has of late years been assumed by our public writers is a notorious circumstance. A political sect has sprung up avowedly adverse to the Estates of the Realm, and seeking by means which, of course, it holds legal, the abrogation of a majority of them. These anti-constitutional writers, like all new votaries, are remarkable for their zeal and activity. They omit no means of disseminating their creed: they are very active missionaries: there is no medium of the public press of which they do not avail themselves: they have their newspapers, daily and weekly, their magazines, and their reviews. The unstamped press takes the cue from them, and the members of the party who are in Parliament lose no opportunity of dilating on the congenial theme at the public meetings of their constituents.

CHAPTER II

Of the Utilitarian System—Its Fallacies.

THE avowed object of this new sect of statesmen is to submit the institutions of the country to the test of UTILITY, and to form a new Constitution on the abstract principles of theoretic science. I think it is Voltaire who tells us that there is nothing more common than to read and to converse to no purpose, and that in history, in morals, and in divinity, we should beware of EQUIVOCAL TERMS. I do not think that politics should form an exception to this salutary rule; and, for my own part, it appears to me that this term, UTILITY, is about as equivocal as any one which, from the time of the Nominalists and Realists to our present equally controversial and equally indefinite days, hath been let loose to breed sects and set men a-brawling. The fitness of a material object for a material purpose is a test of its utility which our senses and necessities can decide; but what other test there is of moral and political utility than the various and varying opinions of mankind I am at a loss to discover; and that this is utterly unsatisfactory and insufficient, all, I apprehend, must agree.

Indeed, I have hitherto searched in vain in the writings of the Utilitarian sect for any definition of their fundamental phrase with which it is possible to grapple. That they pretend to afford us a definition it would be disingenuous to conceal, and we are informed that Utility is "the principle which produces the greatest happiness of the greatest number." Does this advance us in comprehension ? Who is to decide upon the greatest happiness of the greatest number ? According to Prince Metternich, the government of Austria secures the greatest happiness of the greatest number: it is highly probable that the effect of the Austrian education and institutions

may occasion the majority of the Austrian population to
be of the same opinion.   Yet the government of Austria
is no favourite with the anti-constitutional writers of our
own country.   Gross superstition may secure the greatest
happiness of the greatest number, as it has done in Spain
and Portugal: a military empire may secure the greatest
happiness of the greatest number, as it has done in Rome
and France: a coarse and unmitigated despotism may
secure the greatest happiness of the greatest number, as
it does to this day in many regions of Asia and Africa.
Every government that ever existed, that has enjoyed
any quality of duration, must have been founded on this
" greatest happiness principle," for, had not the majority
thought or felt that such were its result, the government
could never have endured.   There have been times, and
those too not far gone, when the greatest happiness of
Christian nations has been secured by burning men alive
for their religious faith; and unless we are prepared to
proclaim that all religious creeds which differ from our
own are in fact not credited by their pretended votaries,
we must admit that the greatest happiness of the greatest
number of mankind is even now secured by believing that
which we know to be false.   If the greatest happiness of
the greatest number, therefore, be the only test of the
excellence of political institutions, that may be the plea
for institutions which, according to the Utilitarians especially, are monstrous or absurd: and if to avoid this conclusion we maintain that the greatest number are not
the proper judges of the greatest happiness, we are only
referred to the isolated opinions of solitary philosophers,
or at the best to the conceited conviction of some
sectarian minority.   UTILITY, in short, is a mere phrase,
to which any man may ascribe any meaning that his
interests prompt or his passions dictate.   With this plea,
a nation may consider it in the highest degree useful
that all the statues scattered throughout the museums of
Christendom should be collected in the same capital, and
conquer Christendom in consequence to obtain their

object; and by virtue of the same plea, some Iconoclastic enemy may declare war upon this nation of Dilettanti to-morrow, and dash into fragments their cosmopolite collection.

Viewed merely in relation to the science of government, the effect of the test of utility, as we have considered it, would in all probability be harmless, and its practical tendency, if any, would rather lead to a spirit of conservation and optimism than to one of discontent and change. But optimism is assuredly not the system of the Utilitarians: far from thinking everything is for the best, they decidedly are of opinion that everything is for the worst. In order, therefore, that their test of utility should lead to the political results which they desire, they have dovetailed their peculiar system of government into a peculiar system of morals, in connection with which we must alone subject it to our consideration. The same inventive sages, who have founded all political science on UTILITY, have founded all moral science on SELF-INTEREST, and have then declared that a system of government should be deduced alone from the principles of human nature. If mankind could agree on a definition of Self-interest, I willingly admit that they would not be long in deciding upon a definition of Utility. But what do the Utilitarians mean by the term Self-interest ? I at once agree that man acts from no other principle than self-interest, but I include in self-interest, and I should think every accurate reasoner must do the same, every motive that can possibly influence man. If every motive that can possibly influence man be included in self-interest, then it is impossible to form a science on a principle which includes the most contrary motives. If the Utilitarians will not admit all the motives, but only some of the motives, then their science of government is not founded on human nature, but only on a part of human nature, and must be consequently and proportionately imperfect. But the Utilitarian only admits one or two of the motives that influence man; a desire of power and a desire of property; and therefore infers that it is the interest of man to tyrannise and to rob.

The blended Utilitarian system of morals and politics, then, runs thus: Man is only influenced by self-interest: it is the interest of man to be a tyrant and a robber: a man does not change his nature because he is a king; therefore a king is a tyrant and a robber. If it be the interest of one man to be a tyrant and a robber, it is the interest of fifty or five thousand to be tyrants and robbers; therefore we cannot trust an aristocracy more than a monarch. But the eternal principle of human nature must always hold good. A privileged class is always an aristocracy, whether it consists of five thousand or fifty thousand, a band of nobles or a favoured sect; therefore the power of government should be entrusted to all; therefore the only true and useful government is a representative polity, founded on universal suffrage. This is the Utilitarian system of morals and government, drawn from their " great works " by one who has no wish to misrepresent them. Granting for a moment their premises, I do not see that their deduction, even then, is logically correct. It is possible to conceive a state of society where the government may be in the hands of a favoured majority; a community of five millions, of which three might form a privileged class. Would not the greatest happiness of the greatest number be secured by such an arrangement ? and, if so secured, would or would not the Utilitarian, according to his theory, feel justified in disturbing it ? If he oppose such a combination, he overthrows his theory; if he consents to such a combination, his theory may uphold tyranny and spoliation.

But I will not press this point: it is enough for me to show that, to render their politics practical, they are obliged to make their metaphysics impossible. Let the Utilitarian prove that the self-interest of man always leads him to be a tyrant and a robber, and I will grant that universal suffrage is a necessary and useful institution. A nation that conquers the world acts from self-interest;

a nation that submits to a conqueror acts from self-interest. A spendthrift and a miser alike act from self-interest: the same principle animated Messalina and Lucretia, Bayard and Byng. To say that when a man acts he acts from self-interest is only to announce that when a man does act he acts. An important truth, a great discovery, calling assuredly for the appearance of prophets, or, if necessary, even ghosts. But to announce that when a man acts he acts from self-interest, and that the self-interest of every man prompts him to be a tyrant and a robber, is to declare that which the experience of all human nature contradicts; because we all daily and hourly feel and see that there are a thousand other motives which influence human conduct besides the idea of exercising power and obtaining property; every one of which motives must rank under the term Self-interest, because every man who acts under their influence must necessarily believe that in so acting he acts for his happiness, and therefore for his self-interest. Utility, Pain, Power, Pleasure, Happiness, Self-interest, are all phrases to which any man may annex any meaning he pleases, and from which any acute and practised reasoner may most syllogistically deduce any theory he chooses. " Such words," says Locke, " no more improve our understanding than the move of a jack will fill our bellies." This waste of ingenuity on nonsense is like the condescending union that occasionally occurs between some high-bred steed and some long-eared beauty of the Pampas: the base and fantastical embrace only produces a barren and mulish progeny.

CHAPTER III

Of Abstract Principles in Politics, and the Degree of Theory that enters into Politics.

WE have before this had an *a priori* system of celestial mechanics, and its votaries most syllogistically sent Galileo to a dungeon, after having triumphantly refuted him. We have before this had an *a priori* system of metaphysics, but where now are the golden volumes of Erigena,[1] and Occam, and Scotus, and Raymond Lully ?[2]   And now we have an *a priori* system of politics.   The schoolmen are revived in the nineteenth century, and are going to settle the State with their withering definitions, their fruitless logomachies, and barren dialectics.

I should suppose that there is no one of the Utilitarian sages who would not feel offended if I were to style him the Angelical Doctor, like Thomas Aquinas ; and I regret, from bitter experience, that they have not yet condescended sufficiently to cultivate the art of composition to entitle them to the style of the Perspicuous ¡Doctor, like Walter Burley.

These reflections naturally lead me to a consideration of the great object of our new school of statesmen in general, which is to form political institutions on abstract principles of theoretic science, instead of permitting them to spring from the course of events, and to be naturally created by the necessities of nations.   It would appear that this scheme originated in the fallacy of supposing that theories produce circumstances, whereas the very converse of the proposition is correct, and circumstances indeed produce theories.   If we survey the career of an

[1] Joannes Scotus Erigena, mediæval philosopher; wrote "De Divisione Naturæ."
[2] William of Occam ("Doctor Invincibilis"), John Duns Scotus ("Doctor Subtilis"), and Raimon Lull ("Doctor Illuminatus"), schoolmen of the thirteenth and fourteenth centuries.

individual, we shall on the whole observe a remarkable consistency in his conduct; yet it is more than possible that this individual has never acted from that organised philosophy which we style *system*. What, then, has produced this consistency ? what, then, has occasioned this harmony of purpose ?   His individual character. Nations have characters as well as individuals, and national character is precisely the quality which the new sect of statesmen in their schemes and speculations either deny or overlook. The ruling passion, which is the result of organisation, regulates the career of an individual, subject to those superior accidents of fortune whose secondary influence is scarcely inferior to the impulse of his nature. The blended influences of nature and fortune form his character; 'tis the same with nations. There are important events in the career of an individual which force the man to ponder over the past, and, in these studies of experience and struggles for self-knowledge, to ascertain certain principles of conduct which he recognises as the cause of past success, and anticipates as the guarantee of future prosperity: and there are great crises in the fortunes of an ancient people which impel them to examine the nature of the institutions which have gradually sprung up among them.   In this great national review, duly and wisely separating the essential character of their history from that which is purely adventitious, they discover certain principles of ancestral conduct, which they acknowledge as the causes that these institutions have flourished and descended to them; and in their future career, and all changes, reforms, and alterations, that they may deem expedient, they resolve that these principles shall be their guides and their instructors. By these examinations they become more deeply intimate with their national character; and on this increased knowledge, and on this alone, they hold it wise to act. This, my Lord, I apprehend to be the greatest amount of theory that ever enters into those political institutions, which, from their permanency, are alone entitled to the consideration of a philosophical statesman; and this moderate, prudent, sagacious, and eminently practical application of principles to conduct has ever been, in the old time, the illustrious characteristic of our English politicians.

CHAPTER IV

Of Magna Charta—Petition of Right.

FROM the days of Magna Charta to those of the Declaration of Right, the same wary boldness is perceptible in the conduct of our leaders. It is the fashion nowadays to depreciate the value of the Great Charter—an ominous sign of the times, in my belief. For he runs a slight chance of being ultimately counted among the false prophets of the realm who predicts that, when the mention of that blessed deed does not command the reverential gratitude of every Briton, evil fortunes are impending for this society. Despots may depreciate it, whether they assume the forms of crowned monarchs or popular tribunes, for it stands alike in their way; but he who really loves freedom and his fatherland will never forget that the signet of the tyrant sealed alike our civil liberty and our national independence. They were great men, my Lord, that Archbishop of Canterbury[1] and that Earl of Pembroke, who, in the darkness of feodal ages, laid this bold and broad foundation of our national liberties; they were great men, and they were great statesmen. They did not act upon abstract principles, luckily for us, principles which the next age might have rejected, and the first schoolman, hired by the King, might have refuted; they acted upon positive conventional right. They set up no new title: they claimed their inheritance. They established the liberties of Englishmen as a life estate which their descendants might enjoy, but could not abuse by committing waste, or

[1] Stephen Langton.

9

forfeit by any false and fraudulent conveyance. They entailed our freedom.

The Magna Charta, at which our new sect of statesmen, the admirers of abstractions, sneer (it would be well if they read it oftener or at all), established an equality of civil rights to all classes of English freemen. It terminated arbitrary imprisonment and arbitrary spoliation. It enacted that justice should neither be sold, nor denied, nor delayed. It virtually established Habeas Corpus. It eminently advanced civilisation by curtailing at the same time the most crying grievances of the feodal tenure, and rendering inviolate the franchises of all mural communities. It checked the forest laws, established the freedom of foreign commerce, and finally secured the speedy execution of justice by virtually rendering the Court of Common Pleas permanent at Westminster, and independent of the Sovereign.

But, my Lord, these great and manifold blessings were not wrested from the Norman oppressor by the Barons of England under the plea of Utility, or with some windy and senseless cry of securing the greatest happiness of the greatest number. Stephen Langton knew the value of words as well as any clerk in Christendom; and he knew also that the right that is founded on words may be subverted by the same machinery; that what is incontestable in the twelfth century may be a subject of great discussion in the thirteenth; that a first principle in one age may become a second principle in a succeeding century, or a twenty-second principle. Whether there were any Utilitarians under the Plantagenets I pretend not to decide. There is generally no lack of political sciolists, and, for aught I know, some predecessor of Condorcet[1] or Bentham may have been innocently dreaming in a cloister; but if these abstract-principle gentlemen had been as active in the reign of John as in that of our own gracious Sovereign, I doubt our great Lord Primate would

[1] Marie Jean Antoine Nicholas Caritat, Marquis de Condorcet (1743–1794), French philosopher.

have placed the State in jeopardy to make it prove and square with their cockbrained fancies. The Barons wished that the liberties they secured for themselves should likewise descend to their posterity; and as therefore they were to become a matter of inheritance, as a matter of inheritance they claimed them. They claimed them as an inheritance which had been too long in abeyance; and, not content with establishing their confirmation by Henry Beauclerk, they traced their glorious pedigree even to the Confessor.

I do not find, my Lord, that at a much later but as momentous a period of our history, Selden and Sir Edward Coke, though they lived in an age which, in the Protestant Reformation and the Revolt of the Netherlands, had witnessed revolutions as awful as any of those which we or our fathers can remember; and had, consequently, the advantage of a far vaster range of political experience than the Stephen Langtons and the great patriots of the reign of John; I do not find, my Lord, that these wise, and spirited, and learned personages saw fit to question the propriety of their great ancestors' conduct. On the contrary, knowing that society is neither more nor less than a compact, and that no right can be long relied on that cannot boast a conventional origin, they were most jealous of our title to our liberties. They lavished all their learning in proving its perfection and completeness. They never condescended to argue; they offered evidence. They were ever ready with their abstract of title, and, with very slight alterations, the language of the famous Petition of Right itself might be transformed into a humble request to a Sovereign for the restoration of some real estate—some patrimony long withheld from a defrauded posterity. In short, all our struggles for freedom smack of law. There is throughout the whole current of our history a most salutary legal flavour. And arbitrary monarchs and rebellious Parliaments alike cloak their encroachments under the sacred veil of right, alike quote precedent and cling to prescription.

CHAPTER V

Of Precedent, Prescription, and Antiquity—Of the Formation of a Free Constitution.

THIS respect for Precedent, this clinging to Prescription, this reverence for Antiquity, which are so often ridiculed by conceited and superficial minds, and move the especial contempt of the gentlemen who admire abstract principles, appear to me to have their origin in a profound knowledge of human nature, and in a fine observation of public affairs, and satisfactorily to account for the permanent character of our liberties. Those great men, who have periodically risen to guide the helm of our government in times of tumultuous and stormy exigency, knew that a State is a complicated creation of refined art, and they handled it with all the delicacy a piece of exquisite machinery requires. They knew that, if once they admitted the abstract rights of subjects, they must inevitably advance to the abstract rights of men, and then that the very foundations of their civil polity would sink beneath them. They held this to be too dear a price for the barren fruition of a first principle. They knew that the foundation of civil polity is Convention, and that everything and every person that springs from that foundation must partake of that primary character. They held themselves bound by the contracts of their forefathers, because they wished their posterity to observe their own agreements. They did not comprehend how the perpetuity of a State could be otherwise preserved. They looked upon the nation as a family, and upon the country as a landed inheritance. Generation after generation were to succeed to it, with all its convenient buildings, and all its choice cultivation, its parks and gardens, as well as its fields and meads, its libraries and its collections of art, all its wealth, but all its incumbrances.

Holding society to be as much an artificial creation as the fields and cities amid which they dwelt, they were of opinion that every subject was bound to respect the established Constitution of his country, because, independent of all other advantages, to that Constitution he was indebted even for his life. Had not the State been created the subject would not have existed. Man with them, therefore, was the child of the State, and born with filial duties. To disobey the State, therefore, was a crime; to rebel against it, treason; to overturn it, parricide. Our ancestors could not comprehend how this high spirit of loyalty could be more efficiently fostered and maintained than by providing that the rights, privileges, and possessions of all should rest on no better foundation than the State itself. They would permit no antagonist principle in their body politic. They would not tolerate nature struggling with art, or theory with habit. Hence their reverence for prescription, which they placed above law, and held superior to reason. It is to this deference to what Lord Coke finely styles " reverend antiquity " that I ascribe the duration of our commonwealth, and it is this spirit which has prevented even our revolutions from being destructive.

I do not see, my Lord, that this reverence for antiquity has checked the progress of knowledge, or stunted the growth of liberty, in this island. We are universally held to be the freest people in Europe, and to have enjoyed our degree of freedom for a longer period than any existing State. I am not aware that any nation can fairly assert its claims to superior learning or superior wisdom; to a more renowned skill in arts or arms; to a profounder scientific spirit; to a more refined or comprehensive civilisation. I know that a year or two back the newspapers that are in the interest of the new sect of statesmen were wont to twit and taunt us with the superior freedom of our neighbours. " The fact can no longer be concealed," announced the prime organ of the party, " the people of France are freer than the people of Eng-

land. The consciousness of this fact will be the last blow
to the oligarchy." Profound publicist ! The formation
of a free government on an extensive scale, while it is assuredly one of the most interesting problems of humanity,
is certainly the greatest achievement of human wit. Perhaps I should rather term it a superhuman achievement ;
for it requires such refined prudence, such comprehensive
knowledge, and such perspicacious sagacity, united with
such almost illimitable powers of combination, that it is
nearly in vain to hope for qualities so rare to be congre-
gated in a solitary mind. Assuredly this *summum bonum*
is not to be found ensconced behind a revolutionary barri-
cade, or floating in the bloody gutters of an incendiary
metropolis. It cannot be scribbled down—this great invention—in a morning on the envelope of a letter by
some charter-concocting monarch, or sketched with ludicrous facility in the conceited commonplace book of a
Utilitarian sage. With us it has been the growth of ages,
and brooding centuries have watched over and tended its
perilous birth and feeble infancy. The noble offspring of
liberty and law now flourishes in the full and lusty vigour
of its proud and perfect manhood. Long may it flourish !
Long be its life, venerable its age, and distant its beatified
euthanasia ! I offer this prayer for the sake of human
nature as much as for my country; not more for Britain
than for the world of which it is the ornament and honour.

CHAPTER VI

Of the Attempts of the French to form a Free Constitution—
    Reasons of their Failure—Fallacy of adopting the English
    Constitution in France.

WHEN the people of France, at the latter part of the last
century, made their memorable effort for the formation
of a free government, they acted on very different principles to those that guided Stephen Langton and Selden.
Their principles, indeed, were as abstract as any Utili-

tarian could desire. They built their fabric, not merely upon the abstract rights of subjects, but the abstract rights of men, and at once boldly seized equality for their basis. We know the result. Equality, anarchy, tyranny, were the necessary gradations of their philosophical system of political regeneration. Wearied with fruitless efforts, and exhausted by long suffering, they at length took refuge in the forced shade of exotic institutions. We witnessed the miserable but inevitable fate of the constitutional studies of the groves of Hartwell;[1] a fate which must ever attend institutions that have not been created by the genius of a country, and with which the national character can never sympathise.

In France, previous to the great revolution, there existed all the elements of a free Constitution, although not of the English Constitution. In its old local divisions, indicated by nature, consecrated by custom, in its ancient States, its Parliaments, its corporations, its various classes of inhabitants, its landed tenure, its ecclesiastical and chivalric orders, there might have been found all that variety of interests whose balanced influences would have sustained a free and durable constitution. The French leaders neglected these admirable materials. To secure equality they decided on indiscriminate destruction : they not only destroyed law and custom, but they destroyed their country. They destroyed Normandy, they destroyed Provence, they destroyed Burgundy, they destroyed Gascony; not in name alone, but in very deed and fact. They measured their land, and divided it into equal geometrical departments, without the slightest regard to difference of soil or population, variety of manners, or diversity of temperament; and in this Laputan state that great country still remains. Why the name of France was preserved it is difficult to comprehend. If for its associations, could not these Utilitarian legislators understand that, in destroying the asso-

[1] Hartwell, a Buckinghamshire village, to which Louis the Eighteenth retired in 1809.

ciations that clung to the name of Brittany and Burgundy, they were destroying so many wholesome elements of vigorous and enduring government ? Their sentiment required that they should still dwell in Paris, beautiful and famous Paris. Were they so blind as not to see that the outraged sympathy, which would have recoiled from styling the capital " the city of the Seine," was equally offended when the old dweller in Touraine found that he was suddenly transformed into an inhabitant of the department of the Loire ?

When Napoleon obtained supreme power France was not a country—it was a camp—a lawless and disorderly camp. Napoleon disciplined it. He found the land geometrically parcelled out, and the French nation billeted on the soil. With such elements of government, even Napoleon could do not more; even with his unlimited authority and indomitable will, all that he could aspire to was to organise anarchy. The Emperor of the French was not one of your abstract-principle gentlemen. His was eminently a practical mind. He looked about for the elements of government, and he could discover no better than those which had been created by the national character, and hallowed by the national habits. Even his sagacious mind deferred to the experience of ages, and even his unconquerable will declined a rivalry with the prescriptive conviction of an ancient people. He reestablished the tribunals; he revived chivalry; he conjured up the vision of a nobility; he created the shadow of a Church. He felt that his empire, like all others, must be supported by institutions.

The rapid vicissitudes of his reign prevented these establishments from maturing into influence and power, and, when Louis the Eighteenth returned to the throne of his fathers, he was called upon to establish a Constitution without being furnished with the elements to form one. The puzzled monarch in despair, with some degree, one would think, of that Rabelaisian humour with which he was not altogether untinctured, presented his subjects

with the Constitution of another country. Could anything be conceived more supremely ludicrous ? Was it
in the power of the most ill-regulated mind to break into
folly more flagrant ? The lunatic with a crown of straw
is as much a sovereign as a country is a free country with
a paper Constitution. France, without an aristocracy of
any kind, was ornamented with an Upper Chamber of
hereditary peers, and a Second Chamber invested with all
the powers with which, after more than five centuries of
graduated practice, we ventured to entrust our House of
Commons, was filled with some hundreds of individuals
who were less capable of governing a country than a
debating society of ingenious youth at one of our Universities. The good Louis presented his countrymen with
a free Constitution—drawn up in a morning. He did
that which the great Napoleon never ventured to do.
Louis the Eighteenth achieved that in one morning
which in less favoured England has required nearly a
thousand years for its accomplishment. This innocent
monarch seems to have supposed that the English Constitution consists merely of two rooms full of gentlemen,
who discuss public questions and make laws in the
Metropolis at a stated season of the year. The King
of France had no idea that political institutions, to be
effective, must be founded on the habits and opinions
of the people whom they pretend to govern; that the
members of a representative body must be composed of
a class to which the people have long looked up with
respect and confidence; and that these representatives
must carry on their affairs in a mode and spirit congenial
and homogeneous with the prescriptive practice of the
community. The King of France, good, easy man, had
forgotten—M. de Lolme[1] had not taught him—that the
Parliament of England was only the last, though loftiest,
gradation in a long flight and series of ascending establishments; that not a man was entrusted with the exer-

─────────
[1] Jean Louis de Lolme (1740–1806), who wrote " The Constitution of England, or an Account of the English Government."

cise of a political suffrage in England who was not already invested with the most precious office in the realm, the duty of deciding upon the fortunes and the lives of his fellow-citizens, and was thus long, early, and accurately practised in the habits of judgment and examination; that nearly every member of the Houses of Parliament was an active magistrate of the realm, and, in taking his legislative seat, bore his quota of local respect to the great aggregate of national reverence; that the vast institution of the Poor Laws alone connected the thoughts and feelings of the unrepresented peasants and populace of England with the Parliament in which the local executors of those statutes as magistrates took their seats as members.

Louis the Eighteenth forgot that in almost every town in England there were corporations which were the express image of the political Constitution of the realm, and vestries in which the local interests were debated by a representative body with an affectation of all the forms and ceremonies of Westminster. Louis the Eighteenth had no idea that his two rooms full of gentlemen, to be obeyed, must actually or virtually, directly or indirectly, represent every important interest in the kingdom. He had no suspicion that it is not in the power of any legislator that ever lived, or that ever will live, to frame a political assembly *a priori* that shall represent all, or even a majority of, the interests of a complicated society. The French Chambers represented none—they were only fitted to be the tools of a faction, and the tools of a faction they became. The two Chambers constituted by the Charter were nothing more than two debating societies. I am only surprised that the ludicrous imposture lasted so long; but we must take into consideration the exhaustion of France when the exotic was introduced and planted in its soil, and the unceasing vigilance and sleepless care with which the delicate graft was tended by the foreign Powers, whose complaisant approval had sanctioned its adoption.

CHAPTER VII

Of the Attempts to establish the English Constitution in the Sicilies and the Peninsula.

If the barren adoption of a form of government by France, styled by courtesy the English Constitution, must be classed among the prime follies of human conduct, what language are we to use when the Anglo-Gallic scheme is gravely introduced to the consideration of the Lazzaroni of Naples and the Hidalgos of Spain; we seem to have arrived at the climax of human absurdity. The classical romance of "Rienzi" was not more ridiculous than the first instance; there is no adventure in " Don Quixote " which can rival the frenzy of the second. In France, thanks to Equality and its crabbed fruits, there were no prejudices to shock; but when we read of the sudden transplantation of institutions gradually established in the course of centuries by the phlegmatic experience of a Saxon people into the most southern soils of Europe, the glittering and barbaric Sicilies, and a country which is the link between Europe and Africa, and which in the fertility of its soil, the temperature of its climate, and the character of its inhabitants, resembles Morocco more than England, we seem to be perusing the mad pages of a political novel poured forth by the wild and mystic genius of some inmate of a German University. Undine or Sintram[1] are more real: the pages of Hoffmann[2] less shadowy and more probable.

I have travelled over Andalusia and Sicily—I travelled on horseback, for there were no roads—I found a feodal nobility and a peasantry untinctured, even in the slightest degree, by letters, and steeped in the grossest superstition: I found agriculture generally neglected, or unchanged

[1] " Sintram and his Companions " and " Undine," by Baron Friedrich Heinrich Karl de la Motte Fouqué (1777–1843).
[2] Ernst Theodor Wilhelm Hoffmann, 1776–1822. Of his fairy tales, "Der Goldene Topf" was translated by Carlyle in 1827.

in its pursuit since the days of Theocritus; a teeming soil, no human energy; no manufactures, no police; mountainous districts swarming with bandits, plains whose vast stillness prepared me for the Syrian deserts; occasionally I reposed in cities where a comparative civilisation had been obtained under the influence of a despotic priesthood. And these are the regions to which it is thought fit suddenly to apply the institutions which regulate the civil life of Yorkshire and Kent! We may celebrate the constitutional coronation of a Bavarian in the Acropolis, and surround his free throne with the bayonets of his countrymen; we may hire Poles and Irishmen as a bodyguard for the Sovereign who mimics the venerable ceremonies of Westminster as she opens the Parliaments of Madrid or Lisbon; but invincible nature will reject the unnatural novelties, and history, instead of celebrating the victory of freedom, will only record the triumph of folly.

CHAPTER VIII

Of the Last Attempt of the French to form a Free Government
—La Fayette and Lord Somers compared.

CHARLES THE TENTH struggled with the futility of the Charter; he passed years in an impracticable attempt and fruitless effort to govern thirty-two millions of people with a silly piece of paper. With good intentions but with no talents, surrounded by creatures destitute of every quality of statesmen, the King at length attempted to rid himself, and the nation, of an imposture which only supplied a faction with a pretext. Charles failed, but even Charles the Tenth nearly succeeded. Louis Philippe at the head of a mob crying, "Vive la République!" established a despotism. Is there no moral in this rapid catastrophe? Are we to be ever deaf and ever blind? Are we never to learn that a Constitution, a real Constitution, is the creation of ages, not of a day, and that when we destroy such a Constitution we in fact destroy a nation ?

Let us bestow a little more examination upon the conduct of the French nation during their last Revolution, their second great effort to establish a free government. Let us contrast La Fayette at the head of France in 1830 with Lord Somers at the head of England in 1688. The parallel will be instructive. When La Fayette had got rid of Charles the Tenth, he found himself precisely in the same situation in which that unfortunate monarch had suffered throughout his reign; he found himself in the precise predicament in which Louis the Eighteenth was placed when he returned from Hartwell; he occupied the exact site of Napoleon when he declared himself First Consul. He found himself at the head of a people without a Constitution, and not possessing any elements to form one. The creative genius of Napoleon instantly devised some expedients, and until they could be called into action he depended upon the teeming resources of his own strong mind, and the devotion of a victorious army. Louis the Eighteenth trusted to his allies for substantial support, and offered the written description of the Constitution of another country as a pretext for the loyal allegiance of his own subjects. Charles the Tenth had neither a confiding army nor foreign allies; he had neither the creative genius of Napoleon nor the epicurean adroitness of Louis. La Fayette called out the National Guard and changed the national colours for present support, and then, that his revolution might be something better than merely a revolution of ribbons, he took refuge again in abstract principles. Equality would not serve the purpose again; that blooming prostitute had shrunk by this time into a most shrivelled and drivelling harridan. For Equality the pupil of Washington substituted the SOVEREIGNTY OF THE PEOPLE. The people shouted in its honour, all was satisfactorily settled, and thirty-two millions were again to be governed by a phrase.

Let me recall to your Lordship the tone and temper
with which the intelligence of these exploits was received
in our own country.   I was indeed then absent; but
although the announcement of this millennium reached me
in the shadow of the Pyramids, and two years elapsed
before I returned to a country which I found so changed,
I returned in time to witness the still exulting and still
palpitating triumph of that party, who are now so anxious,
and so active in their anxiety, to abrogate the clumsy
and chance-born institutions of England, and substitute
in their place their own modish inventions, formed on the
irrefragable basis of Reason and Utility.   There was no
class of persons in England with whom the junior French
Revolution[1]—I mean the riot that placed the House of
Valois[2] on the throne of Paris—was so popular in this
country as our own anti-constitutional writers.   It was
the avowed consummation of all their theoretical wishes :
the practical adoption of the scheme in England was all
that was requisite to secure the completion of their
patriotic satisfaction.   I believe there was no individual
in this country who more ardently admired the conduct
of France at that period than Mr. Bentham.   I have been
assured this on good authority.   Within these last twelve-
months, even, the principal daily organ of this new sect
of statesmen has more than once taunted Englishmen
with the fact that the French were now freer than they,
and has announced that the consciousness of this fact
would be " the last blow to the oligarchy."   I impute no
bad motives to these writers; I condescend to none of
those " vituperative personalities " which their apostle
deprecates; I avoid the " *fallacies ad odium* " which their
evangelist so successfully exposes by fallacies still more
fallacious (" Book of Fallacies," pp. 127-133); I am con-

[1] The Revolution of 1830.
[2] Disraeli, in a letter to his sister (January 9, 1836), writes:
" Eliot . . . wants to know, by-the-by, why I called the Orleans
branch the House of Valois.   I am sure I don't know.   Pray find
out for me, and write your answer, if you catch one, as soon as
possible."

tent ever to take the motives of individuals as I find
them. I give them full credit for sincerity. But judge,
oh ! judge by the result, of their capabilities for government; admire their political prescience, and trust, if you
will, their practical ability.

The Constitution founded on the Sovereignty of the
People has run even a shorter career than the Constitution founded on the Equality of Man: one of the most
gifted and civilised nations that ever existed is enthralled
by an iron despotism; the liberty of the press is utterly
destroyed; trial by jury virtually abrogated; arbitrary
imprisonment in daily practice; the country covered with
Bastiles, and the Bastiles crowded with State victims.

I turn from France in 1830 to England in 1688; from
La Fayette to Lord Somers; from the abstract-principle
politicians eulogised on all occasions by our anti-constitutional writers to practical statesmen on all occasions the
object of their sneers, and whom one of their number has
recently published a quarto volume to decry. No sooner
had the nation got rid of the Popish tyrant than Lord
Somers drew up the famous Declaration of Right. Mark
that title. A Declaration of Right. This document
enumerated and claimed for Englishmen all the rights
and liberties to which they were entitled by laws which
James the Second had violated. So careful were the
leaders of 1688 of not vitiating or injuring the valued title
to our liberties that they omitted in this great remedial
statute all mention of those further guarantees of our
freedom which they had already devised, and which they
immediately afterwards proposed and passed in Parliament. First, and before they made any addition to their
inheritance, they determined to secure themselves in the
clear freehold of their rights. They were careful, while
they were meditating improvements and increase, that
they should not, from present neglect, be forced to bring
actions of ejectment hereafter for property to which they
had become entitled in the times of Charles the First or
the Plantagenets, and which in their hot zeal and hurry

they had now overlooked. The Declaration of Right connected the pedigree of our rights and liberties with the Petition of Right, which again carried them upwards to the Great Charter, in like manner dependent on the charter of Henry Beauclerk and the laws of the Confessor. Whether it ascended further was now a matter of interest only to the antiquary. A pedigree of six centuries was proud enough even for our glorious British freedom. In all this Lord Somers exhibited the same practical wisdom as had animated Stephen Langton and guided Selden. Lord Somers, I doubt not, was as conversant with abstract principles of government as any writer in the *Westminster Review ;* for a quarter of a century before they had been rife enough in England, but Lord Somers knew to what their adoption had eventually and speedily led. He knew that there was a stern necessity in society which would occasionally vindicate its way above all law; his recent experience would have taught him, if nothing else, that occasional revolutions in States were beyond the power of human prevention; but, like all other wise statesmen, he would not look upon these as the course of politics, any more than the earthquake or the hurricane as the course of nature. He blotted their possibility out of the statute book, however he might choose to speculate over them in a political treatise, in Sidney, or Harrington, or Locke. He wished to obliterate from the mind of the nation that awful truth, that a deed may sometimes be necessary which is not lawful. He knew very well that, if a crisis were again to occur that should require such a sacrifice, the native instinct of men would prompt them to the exploit. They would read their purpose in each other's eyes, and do the deed. Far from braying out the sovereignty of the people, or any such perilous stuff, he and his great associates exerted themselves to the utmost to endow King William with a legal and hereditary title. They had consented to the necessary evil of a revolution, but then they had carved the State

" As a dish fit for the gods,[1]
Not hewed it as a carcass fit for hounds."

An English revolution is at least a solemn sacrifice: a French revolution is an indecent massacre.

Lord Somers and the English nation were rewarded for their wisdom and their prudent carriage by securing for this realm nearly a century and a half of the greatest order, prosperity, and glory, that this country, or any other country, ever enjoyed. And this leads me, my Lord, to another great event in our history: the Reform of the House of Commons, to which I shall presently advert.

CHAPTER IX

Of the Constitutional Development of Prussia.

I WISH, however, previously, to call your Lordship's attention to the conduct of a Sovereign who was placed in the same situation as Louis the Eighteenth at the same period; but whose policy, fortunately for himself and for his subjects, materially differed from that of the brother of the unhappy Charles the Tenth. The Sovereign to whom I allude is the present King of Prussia. The King of Prussia, like the King of France, promised his subjects a Constitution; and we all remember for how many rabid years this Sovereign was the object of the virulent invective of our own disaffected writers, who, by-the-by, seem equally anxious to destroy the English Constitution in England, and to substitute it in every other country, for not redeeming his pledge and fulfilling his promise. No news arrived to the geniuses of our gazettes of the holding of any Parliament at Berlin; no advices reached them of any Dukes of Potsdam or Posen moving constitutional addresses in the Prussian House of Lords; there was not

---

[1] " Let's carve him as a dish fit for the gods,
Not hew him as a carcass fit for hounds."
SHAKESPEARE : *Julius Cæsar*, II. i. 173.

even a rumour of any frank having yet been seen in the
handwriting of any honourable representative of Königs-
berg or Erfurt.   What royal treachery !   What base,
despotic, holy-alliance perfidy !   But nations are not to
be deceived, and outraged, and trampled on, with impunity.   The day of retribution was at hand; sooner or
later the hour of popular vengeance would arrive, and
then the perfidious tyrant, in spite of his standing army,
would learn how utterly vain is the struggle with the
spirit of the age, and how futile the final rivalry of force
and freedom.   Prussia was undoubtedly to be the first
victim.

Now this is no misrepresentation, no exaggeration even,
of the tone in which the disaffected writers of this country
indulged for a series of years against the King of Prussia.
I think it expedient to seize an occasional opportunity of
illustrating the sagacity and information which the disaffected writers in this country invariably bring to the
consideration of public subjects, and especially to any
speculations connected with foreign politics.   Abstract
principles and a daily and dexterous practice in the art
of misrepresenting circumstances which, in the imperfect
survey of gradual occurrence, cannot always be fully comprehended even by the wisest heads and the calmest
minds, carry these writers through their domestic lucubrations with a spanking breeze and flying colours; but
when we catch them fishing in strange waters, we are
better enabled to test the value of their barren axioms,
and to gauge the depth and spirit of their acuteness and
information.

And so it happened that, when the party throughout
Europe who, to use the words of Locke, " are the popular
asserters of public liberty and the greatest engrossers of
it too, and not unfitly called its keepers—ambitious men
who pull down well-framed Constitutions, that out of the
ruins they may build themselves fortunes "—when, I say,
it happened that that restless and intriguing minority,
who ever have the greatest happiness of the greatest

number on their lips, succeeded in 1830 in overthrowing
the Bourbon Government and embroiling Europe in that
period of general commotion, when every European State
was more or less shaken with internal convulsions, when
Belgium revolted from Holland and Poland from Russia,
when the tricolor flag was hoisted in Italy, when Spain
summoned its Cortes, and Portugal expelled its Sovereign
with foreign bayonets, when even the Swiss Confedera-
tion shook to its centre, and every minor German State,
from Baden to Brunswick, was the theatre of revolutionary riots—and last of all, but, oh ! indeed not least,
when even Great Britain yielded to the tempest, and at
least a branch of that mighty oak was severed from its
vigorous though ancient trunk; Prussia, enslaved and
indignant Prussia, governed by a perfidious despot, whose
realm was surrounded and even divided in the midst of
its territory by the very States which were most inflamed,
alone sent forth neither a shout nor a murmur, and alone
remained tranquil and undisturbed. How was this ?
How did this accord with the Utilitarian system of government ?   Was Prussia content because it was tranquil ?
Was it the general conviction that the greatest happiness
of the greatest number was secured by the influence of
its polity ?   But that polity was absolute. It is the
interest of every man to be a tyrant and a robber. Was,
then, the King of Prussia neither a tyrant nor a robber ?
Was he mild, merciful, just, beneficent, useful ?   How
did this accord with the Utilitarian system of morals ?

It appears to me that a study of the policy of Prussia
during the last quarter of a century may tend more to a
solution of the great problem of government than any
exercise of reason with which I am acquainted. By it
we may learn how entirely the result of a principle depends
upon its method of application, and that that method of
application, to be beneficent, must be framed in very
strict, though not absolute, deference to the existing
civilisation of the country. That a reforming Minister
must, above all things, be skilful in adaptation is per-

haps but a barren phrase; but this I will observe, that a wise statesman will be careful that all new rights shall, as it were, spring from out old establishments. By this system alone can at the same time the old be purified and the new rendered permanent.

The French Revolution was the death-blow in civilised Europe to the long-declining feudal system. An equality of civil rights was recognised by the King of Prussia and his wise councillors as the basis of their new order of society. And how did they obtain this great end ? Not by a bombastic decree from Potsdam suddenly braying the rights of man into the indefinite ears of the motley subjects of the Prussian Government, and creating, probably, endless riots in consequence; but by a series of wise edicts which, in the course of twelve years, entirely abolished serfage, and effected a complete but gradual revolution in the tenure of land, so that at length the Prussian nobility found themselves with no other privilege but the prefixion of a definite article to their name. Almost simultaneously with the abolition of serfage among the rural population, the citizens were emancipated by a great municipal charter, which introduced the system of popular election into towns, and prepared the inhabitants for the function of even higher duties. I assure you, my Lord, that the municipal constitution of Prussia might have been referred to with profit in those memorable debates, in which you achieved so much general benefit and acquired so much personal honour.

I now arrive at the most important decree of the King of Prussia, and the establishment of which I hesitate not to class among the wisest, the most benevolent, and the most comprehensive institutions on record, and fairly to entitle its illustrious originator to rank among the most eminent legislators that have flourished. Convinced that a practical assembly of national representatives can never be collected except in a country in which the inhabitants have been long versed in the partial administration of affairs, and consequently habituated to the practice of public discussion, and anticipating that the hour would arrive when such an assembly might indeed be holden at Berlin, the King in 1815 decreed the erection of Provincial States, to whose supervision the interests of their respective provinces were intrusted, with full power to take into consideration all measures, whether relating to persons, property, or taxation, and to advise with the King thereon, by the right and process of petition. Here the powers of these States ceased; their province was merely consultative; they were invested with no legislative functions. In this great institution of consultative Parliaments, the King of Prussia, by an analogous wisdom which cannot be too much admired, has adopted as the basis of the future Constitution of his country that system of Remedial, as contradistinguished from Legislative, Representation which was long the custom of England, and to the influence of which upon the character of the nation we mainly owe our efficient legislative representation in the House of Commons.

There is no spectacle in the world more delightful than that of a wisely-governed and well-ordered community, and I could willingly dwell upon the consideration of Prussian policy, were the fortunes of that realm the sole subject of my remarks, instead of being the incidental illustration of an argument. I might show how one of the bravest, best disciplined, and most numerous, armies in the world was a popular force; how the boasted career of merit of the French Empire is reduced to such practical reality in Prussia that to rise to the highest appointments in the State requires only a proportionate degree of talent, industry, honesty, and study; and, lastly, how the most philosophical system of national education with which we are acquainted is preparing the rising generation of the realm for all the duties of good citizens, loyal subjects, and devoted patriots.

Having now, I hope, satisfactorily explained why in the heady tumult of 1830 the subjects of Prussia were alone loyal to their Sovereign, I will ask your Lordship

what would have been the situation of that country, then
and now, had Frederick William, at the same time as
Louis the Eighteenth, presented his subjects with the
same Constitution and a free press, and thus avoided the
diatribes of those enlightened journalists, who for so
many years described and denounced this great and good
man as a perfidious despot. We know very well what
would have happened. A nominally representative
assembly would have met in Berlin, consisting of individuals totally inexperienced in the habits of discussion,
the practice of legislation, and the art of government.
Invested with power which they could not exercise for
any beneficial purpose, and representing the nation in
form only, and not in spirit, they would have soon split
into factions, having no other object but their own aggrandisement. An active click, through the agency of a
violent press, would have enlisted the physical force of
the people on their side by affecting an extraordinary zeal
for popular interests : having obtained a majority in the
Chamber by repeated elections, rendered necessary by
their factious conduct, they would have overthrown a
series of administrations by a series of factious resolutions. When they had rendered the royal government
impracticable, they would have forced the King, in
defence of the nation and his crown, to some necessary
but unconstitutional decrees, and then we should have
had "three glorious and beautiful days " at Berlin.
Perhaps in such a vicinity the conspiracy would have
been crushed, but where now would have been the
prosperity and patriotism and philosophy and real
freedom of Prussia ? The bayonet would have been the
only law, and a military dungeon the only school of national
education. The King of Prussia was as careful that the
rights of his subjects should flow from the royal will, their
ancient government, as Stephen Langton, Selden, and
Lord Somers that the liberties of their countrymen
should be traced to a similar source. All were alike
practical men ; all avoided the barren assertion of abstract

rights; and the same destiny of continued welfare in all
probability awaits Prussia that has long so blessed our
native land.

CHAPTER X

Constitution of the United States exercises the same Fatal Influence over America as that of England over Europe—Mexico,
Chili, Peru, contrasted with France, Spain, and Portugal.

IT appears to me, my Lord, that it is destined to the free
Constitution of the United States of North America to
exercise the same fatal influence over the political society
of the New World as the Constitution of England has
wielded over that of the old. The Constitution of the
United States was applied to the Government of Mexico,
Colombia, Peru, and Chili, by virtue of the same peremptory and abstract principles that had selected the
Constitution of England for the government of France,
Sicily, Spain, and Portugal; and the same results were
acquired. The European and the American States, that
have been the victims of this Quixotic spirit of political
Propagandism, have vied with each other in successive
revolutions, until at length disorder and even disorganisa-
tion have universally prevailed, except where anarchy
has been arrested by despotism.

Why is this ? Why has the republican Constitution
flourished in New England, and failed in New Spain ?
Why has the Congress of Washington commanded the
respect of civilised Europe, and the Congresses of Mexico,
or Lima, or Santiago, gained only its derision or disgust ?
The answer is obvious: The Constitution of the United
States had no more root in the soil of Mexico, and Peru,
and Chili, than the Constitution of England in that of
France, and Spain, and Portugal: it was not founded on
the habits or the opinions of those whom it affected to
guide, regulate, and control. There was no privity
between the legislative institutions and the other establishments of these countries. The electors and the

elected were both suddenly invested with offices for the function of which they had received no previous education and no proper training; and which they were summoned to exercise without any simultaneous experience of similar duties. Had it been the Constitution of England, instead of that of the United States, which they were seeking to establish, these disqualifying circumstances alone would have insured failure; but, in addition to these disadvantages, picture to yourself the frenzy of attempting to establish republican institutions, invented by the Puritans and maintained by their peculiar spirit, not only among an ignorant people educated in Papal despotism, but in revolted colonies possessing a powerful Church establishment and a wealthy aristocracy. In their haste to establish freedom, these rudderless States have not secured independence; their revolutions have degenerated into riots, and, if they be not wise, may yet turn out to be only rebellions.

He is a short-sighted politician who dates the Constitution of the United States from 1780. It was established by the Pilgrim Fathers a century and a half before, and influenced a people practised from their cradles in the duties of self-government. The Pilgrim Fathers brought to their land of promise the laws of England, and a republican religion; and, blended together, these formed the old colonial Constitution of Anglo-America. The transition from such a government to the polity of Washington was certainly not greater in degree than the difference between Great Britain of 1829 and our country at this hour. The Anglo-Americans did not struggle for liberty: they struggled for independence; and the freedom and the free institutions they had long enjoyed secured for them the great object of their severe exertions. He who looks upon the citizens of the United States as a new people commits a moral, if not an historical, anachronism.

Of the Reform of our House of Commons, it is in this place only necessary to observe that the alleged increase

of democratic power was not founded on abstract rights,
but that the leaders and advocates of the Reform ostentatiously, although ignorantly, recommended their scheme
as a restoration of the ancient spirit and a return to the
ancient practice of the Constitution. Whether that
Reform originated in a Continental or a national impulse;
whether it were an expedient or an imprudent measure;
whether it were framed in harmony or in hostility to
our existing institutions; whether it really developed the
democratic elements of the country in their true and
comprehensive sense, or only increased the power and
influence of a sectarian minority; whether that great
settlement, in short, will be conducive to the ultimate
prosperity of the community, the happiness of the people,
and the honour of the Empire, are great questions from
the discussion of which I do not shrink, but they bear
no reference to the point at present under our examination, and are fully treated in a work which for a long
period has engaged my time and study.[1] My object
hitherto has been to prove by reference to the experience
both of the Old and the New World, and of the several
States of which they respectively consist, that political
institutions, founded on abstract rights and principles,
are mere nullities; that the only certain and legitimate
foundation of liberty is law; that if there be no privity
between the old legal Constitution of a country and the
new legislature, the latter must fall; and that a free
government on a great scale of national representation
is the very gradual work of time, and especially of preparatory institutions.

[1] Possibly at this time Disraeli was engaged on "The Spirit
of Whiggism," published in the following year, which briefly
discusses the points mentioned.

CHAPTER XI

Of the "Wisdom of our Ancestors."

IT was a conviction of the soundness of these principles that guided our forefathers in that prudent practice which we have hitherto been in the habit of dignifying by the venerable title of the Wisdom of our Ancestors,[1] a phrase once ever on the grateful lips of Englishmen, but now the object of scorn and ridicule by those who fancy themselves very profound, but who in reality are especially superficial. According to the most eminent of the Utilitarian schoolmen,[2] in his "Book of Fallacies" we have all the wisdom of our ancestors and our own into the bargain. The great detector of the deceits of political logic has here, according to his custom, involved himself in a position as deceptive as any of those from which he intended to dislodge his opponents. The fallacy of the great Utilitarian schoolman consists in confounding wisdom with knowledge. We may have all the knowledge of our ancestors, and we may have more; but it does not follow that we have all the wisdom of our ancestors, and we may have less. In using the phrase "wisdom of our ancestors," we, in fact, refer to the conduct of those of our ancestors who were wise; and when we have recourse to this phrase in reference to political conduct, we especially allude to those of our forefathers, those rare great men, who in seasons of singular emergency, difficulty, and peril, have maintained the State, and framed, fostered, developed, and established, our political institutions.

Let us take a rapid survey of our wise ancestors, in a political sense, since the Reformation. We will commence by a King, that extraordinary being, Henry the

---

[1] First used, according to Brougham, by Sir William Grant (1754–1832).   [2] Bentham.

Eighth, for certainly he must not be omitted; Burleigh claims a place, and Cecil, and assuredly Walsingham; then we may count Sir Edward Coke, and Selden, Strafford, and Pym, the Protector, Lord Clarendon, Sir William Temple, King William, Lord Somers, the Duke of Marlborough, the Duke of Argyll, Sir Robert Walpole, Lord Mansfield, Lord Hardwicke, Edmund Burke. The name of a twentieth great statesman since the Reformation previous to our own age does not easily occur to me, although I would include Lord Bolingbroke for reasons I may hereafter offer; and I have some doubt whether it would be possible, even with research, to fix upon another score. Now, it is possible that, having the benefit of all these men's knowledge, we may actually know more than these men; but suppose we are called upon to act to-morrow, and act, as is very probable, very unwisely, we may then find that we have not all these men's wisdom.

M. Guizot, who is so learned in British history, who writes even our annals, and edits our political memoirs,[1] doubtless, during the three glorious days and the subsequent settlement, inwardly congratulated the French people on being directed by a statesman who had all the knowledge of Lord Somers, "and something more." But where are the French people now, and what is M. Guizot? A striking evidence that a man may be very knowing without being very wise. Throughout the whole of our history we observe that the leading men who have guided the fortunes of our Commonwealth in times of great difficulty and danger have invariably agreed in one line of policy—namely, to eschew abstractions. This resolution is the distinguishing feature of English statesmanship; it is the principal cause of the duration of the English State; and herein eminently consists the " wisdom of our ancestors."

---

[1] " Mémoires relatifs à la Révolution d'Angleterre " (26 vols.).

CHAPTER XII

The " House of Commons " not the " House of the People "—
The Political Institutions of England sprung from its Legal
Institutions — Nature of the Representative Principle —
Original Character of the English Parliament.

BUT, my Lord, to confess the truth, I have my suspicions
that the new school of statesmen, with all their affected
confidence in abstract principles, and all their valorous
determination to construct our coming commonwealth
on a basis of pure political science, have some misgivings
that this great result is not to be entirely obtained by the
virgin influence alone of their boasted philosophy; and
I am confirmed in this imagination by the distrustful
circumstance of their simultaneously condescending,
amid all their theory, to avail themselves, for the purpose
of advancing their object, of a great practical misrepresentation of the form and spirit of our Constitution. For
it is curious to observe that, while they pretend to offer
us an unfailing test of the excellence and expediency of
all political institutions, they are at the same time indefatigable in promulgating the creed that the branch of
our legislature hitherto styled the House of Commons
is, in fact, the House of the People, and that the members
of that assembly are consequently and absolutely representatives of the People. VOX POPULI VOX DEI is a
favourite adage, and ever on these persons' tongues: so
that, if the House of Commons be the House of the People,
it is also the House of God; it is omniscient and omnipotent—a convenient creed ! There was a time when our
Kings affected to rule by Divine right. It cost our fathers
dear to root out that fatal superstition. But all their
heroic labours will prove worse than fruitless if the Divine
right of Kings is to be succeeded by the Divine right
of the House of Commons. In such a belief, I, for one,
see no security for our cherished liberties; and still less

a guarantee for our boasted civilisation : in such a belief it seems to me the prolific seeds are deeply sown of tyranny and of barbarism, and if this principle is to be the foundation of our future polity, it requires, in my opinion, no great gift of inspiration to foretell that all those evils are impending for this country which are the inevitable consequences of its destinies being regulated by a vulgar and ignoble oligarchy.

My Lord, I do not believe that the House of Commons is the House of the People, or that the members of the House of Commons are the representatives of the People.[1] I do not believe that such ever were the characters, either of the House of Commons or the members of the House of Commons ; I am sure that such are not now the characters of that assembly, or of those who constitute it, and I ardently hope that such will never be the characters.

The Commons of England form an Estate of the realm, and the members of the House of Commons represent that Estate. They represent nothing more. It is a very important estate of the realm; it may be the most important estate. Unquestionably it has of late years greatly advanced in power; but at this very moment, even with all the accession of influence conferred upon it by the act of Reform, it has not departed from the primary character contemplated in its original formation ; it consists of a very limited section of our fellow-subjects, invested, for the general advantage of the Commonwealth, with certain high functions and noble privileges. The House of Commons is no more the House of the People than is the House of Lords ; and the Commons of England, as well as the Peers of England, are neither more nor less than a privileged class, privileged in both instances for the common good, unequal doubtless in number, yet both, in comparison with the whole nation, forming in a numerical estimation only an insignificant fraction of the mass.

[1] Compare argument in *Morning Post* articles, 1835.

Throughout these observations, in speaking of the English Constitution, I speak of that scheme of legislative and executive government consisting of the King and the two Houses of Parliament; but this is a very partial view of the English Constitution, and I use the term rather in deference to established associations than from being unconscious that the polity of our country consists of other institutions, not less precious and important than those of King, Lords, and Commons.   Trial by Jury, Habeas Corpus, the Court of King's Bench, the Court of Quarter Sessions, the compulsory provision for the poor, however tampered with, the franchises of municipal corporations, of late so recklessly regarded by short-sighted statesmen, are all essential portions of the English Constitution, and have been among the principal causes of the excellent operation and the singular durability of our legislative and executive Government.   The political institutions of England have sprung from its legal institutions.   They have their origin in our laws and customs.   These have been the profound and perennial sources of their unexampled vigour and benefi-cence; and unless it had been fed by these clear and whole-some fountains, our boasted Parliament, like so many of its artificial brethren, would soon have dwindled and dried up, and, like some vast canal filled merely with epidemic filth, only been looked upon as the fatal folly of a nation.

We talk much at the present day of the Representative principle; yet how little is that principle understood ! An assembly may be representative without being elective. No one can deny that the Church of England is at this day not only virtually, but absolutely, faithfully, and efficiently represented in the House of Lords by the Bishops; yet these Lords of Parliament are not elected by their clergy.   Previous to the Reformation the mitred Abbots took their seat in the Upper House.   Who can deny that these great officers were the direct representa-tives of their powerful and wealthy institutions ?   If a

representative assembly be not necessarily elective, so
also it may be elective without being legislative. Representation may be purely remedial, and such for a long
period was the character of English representation. This
remedial representation arose out of some peculiar
elements of our ancient Parliament, an assembly which,
besides being a great national council, was also a high
court of justice. Our ancient Parliaments, like those of
other feodal countries, were formed by the simultaneous
gathering of a vast number of estates, tribunals, and
public officers, from all parts of the kingdom, who met
to convey to the Sovereign information of the condition
of his realm, and to assist him in the execution of justice
between his subjects. Among those who mingled with
the prelates of the land, and the Earls and Barons of the
kingdom, were certain chosen delegates of the counties,
who were, in fact, elected by a particular order or estate
of the kingdom to act, not as their legislators, but as
their judges. These personages were prepared to afford
immediate information to the Sovereign of the state of
their districts; and previous to their arrival at the great
council they obtained, by the inquisitions of the juries
of the hundreds, an accurate report of the condition of
the county, of the necessities of the lieges, of the " oppres-
sions " to be redressed, and of their ability to contribute
to the exigencies of the State.

CHAPTER XIII

Of the Estate of Knights—Rise of the Towns.

THESE deputies were members of a class of our population which, from the important part it was subsequently
destined to fill in the fortunes of our country, requires
our particular attention. I allude to the estate of THE
KNIGHTS. In spite of some cloudy cavils of Madox,[1]

---

[1] Thomas Madox, English antiquary and royal historiographer
(d. 1727).

our modern inquirers agree with the learned Selden, that every immediate tenant of the Crown in England was a Baron by virtue of his tenure, and as such entitled to be personally summoned to the King's Great Court or Council of Parliament, and therein to take his seat. But in process of time these military tenants of the Crown had, by the alienation and splitting of feofs, become in number so considerable, and in personal influence, in comparison with their high privilege, so moderate, that the Crown neglected to summon them to its councils, and, indeed, the burthen of attendance in Parliament was so grievous to men whose limited estates required their personal supervision that the royal neglect was by themselves considered anything but a grievance. In the thirteenth century these royal tenants formed the great bulk of the freeholders of the kingdom, for I need not remind your Lordship that it was not then uncommon for a tenant *in capite* to hold even a fraction of a knight's fee. These lower nobility, or minor Barons as they were styled, in gradually ceasing to be insignificant Peers, subsided, however, into a most powerful equestrian order, in which the lesser portion of the freeholders, who were only mesne tenants, by degrees also merged. And thus was established the ESTATE of THE KNIGHTS.

The local government of the country was in the hands of this order. In their county court, under the style and title of "The *Community* or Commonalty of the County," a phrase which has been so much misunderstood, but which originally implied nobility, this estate met to elect one of their number as the governor or guardian of the shire, their choice subject, however, to the royal ratification. When the King held his great council, he directed the Sheriff of the county to return two or more knights to present to him the condition of their district. These knights, being sworn, summoned before them the jurors as witnesses of the hundreds, and, having obtained from these inquisitions all necessary information, repaired

to the great council of the kingdom with their quota of
statistical intelligence. The transition from being merely
the selected councillors of their Sovereign to being the
virtual representatives of their order was natural, easy,
and rapid; and thus this important and numerous estate
of the kingdom was in fact represented by deputation
in the great council—a representation, however, merely
remedial, and not legislative: they came to impart knowledge and inferentially to proffer counsel, to present to
the King the state of his realm and the " grievances " of
his subjects, and to assist the monarch in deciding suits
arising in their districts, and in ascertaining the just
apportionment of the general taxation. As from councillors and judges they became representatives, so also
in time their sanction was held necessary to the tax which
originally they had met only to estimate by their information. In time, also, their consent was equally held
necessary to the laws, which, however, they never
originated. It is, indeed, very questionable whether the
great office of legislation was then exercised even by the
more potent estates of the kingdom themselves, who
appeared personally in Parliament, the Clergy and the
Peers. In those days legislation was the province of
the clerk-like councillors of the Sovereign, and I do not
myself infer any degrading inferiority in the estate of
the knights from the circumstance of their Parliamentary
attendance assuming merely a remedial character. Thus,
gradually, a most important constituent portion of our
House of Commons developed itself, and so little has
any preconceived theory ever influenced the formation
of our political institutions, and so entirely have they
emanated from the legal economy of the land, that I have
myself little doubt that this convenient method, by which
the English knights assumed their fitting place in the
council of their Sovereign, was derived from ancient and
analogous, though occasional, customs of our country
which prevailed in England before the Conquest, and
which pervaded the Teutonic jurisprudence in every land.

11

The Court of Echevins[1] alone will occur to those who are learned in British history, and curious in constitutional inquiries.

Thus we find, in the thirteenth century, the King of England surrounded in his council by three estates of his realm—his Prelates, his Peers, and his Knights. We approach now an interesting period in the history of our political Constitution. The reign of Henry the Third is one of the most important in our annals. The great struggle between the Norman King and the feodal aristocracy was at this time conducted on both sides with unexampled energy. Undoubtedly the great body of the nation in these struggles favoured the aristocracy. In England, unlike the Continent, the King was powerful. We owe our liberties to our nobility. But I am inclined to attribute the sympathy which has ever subsisted between the English and their aristocarcy to a more influential cause than the mere power and consequent tyranny of the Crown, and to this cause, which at present flourishes, and to which may be principally ascribed the singular prosperity of this country, I shall hereafter advert.

Under the Norman Kings, and especially under Henry the Second, the English towns had made rapid advances in wealth and population. Charters of incorporation became frequent. In the latter part of the twelfth century it was impossible for a sagacious politician not

[1] Mr. J. H. Round's discovery, " among the manuscripts of the British Museum, of the oath of the ' Commune ' proves for the first time that London in 1193 possessed a fully-developed ' Commune ' of the Continental pattern. From this we learn that the government of the city was in the hands of a Mayor and twelve *échevins* (skivini); both these names, being French, seem for a time to have excluded the Saxon Aldermen. Twelve years later (1205–06) we learn, from another document preserved in the same volume as the oath, that *alii probi homines* were associated with the Mayor and *échevins* to form a body of twenty-four (that is, twelve skivini and an equal number of councillors). Round holds that the Court of Skivini and *alii probi homines* . . . was the germ of the Common Council."—Article on " London," " Encyclopædia Britannica," vol. xvi.; J. H. Round, " The Commune of London and Other Studies," 1899, cited.

to perceive that new and powerful interests were spring-
ing up in the Commonwealth, or to shut his eyes to the
political privileges which awaited the growing wealth
and increasing numbers of the citizens and burgesses of
England. But as, from the very nature and origin of
these mural communities, the Sovereign had the undoubted and unquestioned prerogative of imposing
tallages or taxes on cities and boroughs at pleasure, there
existed no obvious or urgent inducement to summon the
inhabitants to the great council of estates, which principally assembled to apportion the aids to be raised on
their separate orders. Although the Earl of Leicester,[1]
who headed the rebellious Barons, unquestionably possessed many of the eminent qualities becoming the leader
of a great party, I am not disposed to behold any very
revolutionary tendency in his conduct when, mighty as
were the results in his memorable Parliament of 1264,
in addition to the Prelates, the Magnates, and the Knights,
he decided to issue writs of summons to " two honest,
lawful, and discreet " citizens and burgesses from every
city and burgh. I am more inclined to believe that this
great movement was rather dictated by a politic apprehension that, however the nation might be disposed to
view in complacent silence his assumption of many of the
prerogatives of the King, who was his prisoner, they might
perhaps have expected that an exception would be made
in favour of the royal right of arbitrary taxation. I
suspect that he was of opinion that the tallages would
be forthcoming with more readiness if the citizens were
flattered by granting those contributions as a favour
which were before exacted as a right. Certain it is that
De Montfort anticipated in some degree the necessities
of his age; for when, under the vigorous policy of the
next reign, civil peace again flourished, and the legitimate
Sovereign found it convenient to avail himself of the new
machinery which his rebellious subject had introduced,
no privilege ever conferred by a King was ever received

[1] Simon de Montfort.

with more discontent than the right of returning members to his Parliament by his loyal towns. These honest burghers were loth to leave their homes and business for pursuits with which they were little acquainted, and society for which they were unfitted. Petitions to be exempted from the grievance of sending members to Parliament are not uncommon in our early records; many burgesses when appointed declined to serve, and absented themselves from the council; and to remedy these inconveniences the Sheriff was invested with a discretionary power of omitting boroughs in his return. It would seem that, from experience, the inhabitants of towns preferred the arbitrary taxation of their Sovereign to the grants of their representatives, and that these worthy traders were generally cajoled by the great council into contributions more liberal than their calmer moments in their stores and counting-houses approved.

We must, however, guard ourselves from supposing that these citizens and burgesses who were summoned to Parliament were absolutely elected by the inhabitants of the towns as their representatives. Their presence in Parliament is another instance of representation without election. They were often nominated by the Sheriff of the county; and even when that great officer, from negligence or favour, permitted the return to be made by those more interested in the transaction, the nomination was confined to the small governing body, who returned two of their members, in general very unwilling missionaries, to the great council.

CHAPTER XIV

Creation of the Estate of the Commons—The House of Commons an Equestrian Chamber—Why the Equality of Civil Rights was established in England at so Early a Period in our History.

AT first the three Estates of the realm held themselves aloof; the Knights by right and custom taking their seats among the Peers, while the citizens and burgesses re-

mained in humble attendance, and, after settling the
amount of their tallages, gave themselves no further
concern with the public business, but cheerfully returned
to their homes and affairs. But the two great causes
which had simultaneously degraded the lower nobility
into mere gentry, and raised the burghers into comparative importance, still operated; the increased division of
land rendered the first class less influential and more
numerous, the increase of commerce the last more powerful and more wealthy. The chasm between the magnates
and the lower nobility or Knights became each year wider
and more profound, the boundary that separated the
Knights from the burghers each year less marked and
definite. It is impossible to fix nicely the period when
Parliament was divided into two Houses, but I am inclined to place it towards the end of the reign of Edward
the First. It is easier to ascertain the principles on
which the memorable division was established. Between
the Prelates and the Magnates on the one hand, and the
Knights and Burgesses on the other, there existed this
memorable distinction. The first were in themselves
estates of the realm; the last were only representatives
of estates. To induce the Knights, however, to quit
their noble companions, of whom the law still held them
as the personal equals, and mix with the humble burghers,
required some politic dexterity. It was at length settled
that a new estate of the realm should be created, styled
the Estate of the Commons or Commonalty, a title, as
I have before observed, of great dignity, implying nobility,
and formerly confined to the landed proprietors. The
burghers were flattered by merging into the landed gentry
of the country, and thus obtaining the dignity of the
lesser nobility, and the Knights were compensated for
the sullen sacrifice on their part by giving their title to
the new estate, and impressing their peculiar character
on the new chamber in which, for a very long period of
our history, they naturally took the lead. Yet even then
some time elapsed before the Knights condescended to

renounce their old privilege of apportioning the tax of their original order, and blending the aids of the Lower House of Parliament.

Thus have I traced, my Lord, and I assure you not without some difficulty, the history of the formation of our House of Commons. And now to what did this great revolution in the Constitution of our country amount ? To nothing more nor less than the establishment of AN EQUESTRIAN CHAMBER. If such were its original character, that character has been maintained throughout the whole of our history, and that character, as I will shortly show, has not been affected by the recent Act of Reform. It never was the House of the People; it is not the House of the People. The members of the House of Commons never were the representatives of the people. They are not the representatives of the people. They always were, and they are still, the representatives of the Commons, an estate of the realm privileged as the other estates, not meeting personally for the sake of convenience, but by its representatives, and constituting, even with its late considerable accession of members, only a small section of the nation. We have a curious instance how accurately this distinction was observed in the time of Henry the Fourth, and how perfect was the order of Parliament in that reign. For when the King met his Parliament, and, having addressed the estates of the Lords Spiritual and Temporal, then turned to the House of Commons, he promised that he " would do nothing *against the liberty of the estate for which they had come to Parliament*, nor against the liberties of the Lords Spiritual and Temporal." The impudent misrepresentation of our anti-constitutional writers originates in an ignorant misconception of words. If the House had been called the House of Knights, or rather the House of Squires, which is the literal meaning of the word Commons, we should have heard nothing of this dangerous nonsense by virtue of which it is sought that the whole power of the realm shall be concentrated in one of the estates, and that, too, one recently remodelled for factious purposes. An Estate of the People involves a contradiction in terms, for an estate is a popular class established into a political order. If, therefore, the Sovereign had established the Lower House as the estate of the people, he would have virtually declared that the clergy and the nobles, the most influential part of the nation, were not a portion of the people. Far from this, the cautious monarch refrained from even establishing the citizens into a separate estate; instead of doing this, he flattered their vanity while he checked their independence, and while he raised them to the rank of Commons, he secured, to use the epithet in its popular—not its correct—sense, an aristocratic character for each estate of his realm. As the Upper House consisted of two estates of the realm, the Clergy and the Peers, so also the Lower House might equally have consisted of the representatives of two estates of the realm, the Knights and the Burgesses. But this was avoided. Yet suppose the Sovereign had thought fit to establish a separate estate of the citizens, would the Lower House any more have represented the people ? By no means. Other classes of the people would still have remained unrepresented, and classes the most numerous—for instance, the peasantry. Such estates were not unknown in the Middle Ages, and even at this day an Estate of the Peasantry meets in the Diets of Sweden and the Storthings of Norway.

By this final constitution of the English Parliament the seal was set to that glorious characteristic of our laws which various causes had been for a long period silently combining to create; to which I mainly attribute the freedom, honour, and prosperity of our country, and our singular preservation from that whirlwind of outraged passion and opinion which swept over Europe during the end of the last century, and still threatens Christendom, with its wild and moaning wail. This glorious characteristic of our laws is our equality of civil rights. By the formation of the House of Commons, the great body of the lesser nobility of England formally renounced those rights of peerage, the practical enjoyment of which had been long escaping them; and instead of that gallant but adventurous swarm of personages who, under the perplexing title of nobles, abounded in Europe before the great French Revolution gave the last blow to the crumbling Gothic edifice of feodal polity, men who were distinguished from ordinary freemen by privileges inherent in their blood, and held their pedigrees, often their only muniments, as valid exemptions from the toils and cares of honest industry; men who were free from contributing to the public burthens; who alone might draw the sword; and whose daughters were defended by law from profaning alliances with *roturiers*—arose in this our favoured land of Albion, a class of individuals noble without privilege, noble from the generosity of their nature, the inspiration of their lineage, and the refinement of their education; a class of individuals who, instead of meanly submitting to fiscal immunities, support upon their broad and cultivated lands all the burthens of the State; men who have conquered by land and sea, who have distinguished themselves in every honourable profession, and acquired fame in every department of learning and in every province of science and of art; who support the poor instead of plundering them, and respect the court which they do not fear; friends alike to liberty and order, who execute justice and maintain truth—the gentlemen of England; a class of whom it is difficult to decide whether their moral excellence or their political utility be most eminent, conspicuous, and inspiring.

In due and sympathising deference to the lesser nobility, their former equals who subsided into gentry, the magnates were careful to arrogate to themselves no privileges which were not necessary and incidental to them in their character of an estate of the realm, and their capacity of hereditary legislators of a free people. So that even their blood was not ennobled, and their children ranked only as Commons; thus distinctly announcing that their rank was a political institution for the public weal, and not a privilege for their private gratification. Indeed, it would not be too much to affirm that the law of England does not recognise nobility. It recognises the peerage, and it has invested that estate with august accessories; but to state that a man's blood is ennobled is neither legal nor correct, and the phrase, which has crept into our common parlance, is not borrowed from the lawyers, but from the heralds. Thus, I repeat, was consummated that glorious characteristic of our laws, the equality of our civil rights, and to this cause I refer the sympathy which has ever subsisted between the great body of the English nation and their aristocracy.

CHAPTER XV

Why Liberty flourished under the Plantagenets—Why Liberty declined under the Tudors—Primary Effect of Protestantism in England not Favourable to our Civil Liberties.

LIBERTY flourished under the Plantagenets—and for this reason, that the aristocracy headed the nation, and the House of Commons soon learnt to combine with the discontented party among the Peers. The remedial character of our representation rapidly expanded into the legislative, and the judge matured into a law-maker. Seldom has the crown of this realm circled a more able and vigorous brow than that of our third Edward: his reign, too, was long and eminently prosperous. Yet as early as this reign the illegality of raising money without consent of Parliament was firmly and practically established, as well as the necessity of the concurrence of the two Houses in any alteration of the law. In this reign, too, for the first time, the councillors of the Crown were impeached by the Commons, though there is little doubt that the Lower House would not have ventured on so bold an advance in authority had they not been secretly stimulated by the Prince of Wales, and upheld by the majority of the Peers, jealous of the intrigues of the Duke of Lancaster against the interests of the heir-apparent. The Parliament that had ventured to resist an Edward dared to control a Richard. The Commons now inquired into the public expenditure, and even regulated the economy of the royal household. The Lancastrian Kings owed their throne to the Parliament, and the Parliament was mindful of the obligation. Under these three Sovereigns the present Constitution of England was amply, if not perfectly, developed. The right of taxation in the two Houses was never questioned; the direction of the public expenditure was claimed and practised; the illegality of royal ordinances declared; Ministers, too, were impeached and punished, and finally the privileges of Parliament for the first time established. But perhaps the most important change in our constitutional system was the introduction, in the reign of Henry the Sixth, of complete statutes of the Commons, under the title of Bills, instead of their old method of Petitions. By these means the Sovereign was obliged to sanction or to reject the propositions of his Parliament without qualification; and as it had been previously a maxim of Parliamentary practice that all laws should originate in the form of petitions from the Lower House, the legislative right of the Commons was now completely and firmly established.

If liberty flourished under the Plantagenets, it faded under the Tudors. How was this ? Compare the reigns of the third Edward or the second Richard with those of Henry the Eighth and Elizabeth, and no one can shut his eyes to the vast progression which our country has made in all the elements of civilisation. We were much more populous, infinitely wealthier. We enjoyed a great commerce, our manufactures were considerable, our ancient military reputation maintained, our advance in arts indisputable. Why were we less free ? Why had that bold House of Commons, to whom the warlike and impatient Edward had to bow before he could carry on a struggle flattering to the fame of England, sunk into a servile crew, who witnessed without a murmur the forced loans of a Privy Seal and a benevolence ? Where were the men who, under the wily Henry the Fourth, had declared the royal ordinances illegal ? Humbling themselves before royal proclamations, crushed by the oppression of the Star Chamber, and yielding without even a remonstrance to the enormity of the Council. Who now dared to inquire into the public administration ? Why were not Wolsey and Burleigh impeached as well as Lord Latimer and Suffolk ? Who remembered the statute of Henry the Sixth, " for the punishment of such as assault any on their way to the Parliament," when any member who offended the Sovereign or the Minister was, in scornful defiance of his privilege, instantly imprisoned; and Henry the Eighth vowed he would behead any of the Commons who opposed his will ? We cannot account for this extraordinary change in the character of our House of Commons by the usual reason of a standing army. Henry the Eighth commanded fifty beefeaters, and Elizabeth trusted to the guardianship of the trained bands. The truth is, the House of Commons was no longer supported by the Peers, and the aristocracy no longer headed the nation. The great advance in public liberty under the Plantagenets was carried on by a Parliament in which a perfect understanding subsisted between the two Houses. We owe that bold scheme of popular government to which Selden and Pym in other days were content to appeal to " the wisdom of their ancestors," and to the united and harmonious efforts of the three estates of the realm.

The Wars of the Roses were mortal to the great Peers and chivalric commons of England, and the tints of those fatal flowers were only emblematic of the terror and the blood that they occasioned. Unquestionably these evils in the course of time might have been remedied, and, doubtless, in the natural order of events a new race of great national leaders would have arisen, who might have restored that noble freedom and that sweet equality

which rose under the Plantagenets, struggled under the
Stuarts, and triumphed under the benignant sway of the
House of Brunswick : but when, in the reign of Henry the
Eighth, the aristocracy afforded some indications of
reviving power, a new feature appeared in European, and
especially in English, politics, which changed the whole
frame and coloured the complete aspect of our society—
RELIGIOUS DISSENSION. It was by balancing the great
parties in which this new spirit, so fertile in discord,
divided the nation, that the Tudors, and especially
Elizabeth and her statesmen, succeeded in establishing
her power, until they delivered over to her successor the
sceptre of a despot. I have myself no doubt that,
although in its nature intimately and essentially connected with the cause of civil liberty, the immediate
effect of the reformation on our English polity was anything but favourable to the growth of our liberties and
the establishment of our political. institutions. The civil
despotism of the King was in that age the consequence
of his religious supremacy. The creation of the High
Commission Court alone, and the sanction which the
religious passions of a large party in the nation gave to
that dark tribunal, afforded a fatal precedent for an
application of analogous discipline to civil affairs which
in practice reduced our Constitution to a polity befitting
the meridian of Madrid, or even Constantinople.

CHAPTER XVI

Of the Constitution of the House of Commons under the Tudors,
and of the System of Borough Representation.

IF we survey the constitution of the House of Commons
under the Tudors, we shall find that, although it experienced several very considerable changes, they were far
from effecting any departure from the original character
of that assembly. It did not in any degree more become

the House of the People. It still remained the representative of an estate of the realm, an estate in number, I apprehend, not very considerable; inferior probably to the fleeting population of any of the large fairs then common in the country, and at this day not superior to the population of a second-rate capital. The House, when it was first established, consisted of seventy-four knights, and, for the causes I have before stated, of a very fluctuating number of burgesses : in early times they amounted to two hundred and sixty. The knights, in spite of their minority, seem to have indulged in no jealousy of their humbler brethren, but appear to have exercised in the chamber which had derived from them its name all that superior authority to which their noble lineage and territorial possessions entitled them. It is curious that the idea of representation, as relative to population, never appears to have entered into the consideration of our ancestors : York and Rutland returned the same number of representatives. I ascribe the apparent anomaly to the circumstance of the constituent body being generally very limited, and particularly so in the northern counties. It was never intended that the population should be represented, but a particular class of it, and, as the spirit of the body pervaded all the county representatives, a knight of Rutland doubtless considered himself virtually as much the guardian of the knights of the county of York or Lancaster as of his own shire or that of Huntingdon. Moreover, there are reasons to believe that earlier than is usually imagined the English knights were in the habit of being returned for boroughs; and I apprehend that the majority of the House of Commons in the reigns of the Lancastrian Kings consisted of the descendants of our former minor Barons.

On the accession of Henry the Eighth, the burgesses were in number two hundred and twenty-four. Henry extended county representation to Wales, Chester, and Monmouth, and even summoned burgesses from his Scotch town of Berwick and his French garrison of Calais.

Edward the Sixth created fourteen boroughs and revived
ten : Mary added twenty-one, and Elizabeth sixty. In
most of these instances the right of representation was
conceded to insignificant places and confined to mere
nomination. Elizabeth was the first who worked on an
extensive scale the great Parliamentary mine of Cornwall,
and liberally enfranchised fishing-towns and miserable
villages. The object of the Tudor Sovereigns in this
increase of the House of Commons was to command
majorities on the great religious questions. Arbitrary
in every other respect, they were not unwilling to share
with the compliant orthodoxy of their Parliament the
responsibility of those extraordinary statutes which form
an epoch in the philosophy of legislation.

But the Tudors, in this extensive exercise of the power
of Parliamentary appointment, introduced no heretical
elements into the constitution of our House of Commons.
As early as Edward the Second the representatives of
more than twenty boroughs had been added by the King
to the members of that assembly. I do not believe that
the representation of our boroughs was originally elective.
Far from being of opinion that the popular character of
the third estate had gradually become corrupt and diminished previous to the late Act of Reform, I believe, on the
contrary, that since the accession of the Stuarts it had
gradually become more vigorous and more comprehensive.
Our Parliament long possessed, and indeed in some degree
still retains, its original character of a royal council.
The object of our Sovereigns was to surround themselves
by the notable subjects of their realm, and they proceeded
in the shortest and simplest manner to obtain their
purpose. The elective character of the Parliamentary
knights arose from the peculiar circumstances of their
order and the ancient juridical customs of their shires.
But these circumstances bore no relation to the Parliamentary burgesses, and although, *honoris causâ*, they
were incorporated with the noble Commons of the realm,
the machinery of their selection was far less nice and com-

plicated. In general these returns were made by the small governing body which must exist in all mural communities, whether incorporated or not; probably in corporations the Aldermen or capital burgesses served by rotation. Sometimes, when no leading member of the society could be induced to undergo the inconvenience of quitting his home and neglecting his affairs, a neighbouring squire was substituted : sometimes the return was at once made by the Sheriff from his knowledge of the leading personages of the borough; sometimes the future members were recommended by the Privy Council; sometimes the same representatives at once returned to a new Parliament, without any intervening ceremony, who had been seated in the last. The towns in royal demesne were probably always represented by officers of the Crown, and, indeed, this class of individuals abounded in the Tudor Parliaments. If this loose practice of borough representation were occasionally in turbulent or careless times drawn into a dangerous precedent for the return of knights for shires without the due and legal convocation of the county court, it is certain that eventually the more formal and comprehensive scheme of county representation exercised a far more decided influence on that of the boroughs. As these increased in population and intelligence, and the privilege of being represented in the royal council became to be more generally understood and more finely appreciated, the system of representation by election, always more or less maintained by the return of the knights, afforded, as the origin of institutions became darker, at the same time a precedent for those inhabitants who sought a participation in the now envied privilege, and a plan by which their wishes might be accomplished. Thus the freeholders in boroughs by the right of their burgage tenure,[1] the freemen of the corporations, and sometimes the inhabitants at large, where burgage tenure was rare, and the towns, though flourish-

---

[1] A tenure by which lands or tenements in cities and towns were held of the King or other lord for a certain yearly rent.

ing, had not been incorporated, gradually established their right to the exercise of a suffrage, and thus in the course of time the House of Commons came to consist of county members elected by the freeholders; representatives of cities and boroughs chosen by a popular constituency where a popular constituency existed; and representatives of the same class who retained the old exemption from election, because, in fact, the unimportant places for which they appeared in Parliament had never emerged from their original insignificance, or produced a population bold and flourishing enough to usurp the return of their representatives from the hands of the governing body.

This I believe to be a very just, as I am sure it is a very impartial, view of the formation of our House of Commons; and if the history of our country and our Constitution had ever been anything better than a turbulent theatre for the gladiatorial struggle of party writers, it is one, I believe, which long ere this would have been adopted : for it has the merit of being not only consistent with human nature and consonant with that profounder knowledge of the origin of our political institutions which is the privilege of the present day, but it reconciles all the characteristics and all the difficulties which have been proved and promulgated by the four great theories of borough representation that have so long puzzled our lawyers and perplexed our antiquaries.

Those who may imagine that I derive any satisfaction in establishing the narrow origin of our present more popular representation greatly mistake my feelings and opinions. I am not one of those who believe that the safety of the Constitution is consulted by encouraging an exclusive principle in the formation of the constituency of our third estate. It is not the supposed democratic character which it has assumed under the new arrangement—I wish I could call it settlement—that fills me with any apprehensions. On the contrary, I wish it were even more catholic, though certainly not more Papist.

It is its sectarian quality in which I discover just cause of
alarm. But it has been necessary for me to show what
was the original character of our Lower House, and the
primary intention of the founders of our Constitution.
In creating a third estate of the realm, they established
an order of men, limited in number and highly privileged,
styled the Commons. Although we have increased the
number of these Commons, we have not increased their
privileges or enlarged their political capacity. They still
remain an estate of the realm, and only an estate of the
realm—in spirit as well as in law. For although their
representatives may be chosen by three hundred thousand
men instead of one hundred thousand, they are still only
the representatives of a limited and favoured class of the
kingdom. The House of Commons is not a jot more the
House of the People, unless we exclude from our definition
of the people many of the most essential and most important elements of a nation. I shall have occasion in
due season to speak further of the great reformingscheme
of 1830. Here I will only observe that, in a hasty and
factious effort to get rid of representation without election, it will be as well if eventually we do not discover
that we have only obtained election without representation.

CHAPTER XVII

Anecdote of the Pacha of Egypt—Representation without Election
illustrated.

THE current of these observations reminds me of an
anecdote which may perhaps amuse your Lordship, nor
be found altogether devoid of instruction. When I was
in Egypt the Pacha of that country, a personage, as is
well known, of rare capacity, and influenced by an almost
morbid desire of achieving in an instant the great and
gradual results of European civilisation, was extremely
desirous, among other objects of passion or of fancy, of

obtaining a Parliament.   Emulous of the prosperity and popular power of our Kings, his Highness was eager to obtain the means by which, on reflection, he was convinced not only that our country so eminently flourished, but by which our Sovereign succeeded in commanding at the same time obedience and affection.   It so happened that a young English gentleman, who was on his travels,[1] was at this period resident in Cairo, and as he had more than once had the good fortune in an audience of engaging the attention of the Pacha by the readiness or patience of his replies, his Highness determined to do the young Englishman the honour of consulting him.

Our countryman received the summons, which all instantly obey, and immediately repaired to the Divan of the citadel.   He found the Pacha surrounded by his courtiers, his engineers, his colonels, and his eunuchs. At length his Highness clapped his hands, and the chamber was cleared, with the exception of a favourite Minister and a faithful dragoman.   The surprise of our countryman when he received the communication of the Pacha was not inconsiderable; but he was one of those who had seen sufficient of the world never to be astonished, not altogether untinctured with political knowledge, and gifted with that philosophical exemption from prejudice which is one of the most certain and the most valuable results of extensive travel.   Our countryman communicated to the Egyptian ruler with calmness and with precision the immediate difficulties that occurred to him, explained to the successor of the Pharaohs and the Ptolemies that the political institutions of England had been the gradual growth of ages, and that there is no political function which demands a finer discipline, or a more regulated preparation, than the exercise of popular suffrage.   The Pacha listened in silence, nodding his head in occasional approbation : then, calling for coffee, instead of looking at his watch like a European Sovereign, delicately terminated the interview.

[1] Disraeli himself (see "Home Letters," Cairo, May 28, 1831).

Some short time afterwards the young Englishman repaired, as was his occasional custom, to the levee of the Egyptian ruler. When the Pacha perceived him, he welcomed him with a favouring smile, and beckoned to him to advance to the contiguous divan.

"God is great!" said Mehemet Ali to the traveller; "you are a wise man—Allah! kerim, but you spit pearls. Nevertheless I will have a Parliament, and I will have as many Parliaments as the King of England himself. See here!" So saying, his Highness produced two lists of names, containing those of the most wealthy and influential personages of every town and district in his dominions. "See here!" said he, "here are my Parliaments; but I have made up my mind, to prevent inconvenience, to elect them myself."

Behold, my Lord, a splendid instance of representation without election! In pursuance of this resolution of Mehemet Ali, two chambers met at Cairo, called in the jargon of the Levant the *alto Parliamento*, and the *basso Parliamento*. The first consisted of the Pachas and chief officers of the capital, the second really of the most respectable of the provincial population. Who can doubt that the *basso Parliamento* of Cairo, if the invasion of Syria had not diverted the attention of Mehemet Ali from domestic politics, might have proved a very faithful and efficient national council, and afforded the governor of the country very important information as to the resources, necessities, and grievances of his subjects? Who can hesitate in believing that there was a much greater chance of its efficiency and duration when appointed by the Pacha himself than when elected by his subjects in their present condition? Who does not recognise in such an assembly the healthy seeds of a popular government? I for one should have much more confidence in the utility and duration of the Parliament of Cairo than in that of Naples or Madrid; especially as, it is but candid to confess, Mehemet Ali had further secured a practical term of political initiation for his future legislators by two capital rules: first, that the *basso Parliamento* should only petition and not debate; and, secondly, that the *alto Parliamento* should only debate and not vote !

CHAPTER XVIII

Why the Political Consequences of the Protestant Religion on the Continent were Different to those in England, and why Favourable to Civil Liberty—Protestantism creates a Republican Religion—Introduction of the Phrase "The People," into European Politics.

THE Protestant Reformation, which, in a political point of view, had only succeeded in dividing England into two parties and establishing arbitrary power, had produced far different effects on the Continent of Europe. There it had created a Republican religion: for such was the ecclesiastical polity of Calvin. The English Protestants, who, flying from the Marian persecution, sought refuge at Geneva, in the agony of their outraged loyalty renounced their old allegiance, applied to civil polity the religious discipline of their great apostle, and returned to their native country political republicans. Kings were the enemies of Protestantism, and Protestants naturally became the enemies of monarchy. The Hebrew history, which they studied as intently as the Christian Gospels, furnished them with a precedent and a model for a religious republic. Judges ruled in Israel before the royal dynasties of Saul or David. The anti-monarchical spirit of Protestant Europe was notorious and incontestable as early as the middle of the sixteenth century. The regicides of Holy Writ are the heroes of the turbulent tractates of the early missionaries of spiritual democracy: the slayer of Sisera, or he who stabbed the fat King of Moab in his chamber. Samuel, the prophet of the Lord, deposed Kings: Calvin and Knox were the successors of Samuel. The bloody massacre of Saint Bartholomew, occasioned by the promulgation of this dangerous political religionism, aggravated the danger and determination of its votaries. The press of Europe swarmed with republican treatises composed by the ablest writers. Books are great landmarks in the history of human nature. Now was heard, for the first time, of the paramount authority of "THE PEOPLE." This is the era of the introduction into European politics of that insidious phrase, by virtue of which an active and unprincipled minority have ever since sought to rule and hoodwink a nation. In 1579 appeared the famous "Vindiciæ contra Tyrannos" of Languet,[1] and the revolt of Holland and the League of Utrecht, which terminated in the establishment of the Dutch Republic, formed a practical commentary on its virulent and fervent pages.

The Republican Religion, which revolutionised Holland, triumphed in Scotland under Knox, and in France long balanced the united influence of the crown and the tiara. Even as late as 1621 the genius of Richelieu alone prevented France from being formed into a Federal Republic, and from being divided into circles.

Such was the spirit of the European movement when the aristocracy of England, refreshed and renovated by more than half a century of prosperity and peace, deemed the accession of Charles the First a fitting season for a struggle to restore the ancient liberties of the nation, and to regain and complete the Constitution of the Plantagenets. For nearly two centuries that Constitution had been suspended, like an old suit of armour, crusted with the blood of the civil wars, and covered with the dust of theologic logomachies: but the great spirits of the seventeenth century recognised the suit as of good proof, and, though somewhat antiquated in its style and fashion, possessing all necessary powers of protection and o`ence. The history of the age of Charles the First has been the literary arena of the passions of all parties. The far vaster range of political experience which, from the great

[1] Hubert Languet (1518-1581).

French Revolution and its consequences, we enjoy than our forefathers, our increased, yet not too considerable, distance from the passionate period in question, and our decreased dependence upon its incidents as the once solitary precedents for all popular movements, the researches of ingenious scholars, and the publication of contemporary memoirs, have all combined to render us more competent to decide upon the character of the most memorable transactions of our annals.

Until the meeting of the Long Parliament, the King appears to have had no party in the nation, and solely to have depended upon his courtiers and his Bishops. There was a general feeling throughout the leading classes of the country that the time had arrived when the settlement of the State on a broad basis of constitutional liberty was indispensable. The aristocracy of England, also, was no longer that unlettered class of mere warriors who, however great might be their political power or ardent their love of public liberty, were necessarily debarred by their habits and want of education from practising the arts of government and legislation. The cultivated intellect of England required a theatre for its display and exercise; it found this in some degree in its Parliament, but sought it more decidedly in the administration of the Empire. The time had arrived when a prelate could no longer conduct the affairs of the realm from his monopoly of learning. The age of royal favourites was about to be closed for ever. The monarch, though apparently almost a despot, was fast approaching the simplicity of his executive capacity: it not only might be then obvious to the contemplative, but it was absolutely determined by practical men, that the administration of the kingdom should soon be conducted by those of the subjects who were most eminent and distinguished in the great national council.

CHAPTER XIX

Attempts of the English Aristocracy to restore the Constitution
   of the Plantagenets under Charles the First—Constitutional
   Reformers and Root and Branch Reformers—The Root and
   Branch Reformers attack the Church and alarm the Constitutional Reformers—The Root and Branch Reformers, deserted
   by the Constitutional Reformers, form an Anti-national
   Alliance with the Scotch Covenanters.

THE two Houses of the first Parliament summoned by
Charles contained the flower of his kingdom—men of
the highest lineage, the largest estates, the most distinguished learning, and the most illustrious accomplishments. The Opposition in the House of Commons, led
by Eliot, and supported by the Peers, succeeded, as early
as the third year of Charles's reign, in obtaining the
Petition of Right. But this concession did not satisfy
the Parliament; they wished to dislodge the favourite;
to change the Ministry as well as establish the Constitution. Charles recoiled from the novel heresy of not being
the master of his own servant, a heresy soon doomed to
become orthodox: he determined to support his friend,
and the King resolved to reign without a Parliament.

It is singular that the King could have contrived to
reign ten years without one, but the truth is the state
of the country, as is admitted and celebrated by all
foreign writers, was of a prosperity so extraordinary that
it was difficult to excite discontents among the great
body of the nation. In this dilemma, the leaders of the
Opposition among the Commons, Hampden and Pym,
but concealing their masterly machinations from the
more numerous and moderate portions of their party, intrigued with the Scotch, and held out to the Presbyterian
leaders of that nation the prospect of the English Opposition assisting them in their favourite project, the overthrow of the Church of England in Scotland. The consequent troubles in Scotland plunged the King in a war,

and was the occasion of the summons of the Long Parliament.

The spirit of the King when he met this famous assembly was quite broken. He was ready to make any concession consistent with the maintenance of a limited monarchy. Experience had taught him that the whole body of the aristocracy was opposed to him, and we know that Charles was perfectly aware of the sacrifices which would be demanded of him, and which he was prepared to grant without resistance. The objects of the King at this time were to obtain the establishment of a limited monarchy by constitutional concessions, and then to form a Parliamentary administration from the most eminent of his previous opponents, in which conduct alone he recognised any security for a strong government, and the only prevention of further movement.

The Long Parliament in a few months restored the Constitution of the Plantagenets. It secured the frequent assemblage of Parliaments : it terminated for ever arbitrary taxation : it abolished the Star Chamber and the High Commission Court. The concessions of Charles the First during the two sessions of this Parliament, previous to the Civil War, were so ample that the Revolution of 1688 added no important feature to our political system. Faithful to their purpose, the leaders of this famous Opposition not only established our liberties, but impeached the Ministers, and this brought about a result not less anxiously and eagerly sought after than the abolition of Ship Money: a formal attempt by the King, for which he had been long prepared, to form a Government of the more moderate portion of the Parliamentary party. I cannot believe that the death of the Earl of Bedford could alone have occasioned the failure of this intended arrangement; it is more probable that the dissensions which soon broke out in the great body of the Commons had already covertly appeared. The Parliament, although both Houses and the vast majority of the Lower had been previously opposed to the King—

for we must not forget that even Hyde and Falkland were originally members of opposition—had now become divided into two parties : the Constitutional Reformers, and the Root and Branch Reformers ; Pym and Hampden headed the latter. The Constitutional Reformers were alarmed by the attack on the Church: the Lords threw out the Bill which sought to deprive the Bishops of their Parliamentary suffrage. This was the first check that the Commons had received from the Upper House. Pym and Hampden, deserted by the Constitutional Reformers, had thrown themselves into the hands of the Puritans and Root and Branch men. Instead of political unions, they appealed to the city apprentices, and the trained bands; mobs were hired, petitions forged, all the arts of insurgency practised. The Peers were daunted, the King frightened; Strafford was executed, the Bishops expelled the House of Lords, the House of Commons itself rendered independent of the King and its constituents by the act which made its dissolution consequent on its own pleasure. At length, by the Remonstrance and the Propositions the very abrogation of the monarchy being attempted, the King raised his standard, and so completely had the unhappy monarch by his conduct placed the Commons in the wrong, that the very personage who, two years before, had absolutely no party in the nation found himself supported by a considerable majority of his people, and nearly the whole of the Peerage; while the vote which virtually occasioned the struggle, and was the trial of strength of the two parties in the House of Commons, was only carried by a majority of eleven. The success of the royal arms, and the unexpected strength of the royal party, filled the Commons with consternation. The moderate members continued to flock to the King. Pym and Hampden, finding that they were deserted by their aristocratic companions, and that the Puritans and Root and Branch men were not powerful enough to support them, made an open and absolute alliance with the Scotch Presbyterians, with whom they had always had a secret understanding, swallowed the Covenant which they had before disfavoured, decreed the extermination of the Church of England, beheaded Laud, called in a Scotch army, and maintained their cause by a connection offensive to their countrymen.

CHAPTER XX

Parallel between passing Events and the Reign of Charles the First —Government of " the People " established in England—Its Practical Consequences—The Nation seeks Refuge from " the People "—Public Opinion not less Influential in the Age of Charles the First than at the Present Day—European Movement described—Of the Latter Stuarts.

AM I indeed treating of the reign of Charles the First ? or is it some nearer epoch that I am commemorating ? Am I writing of the affairs of the seventeenth or the nineteenth century ?   There is such a marvellous similarity between the periods that, for my part, I find great difficulty in discriminating between the two Dromios. In both instances the Church of England is the great victim, and at both seasons the vast majority of the English people were warmly and tenderly attached to their establishment.   In both cases the aristocratic leaders of the movement thought fit to secede from their own party, while in both cases their more determined or desperate associates compensate themselves for the desertion by the alliance of revolutionary or anti-national support.   In one instance the Radicals, in the other the Root and Branch men; in one instance the Dissenters, in the other the Puritans.   And in both instances, when Radicals and Dissenters in the one case and Puritans and Root and Branch men in the other fail in making up with their influence for the loss of the aristocratic connections of the leaders who had summoned them, we find the same desperate and treasonable compact, made in one age with the Scotch Presbyterians, and in the other

with the Irish Papists; the Solemn League and Covenant
so long repudiated swallowed as the condition in the first
instance, and the Irish Church scheme, once so warmly
opposed, gulped down in the other.

The Bishops expelled from the House of Lords, the
King defied, then imprisoned, and then decapitated, the
House of Lords disregarded, and then formally abolished,
voted " a nuisance, and of no use "—you see, my Lord,
there were Utilitarians even in those days—behold the
great object at length consummated of concentrating
the whole power and authority of the government in one
estate of the realm. The verbal process by which the
revolution was effected was very simple and very logical
if we only grant the premises; the schoolmen themselves
could not have reasoned with more invincible accuracy.
The House of Commons, having first declared "that the
people are the origin of all just power "—an axiom to
which any person may annex any meaning of his fancy—
next enunciated that the House of Commons, being
chosen by the people and representing them, are the
supreme authority of the nation, and that consequently
whatever is declared to be law by the House of Commons
hath the force of law without the consent of the King or
the House of Peers.   First, the constituency of the House
of Commons, a small fraction of the nation, is declared
to be the People; their power then becomes invested in
their representatives; the majority of those representatives, acting by their supreme authority, then expel from
their numbers the minority who oppose their projects;
and then, still acting by their supreme authority, vote the
power of the triumphant majority perpetual. This is
the simple process by which we at length obtain a tolerably
definite idea of what is meant by the phrase " the People,"
and the easy machinery by which a band of two or three
hundred individuals obtain and exercise despotic power
over the lives, liberties, and property of a whole nation.

We still remember in this country the tender and happy
consequences of being governed by " the People." We

have not forgotten that " the People " established Courts more infamous than the Star Chamber in every county of England, with power of fining, sequestrating, imprisoning, and corporally punishing all who opposed or even murmured against their decrees; that under the plea of malignancy " the People " avenged their private hatreds, and seized for their private gain and gratification any estates or property to which they took a fancy; that " the People " consigned to Bastiles and perpetual imprisonment all those who refused to answer their illegal inquiries, and bored red-hot irons through the tongues of the contumacious; that not an appearance of law or liberty remained in the land; that " the People " enlarged the laws of high-treason so that they comprehended verbal offences and even intentions; that " the People " practised decimation; that " the People " voted trial by Jury a breach of Parliamentary privilege; that " the People " deprived of authority all persons of family and distinction who had originally adhered to their party, because men of blood and breeding would not submit to be their disgraceful and ignoble tools, and filled every office under them with the scum of the nation; that the very individuals who had suffered and struggled under the Star Chamber were visited by " the People " with punishments and imprisonments infinitely more bloody and more grievous; that " the People " sequestrated nearly one-half of the goods and chattels of the nation, and at least one-half of its rents and revenues; that in seven years " the People " raised the taxation of the country from £800,000 per annum to £7,000,000 per annum; that " the People " invented the Excise, and applied that odious impost even to provisions and the common necessaries of life; that " the People " became so barefaced in their vile extortions that one morning they openly divided £300,000 amongst themselves, and settled an annuity of £4 a day on each of their number; that " the People " committed all these enormities in the teeth of outraged England, by the aid of an anti-

national compact with the Scottish Covenanters; and
that finally the Nation, the insulted and exhausted
Nation, sought refuge from the Government of "the
People " in the arms of a military despot.

I hear much in the present day of the march of intellect, and the diffusion of knowledge, and the influence
of public opinion, and there are those who would assure
us that in these circumstances and qualities we may
safely count upon finding ample guarantees for not only
the maintenance but the increase of our liberties, and
very able securities for every species of good government.
It will be as well for us, however, to turn aside, if possible,
for a moment from the exciting tumult in which it is
the destiny of the present age to flourish, and calmly
condescend to spare a few moments of consideration to
the history of that not less agitated and consequential
age which elapsed from 1550 to the middle of the seventeenth century. The Protestant Reformation and its
great political consequences, especially the formation of
the Dutch Republic, had agitated men's minds in a
degree not inferior to the influence exercised over the
spirit of the eighteenth and present centuries by the
French Revolution. The nature and origin of Power
were not less severely scrutinised; the object and influence of Establishments not less sharply canvassed.
There was as much public intelligence, as much public
opinion, and as much public spirit, in Europe then as at
the present hour. The exclusive and local character of
nations was fast disappearing; patriotism was fast
merging into philanthropy; a cosmopolite spirit pervaded
Christendom: Geneva communicated with Edinburgh or
Paris; there was a constant spiritual correspondence
between Amsterdam and La Rochelle and London. The
political movement in England originated with the aristocracy; it was supported and advanced by the great
body of the nation. If the influence of the press were
less considerable than at the present day, though I much
doubt it, and the British Museum, which contains so many

thousand pamphlets of the times of Charles the First, a
fraction only of the fugitive effusions, confirms my
scepticism—Public Opinion had yet another and more
powerful organ, and was influenced by even a more
potent and passionate medium.   If there were ten
thousand pamphlets, certainly there were ten thousand
pulpits.

There was as much communication in 1640 as there is
likely to be in 1840; if we had no rail-roads, we had men
who rode " post haste "; there were as many committees,
there was as complete an organisation; the arts of insurgency reached such a zenith of perfection that the
unlicensed imagination and unbridled devices of Jaco-
binical France only imitated and never surpassed them;
and, more important than all, the Government was much
weaker.   Yet, although the flame of popular liberty was
fed by such various and vigorous fuel, and although the
ranks of the popular party were marshalled and led on
during the contest by statesmen inferior in station,
capacity, and accomplishment, to none who ever figured
in this land, the mighty impulse, like the most beautiful
river of Germany, which, after renovating a country and
commanding the admiration of a nation, never reaches
the ocean, but sinks into the swamps of Brabant—the
mighty impulse achieved only destruction, and the movement ended in mud.

The reigns of the latter Stuarts are the most disgraceful
in our annals, but as much from the character of the
nation as the character of those monarchs.   The public
spirit was broken and the public mind corrupted.   Good
laws are of little avail without good manners, and unless
there be a wholesome state of mind in the nation to
regulate their exercise.   Trial by Jury in the time of
Charles the Second was a tyranny as fearful as the Star
Chamber; and without any formal violation of our written
Constitution, it is probable that the government of the
Tudors would have been re-established in England, had
not James the Second alarmed the Protestant spirit of

the country, and the aristocracy seized the opportunity of again establishing our liberties.

The consequences of the famous revolution which raised the Prince of Orange to the throne of these realms were very important, but, as they did not affect the form or elements of the House of Commons, the remarks which it may be necessary to make upon that event will more naturally occur to me when I come to consider the nature of the executive branch of our Constitution, and the character of the kingly office. The history of England from that period until 1830 is rather political than constitutional, and, although extremely interesting to a statesman, relates to the struggles of rival parties for power instead of the more inspiring contest between royal prerogative and Parliamentary privilege, and that more noble conflict for their liberties between a nation and a Sovereign. The struggles of parties also, as connected with Ministerial responsibility, are naturally linked with the yet untouched topic of the Crown.

CHAPTER XXI

Blunders of the Whigs in their Reform of the House of Commons —But the Original Character of the House of Commons still retained—Not the House of the People—Of the Constitution of the House of Lords.

VIEWING the Reform Bill of 1830 as the *coup d'état* of a party who, having obtained power, found themselves opposed by all the estates of the realm, and supposing that their only object was to establish themselves in power by conceding a preponderating influence in the constituency to a sectarian minority in the State favourable to their views and policy, the intended measure is very intelligible; but, dismissing for the moment from our consideration all factious imputations, it must be admitted that this reform was conceived and prosecuted in a profound ignorance of the nature of our Constitution, to which we may ascribe all the mischiefs that have occurred and that threaten us.

That the reconstruction of the third estate of the realm was necessary is an intelligible proposition; and, had it been proved, all that we had to consider was the mode by which it should be attained. But the Whigs set out with reforming the representatives of the estate instead of the estate itself, and the consequences of this capital blunder pervade the whole of their arrangement. If the proposition of the necessity had been proved, then we had to consider the principle on which the Reform should be conducted, as population, fiscal contribution, or peculiar class. But by reforming the representatives instead of the estate, no principle could be adopted, or at least could only partially be applied. Hence the present system is as anomalous as the late one: communities of two or three hundred electors return as many representatives as communities of fourteen thousand; a man who rents a £10 house in a town enjoys a suffrage, a man who lives in a £40 house out of a town is not an elector. It might be undeniable that, if the third estate were to be reformed, the principle of representation without election no longer suited the present state of society: but why then cling to that part of the ancient scheme which gave a preponderating influence in numbers to the citizens and burgesses because, in fact, they were not elected, but only nominated? All this originated in the fallacy of supposing that the state of our representation in many towns was the consequence of decay, instead of original intention. Thus whole and important districts of the country, and considerable classes of the community, are not represented, and the land, which originally formed the third estate, assumes only a secondary character in its present elements.

Nevertheless, constituted as the third estate now is, and changed as may be its elements, has it in a political capacity deviated from its original character? The Commons form still only an estate of the realm, a privileged and limited order of the nation, in numbers a fraction of the mass, and their representatives can only be invested with the qualities of their constituents. To maintain that an estate of the realm is the People involves a contradiction in terms, for an estate implies a class of the People. The Commons of England are not the People unless we declare that every person who is not a Parliamentary constituent is without the pale of national definition. If we agree to this, the people of England consists of three or four hundred thousand persons, divided into almost equal classes professing the most contrary opinions. The absurdity of such a conclusion is evident. The House of Commons is not the House of the People, and the members of the House of Commons are not the representatives of the People.

I proceed to consider the Constitution and the character of the Upper House of Parliament. The House of Lords is the most eminent existing example of representation without election. As an estate of the realm which, from its unlimited numbers, can with convenience personally appear and assemble, the Peers of England do not meet at Westminster by their trustees, or deputies, or delegates. But this House is nevertheless representative. The House of Lords represents the Church in the Lord Bishops, the law in the Lord Chancellor and often the Lord Chief Justice, the counties in the Lord Lieutenants, the boroughs in their noble Recorders. This estate, from the character of the property of its members, is also essentially the representative chamber of the land; and as the hereditary leaders of the nation, especially of the cultivators of the land, the genuine and permanent population of England, its peasantry.

In ruder times, when the King desired to call a great council which should represent the interests and consult over the welfare of his kingdom, he summoned the Barons or chief subjects of his realm. These great councils, which were the origin of our Parliaments, and so styled before they assumed a legislative character, assembled

13

for the administration of justice. They formed a high court of law whither in time repaired, as I have before described, deputations of the provincial tribunals and the local executors of the law. The Barons originally held their Parliamentary privilege by tenure, but the King soon mingled among them by his writ of summons such individuals as he deemed fit and competent to assist them in their great office. Such was the origin of baronies by writ; and peerages by patent were also introduced as early as the reign of Richard the Second. Gradually, as the country advanced in civilisation, and the affairs of its population became more complicated, the Sovereign delegated portions of his judicial power to appointed and permanent tribunals of his palace, presided over by his selected councillors, and in time by professional lawyers. Such was the origin of our great courts of law—of King's Bench, of Common Pleas, and of Exchequer; but the House of Lords, even when the formal and present constitution of Parliament occurred, still retained, independent of the legislative functions of their estate, their original character of a high court of justice, which has descended to their successors, who to this day form the supreme and efficient Court of Appeal of the kingdom. It was this character, indeed, which rendered in old days the intermission of Parliaments so great a grievance. By not assembling the House of Lords, justice was delayed, and when we read in the reigns of the Plantagenets of the murmurs of the nation at the King not calling his Parliament, it was, in fact, the meeting of the Peers which the nation invoked with such loud complaints.

The House of Lords strictly consists of two estates of the realm: the Lords Spiritual and Temporal. Originally the Lords Spiritual exceeded the Temporal Peers in number. In the last Parliament that was held before the struggles between the Houses of York and Lancaster, so fatal to our ancient Peerage, only fifty-three Temporal Lords appeared in Parliament: the Spiritual Lords, on the

other hand, numbered twenty-one Bishops and thirty-six
mitred Abbots and Priors. Henry the Seventh could only
summon to his first Parliament twenty-nine Temporal
Lords, and even in the reign of Henry the Eighth the
Temporal Peers did not equal the representatives of the
Church and the great ecclesiastical corporations. The
dissolution of the monasteries, which expelled the mitred
Abbots and Priors from the Upper House, reduced the
number of the Spiritual Peers to twenty-six, five new
bishoprics having been created as a species of representative compensation to the new Church. From this period
the political influence of the Lords Spiritual in the Upper
House has never been of a preponderating character; and
although they retained their ancient privilege as a
separate estate, and the precedence to which they were
originally entitled, they have in fact, by blending their
votes with their temporal brethren, contributed to the
formation of one estate of the realm, in which they have
long virtually, although not formally, merged.

CHAPTER XXII

Of the Spiritual Lords—The Bench of Bishops a Democratic
Institution—Of the Temporal Lords.

I THINK, my Lord, this is not an inconvenient opportunity
of considering the policy of the presence of these right
reverend personages in the Upper House of Parliament,
a policy so unpopular with the anti-constitutional party
of this country. Whenever the factious leaders of the
third estate attempt to obtain a preponderating influence
in the Constitution for the House in which they sit as
representatives of their order, and to usurp the entire
government of the country, and exercise despotic control
over the lives and liberties, the persons and properties,
of their fellow-subjects, the attack upon the independence
and influence of the House of Lords is invariably com-

menced by an assault upon the ecclesiastical elements of its composition.   Thus, in the time of Charles the First the factious leaders of a majority of the representatives of that limited and privileged order of the nation called the Commons succeeded, after repeated efforts, in expelling the Bishops, or first estate, from the Upper House; and thus certain persons at the present day, who inherit all the faction of Pym and Hampden, though none of their genius, being as like to them as Butler's Hudibras is like to Milton's Satan, have, in a manner at once indecent and unconstitutional, and which, if I have any knowledge of the laws of my country, subjects them to a præmunire, soiled the notice book of the proceedings of the next session of the House of Commons with a vile and vulgar menace of this exalted order.

The great art in creating an efficient Representative Government is to secure its representation of those interests of the country which are at the same time not only considerable, but in their nature permanent.   To bind up with our form of polity the feelings of vast and influential classes of the nation obviously tends to the perpetuity of the State; though the danger of making sudden and slightly considered additions to the elements of our political estates need not be enlarged upon, nor the fatal blunder of mistaking an evanescent for a permanent interest.   Independent of all those spiritual considerations, which hitherto have been held as justly and wisely influencing the elements and character of the English Constitution; dismissing for a moment from our thoughts that union of Church and State which hitherto has consecrated the commonwealth of England; granting for an instant that that religious connection, which has so long tempered power and so often elevated its exercise, should indeed cease, and that the authority of the Church of England should only be supported by the affections and voluntary succour of its votaries; I have yet to learn that the presence in the House of Peers of an order of individuals who, in the independence of their means, I may say the vastness of their possessions, are inferior to none, can be enumerated among the less desirable elements of a Senate. To me it seems that a Bishop of Durham or of Winchester affords, from his position, the probable materials of as efficient a member of the Upper House as any Earl or Marquis who bears those names.

But when I recall to my recollection the virulent antipathy of the anti-constitutional writers of the present day against what they style the Hereditary Peerage, and the unqualified legislators, who, they pretend, must be the inevitable consequences of its institution, I confess that I am somewhat astonished that their first and fiercest attack should be made on that portion of the House of Lords whose office is not hereditary, who in general spring from the humbler classes of the community, and who, from the nature of their qualification to sit in that august assembly, must necessarily be men distinguished for their learning, their talents, and their virtues. Of the many popular elements of the House of Lords, I have always considered that the bench of Bishops was the most democratic.

I have not concealed my conviction, for I plead only the cause of Truth, that the Protestant Reformation in England originally tended to the establishment of arbitrary power, and of that despotism of the Tudors of which Charles the First was the victim. The Church transferred their allegiance from the Tiara to the Crown; the people followed the example of their national ecclesiastics. But these were the inevitable consequences of unparalleled events. The Church is part of our Constitution, and its character has changed in unison with that Constitution; the clergy in this country, thanks to that Reformation whose good fruits we have long enjoyed, both political and spiritual, are national; they are our fellow-subjects. and they have changed with their fellow-countrymen. Their errors were the errors of their age and of their nation; they were no more. The Bishops who, under

James the First, maintained the High Commission Court, under James the Second were the first champions of our liberties; the Establishment which, under Laud, persecuted to obtain Conformity, is now certainly our surest, perhaps our only, guarantee of Toleration.

The English Constitution, while it has secured that toleration, absolute and illimitable, has also consecrated the State; it has proved that religious government and religious liberty are not incompatible. It is one of the leading principles of our polity that the religious discipline and future welfare of our citizens are even of greater importance than their political and present well-being. And although the pious and private munificence of an ancient people has, in the course of ages, relieved the State from the fiscal burthen of a dependent Clergy, invested that godly and learned and devoted body with a noble and decorous inheritance, and covered our land with schools and churches, with sublime temples, and august and unrivalled universities; the State has nevertheless stepped in as the trustee and guardian of the ministers of our religion, adopted them as its children, and established their order into an estate of the kingdom.

The Stuarts were prodigal in the creation of Temporal Peers; one hundred and nineteen met in the Parliament of 1640, but in 1661 the number had scarcely increased. The Peers of England led the movement against the unhappy son of James the First. A Peer was one of the five members whom the King attempted to seize; but when all those concessions were obtained from the Sovereign, which would have left the estates, and the nation at large, in the possession of even greater privileges than we enjoy at this day; when it was discovered that the monarchy itself was aimed at, and that Reform was fast approaching Revolution, the great body of the Peerage, in unison with the great body of their fellow-subjects, withdrew themselves from the Parliament and adhered to the King. So that when the Upper House was formally abolished by the vote of the House of Commons, the customary attendance of Lords was not more than six or eight. Little more than a quarter of a century after the restoration of the Stuarts, the nation, headed by the Peers, expelled them, and established the security of a Protestant throne.

CHAPTER XXIII

Of the Peerage Bill—Attempts of the Whigs to establish an Oligarchy—Irresponsibility of the House of Lords considered —The Lords not more Irresponsible than the Commons—The Qualification of the Peers the same as the Commons, Hereditary—Hereditary Legislators not more Absurd than Hereditary Electors—The Principle of Hereditary Legislation not constitutionally Anomalous—The Principle of Hereditary Legislation not abstractedly Absurd.

FROM the accession of William the Third to the accession of William the Fourth, a period of upwards of one hundred and forty years, the House of Lords has not only exercised an independent, but a considerable, and, as some have held, a preponderating, influence in the government of the country. The Whigs under George the First, in pursuance of their plan of reducing the English monarch to the character of a Venetian Doge, succeeded in carrying a Bill through the Upper House to deprive the King of his prerogative of creating further Peers, and thus to convert the free and democratic Peerage of England into an odious oligarchy of exclusive privilege; but the House of Commons, led by the Tory country gentlemen, rejected the proposition with becoming decision. Since that time, and especially during the active reigns of the Third and Fourth Georges, the royal prerogative has been exercised with a liberality which by some has been warmly, but I think unwisely, stigmatised. The ranks of our second estate have been periodically strengthened by an accession of some of the best blood, the greatest wealth, and the most distinguished talent, of the community, and its due influence alike in the legislature and in national opinion has thus been efficiently maintained.

The increased strength of the third estate, in consequence of its recent reconstruction, having filled the imaginations of certain factious leaders with the old and disastrous machination of establishing the supremacy of its representative chamber, and that result not being possible unless the independence of the Upper House of Parliament is first destroyed, an attack is now made with equal violence and perseverance upon the hereditary principle of its institution as productive of irresponsibility, and thus affording not only a most injurious, but an anomalous, feature in the scheme of our legislative and executive government.

Who has not heard of the fatal and anomalous irresponsibility of the House of Lords ? Of what Whig journal does it not form the subject of the choice and cockbrained leading article ? Is there a tavern Cleon from whose foaming lips its anathema does not flow in rabid sentences of seditious folly ? Is there a plebeian oracle of a metropolitan vestry who does not warn the Peers of England with the solemn stolidity of his Delphic utterance ? Nay, the authorised agitator of the administration itself is sent upon a provincial tour of treason to open the minds of the King's lieges on this urgent point of constitutional revelation—the vagabond and overrated rebel—vomiting his infamous insolence in language mean as his own soul !

And yet this fatal and anomalous irresponsibility is no more the characteristic of the House of Lords than of that third estate itself, in whose supremacy the anticonstitutional writers teach us we are alone to find a security for good government.

The estate of the Peers is in no greater degree irresponsible than the estate of the Commons. Both are alike popular classes—that is, sections of the nation, established for the public and common good into political orders or estates. For this reason are they privileged, and for no other; nor is there any privilege of importance which the Lords enjoy which the Commons do not share;

though there are very many, and those, too, very important, privileges which the Commons in the course of time have acquired, and which they have jealously monopolised. The Commons, for their own convenience, meet in Parliament by their representatives; the Lords, from their limited number, meet personally. Yet a Peer is allowed to vote by proxy on the same principle that the Commons are allowed to vote by their proxies or representatives; it ever being the wish and intention and genius of our Constitution that the three estates shall be as completely and constantly consulted on all subjects, and their consent to all laws as perfectly obtained, as human wit could devise. This is the real and original cause of the Peers voting by proxy, an analogous privilege with that enjoyed by the Commons; yet in these days of profound constitutional learning even this vote by proxy is held " an anomaly," and no less a personage than an exalted member of the Upper House itself, eager to obtain a little vulgar popularity by falling in with the superficial humours of the day, has been found anxious to deprive his own order to an ancient, and, as I have shown, not a peculiar, privilege.

A political estate is in its nature complete, and therefore, whatever may be the amount of privileges or the degree of power with which it is invested, it is necessarily independent. Now, all power that is independent must be irresponsible. If the state of the Peers be independent and irresponsible, and undoubtedly and necessarily it is so, to whom is the estate of the Commons responsible ? To whom is that privileged order of the kingdom, who at the last General Election, to the amount of three hundred thousand men, voted for the representatives of their order in Parliament—to whom are they responsible ? What political dependence have they upon the nation at large ? What do they care for what the unrepresented mass may think of their resolves and conduct ? Are they amenable for their political behaviour to any public tribunal ? Have they not, if they agree among them-

selves and return their representatives to that effect,
the power, as far as the assent of their estate is concerned,
the power to deprive all those who are not of their privileged order of their rights and liberties ? What lawyer
can doubt such a right in the Commons, or dispute their
power, if they choose to exercise it ? Have not the
majority of their representatives, in fact, often exercised
the delegated power of their order to this effect ? Why
has the House of Commons often been unpopular with
the great body of the nation ? Because their conduct
opposed its interests or inclinations. Was the House of
Commons dependent on the nation ? No ! They were
dependent on their order, on their privileged constituents,
who sent them to their chamber, and who, in their turn,
are responsible to no class whatever. If the question of
responsibility be mooted, what satisfaction or increased
security to a nation of many millions is it that the
privileged order of Commons consists of three hundred
thousand, instead of two hundred thousand, or even one
hundred thousand persons ? Is a privileged order of
three hundred thousand individuals, represented by their
deputies, likely to be more responsible than a privileged
order of three hundred individuals appearing by themselves ? On the contrary, everyone sees and feels in
an instant that, as far as the nation is concerned, the
more limited order, who appear for themselves, and are
more in the eye of the world, are in fact in a moral point
of view much more responsible to the general body of the
people than the more numerous and more obscure class,
who shuffle off that moral responsibility on their representatives.

So much for the anomalous irresponsibility of the House
of Lords. You will perceive, my Lord, that nothing but
the two capital blunders prevalent among the anti-
constitutional writers of the present day—namely, in the
first place, confounding the representatives of an estate
with that estate itself, and, secondly, supposing that their
presumed estate was in fact representative of no less a

body than the nation itself, between whom and the House of Commons there really exists no privity—I repeat, nothing but these two capital blunders in our profound political instructors can account for the perverse absurdities of their lucubrations, or the conceited complacency with which they develop their ill-seasoned theories.

If the estate of the Peers be not more irresponsible in the exercise of the power with which it is invested than the estate of the Commons, so also the qualification by which the Peers exercise their power is in its nature the same as the qualification by which the Commons exercise their power. If the institution of hereditary legislators be absurd, I do not see that that of hereditary electors is less so. If it be absurd to enact that a man in the most elevated and cultivated class of the community should be born with a right of becoming, at a legal age, an English legislator, so is it equally absurd to maintain that a man in one of the humbler and less educated classes of the community should be born with the right of becoming, at a legal age, the nominator of a legislator. Yet the qualification of a majority of the English Commons is hereditary.

So you see, my Lord, it turns out, on a little dispassionate examination, that the " anomalous " institution of the House of Lords is not quite so irregular, so flagrantly out of rule, so absolutely alien to the genius of our Constitution, as, were we to place credit in our profound disquisitionists and reformers, we might too hastily imagine.

The Lords, it seems, in a legal point of view, are not a jot more irresponsible than the other limited and privileged and purely conventional order of the State; in a mere moral point of view, indeed, are more amenable to the influence of public opinion than their obscurer rivals; while the qualification both of the Lords and Commons is to a great amount identical, and the Commons hold and enjoy their privileges by the very same odious principle which frights the orators of the Crown and

Anchor from their propriety, and stimulates the kennel orators of Westminster and Marylebone, in the enthusiasm of their rhetoric slang, to denounce the "absurd and anomalous authority of the Lords"; to wit, that very same, that odious hereditary principle, which pervades the whole frame of our society, which has conduced more than any other principle to the perpetuity of our State, and which at the present day is so greatly abused and so little understood.

But although the exposition into which I have entered of the real principles and the genuine nature of the English Constitution has destroyed for ever, as far as reason can influence and truth prevail, the revolutionary objection which it is now the fashion to urge against the hereditary principle of the second estate of this kingdom, I am far from wishing to avoid the abstract discussion of the fitting elements of a senate in which our modern anti-constitutional writers, the gentlemen who admire abstract principles, and would build up their political fabric on a system of pure science, so freely and frequently indulge. And therefore I will at once admit that, if I were called upon to construct a Constitution *a priori* for this country, of which a senate, or superior chamber, was to be a constituent part, I am at a loss to conceive where I could obtain more suitable materials for its construction than in the body of our hereditary Peerage. So far from considering that there is anything absurd or objectionable in the principle of political inheritance, as a statesman who wished to study the perpetuity of his State it is the very principle of which I should eagerly avail myself, and to which I should cling. Assuredly I cannot understand how an efficient senate is to be secured by merely instituting another elective chamber, the members of which, being the deputies of their constituents, must either be the echo of the Lower House, or, if returned by a different class, the factious delegates of an envious and hostile section of the community. Would the difficulty be removed, and the object obtained, by

allowing the members of the senate to be chosen from
the body of the Lower House itself ? The trial of
strength then would be elevated from the choice of a
Speaker to the election of a House of Lords. This would
indeed be a struggle ! What a prize for an ambitious
Minister ! What a noble quarry for the falcon glance of
a keen Opposition ! After the division, after the high
blood excited by such an encounter, we might, I think,
retire to our homes, and return to our constituents at
once, and leave the victorious party to record their
decrees without the affectation of discussion and the
mockery of control.

What chance do these wild schemes hold out of an
effective senate ? But would you then cling to your
hereditary legislators ? Why not ? But the very idea
of an hereditary legislator is absurd ; who ever heard of an
hereditary physician, or an hereditary surgeon, or an
hereditary apothecary ? Such an idea would be absurd ;
therefore the idea of an hereditary legislator is absurd.
Granted, if legislators be apothecaries. Before we can
decide whether the idea of an hereditary legislator be
absurd, we must first ascertain what is meant by the
word "legislator," and what are the public duties of this
personage which we are about to make a matter of
inheritance to his posterity. If by the word "legislator"
we mean one of those original and organising minds who
occasionally arise to frame commonwealths, and to mould
the minds of nations, I willingly concede that it would
be very absurd to invest such a character with the necessary power to fulfil his grand objects, and simultaneously
to entail the enjoyment of the same power on his posterity ; I freely admit that it is not very probable that
the entailed legislator, like his sire, would prove either
a Moses or a Minos, a Numa or a Solon, a Saxon Alfred
or a Russian Peter. But at the same time I am equally
of opinion that it is just as probable that the legislative
descendant of the great legislator would rival his powers,
as that a Moses or a Minos, a Numa or a Solon, a Saxon

Alfred or a Czar Peter, should be returned to Parliament as their representative by any body of ten-pounders in the kingdom. Such characters are so rare that we do not count upon their force and impulse in arranging the economy of a State. If the conduct of public affairs depended upon the constant presence in the commonwealth of such characters, the State would enjoy no quality of duration. It seems, therefore, that we must be content to require from our legislators a somewhat more moderate portion of sagacity and science. And the question then naturally arises, What portion? Whether, in fact, the qualities of a legislator in an ancient and free and highly civilised and experienced State will not be necessarily found among individuals of average intelligence and high education; and whether an order of men who, from their vast possessions, have not only a great, a palpable, and immediate interest in the welfare of a country, but by ease, and leisure, and freedom from anxiety, are encouraged to the humanising pursuits of learning and the liberal love of arts; an order of men who are born honoured, and taught to respect themselves by the good fame and glory of their ancestors; who from the womb to the grave are trained to loathe and recoil from everything that is mean and sordid, and whose honour is a more precious possession than their parks and palaces; the question is, whether an order of men thus set apart in a State, men refined, serene, and courteous, learned, brave, travelled, charitable, and magnificent, do not afford the choicest elements of a senate, especially when they are distinguished from their fellow-citizens by no civil privileges, and the supreme power in the State has the capacity of adding to their numbers at his will any individuals, however humble and plebeian their origin, whose wisdom will in his opinion swell the aggregate capacity of their assembly?

CHAPTER XXIV

Political Institutions must be judged by their Results—The
Hereditary Peerage contributes to the Stability of the State
—The House of Lords in Ability always Equal to the House
of Commons—Superior since the Reform—The Principle of
Hereditary Legislation prevalent in the House of Commons,
and sanctioned by the National Character.

POLITICAL institutions must be judged by their results.
For nearly five centuries the hereditary Peerage, as at
present constituted, has formed an active and powerful
branch of our legislature. Five centuries of progressive
welfare are good evidence of the efficient polity of the
advancing country. No statesman can doubt that the
peculiar character of the hereditary branch of our legislature has mainly contributed to the stability of our
institutions, and to the order and prosperous security
which that stability has produced. Nor can we forget
that the hereditary principle has at all times secured a
senate for this country inferior in intelligence to no
political assembly on record. If we survey the illustrious
history of our Parliament since 1688, whether we consider its career in reference to the patriotic energy that
has at all times distinguished its councils, its unceasing
vigilance, its indefatigable industry, its vast and various
knowledge, its courageous firmness, its comprehensive
sympathy with all classes of the community, its prescient
and imperial ambition, or the luminous and accomplished
eloquence in which its counsels and resolves have been
recommended and expressed; assuredly the hereditary
branch of our legislature need not shrink from a comparison with its elective rival. I do not think, my Lord,
that anyone will be bold enough to assert—or, if bold
enough to assert, skilful enough to maintain—that the
late Reform, which was to open the doors of the House
of Commons to all the unearthed genius of the country,
has indicated as yet any tendency to render this rivalry

on the part of the Peers of England a matter of greater
venture. If in old times the hereditary senate has at
least equalled in capacity the elective chamber, no impartial observer at the present day can for a moment
hesitate in declaring that, not only in the higher accomplishments of statesmen, in elevation of thought and
feeling, in learning and in eloquence, does the hereditary
assembly excel the elective, but, in truth, that for those
very qualities for the possession of which at first sight
we should be most disposed to give a House of Commons
credit, that mastery of detail and management of complicated commonplaces which we style in this country
"business-like habits," the Peers of England are absolutely more distinguished than the humbler representatives of the third estate.

But the truth is, my Lord, that the practical good sense
of this country has long ago disposed of the question of
the principle of hereditary legislation, even if its defence
merely depended on its abstract propriety. For if we
examine the elements of the House of Commons with a
little attention, we shall soon discover that hereditary
legislators are not confined to the House of Lords, and
that the inclination of the represented to make representation hereditary is very obvious and very natural.
The representative of a county is selected from one of
the first families in the shire, and ten years after the son
of this member, a candidate for the same honour, adduces
the very circumstances of his succession to his father as
an increased claim upon the confidence of the constituency. Those who are versed in elections know that
there is no plea so common and so popular. Such
elections prove that, far from holding the principle of
hereditary legislation absurd, public opinion has decided
that the duties of an English legislator are such as, on
an average of human capacity, may descend from sire
to son; and that, while there is nothing to shock their
reason in the circumstance, there is much at the same
time to gratify the feelings and please the associations

of an ancient people, who have made inheritance the
pervading principle of their social polity, who are proud
of their old families and fond of their old laws.

CHAPTER XXV

The Hereditary Principle must not be considered abstractedly—
The French Senate examined—Why an Hereditary Senate,
composed of the Ablest Men, may be a Political Nonentity—
Necessary Qualities of an Assembly like the English House
of Lords.

THE hereditary character of our Peerage must be considered in relation to the other qualities of that illustrious
body.   No one competent to form an opinion upon public
affairs can doubt for an instant that, whether the nominal
honours of those insignificant personages, who at this
present hour meet in the senatorial chamber of the
Luxembourg, devolve upon their posterity or not, the
circumstance one way or the other can neither increase
nor diminish their public and political authority.   The
Peers of France are nonentities, and nonentities they
have ever been, as insignificant before the junior French
Revolution as they are after that bloody riot.   If the
hereditary principle could not render the French Peerage
more powerful, it is equally true that the intellectual
qualifications of its members, however eminent, were
equally unproductive of that result.   The Chamber of
Peers in France since the Restoration has numbered
amongst its members the most illustrious warriors and
the most celebrated diplomatists of the kingdom, the
ablest writers of the day, the most distinguished scientific
men, marshals, ambassadors, editors of newspapers, wits,
travellers, authors, mathematicians, chemists: had it
been selected by a Westminster Reviewer himself, the
Senate of France could not have consisted of men more
qualified to develop and demonstrate all "the science
of legislation."   Why, then, are they so insignificant ?

14

Formed of all the talent of the country, the Chamber has no authority. What can be the cause ? The hereditary principle, to be sure—the fatal, the absurd, the anomalous hereditary principle. The hereditary principle is destroyed ! Yes, a revolution is got up to achieve, among other great objects, the destruction of the fatal, absurd, and anomalous principle of hereditary legislation in the French Charter; and the French House of Peers in consequence becomes, if possible, more odious and more contemptible.

It is not, then, necessarily the hereditary principle which renders the influence of our House of Lords so injurious to the commonweal; and it is not, then, a collection of all the clever men of a country, under the august title of a Senate, which necessarily must be productive of good government. The truth is, a nation will not allow three hundred men, however ingenious, to make laws for them because the sovereign power of the State chooses to appoint that such a number of its subjects shall possess this privilege, and meet in a room to register their decrees. The King of England may make Peers, but he cannot make a House of Lords. The order of men of whom such an assembly is formed is the creation of ages. In the first place, they must really be an estate of the realm, a class of individuals who, from their property and personal influence alone, form an important section of the whole nation. The laws and customs of England have compensated its Peers for the loss of their feudal splendour. A strong current of property and influence from the wide ocean of national prosperity perpetually flows into our House of Lords. They still form the most eminent class in the State; and, instead of the position of the Peers at the present day bearing a diminished importance, compared with the attitude of the remaining classes of the community, as the superficial vulgarly imagine, I shall be surprised that, if the subject be more profoundly inquired into, if the power and privileges with which the Constitution has invested him be duly considered, and the indirect support which he receives from his alliances with the great Commons and the aristocratic classes which have sprung up around him be not omitted in the estimate, the influence of a great Peer of the present day—a Duke of Buccleugh or a Duke of Devonshire—be ascertained to be much inferior to that of an Earl of Pembroke in the time of John, or an Earl of Leicester in the reign of his successor. A House of Lords must consist of men whose influence is not felt merely in their chamber of Parliament. They must be an order of individuals whose personal importance crosses us in all the transactions of life, and pervades the remotest nook and corner of the country, an importance, also, which we find to arise as much from the hallowed associations, or even the inveterate prejudices of society, as from their mere public privileges and constitutional and territorial importance. Their names, office, and character, and the ennobling achievements of their order, must be blended with our history, and bound up with our hereditary sentiment. They must be felt and recognised as the not unworthy descendants or successors of a class that has always taken the lead in civilisation, and formed the advanced guard in the march of national progress. Vast property, and the complicated duties which great possessions entail upon their owners, the inspiring traditions of a heroic history, the legendary respect of ages, the fair maintenance in the order itself of that civility of manners, that love of liberal pursuits, and that public spirit which become the leaders of a free people, and a strong conviction in the nation generally that, under the constitution of which this order forms a branch, they have flourished for a longer period, and in a greater degree, than any existing commonwealth—such are some of the elements of which a Senate must be formed that attempts to cope with the House of Lords of England.

The English nation has thought that there is a greater certainty of securing a Senate of this high character by entailing its functions on the most important order of its members than by trusting to the periodical selection of any body of individuals whatsoever. It has supposed that the chance production of its carefully cultivated aristocracy may offer, on the whole, senatorial elements preferable to the selected materials of popular choice. It has desired that there should be one portion of its legislature free from the turbulent and overwhelming passions that occasionally assail the less guarded structure of its more popular assembly; and to secure all these great purposes, to contrive at the same time, in establishing this chamber, its power and its perpetuity, its independence and its ability, it has not comprehended how a more practical system could be adopted than to establish the hereditary legislation of a democratic Peerage.

CHAPTER XXVI

Causes of the Harmony between the Two Houses—The Hereditary Principle must also be considered in Reference to the System of Parties in this Country—Summary—That the Principle of Hereditary Legislation is neither constitutionally Anomalous, nor abstractedly Absurd, nor practically Injurious, but the Reverse.

THIS, my Lord, is, I think, one of those cases in which " the wisdom of our ancestors " has been conspicuous, and the harmony which throughout our history has on the whole so remarkably subsisted between our two Houses of Parliament, and the effective manner in which the machinery of our legislature has consequently operated, prove the sound judgment of the national mind that has required and sanctioned a Senate thus constituted. So profound, indeed, is and ever must be the reciprocal sympathy between the Peers and Commons of England, that, even after the late factious reconstruction of the third estate, a majority of the representatives of the English Commons upheld the independence of our

august Senate. I ascribe this sympathy to a cause I
have before indicated, to the principle which is the basis
of our social fabric, our civil equality. It is this great
principle which has prevented the nobility of England
from degenerating into a favoured and odious sect; it is
this great principle which has placed the Peers at the
head of the People, which has surrounded them with a
popular aristocracy, and filled the chamber of the third
estate with representatives connected with our senators
not only by sympathy of feeling and similarity of pursuits, but by the most intimate relations of birth and
blood.

Again, my Lord, the question of our hereditary Peerage
must be viewed in reference to the state and system of
parties in this country. It results from the system of
parties in this country that both Houses of Parliament
are led and directed by a very few members, and those
the most eminent for talents, and character, and station,
in the respective assemblies. Thus the extreme cases,
which the anti-constitutional writers are ever urging, of
the legislative function devolving through the medium
of an hereditary institution to individuals incompetent
to discharge this high office, never in fact practically
occur. By ranging himself under one of the political
banners of the State, every legislator avails himself of the
intelligence of his leaders; to guide his judgment and
form his opinion, he has the advantage of the finest talents
in the country. Thus an individual, abstractedly very
incompetent, may become practically very useful, and
thus even a weak brain may assist in passing a wise law.

Thus we have seen, my Lord, that, viewed in reference
to the complete scheme of our legislature, the hereditary
principle of the House of Lords, far from being " anomalous," is in perfect harmony with the constitution of the
other estate of the realm; that if it were as " anomalous "
as it is regular and consistent, far from being " absurd,"
the application of the principle is extremely rational;
and that, inasmuch as it is not either constitutionally

" anomalous " or abstractedly " absurd," its practical
results have been such as might have been anticipated
from an institution suited to the genius of the country,
in harmony with all its political establishments, and
founded, not only on an intimate acquaintance with the
national character, but a profound knowledge of human
nature in general.

CHAPTER XXVII

Of the Kingly Office—Unsuccessful Attempts of the Whigs to
  establish an Oligarchy under William the Third—Reign of
  Anne—Its Influence on Parties—More Successful Attempts
  of the Whigs to establish an Oligarchy under George the First
  —They establish the Cabinet, and banish the King from his own
  Council; pass the Septennial Act, and introduce the Peerage
  Bill—Oligarchical *Coups d'État*—Policy of the Whigs under
  George the First compared with their Policy at the Present
  Day.

IN these observations on the character and history of our
two Houses of Parliament, I have already incidentally
traced, or referred to, the character and history of the
monarchy. We have seen the Kings of England, in the
reigns of the Plantagenets, exercising a sovereign power,
limited, however, in its use by the privilege estates of
the kingdom, who, although they held the right of
legislation in its fullest extent, from the imperfect civilisation of the times assumed on the whole rather the office
of powerful councillors of the Sovereign than that of
the administrators of the kingdom. We have seen the
same King, in the reigns of the Tudors, an arbitrary
monarch. We have witnessed the same King, in the
reigns of the Stuarts, engaged in a continual struggle
with the reviving and at length preponderating power
of the long-dormant and paralysed estates. From the
accession of the Prince of Orange the character of our
history changes. The old contest between prerogative
and privilege, between the power of the Crown and the
liberty of the subject, ceases for ever, and the war of

parties succeeds to the struggles of Kings and Parliaments.

The English Constitution under William the Third did not secure greater power and privileges to our Parliament than it possessed under the reign of Henry the Fourth; but the Lords and great Commons of England had since that time become the most civilised and highly cultured body in Europe; men exceeding the superior classes of all nations in learning, eloquence, and public spirit, in practical skill and theoretic wisdom. It is not difficult to comprehend that such a body of men in absolute and unquestioned possession of the legislature should no longer be content that the executive and administrative province of the Constitution, with all its pomp and circumstance, should be monopolised by a single individual and his personal retainers. Here, then, commences the age when the influence of the Court rapidly declined, when Ministers were virtually appointed by the Parliament instead of the Sovereign, and when, by the institution of the Cabinet, the scheme and policy of the administration devolved upon a Parliamentary committee, and the King was, in fact, excluded from his own council.

If it be perhaps too strong an expression to say that William the Third was called to the throne by the voice of the whole nation, it is certain that the whole nation ratified the abdication of James the Second. Whig and Tory, Churchman and Dissenter, had alike required, and alike assisted in, his expulsion. When the excitement of this great event had a little subsided, when the rights and liberties of the nation had been secured by its Parliament, the leaders of the Whigs, including many of the most powerful and ancient families of the kingdom, commenced a favourite scheme of that party, which was to reduce the King of England to the situation of a Venetian Doge. But William the Third, like Louis Philippe, was resolved to be his own Minister, and it is not very easy to comprehend how in a perilous and revolutionary period a Sovereign of great capacity will consent to be deprived of the benefit of his own sagacity. The Whigs therefore were obliged to postpone until a more favourable opportunity the series of measures by which their great result was to be obtained; and for the present indicated their spleen by opposing the Sovereign, to whom certainly that party had originally attracted the attention of the English nation. But William, whose administrative talents were of a high order, succeeded, by his adroit balance of parties, in keeping the Whigs in check, and throughout his reign in maintaining his authority.

The reign of Anne, which proved that the reign of a Stuart might at the same time be glorious, Protestant, and prosperous, completely unsettled the public mind of England, and made nine-tenths of the people yearn after the lost dynasty of their native Sovereigns. The leaders of both parties were in secret communication with St. Germains, and one circumstance alone prevented the son of James the Second from regaining the throne of his ancestors—his absolute incompetence. The Pretender was an incapable bigot, totally devoid of that talent which in some degree had always characterised his family.

The Hanoverian accession was secured by the bold conduct of the Dukes of Somerset and Argyle. These great Whig Peers had the hardihood to attend a Privy Council, without being summoned, while the Queen was lying in a state almost of lethargy, and absolutely forced Her Majesty to appoint the Duke of Shrewsbury Lord Treasurer. This is one of the most dramatic scenes in our political history: the unexpected arrival of the two Dukes, the Queen's desperate state, Bolingbroke's baffled hopes, the troops summoned to London, the heralds kept in waiting with a company of guards to proclaim the new King the moment the throne was vacant. The Elector of Hanover ascended the throne of England by the sufferance rather than the consent of the nation. Unsupported by the mass of the people, ignorant of our language, phlegmatic in temperament, George the First entirely depended upon the Whig Peers, and the Whig Peers resolved to compensate themselves for the disappointment they had experienced under William the Third. They at once established the Cabinet on its present basis. It is curious to trace the kingly office from the era of the Plantagenets, when the characters of a royal council and a legislative chamber were so blended together in the House of Lords that the monarch always presided over his Parliament, to the moment when the Sovereign under the Brunswicks was virtually excluded from his own council. Having thus by the establishment of the Cabinet obtained in a great degree the executive power of the State, the Whig Peers ventured to propose a measure, in order to consolidate and confirm their strength, which is perhaps unequalled by any of the machinations of a party so remarkable in all periods of our history for the unscrupulous means with which they satisfy their lust of power. This measure was the famous Peerage Bill, proposed and supported in the House of Lords by those very Dukes of Somerset and Argyle who had forced a Queen to appoint a Prime Minister on her death-bed. This Bill, if passed into a law, would have deprived the King of his prerogative of making further Peers, and would have occasioned a virtual revolution in our government, which from that moment would have become oligarchical. George the First assented to the Bill, and the House of Lords passed it; but the Tory country gentlemen in the House of Commons, aided on this occasion by some unusual allies, succeeded in rejecting the measure. The Peerage Bill, my Lord, made as much noise in its day as the Reform Bill in our own. There was as great a " crisis," as vehement a " collision " in 1718, as any we have lately witnessed stalking about in their lions' skins; and the press teemed then with more pamphlets about " the Lords " than even at this hour, when every briefless barrister smells out that the surest road to a commissionership or other base job is to denounce that House of Parliament which will not truckle to a rapacious and unprincipled faction. The Whigs in 1718 sought to govern the country by "swamping" the House of Commons: in 1835 it is the House of Lords that is to be "swamped." In 1718 the *coup d'état* was to prevent any further increase of the Lords; in 1835 the Lords are to be outnumbered. Different tactics to obtain the same purpose; and the variance to be accounted for by the simple circumstance that the party which has recourse to these desperate expedients is not a national party, influenced by any great and avowed principles of public policy and conduct, but a small knot of great families who have no other object but their own aggrandisement, and who seek to gratify it by all possible means.

CHAPTER XXVIII

George the Second unsuccessfully struggles against the Whig Oligarchs—George the Third emancipates the Nation from them—Of Whigs and Tories—Their Origin explained, and their Real Character ascertained.

ALTHOUGH the House of Commons, supported by a roused and indignant nation, rejected the Peerage Bill, still the power of the Whig aristocracy, increased by the Septennial Act, was so considerable that they monopolised the administration of this realm for upwards of half a century. George the Second, indeed, struggled for a time against these Venetian magnificoes, but when he found himself forced to resign his favourite Minister, the brilliant Carteret, to the demands of the Pelhams and their well-organised connections, the King gave up the effort in despair. It was the clear sense and the strong spirit of his able grandson that emancipated this country from the government of " the great families." The King put himself at the head of the nation; and, encouraged by the example of a popular monarch in George the Third, and a democratic Minister in Mr. Pitt, the nation elevated to power the Tory or national party of England, under whose comprehensive and consistent, vigorous and strictly democratic system, this island has become the metropolis of a mighty Empire, its Sovereign at the same time the most powerful and its people the most free, and second to no existing nation in arts or arms, in internal prosperity, or exterior splendour.

There is no political subject, my Lord, on which a greater confusion of ideas exists, and none on which it is more desirable that we should possess very accurate conceptions, than respecting the nature and character of the two great political parties in which England, for the last century and a half, has been divided—the WHIGS and the TORIES. The people of England in the reign of George the First formed a community as distinguished for their public spirit as any people with which we are acquainted. How happened it, then, that nine-tenths of the nation were the avowed admirers of arbitrary power, of the Divine right of Kings, of the doctrine of non-resistance, and of the duties of passive obedience ? How came it that the upholders of this servile creed, instead of imbibing it from the Court, maintained it in defiance of the Court ? How happened it that the supporters of the Court themselves were the avowed admirers of the most popular opinions, of the sovereignty of the people, of the right and duty of resistance, of toleration, and of the cause of civil and religious liberty ? How came it that the upholders of these popular opinions, instead of adopting them to flatter the bulk of the people, maintained them in defiance of the people ? And, lastly, how came it that, while the professors of arbitrary opinions exhibited on every great occasion an unquestioned and undisguised love of freedom and their rights, and expelled from the throne the Sovereign who menaced them, the professors of popular opinions, on the other hand, seized every opportunity of curtailing popular power and abridging popular privileges, introduced a Peerage Bill in the House of Lords, carried a Septennial Act in the House of Commons, and finally organised a system of political corruption throughout the Parliament and the country from the taint of which, it is not too much to assert, the national character has never absolutely recovered ?

The consequences of the Great Rebellion, Parliamentary tyranny, and sectarian fanaticism, had occasioned in due season a strong reaction throughout the country in favour of the Crown and the Church. Gradually there developed themselves two sections of the nation respectively hostile to one of these institutions—sections connected together by no other similarity of feeling or situation, yet finally co-operating for the purpose of reciprocal assistance in a united attack upon the Monarchy and the Establishment: these were a powerful party of the Lords and the Non-conformists. A republican feeling united the haughtiest of the Peers with the lowest of the Puritans; but the republican model of the House of Russell was Venice; of their plebeian allies, Geneva. The Peers, to reduce the power of the Crown, now supported by the great majority of the nation, called in the aid of the Puritans, and to obtain the aid of the Puritans attacked the Church: the Puritans, to insure the destruction of the religious establishment, allied themselves with the Peers in their assault upon the King, whose office, apart from the ecclesiastical polity, they were inclined to respect, and even to reverence. The Puritans, headed by the Peers, formed a small minority of the nation, but at the same time a party formidable from their leaders and their organisation, for the Non-conformists abounded in the metropolis, and were chiefly resident in towns. Their cry was, " Civil and Religious Freedom "—that is, a Doge and no Bishops: advocating the liberty of the subject, the Peers would have established an oligarchy; upholding toleration, the Puritans aimed at supremacy. This is the origin of the Whig party in our country.

CHAPTER XXIX

Why the Advocacy of Divine Right, Non-Resistance, and Passive
Obedience by the Tories in the Reign of George the First were
Evidences of the Democratic Character of the Party—The
Whigs an Oligarchical Faction—The Tories a National Party
—Why the Whigs are, ever have been, and ever must be,
Odious to the English Nation—Why the Whigs are Hostile to
the Establishments of the Country.

THE mass of the nation still smarting under the seques-
trations and imprisonments of Parliamentary committees,
and loathing the recollection of the fanaticism and the
hypocrisy of the Roundhead apostles of the tub, clung
to the national institutions. The clergy, jealous of the
Non-conformists, and fearful of another deprivation,
exaggerated the power and character of the Crown, in
which they recognised their only safeguard. Hence
Divine right and passive obedience resounded from our
Protestant pulpits, echoed with enthusiasm by a free
and spirited people, who acknowledged in these phrases
only a determination to maintain the mild authority of
their King and of their Church. This is the origin of the
Tory party in our country.

On the one hand civil and religious liberty; on the
other, Divine right and passive obedience; both mere
phrases, both the sheer cries of a party, both the mysti-
fying pretexts that concealed a pregnant cause. The
avowed upholders of Divine right and passive obedience,
headed by the national clergy that promulgated these
doctrines, were the first to expel the Sovereign who aimed
at their rights and liberties; the avowed advocates of
civil and religious freedom, when they finally obtained
power, hazarded a blow at the only foundation of freedom,
the equality of civil rights, " swamped " the House of
Commons by the Septennial Act, and nearly concentrated
the whole powers of the State in the House of Lords by
the Peerage Bill.

It was the intention of the Whigs to have raised the Prince of Orange to the throne by the aid of a cabal. By this means the Sovereign would have been in their power, and they could have realised the object at which they had been long aiming. The insurrection of the Tories or the national party against James frustrated this project: the movement became national, and the settlement, instead of being factious, was patriotic. The powerful capacity of William the Third was not content with the limited authority destined for him: he encouraged the Tories, he balanced parties, and he maintained his throne with all the artifices of a practised politician. The reign of Anne, a Stuart, yet strictly Protestant and eminently prosperous, broke up in a great degree the strong lines of political demarcation, and occasioned the blending of parties. In spite of the Act of Settlement, the whole nation was prepared for the restoration of the ancient line; Whigs and Tories alike corresponded with St. Germains, and served together in the same administration at home. So weak was the tie of party in this reign, that it was not then considered a point of political honour to resign your post on a change of administration which substituted a Prime Minister of different opinions to your own, and to those through whose influence you had yourself acceded to office.

The Whigs secured the Hanoverian succession by a *coup d'état*. But when the nation had recovered from its surprise, the rage of parties increased to a degree unprecedented in our history, and that formal and organised division of public men occurred which has ever since been observed in the world of politics. The dislike of the Tories to the new dynasty was, if possible, aggravated by the conviction of the impolicy of recalling the old. The truly Protestant spirit of England forbade such a recourse. The House of Brunswick was supported by the great Whig families, the Non-conformists, and what was then for the first time called " the money interest," the fungus spawn of public loans, who began to elbow the country gentlemen, and beat them out of the representation of their boroughs by the long purses of a Plutocracy. The rest of the nation—that is to say, nine-tenths of the people of England—formed the Tory party, the landed proprietors and peasantry of the kingdom, headed by a spirited and popular Church, and looking to the kingly power in the abstract, though not to the reigning King, as their only protection from an impending oligarchy. The Whig party has ever been odious to the English people, and, in spite of all their devices and combinations, it may ever be observed that, in the long-run, the English nation declares against them. Even now, after their recent and most comprehensive *coup d'état*, they are only maintained in power by the votes of the Irish and the Scotch members.

CHAPTER XXX

Probable Consequences of Whiggism, and Degrading Effects of Centralisation—Democratic Character of Toryism developed —Why Parties sometimes change their Names and Cries.

THE reason of this is that the Whigs are an anti-national party. In order to accomplish their object of establishing an oligarchical republic, and of concentrating the government of the State in the hands of a few great families, the Whigs are compelled to declare war against all those great national institutions the power and influence of which present obstacles to the fulfilment of their purpose. It is these institutions which make us a nation. Without our Crown, our Church, our Universities, our great municipal and commercial Corporations, our Magistracy, and its dependent scheme of provincial polity, the inhabitants of England, instead of being a nation, would present only a mass of individuals governed by a metropolis, whence an arbitrary senate would issue the stern decrees of its harsh and heartless despotism. A class

of the subjects, indeed, might still possess the fruitless
privilege of electing its representatives in Parliament,
but without any machinery to foster public spirit and
maintain popular power, the whole land a prey to the most
degrading equality, the equality that levels, not the
equality that elevates, we should soon see these mock
representatives the mere nominees of a Præfect, and the
very first to tamper with our privileges and barter away
our freedom. In such a state of society, a state of society
which France has accomplished, and to which the Whigs
are hurrying us, no public avenues to wealth and honour
would subsist save through the Government. To that
government all the ambition and aspirations, all the
talent and the energy of the subject, would be devoted;
and from the harsh seat of the provincial governor, to
the vile office of the provincial spy, every place would be
filled by the ablest and most unprincipled of a corrupted
people.

The Tory party in this country is the national party;
it is the really democratic party of England. It supports
the institutions of the country because they have been
established for the common good, and because they secure
the equality of civil rights, without which, whatever
may be its name, no government can be free, and based
upon which principle every government, however it
may be styled, is in fact a Democracy. The Whig
leaders at the commencement of the last century,
men of consummate ability and great experience in
affairs, were not blind to the advantage which might
be obtained by enlarging on the apparent unpopular
character of Tory tenets. In the reign of George the
First, both parties in their eagerness had recourse to
their old cries, without reflecting that the circumstances
of their respective positions had considerably changed;
that the advocates of enlarged and comprehensive freedom were now attempting to establish an oligarchy on
the ruins of the national institutions, and that the votaries
of Divine right and passive obedience were prepared to

rebel against the Sovereign whose authority, by the original Act of Settlement, they themselves had mainly contributed to establish. However inconsistent might be the practice and the professions of the respective parties, it was obvious that, in the mutual misrepresentations, the Whigs had the advantage. An oligarchy sought to establish itself by the plea of public freedom; a nation struggled to maintain its rights on the principles of arbitrary power. This was, indeed, a false position; yet so clear-sighted was the people of England, and so apt to distinguish their cause from their pretext, that its inconvenience was for a long time unfelt, and in the preceding reign the nation had sympathised with the triumph of Sacheverell, and ridiculed the false pretensions of the Whigs to the advocacy and trusteeship of the popular cause.

When, however, the Tory party—that is, the English nation—had renounced all hope or wish for the restoration of their native Sovereigns; when, in their Protestant feeling, they had taught themselves to look upon the establishment of the Hanoverian succession as indispensable to the maintenance of their liberties, and had thus authorised and ratified, without redress or appeal, the very political opinions which they had hitherto opposed, the inconvenience became more apparent. There are periods when the titles and watchwords of political parties become obsolete; and when, by adhering to an ancient and accustomed cry, a party often appears to profess opinions less popular than it really practises, and yields a proportionate advantage to its more dexterous competitor. In times of great political change and rapid political transition, it will generally be observed that political parties find it convenient to rebaptise themselves. Thus, in the present day, Whigs have become Reformers, and Tories Conservatives. In the early part of the last century, the Tory party required a similar reorganisation to that which it has lately undergone; and as it is in the nature of human affairs that the in-

15

dividual that is required shall not long be wanting, so, in the season of which I am treating, arose a man remarkable in an illustrious age, who, with the splendour of an organising genius, settled the confused and discordant materials of English faction, and reduced them into a clear and systematic order. This was Lord Bolingbroke.

CHAPTER XXXI

Character of Lord Bolingbroke—His Influence on our History— Reorganises the Tory Party—Founder of Modern Toryism— The Whigs pursuing the Same Machinations now as under George the First.

GIFTED with that fiery imagination, the teeming fertility of whose inventive resources is as necessary to a great statesman or a great general as to a great poet; the ablest writer and the most accomplished orator of his age, that rare union that in a country of free Parliaments and a free press insures to its possessor the privilege of exercising a constant influence over the mind of his country, that rare union that has rendered Burke so memorable; blending with that intuitive knowledge of his race, which creative minds alone enjoy, all the wisdom which can be derived from literature, and a comprehensive experience of human affairs—no one was better qualified to be the Minister of a free and powerful nation than Henry St. John; and Destiny at first appeared to combine with Nature in the elevation of his fortunes. Opposed to the Whigs from principle, for an oligarchy is hostile to genius, and recoiling from the Tory tenets, which his unprejudiced and vigorous mind taught him at the same time to dread and to contemn, Lord Bolingbroke, at the outset of his career, incurred the common-place imputation of insincerity and inconsistency, because, in an age of unsettled parties with professions contradictory of their conduct, he maintained that vigilant and meditative independence which is the privilege of an original and

determined spirit. It is probable that in the earlier
years of his career he meditated over the formation of
a new party, that dream of youthful ambition in a perplexed and discordant age, but destined in English
politics to be never more substantial than a vision. More
experienced in political life, he became aware that he
had only to choose between the Whigs and the Tories,
and his sagacious intellect, not satisfied with the superficial character of these celebrated divisions, penetrated
their interior and essential qualities, and discovered, in
spite of all the affectation of popular sympathy on one
side, and of admiration of arbitrary power on the other,
that this choice was in fact a choice between oligarchy
and democracy. From the moment that Lord Bolingbroke, in becoming a Tory, embraced the national cause,
he devoted himself absolutely to his party : all the energies
of his Protean mind were lavished in their service; and
although the ignoble prudence of the Whig Minister
restrained him from advocating the cause of the nation
in the senate, it was his inspiring pen that made Walpole
tremble in the recesses of the Treasury, and in a series
of writings, unequalled in our literature for their spirited
patriotism, their just and profound views, and the golden
eloquence in which they are expressed, eradicated from
Toryism all those absurd and odious doctrines which
Toryism had adventitiously adopted, clearly developed
its essential and permanent character, discarded *jure
divino*, demolished passive obedience, threw to the winds
the doctrine of non-resistance, placed the abolition of
James and the accession of George on their right basis,
and in the complete reorganisation of the public mind
laid the foundation for the future accession of the Tory
party to power, and to that popular and triumphant
career which must ever await the policy of an administration inspired by the spirit of our free and ancient institutions.

Upwards of a century has elapsed since the Whigs,
by a series of *coups d'état*, attempted to transform the

English Constitution into an oligarchy. George the Third routed the Whigs; but had their India Bill been more fortunate than their Peerage Bill, all the energy of that spirited Sovereign would have been fruitless. Stung to the quick by their long and merited exclusion from power, the Whigs are now playing the same great game which was partially successful at the commencement of the last century. They have again formed a close and open alliance with the Dissenters, and again declared war against the national institutions. Instead of " swamping " the Tory House of Commons by a Septennial Act, they have moulded it to their use and fancy by a reconstruction which has secured a preponderating influence to their sectarian allies: instead of restricting the royal prerogative in the creation of Peers, they have counselled its prodigal exercise; but before they had only to confirm their power in the House of Lords, now they have to create their power. They boast that they hold the King in *duresse*, and probably their boast is not ill-founded, but let us hope that our gracious Sovereign may take warning from the first of his house that ruled these realms, and follow the example of George the Third rather than George the First. The House of Commons remodelled, the House of Lords menaced, the King unconstitutionally controlled, the Church is next attacked, then the Corporations, and they do not conceal that the Magistracy is to be the next victim: and the nation is thus mangled and torn to pieces, its most sacred feelings outraged, its most important interests destroyed, by a miserable minority arrogating to themselves the bewildering title of " the People," and achieving all this misery and misfortune, all this havoc and degradation, in the sacred name of liberty, and under the impudent pretence of advancing the great cause of popular amelioration, and securing the common good and general happiness. My Lord, the Whigs invoke " the People "; let us appeal to the nation.

Mark these friends of " the People " installed in power.

What are their great measures ?   The Poor Law Bill and
the projected disfranchisement of all the freemen of
England.   Is this their service to the " People "?   Are
these their measures of popular amelioration ?   Is this
their scheme to secure the happiness and increase the
power of " the People "?   Who does not in an instant
detect that " the People " of the Whigs is that part of
the constituency or Commons of England who yield
them the advantage of their suffrages ?   Now, at the last
General Election, warm as was the contest, there were not
more—I doubt whether as many—than one hundred and
fifty thousand votes polled in favour of the Whigs.   And
this, too, after they had remodelled the third estate with
a mere view to the consolidation of their own interest.
So, then, " the People " of the Whigs is about one hundred
and fifty thousand persons, and of these, too, the great
majority sectarians, a class necessarily hostile to our
Constitution, and long excluded by the nation from the
exercise of political power for that very reason.   It might
have been very odious, it might have been very illiberal,
it might have been very unwise, to exclude the Dissenters
from the exercise of political power; but is it less odious,
is it more liberal, is it wiser, to carry on the government
of the State by the aid of the Dissenters alone ?

CHAPTER XXXII

Three Points to which the Tories must at the Present Moment
    apply themselves—Tories vindicated from the Charge of
    Corruption, Bigotry, and Hostility to Improvement—Causes
    and Consequences of Political Conciliation.

IF the Whigs at this moment be pursuing the same
desperate and determined policy that they prosecuted
so vigorously a century back, it will be well for their rivals
to adopt the same cautious yet energetic system of
conduct which, developed at the same period by the
genius of a Bolingbroke, led in due season to the ad-

222 VINDICATION OF ENGLISH CONSTITUTION [1835

ministration of a Pitt. In the conduct of the Tory party
at this moment, it appears to me that there are three
points to the furtherance of which we should principally
apply ourselves: First, that the real character and nature
of Toryism should be generally and clearly comprehended:
secondly, that Toryism should be divested of all those
qualities which are adventitious and not essential, and
which, having been produced by that course of circumstances which are constantly changing, become in time
obsolete, inconvenient, and by the dexterous misrepresentation of our opponents even odious: thirdly, that the
efficient organisation of the party should be secured and
maintained.

The necessity of the third point has already been
anticipated by the party; but they have blundered in the
second, and totally neglected the first.

Toryism, or the policy of the Tories, being the proposed
or practised embodification, as the case may be, of the
national will and character, it follows that Toryism must
occasionally represent and reflect the passions and prejudices of the nation, as well as its purer energies and its
more enlarged and philosophic views. In a perilous age
of war and revolution, throughout the most terrible
struggle of modern history, the destiny of England was
regulated by the Tories. They carried us through the
sharp and flaming ordeal to transcendent triumph and
unparalleled prosperity. A factious and anti-national
Opposition, who predicted our discomfiture in every
engagement, and exaggerated and extolled on every
occasion the power and pre-eminence of our foe, raised
a cry of corruption against the Tories during this mighty
contest because, in the creation of our colonial empire,
immense establishments were necessarily raised, the
details of which in the desperate heat of war could not
be severely scanned; raised a cry of enmity to improvement against the Tories during this mighty contest,
because they opposed any examination or remodelling
of our ancient institutions and domestic polity at a time

when all the attention and energies of the nation and its
rulers should be devoted to their foreign enemy, the
most terrible for his power, his resources, his talents, and
his activity, which England had ever encountered; raised
a cry of narrow-minded bigotry and hostility to civil and
religious liberty against the Tories during this mighty
contest, because at such a moment they refused to sanction
extensive alterations in the Constitution of the country,
and declined the responsibility of entrusting, at a season
ill-suited for experiments, new classes of their fellow-
subjects with the exercise of political power. Corruption, bigotry, hostility to all improvement—these were
the false cries raised by the Whigs against the national
party during the immortal struggle between Toryism and
Napoleon. Yet were the Tories advocates of corruption
when they introduced a Bill into the House of Commons
for the banishment of all placemen from that assembly,
and denounced Walpole ? Were the Tories hostile to
civil and religious liberty when they crushed the Papacy,
opposed a standing army, cherished free elections, upheld
short Parliaments ? Were the Tories inimical to national
improvement when, under Pitt, they first applied philosophy to commerce, and science to finance; when, under
their auspices, the most severe retrenchment was practised
in every department of the public expenditure; when a
Bill for the Commutation of Tithes was not only planned,
but printed; and when nothing but the violence of the
French Revolution prevented the adoption of a matured
scheme of Ecclesiastical Reform, which would not have
left our revolutionary oligarchs a single pretext to veil
their present plundering purpose ? Why ! the cry of
Parliamentary Reform was first raised by a Tory Minister,
struggling against the bigoted and corrupt authority of
the Whig oligarchy; and it was not until the united efforts
of the Sovereign, the Minister, and the nation, succeeded
in piercing the serried ranks of the anti-national faction,
that the Whigs, alarmed at the Tories beginning, by their
acquisitions, to neutralise the only ill effects of the close

borough system, borrowed the watchword of their patriotic opponents, became friends of "the People" and Parliamentary Reformers. Corruption, bigotry, hostility to improvement, may be but other names for the just and decent influence of a vigorous government, a determination to uphold the religious establishment of the country, and a resolution to oppose the crude and indigested schemes of adventurous charlatans. However this may be, it is sufficient for me to show that the qualities popularly associated with these titles are not peculiar to Toryism, that they form no essential portion of that national policy, and that when from the course of circumstances they have been temporarily adopted by the Tories in power, it has been in deference to the national voice, of which Toryism is the echo; for we must not forget that the war, and all its concomitant expenditure, was heartily sanctioned by the English nation, and that that sagacious community discountenanced with an almost unanimous expression any experimental tampering with our civil or religious establishments, or the general scheme of our domestic polity, during the war of the Revolution.

When that war terminated, the alleged advocates of "corruption" pursued so vigorous a system of retrenchment that, when their rivals entered office, pledged to such marvels of financial regeneration, they were absolutely baffled to surpass their misrepresented predecessors; the opposers of "national improvement" reformed our criminal code, revised our currency, remodelled our commercial system; the enemies of civil and religious freedom relieved the Dissenters, and emancipated the Papists. Far from being corrupt, far from cherishing abuses, far from withstanding improvement and upholding a system of exclusive bigotry, we know now, and we know it too well, that Toryism had unwisely weakened the indispensable influence of government, that it indulged in a dangerous liberality, in a fallacious conciliation, in fantastic empiricism and unnecessary concession.

But this was not the fault of the Tory leaders; it was the fault of the party—of Toryism—of the nation. The triumph of the national party at the Peace of Paris over their anti-English opponents was so complete that they fancied, in the fulness of their pride, that all future competition was impossible, so the Tories became merciful and condescendingly lenient. Conciliation was the national motto from the Parliament to the Vestry, and Conciliation conducted us in due time to a Revolution. The supineness of the nation forced the Tory leaders to yield much of which they disapproved. At length the reconstruction of the third estate was demanded, and of such a change the Tory leaders would not incur the responsibility. The old Whig party took advantage of the dissensions which it had deeply sown and sedulously watched, and appeared again upon the public stage to play the old game of a century back, with their mouths full of the People, Reform, and Liberty, and their portfolios bursting with oligarchical *coups d'état*.

The English nation has now recovered its senses, and Toryism has resumed its old healthy complexion. The social power of a national party can never be destroyed, but a State trick may terribly curtail its political power. So it is with the Tories. I do not think there ever was a period in our history when the English nation was so intensely Tory in feeling as at the present moment; but the Reform Act has placed the power of the country in the hands of a small body of persons hostile to the nation, and therefore there is no due proportion between the social and the political power of the national party.

CHAPTER XXXIII

Vindication of the Recent Policy of Sir Robert Peel and his
Cabinet—The Political Power of the Tories distinguished
from their Social Power—The Political Power maintained at
Present by a Series of Great Democratic Measures.

IF, in confirmation of the argument which I have been
pursuing, I appeal to the measures brought forward by
Sir Robert Peel and the Cabinet, in which your Lordship
held the Great Seal of England, as evidence that the
Tories are not opposed to measures of political amelioration, I shall perhaps be met with that famous dilemma
of insincerity or apostacy which was urged during the
last General Election on the Whig hustings, with an air
of irrefutable triumph, which, had it been better grounded,
had been less amusing. I will grant that Sir Robert
Peel and his colleagues had previously resisted the
measures which they then proposed. But in the interval
the third estate of the realm had been reconstructed, and
a preponderating influence had been given to a small class
who would not support any Ministry unprepared to
carry such measures. If once the Tories admitted that
it was impossible for them to propose the adoption of
these measures they simultaneously admitted that they
could never again exercise power; they conceded to the
Whigs a monopoly of power, under the specious title of
a monopoly of Reform; and the oligarchy against which
we had so long struggled would finally have been established. Was this the duty of Sir Robert Peel and his
colleagues ? If they had held it to be such, the nation
would have rejected them for its leaders. The nation,
struggling with a sect, menaced by an insolent minority
of its members, recognised the absolute necessity of such
concessions on the part of its leaders as would deprive this
hostile and privileged minority of every just or plausible
ground of opposition to the national will. The determination of Sir Robert Peel and his colleagues to carry

these measures has already shaken the oligarchy to its centre; it has forced it, only four years after having reconstructed the third estate for its purposes, to rely upon the treasonable support of a foreign priesthood; and it has prepared the way for the regeneration of the national character. This great deed therefore, instead of being an act of insincerity or apostacy, was conceived in good faith, and in perfect harmony with the previous policy of the party: it was at the same time indispensable, and urged alike by the national voice and the national interests, and history will record it as the conduct of patriotic wisdom.

I think, my Lord, that I have now shown how unjust are those, and how liable to error, who form their opinion of Toryism from those accidental qualities which are inseparable from all political parties that have been long in power, and have exercised that prolonged authority under circumstances of extreme difficulty and danger. And it is curious to observe that, so difficult is it to destroy the original character and eradicate the first principles of human affairs, those very members of the Tory party who were loudest in upbraiding the Whig Reform Act as a democratic measure were simultaneously, and have ever since been, urging and prosecuting measures infinitely more democratic than that cunning oligarchical device. However irresistible may be the social power of the Tory party, their political power, since 1831, has only been preserved and maintained by a series of democratic measures of the greatest importance and most comprehensive character. No sooner was the passing of the Whig Reform Act inevitable than the Tories introduced a clause into it which added many thousand members to the estate of the Commons. No sooner was the Whig Reform Act passed, and circumstances had proved that, with all their machinations, the oligarchy was not yet secure, than the Whigs, under the pretence of reforming the corporations, attempted to compensate themselves for the democratic increase of the third estate, through the Chandos clause, by the political destruction of all the freemen of England; but the Tories again stepped in to the rescue of the nation from the oligarchy, and now preserved the rights of eighty thousand members of the third estate. And not content with adding many thousands to its numbers, and preserving eighty thousand, the Tories, ever since the passing of the oligarchical Reform Act of the Whigs, have organised societies throughout the country for the great democratic purpose of increasing to the utmost possible extent the numbers of the third estate of the realm. The clause of Lord Chandos, your Lordship's triumphant defence of the freemen of England, and the last Registration, are three great democratic movements, and quite in keeping with the original and genuine character of Toryism.

CHAPTER XXXIV

General View of the English Constitution—Shown to be a Complete Democracy—English and French Equality contrasted — Conclusion.

IF we take a superficial view of the nature of the English Constitution, we shall perceive that the government of the country is carried on by a King and two limited orders of his subjects : but if we indulge in a more profound and comprehensive survey—if we examine not only the political Constitution, but the political condition of the country—we shall in truth discover that the state of our society is that of a complete democracy, headed by an hereditary chief, the executive and legislative functions performed by two privileged classes of the community, but the whole body of the nation entitled, if duly qualified, to participate in the exercise of those functions, and constantly participating in them.

The basis of English society is Equality. But here let us distinguish. There are two kinds of equality: there is the equality that levels and destroys, and the equality that elevates and creates. It is this last, this sublime, this celestial equality, that animates the laws of England. The principle of the first equality, base, terrestrial, Gallic, and grovelling, is that no one should be privileged; the principle of English equality is that everyone should be privileged. Thus the meanest subject of our King is born to great and important privileges; an Englishman, however humble may be his birth, whether he be doomed to the plough or destined to the loom, is born to the noblest of all inheritances, the equality of civil rights; he is born to freedom, he is born to justice, and he is born to property. There is no station to which he may not aspire; there is no master whom he is obliged to serve; there is no magistrate who dares imprison him against the law; and the soil on which he labours must supply him with an honest and decorous maintenance. These are rights and privileges as valuable as King, Lords, and Commons; and it is only a nation thus schooled and cradled in the principles and practice of freedom which, indeed, could maintain such institutions. Thus the English in politics are as the old Hebrews in religion, " a favoured and peculiar people." As Equality is the basis, so Gradation is the superstructure; and the English nation is essentially a nation of classes, but not of castes. Hence that admirable order, which is the characteristic of our society; for in England every man knows or finds his place; the law has supplied every man with a position, and nature has a liberal charter to amend the arrangement of the law. Our equality is the safety-valve of tumultuous spirits; our gradation the security of the humble and the meek. The latter take refuge in their order; the former seek relief in emancipating themselves from its rank. English equality calls upon the subject to aspire; French equality summons him to abase himself. In England the subject is invited to become an object of admiration or respect; in France he is warned lest he become an object of envy or of ridicule. The law of

England has invested the subject with equality in order that, if entitled to eminence, he should rise superior to the mass. The law of France has invested the subject with equality, on condition that he prevent the elevation of his fellow. English equality blends every man's ambition with the perpetuity of the State; French equality, which has reduced the subject into a mere individual, has degraded the State into a mere society. English equality governs the subject by the united and mingled influences of reason and imagination; French equality, having rejected imagination and aspiring to reason, has, in reality, only resolved itself into a barren fantasy. The Constitution of England is founded not only on a profound knowledge of human nature, but of human nature in England; the political scheme of France originates not only in a profound ignorance of human nature in general, but of French human nature in particular; thus in England, however vast and violent may be our revolutions, the Constitution ever becomes more firm and vigorous, while in France a riot oversets the government, and after half a century of political experiments one of the most intellectual of human races has succeeded in losing every attribute of a nation, and has sought refuge from anarchy in a despotism without lustre, which contradicts all its theories and violates all the principles for which it has ever affected to struggle.

The English nation, to obtain the convenience of monarchy, have established a popular throne, and, to enjoy the security of aristocracy, have invested certain orders of their fellow-subjects with legislative functions : but these estates, however highly privileged, are invested with no quality of exclusion; and the Peers and the Commons of England are the trustees of the nation, not its masters. The country where the legislative and even the executive office may be constitutionally obtained by every subject of the land is a democracy, and a democracy of the noblest character. If neither ancient ages nor the more recent experience of our newer time can supply

us with a parallel instance of a free government, founded
on the broadest basis of popular rights, yet combining
with democratic liberty aristocratic security and monarchical convenience; if the refined spirit of Greece, if the
great Roman soul, if the brilliant genius of feodal Italy,
alike failed in realising this great result, let us cling with
increased devotion to the matchless creation of our
ancestors, and honour with still deeper feelings of gratitude and veneration the English Constitution. That
Constitution, my Lord, established civil equality in a
rude age, and anticipated by centuries, in its beneficent
practice, the sublime theories of modern philosophy:
having made us equal, it has kept us free. If it have
united equality with freedom, so also has it connected
freedom with glory. It has established an Empire which
combines the durability of Rome with the adventure of
Carthage. It has at the same time secured us the most
skilful agriculture, the most extended commerce, the
most ingenious manufactures, victorious armies, and invincible fleets. Nor has the intellectual might of England,
under its fostering auspices, been less distinguished than
its imperial spirit, its manly heart, or its national energy.
The authors of England have formed the mind of Europe,
and stamped the breathing impression of their genius
on the vigorous character of a new world. Under that
Constitution the administration of justice has become so
pure that its exercise has realised the dreams of some
Utopian romance. That Constitution has struggled
successfully with the Papacy, and finally, and for the first
time, proved the compatibility of sectarian toleration
and national orthodoxy. It has made private ambition
conducive to public welfare, it has baffled the machinations
of factions and of parties, and when those more violent
convulsions have arisen, from whose periodic visitations
no human institutions can be exempt, the English Constitution has survived the moral earthquake, and out-
lived the mental hurricane, and been sedulous that the
natural course of our prosperity should only be dis-

turbed, and not destroyed. Finally, it has secured for every man the career to which he is adapted, and the reward to which he is entitled; it has summoned your Lordship to preside over Courts and Parliaments, to maintain law by learning, and to recommend wisdom by eloquence: and it has secured to me, in common with every subject of this realm, a right the enjoyment of which I would not exchange even for

" The ermined stole,
The starry breast, and coroneted brow "

—the right of expressing my free thoughts to a free people.

THE LETTERS OF RUNNYMEDE

[THE LETTERS OF RUNNYMEDE, written while Disraeli was yet in the wilderness, appeared in the *Times* during the first half of 1836, and were republished anonymously in July, with the following lines on the title-page:

> " Neither for shame nor fear this mask he wore
> That like a vizor on the battle-field
> But shrouds a manly and a daring brow."

Disraeli's authorship of the letters was never acknowledged by him; doubtless as the years passed, and his knowledge of the men with whom he had dealt so unsparingly became more intimate, he regretted their publication. They were mainly a curious compost of abuse and panegyric—invective against political foes, adulation of political friends. But the Letters have an abiding reputation, and, like the *Morning Post* articles, to which they have a close kinship, they could not be omitted from a volume of his earlier political writings. They formed an integral portion of his campaign in behalf of Lord Lyndhurst against the Whigs.

It will be convenient, for the better understanding of the Letters, to give here the composition of the Ministry of the day:

Prime Minister	Viscount Melbourne.
Lord President of the Council	The Marquis of Lansdowne.
Lord Privy Seal	Viscount Duncannon.
Chancellor of the Exchequer	Mr. T. Spring Rice (afterwards Lord Monteagle).
Home Secretary	Lord John Russell.
Foreign Secretary	Viscount Palmerston.
Colonial Secretary	Lord Glenelg.
First Lord of the Admiralty	Lord Auckland; Lord Minto.
President of the Board of Control	Sir John Cam Hobhouse (afterwards Lord Broughton).

16

Secretary at War	Viscount Howick (afterwards Earl Grey).
Board of Trade	Mr. C. Poulett Thomson (afterwards Lord Sydenham).
Chancellor of the Duchy of Lancaster	Lord Holland.
Lord Chancellor	In Commission; afterwards Lord Cottenham.
Irish Secretary	Viscount Morpeth.

Sir John Campbell (afterwards Lord Campbell) was Attorney-General, and the Earl of Mulgrave (afterwards Marquis of Normanby) was Lord-Lieutenant of Ireland.]

DEDICATION:

TO THE RIGHT HONOURABLE

SIR ROBERT PEEL, BARONET, M.P.

SIR,—I have the honour to dedicate to you a volume illustrative of WHIGS and WHIGGISM. It has been my object to delineate within its pages not only the present characters and recent exploits of the most active of the partisans, but also the essential and permanent spirit of the party. It appeared to me that it might be advantageous to connect the criticism on the character of the hour with some researches into the factious idiosyncrasy of centuries. Political parties are not so inconsistent as the superficial imagine; and, in my opinion, the Whig of a century back does not differ so materially as some would represent from the Whig of the present day. I hope, therefore, that this volume may conduce, not only to the amusement, but to the instruction of my countrymen.

It is now, Sir, some six months past since I seized the occasion of addressing you another letter, written under very different auspices.[1] The session of Parliament was then about to commence; it is now about to close. These six months have not been uneventful in results. If they have not witnessed any legislative enactment eminently

[1] Letter V., January 26, 1836.

tending to our social welfare, they have developed much
political conduct for which our posterity may be grateful:
for this session, Sir, has at least been memorable for one
great event—an event not inferior, in my estimation, in
its beneficial influence on the fortunes of the country, to
Magna Charta itself—I mean the rally of the English
Constitution; I might use a stronger phrase, I might say
its triumph.[1]

And it has triumphed because it has become understood. The more its principles have been examined, the
more the intention of its various parts has been investi-
gated and its general scope comprehended, the more beneficent and profound has appeared the polity of our fathers.
The public mind of late has been cleared of a vast amount
of error in constitutional learning. Scarcely a hired
writer would have the front at this day to pretend that
a difference of opinion between the two Houses of Parliament is a collision between the Peers and the People.
That phrase " the People " is a little better comprehended
now than it used to be; it will not serve for the stalking
horse of faction as it did. We know very well that the
House of Commons is not the House of " the People ";
we know very well that " the People " is a body not intelligible in a political sense; we know very well that the
Lords and the Commons are both sections of the Nation,
and both alike and equally representative of that great
community. And we know very well that if the contrary
propositions to all these were maintained, the government of this English Empire might, at this moment, be
the pastime and plunder of some score of Irish adventurers.

When, Sir, you quitted Drayton in February, the vagabond delegate of a foreign priesthood[2] was stirring up
rebellion against the Peers of England, with the implied,
if not the definite, sanction of His Majesty's Ministers.
Where is that hired disturber now ? Like base coin de-

---

[1] Compare passage in final article of the *Morning Post* series,
p. 107.   [2] O'Connell.

tected by the very consequences of its currency, and
finally nailed against the counter it has deceived, so this
bad politician, like a bad shilling, has worn off his edge
by his very restlessness. Parliament met, and the King's
Ministers exhibited with a flourish their emblazoned catalogue of oligarchical *coups-d'état*, by which they were to
entrench themselves in power under the plea of amelio-
rating our society. Not one of these measures has been
carried. Yet we were told that their success was certain,
and by a simple process—by the close and incontestable
union between all true reformers. The union between all
true reformers has terminated in the mutiny of Downing
Street.

I believe that I have commemorated in this volume
that celebrated harangue, which the Chancellor of the
Exchequer, at the commencement of the session, addressed at a dinner to his constituents.[1] You may perhaps
remember, Sir, the glowing promises of that Right
Honourable Gentleman: they seemed almost to announce
the advent of a political millennium. "First and foremost," announced the Right Honourable Chancellor,
"we shall proceed in our great work of the reform of the
Court of Equity "—the *opus magnum* of the gifted Cottenham ! It seems the course of nature was reversed
here, and the butterfly turned into a grub. "Our earnest
attention will then be directed," quoth Mr. Rice, "to
the entire and complete relief of our Dissenting brethren
and fellow-subjects." How liberal, how condescending,
and how sincere ! The Dissenters are absolutely our
fellow-subjects. None but a Whig, a statesman almost
eructating with the plenary inspiration of the spirit of the
age, could have been capable of making so philosophical
an admission. In the meantime six months have passed,
and nothing has been done for our unhappy "fellow-
subjects," while the Dissenting organs denounce even the
projected alleviations as a miserable insult. To justice
to Ireland Mr. Rice of course was pledged, and most

[1] Mr. Spring Rice's speech at Cambridge.

determined to obtain it; but his Bills have been dishonoured nevertheless. And the settlement of the Irish
Tithe and the Reform of the Irish Corporations are about
as much advanced by this great Whig Government as the
relief of the Dissenters and the reform of the Court of
Chancery. What have they done then ? What pledge
have they redeemed ? The Ecclesiastical Courts remain
unpurged. Even the Stamp Act, through the medium
of which the Whigs, as usual, have levelled a blow at the
liberty of the press, has not passed yet, and in its present
inquisitorial form can never become a law. What then,
I repeat, have they done ? They promised indeed to
break open the prisons like Jack Cade; but as yet the
grates are barred; the pensions are still paid, and the
soldiers still flogged. Oh, ye Scribes of the Treasury
and Pharisees of Downing Street !

Supported in the House of Lords by a body inferior in
number to the Peers created by the Whigs during the
last five years, upheld in the House of Commons by a
majority of twenty-six, Lord Melbourne still clings to his
mulish and ungenerative position of place without
power; and with a degree of modest frankness and constitutional propriety equally admirable pledges himself
before his country, that, as long as he is supported by a
majority of the House of Commons, he will remain
Minister.[1] I apprehend the ratification of a Ministry is
as necessary by one House of Parliament as by the other;
but I stop not to discuss this. The choice of Ministers
was once entrusted to a different authority than that of
either Lords or Commons.

But this is an old almanack; and I leave Lord Viscount
Melbourne to shake its dust off at his next interview with
his projected Doge of Windsor.

RUNNYMEDE.

July 27, 1836.

---

[1] "I conscientiously believe," Lord Melbourne declared, "that
the well-being of the country requires that I should hold my
present office—and hold it I will till I am constitutionally removed
from it."

LETTER I

To Viscount Melbourne

My Lord,—The Marquis of Halifax[1] was wont to say of his Royal Master, that, " after all, his favourite Sultana Queen was sauntering." It is, perhaps, hopeless that your Lordship should rouse yourself from the embraces of that Siren Desidia to whose fatal influence you are not less a slave than our second Charles, and that you should cease to saunter over the destinies of a nation, and lounge away the glory of an empire. Yet the swift shadows of coming events are assuredly sufficiently dark and ominous to startle from its indolence even

" The sleekest swine in Epicurus' sty." [2]

When I recall to my bewildered memory the perplexing circumstance that William Lamb is Prime Minister of England, it seems to me that I recollect with labour the crowning incident of some grotesque dream, or that in some pastime of the season you have drawn for the amusement of a nation a temporary character, ludicrously appropriate only from the total want of connection and fitness between the festive part and the individual by whom it is sustained. Previous to the passing of the famous Act of 1832, for the amendment of popular representation, your reputation, I believe, principally depended upon your talent for prologue writing. No one was held to introduce with more grace and spirit the performances of an amateur society. With the exception of an annual oration against Parliamentary reform, your career in the House of Commons was never remarkably distinguished. Your Cabinet, indeed, appears to have been constructed from the materials of your old dramatic company. The

---

[1] Sir George Savile, Marquis of Halifax (1633–1695), a prominent figure in the reign of Charles the Second.

[2] " Me pinguem et nitidum bene curata cute vises . . . Epicuri de grege porcum " (Horace, "Epistles," Book I., iv. 15, 16).

domestic policy of the country is entrusted to the celebrated author of " Don Carlos "; the Fletcher of this
Beaumont, the author of the " Siege of Constantinople "[1]
(an idea apparently borrowed from your Russian allies),
is the guardian of the lives and properties of the Irish
clergy, under the charitable supervision of that " first
tragedy man," the Lord of Mulgrave; Lord Glenelg admirably personifies a sleepy audience; while your Chancellor of the Exchequer beats Mr. Power;[2] and your Secretary for Foreign Affairs, in his mimetic sympathy with
French manners and intimate acquaintance with French
character, is scarcely inferior to the late ingenious Charles
Mathews. That general adapter from the Spanish, Lord
Holland, gives you all the advantage, in the affairs of the
Peninsula, of his early studies of Lope de Vega,[3] and,
indeed, with his skilful assistance you appear, by all
accounts, to have woven a plot absurd and complicated
enough even for the grave humour of Madrid or the gay
fancy of Seville. For yourself is still reserved a monopoly
of your peculiar talent, and doubtless on February 4 you
will open your House with an introductory composition
worthy of your previous reputation.

I remember some years ago listening to one of these
elegant productions from the practised pen of the present
Prime Minister of Great Britain, if not of Ireland. I
think it was on that occasion that you enunciated to your
audience the great moral discovery that the characteristic of the public mind of the present day was

" A taste for evil."

Our taste for evil does not seem to be on the wane, since
it has permitted this great empire to be governed by the
Whigs, and has induced even those Whigs to be governed

[1] Viscount Morpeth (afterwards seventh Earl of Carlisle),
author of " The Last of the Greeks, or the Fall of Constantinople,"
1828.

[2] Tyrone Power.

[3] Lord Holland published in 1806 anonymously, and in 1817
over his own name, a short Life of Lope Felix de Vega Carpio;
and in 1807 " Three Comedies from the Spanish."

by an Irish rebel. Your prologue, my Lord, was quite prophetic.

If your Royal Master's speech at the opening of his Parliament may share its inspirations, it will tell to the people of England some terrible truths.

It will announce, in the first place, that the policy of your theatrical Cabinet has at length succeeded in dividing the people of England into two hostile camps, in which numbers are arrayed against property, ignorance against knowledge, and sects against institutions.

It will announce to us that your theatrical Cabinet has also been not less fortunate in maturing the passive resistance of the enemy in Ireland into active hostility, and that you have obtained the civil war from which the Duke of Wellington shrank, without acquiring the political security which might have been its consequence.

It will announce to us that in foreign affairs you and your company have finally succeeded in destroying all our old alliances without substituting any new ones; and that, after having sacrificed every principle of British policy to secure an intimate alliance with France, the Cabinet of the Tuileries has even had the airy audacity to refuse its co-operation in that very treaty in which its promises alone involved you; and that, while the British Minister can with extreme difficulty obtain an audience at St. Petersburg, the Ambassador of France passes with a polite smile of gay recognition the luckless representative of William the Fourth, who is lounging in an ante-chamber in the enjoyment of an indolence which even your Lordship might envy.

It will announce to us that in our colonial empire the most important results may speedily be anticipated from the discreet selection of Lord Auckland[1] as a successor to our Clives and our Hastings; that the progressive improvement of the French in the manufacture of beetroot may compensate for the approaching destruction of our West Indian plantations; and that, although Canada

---

[1] Succeeded Lord William Bentinck as Governor-General of India.

is not yet independent, the final triumph of liberal principles, under the immediate patronage of the Government, may eventually console us for the loss of the glory of Chatham and the conquests of Wolfe.

At home or abroad, indeed, an agreeable prospect on every side surrounds you. Your Lordship may exclaim with Hannibal: " Behind us are the Alps, before us is Eridanus !" And who are your assistants to stem the profound and impetuous current of this awful futurity ? At an unconstitutional expenditure of four coronets,[1] which may some day figure as an article in an impeachment, the Whigs have at length obtained a Lord Chancellor as a lawyer not illustrious, as a statesman a nonentity. The seals of the principal office of the State are entrusted to an individual who, on the principle that good vinegar is the corruption of bad wine, has been metamorphosed from an incapable author into an eminent politician.[2] His brother Secretaries[3] remind me of two battered female sinners; one frivolous, the other exhausted; one taking refuge from conscious scorn in rouge and the affected giggle of fluttering folly, and the other in strong waters and devotion. Then Mr. Spring Rice waves a switch, which he would fain persuade you is a shillelagh; while the Rienzi of Westminster smiles with marvelling complacency at the strange chapter of accidents which has converted a man whose friends pelted George Lamb with a cabbage-stalk, into a main prop of William Lamb's Cabinet.

Some yet remain; the acute intelligence of Lansdowne, the polished mind of Thomson, Howick's calm maturity,[4] and the youthful energy of Holland.

[1] In a later letter the " expenditure " of coronets is reduced to three. Sir Christopher Pepys, Master of the Rolls, received the Great Seal, with the title of Earl of Cottenham; Bickersteth, with the title of Lord Langdale, succeeded him as Master of the Rolls; and Lady Campbell, wife of Sir John Campbell, Attorney-General, was made a peeress in her own right.

[2] Lord John Russell (see Introduction, p. 10).

[3] Lord Palmerston and Lord Glenelg.

[4] Mr. Poulett Thomson and Viscount Howick had just been admitted to the Cabinet.

And this is the Cabinet that controls the destinies of a far vaster population than owned the sway of Rome in the palmiest hour of its imperial fame ! Scarron[1] or Butler should celebrate its political freaks, and the shifting expedients of its ignoble statecraft. But while I watch you in your ludicrous councils, an awful shade rises from behind the chair of my Lord President. Slaves ! it is your master; it is Eblis[2] with Captain Rock's[3] bloody cap shadowing his atrocious countenance. In one hand he waves a torch, and in the other clutches a skull. He gazes on his victims with a leer of fiendish triumph. Contemptible as you are, it is this dark connection that involves your fate with even an epic dignity, and makes the impending story of your retributive fortunes assume almost a Dantesque sublimity.

January 18, 1836.

LETTER II

To Sir John Campbell [4]

Sir,—I have always been of opinion—an opinion I imbibed early in life from great authorities—that the Attorney and Solicitor-General were not more the guardians of the honour and the interests of the Crown than of the honour and the interests of the Bar. It appears to me that you have failed in your duty as representative of this once illustrious body, and therefore it is that I address to you this letter.

Although your political opponent, I trust I am not

[1] The burlesque poet, who married Mademoiselle d'Aubigné, afterwards so well known as Madame de Maintenon.

[2] The chief of the fallen angels.

[3] The fictitious name of the leader of the Irish insurgents in 1822. Maclise's "Installation of Captain Rock" was exhibited in 1834.

[4] The Attorney-General, afterwards Lord Campbell. As a solatium for being passed over in the appointments of Master of the Rolls and Lord Chancellor, Sir John secured the elevation of his wife to the peerage as Lady Stratheden.

incapable of acknowledging and appreciating your abilities and acquirements. They are sound, but they are not splendid. You have mastered considerable legal reading, you are gifted with no ordinary shrewdness, you have enjoyed great practice, and you have gained great experience; you possess undaunted perseverance and invincible industry. But you can advance no claim to the refined subtlety of an Eldon, and still less to the luminous precision, the quick perception, the varied knowledge, and accomplished eloquence of a Lyndhurst. In profound learning you cannot cope for a moment with Sir Edward Sugden;[1] as an advocate you can endure no competiton with your eminent father-in-law,[2] or with Sir William Follett, or—for I am not writing as a partisan—with Mr. Serjeant Wilde. As a pleader I believe you were distinguished, though there are many who, even in this humble province, have deemed that you might yield the palm to Mr. Baron Parke and Mr. Justice Littledale.

But, whatever be your merits or defects, you are still the King's Attorney-General, and as the King's Attorney-General you have a prescriptive, if not a positive, right to claim any seat upon the judgment bench which becomes vacant during your official tenure. This prescriptive right has never been doubted in the profession. It has been understood and acted upon by members of the bar, of all parties, and at all times. In recent days, Sir Robert Gifford,[3] though a common law lawyer, succeeded to the equity tribunal of Sir Thomas Plomer. It is true that Sir Robert Gifford, for a very short time previous to his accession, had practised in the Court of Chancery, but the right of the Attorney-General to succeed, under any circumstances, was again recognised by Lord Eldon, when Sir John Copley,[4] who had never been in an Equity Court in his life, became Master of the Rolls. On this occasion it is well known that Leach,[5] the Vice-

---

[1] Afterwards Lord St. Leonards and Lord Chancellor.
[2] Sir James Scarlett, afterwards Lord Abinger.
[3] Afterwards Lord Gifford.
[4] Lord Lyndhurst.   [5] Sir John Leach.

Chancellor, was anxious to succeed Lord Gifford, but his request was not for a moment listened to in preference to the claim of the Attorney-General.

In allowing a judge, who a very short time back was your inferior officer, to become Lord Chancellor of England, and in permitting a barrister, who had not even filled the office of Solicitor-General, to be elevated over your head into the seat of the Master of the Rolls; either you must have esteemed yourself absolutely incompetent to the discharge of those great offices, or you must have been painfully conscious of your marked inferiority to both the individuals who were promoted in your teeth; or last, and bitterest alternative, you must have claimed your right and been denied its enjoyment. In the first instance, you virtually declared that you were equally unfit for the office you at present hold, and what should have been your consequent conduct is obvious; in the second, you betrayed the interests of the bar; and in the third, you betrayed not only the interests of the bar, but its honour also.

Without imputing to Sir John Campbell any marvellous degree of arrogance, I cannot bring myself to believe that he holds himself absolutely unfit for the discharge of the offices in question. I will not even credit that he has yielded to his unfeigned sense of his marked inferiority to the supernatural wisdom and miraculous acquirements of my Lord Cottenham, or that his downcast vision has been dazzled by the wide extended celebrity that surrounds with a halo the name of Bickersteth! No, Sir, we will not trench upon the manorial right of modesty which is the monopoly of your colleague, Sir Monsey Rolfe,[1] that public man on the *lucus a non lucendo* principle, that shadowy entity which all have heard of, few seen. An individual, it would appear, of a rare humility and admirable patience, and born, as it were, to exemplify the beauty of resignation.

I believe, therefore, that you claimed the office—that

---

[1] Afterwards Lord Cranworth and Lord Chancellor.

you claimed your right, and that you were refused it.
That must have been a bitter moment, Sir John Campbell
—a moment which might have made you recollect, perhaps even repeat, the Johnsonian definition of a Whig.[1]
You have not hitherto been held a man deficient in spirit,
or altogether uninfluenced by that nobler ambition which
spurs us on to great careers, and renders the esteem of
our fellow-countrymen not the least valuable reward of
our exertions. When therefore you were thus insulted,
why did you not resent the insult ? When your fair
ambition was thus scurvily balked, why not have gratified
it by proving to a sympathising nation that you were
at least worthy of the high post to which you aspired ?
He who aims to be the guardian of the honour of the
Crown should at least prove that he is competent
to protect his own. You ought not to have quitted
the Minister's ante - chamber the King's Attorney-
General.

Why did you, then ? Because, as you inform us, your
lady is to be ennobled. Is it the carnival, that such jests
pass current ? Is it part of the code of etiquette in this
saturnalia of Whig manners that the honour of a man is
to be vindicated by a compliment to a woman ? One
cannot refrain from admiring, too, the consistent propriety of the whole arrangement. A gentleman, whom
his friends announce as a resolved republican, and to
whom, but for this slight circumstance, they assert would
have been entrusted the custody of the Great Seal, is
to be hoisted up into the House of Lords in the masquerade
of a Baron; while yourself, whose delicate and gracious
panegyric of the Peers of England is still echoing from
the Movement benches of the House of Commons to the
reeking cellars of the Cowgate, find the only consolation
for your wounded honour in your son inscribing his name
in the *libro d'oro* of our hereditary legislators. Why, if
Mr. O'Connell were but simultaneously called up by the

[1] Johnson, in his Dictionary, defined " Whig " as " the name
of a faction."

title of Baron Rathcormac, in honour of his victory, the batch would be quite complete.

What compensation is it for the injured interests, and what consolation to the outraged honour, of the bar, that your amiable lady is to become a peeress ?   On the contrary, you have inflicted a fresh stigma on the body of which you are the chief.   You have shown to the world that the leading advocate of the day, the King's Attorney-General, will accept a bribe !   Nay ! start not. For the honour of human nature, for the honour of your high profession, of which I am the friend, I will believe that in the moment of overwhelming mortification you did not thus estimate that glittering solace, but such, believe me, the English nation will ever esteem the coronet of Strath-Eden.

Was the grisly spectre of Sir William Horne[1] the blooming Eve that tempted you to pluck this fatal fruit ? Was it the conviction that a rebellious Attorney-General might be shelved that daunted the hereditary courage of the Campbell ?   What, could you condescend to be treated by the Minister like a froward child—the parental Viscount shaking in one hand a rod, and in the other waving a toy ?

I have long been of opinion that, among other perfected and projected mischief, there has been on the part of the Whigs a systematic attempt to corrupt the English bar.   I shall avail myself of another and early opportunity to discuss this important subject.   At present I will only observe that, whether they do or do not obtain their result, your conduct has anticipated the consequence of their machinations: the Whigs may corrupt the bar of England, but you, Sir, have degraded it.

January 19, 1836.

---

[1] Attorney - General in Grey's Ministry ; a " victim to the trickery and shuffling of the Chancellor (Lord Brougham), who wanted to get him out, and did not care how " (Greville's "Memoirs," February 26, 1834).

LETTER III

To Mr. Thomas Attwood, M.P.[1]

Sir,—You may be surprised at this letter being addressed to you; you /may be more surprised when I inform you that this address is not occasioned by any conviction of your political importance. I deem you a harmless, and I do not believe you to be an ill-meaning, individual. You are a provincial banker labouring under a financial monomania. But amid the seditious fanfaronade which your unhappy distemper occasions you periodically to vomit forth, there are fragments of good old feelings which show you are not utterly denationalised in spite of being " the friend of all mankind," and contrast with the philanthropic verbiage of your revolutionary rhetoric like the odds and ends of ancient art which occasionally jut forth from the modern rubbish of an edifice in a classic land—symptoms of better days, and evidences of happier intellect.

The reason that I have inscribed this letter to your consideration is that you are a fair representative of a considerable class of your countrymen—the class who talk political nonsense; and it is these with whom, through your medium, I would now communicate.

I met recently with an observation which rather amused me. It was a distinction drawn in some journal between high nonsense and low nonsense.[2] I thought that distinction was rather happily illustrated at the recent meeting of your Union,[3] which, by-the-bye, differs from its old state as the drivellings of idiotism from

[1] Member for Birmingham ; a Reform leader, and father of the Political Unions; the " King Tom " of Cobbett's *Political Register*.
[2] Disraeli's own letter to the *Times*, December 31, 1835: " I have often observed that there are two kinds of nonsense—high nonsense and low nonsense."
[3] Birmingham Political Union, January 18, 1836, presided over by Mr. Muntz.

the frenzy of insanity. When your chairman, who, like yourself, is "the friend of all mankind," called Sir Robert Peel "an ass," I thought that Spartan description might fairly range under the head of low nonsense; but when you yourself, as if in contemptuous and triumphant rivalry with his plebeian folly, announced to us that at the sound of your blatant voice 100,000 armed men would instantly rise in Birmingham, it occurred to me that Nat Lee[1] himself could scarcely compete with you in your claim to the more patrician privilege of uttering high nonsense. If, indeed, you produce such marvels, the name of Attwood will be handed down to posterity in heroic emulation with that of Cadmus; he produced armed men by a process almost as simple, but the teeth of the Theban King must yield to the jaw of the Birmingham delegate, though I doubt not the same destiny would await both batches of warriors.

But these 100,000 armed men are only the advanced guard, the imperial guard of Brummagem, the heralds of a mightier host. Nay, compared with the impending legions, can only count as pioneers, or humble sappers at the best. Twenty millions of men are to annihilate the Tories. By the last census, I believe the adult male population of Great Britain was computed at less than 4,000,000. Whence the subsidiary levies are to be obtained, we may perhaps be informed the next time some brainless Cleon, at the pitch of his voice, bawls forth his rampant folly at the top of New Hall Hill.

Superficial critics have sometimes viewed, in a spirit of narrow-minded scepticism, those traditionary accounts of armed hosts which startle us in the credulous or the glowing page of rude or ancient annals. But what was the Great King on the heights of Salamis or in the straits of Issus, what was Gengis Khan, what Tamerlane, compared with Mr. Thomas Attwood of Birmingham! The leader of such an army may well be "the friend of all

---

[1] Nathaniel Lee, the dramatist.

mankind," if only to recruit his forces from his extensive connections.

The truth is, Xerxes and Darius, and the valiant leaders of the Tartars and the Mongols, were ignorant of the mystical yet expeditious means by which 20,000,000 of men are brought into the field by a modern demagogue, to change a constitution or to subvert an empire. When they hoisted their standard, their chieftains rallied round it, bringing to the array all that population of the country who were not required to remain at home to maintain its order or civilisation. The peasant quitted his plough and the pastor his flock, and the artisan without employ hurried from the pauperism of Babylon or the idleness of Samarcand. But these great leaders, with their diminutive forces which astounded the Lilliputian experience of our ancestors, had no conception, with their limited imaginations, of the inexhaustible source whence the ranks of a popular leader may be swollen; they had no idea of "THE PEOPLE." It is "the people" that is to supply their great successor with his millions.

As in private life we are accustomed to associate the circle of our acquaintance with the phrase "THE WORLD," so in public I have invariably observed that "THE PEOPLE" of the politician is the circle of his interests. The "people" of the Whigs are the ten-pounders who vote in their favour. At present the municipal constituencies are almost considered by Lords Melbourne and John Russell as, in some instances, to have afforded legitimate claims of being deemed part and parcel of the nation; but I very much fear that the course of events will degrade those bodies from any lengthened participation in this ennobling quality. It is quite clear that the electors of Northamptonshire have forfeited all right to be held portion of "the people," since their return of Mr. Maunsell;[1] the people of Birmingham are doubtless those of the inhabitants who huzza the grandiloquence of

---

[1] Mr. T. P. Maunsell, Conservative Member for North Northamptonshire.

Mr. Attwood; and the people of England, perchance, those discerning individuals who, if he were to make a provincial tour of oratory, might club together in the different towns to give him a dinner. I hardly think that, all together, these quite amount to 20,000,000.

Yourself and the school to which you belong are apt to describe the present struggle as one between the Conservatives and the people—these Conservatives consisting merely of 300 or 400 peers and their retainers. You tell us in the same breath, with admirable consistency, that you possess the name, but not the heart, of the King; that the Court is secretly, and the Peerage openly, opposed to you; the Church you announce as even beholding you with pious terror. The Universities, and all chartered bodies, come under your ban. The Bar is so hostile that you have been obliged to put the Great Seal in commission for a year,[1] and have finally, and from sheer necessity, entrusted it to the custody of an individual whom by that very tripartite trusteeship you had previously declared unfit for its sole guardianship. The gentlemen of England are against you to a man because of their corn monopoly; the yeomanry from sheer bigotry; the cultivators of the soil because they are the slaves of the owners, and the peasantry because they are the slaves of the cultivators. The freemen of the towns are against you because they are corrupt; the inhabitants of rural towns because they are compelled; and the press is against you because it is not free. It must be confessed that you and your party can give excellent reasons for any chance opposition which you may happen to experience. You are equally felicitous in accounting for the suspicious glance which the fundholder shoots at you; nor can I sufficiently admire the

---

[1] When Melbourne returned to office in April, 1835, it was determined, after the conduct of Brougham in the previous Melbourne Administration, not to have him among them again; and to soften the blow to Brougham, the Great Seal was put in Commission until the appointment of Pepys in the following year, the Commissioners being Sir Charles Pepys (Master of the Rolls), Vice-Chancellor Shadwell, and Mr. Justice Bosanquet.

admirable candour with which the prime organ of your faction has recently confessed that every man who possesses £500 per annum is necessarily your opponent. After this, it is superfluous to remark that the merchants, bankers, and ship-owners of this great commercial and financial country are not to be found in your ranks, and the sneers at our national glory and imperial sway which ever play on the patriotic lips of Whigs, both high and low, only retaliate the undisguised scorn with which their anti-national machinations are viewed by the heroes of Waterloo and the conquerors of Trafalgar. Deduct these elements of a nation, deduct all this power, all this authority, all this skill, and all this courage, all this learning, all this wealth, and all these numbers, and all the proud and noble and national feelings which are their consequence, and what becomes of your " people " ? It subsides into an empty phrase, a juggle as pernicious and as ridiculous as your paper currency !

But if you and your friends, " the friends of all mankind," have, as indeed I believe you have not, the brute force and the numerical superiority of the population of this realm marshalled under your banners, do not delude yourselves into believing for a moment that you are in any degree more entitled from that circumstance to count yourselves the leaders of the English people. A nation is not a mere mass of bipeds with no strength but their animal vigour, and no collective grandeur but that of their numbers. There is required to constitute that great creation, a people, some higher endowments and some rarer qualities—honour, and faith, and justice; a national spirit fostered by national exploits; a solemn creed expounded by a pure and learned priesthood; a jurisprudence which is the aggregate wisdom of ages; the spirit of chivalry, the inspiration of religion, the supremacy of law; that free order, and that natural gradation of ranks which are but a type and image of the economy of the universe; a love of home and country, fostered by traditionary manners and consecrated by customs that embalm

ancestral deeds; learned establishments, the institutions
of charity, a skill in refined and useful arts, the discipline
of fleets and armies; and above all, a national character,
serious and yet free, a character neither selfish nor conceited, but which is conscious that as it owes much to its
ancestors, so also it will not stand acquitted if it neglect
its posterity;—these are some of the incidents and qualities of a great nation like the people of England. Whether
these are to be found in " the people " who assemble at
the meetings of your union, or whether they may be more
successfully sought for among their 20,000,000 of brethren
at hand, I leave you, Sir, to decide. I shall only observe,
that if I be correct in my estimate of the constituent
elements of the English people, I am persuaded that in
spite of all the arts of plundering factions and mercenary
demagogues, they will recognise, with a grateful loyalty,
the venerable cause of their welfare in the august fabric
of their ancient constitution.

January 21, 1836.

LETTER IV

To Lord Brougham

My Lord,—In your elaborate mimicry of Lord Bacon,
your most implacable enemies must confess that, at least
in one respect, you have rivalled your great original—
you have contrived to get disgraced. In your Treatise
on Hydrostatics you may not have completely equalled
the fine and profound researches of " the Lord Chancellor
of Nature "; your most ardent admirers may hesitate in
preferring the *Penny Magazine* to the "Novum Orga-
non "; even the musings of Jenkins and the meditations
of Tomkins may not be deemed to come quite as much
home " to men's business and bosoms " as the immortal
Essays; but no one can deny, neither friend nor foe, that
you are as much shunned as their author—almost as
much despised.

Whether the fame of his philosophical discoveries and the celebrity of his literary exploits may console the late Lord Chancellor of William the Fourth in the solitude of his political annihilation, as they brought balm to the bruised spirit of the late Lord Chancellor of James the First in the loneliness of his sublime degradation, he best can decide who may witness the writhings of your tortured memory and the restless expedients of your irritable imagination. At present, I am informed that your Lordship is occupied in a translation of your Treatise of Natural Theology into German, on the Hamiltonian system. The translation of a work on a subject of which you know little, into a tongue of which you know nothing, seems the climax of those fantastic freaks of ambitious superficiality which our lively neighbours describe by a finer term than quackery. But if the perturbed spirit can only be prevented from preying on itself by literary occupation, let me suggest to you, in preference, the propriety of dedicating the days of your salutary retirement to a production of more general interest, and, if properly treated, of more general utility. A memoir of the late years of your career might afford your fellow-countrymen that of which at present they are much in want—a great moral lesson. In its instructive pages we might perhaps learn how a great empire has nearly been sacrificed to the aggrandisement of a rapacious faction; how, under the specious garb of patriotism, a band of intriguing politicians, connected by no community of purpose or of feeling but the gratification of their own base interests, forfeited all the pledges of their previous careers, or violated all the principles of their practised systems ; how, at length, in some degree palled with plundering the nation, according to the usual course, they began plundering themselves; how the weakest, and probably the least impure, were sacrificed to those who were more bold and bad; and, finally, how your Lordship, especially, would have shrouded yourself in the mantle, while you kicked away the prophet.

If your Lordship would have but the courageous candour to proceed in this great production, you might,
perhaps, favour us with a graphic narrative of that
memorable interview between yourself and the present
Premier, when, with that easy elocution and unembar-
rassed manner which characterise the former favourite of
Castlereagh, the present First Lord of the Treasury,
robbing you of the fruit after you had plundered the
orchard, broke to your startled vision and incredulous
ear the unforeseen circumstance that your Lordship was
destined to be the scapegoat of Whiggism, and to be
hurried into the wilderness with all the curses of the
nation and all the sins of your companions. This animated sketch would form an admirable accompaniment
to the still richer picture when you offered your congratulatory condolence to Earl Grey on his long meditated
retirement from the onerous service of a country as grateful as his colleagues.

Your Lordship, who is well informed of what passes in
the Cabinet, must have been scarcely less astonished than
the public at the late legal arrangements. Every post,
till of late, must have brought you from the metropolis
intelligence which must have filled you with anxiety
almost maturing into hope. But the lion was suddenly
reported to be sick, and the jackals suddenly grew
bold. The Prime Minister consulted Sir Benjamin;[1] the
Serjeant-Surgeon shook his head, and they passed in
trembling precipitation the paltry Rubicon of their spite.
When we remember that one voice alone decided your
fate, and that that voice issued from the son of Lord Grey,
we seem to be recalled to the days of the Greek drama.
Your Lordship, although a universalist, I believe, has not
yet tried your hand at a tragedy; let me recommend this
fresh illustration of the sublime destiny of the ancients.
You have deserved a better fate, but not a degrading one;
though Achilles caused the destruction of Troy, we deplore
his ignoble end from the unequal progeny of Priam.

[1] Benjamin Collins Brodie, appointed Serjeant-Surgeon to the
King in 1832, and afterwards knighted.

And is it possible—are you indeed the man whose scathing voice, but a small lustre gone, passed like the lightning in that great Assembly where Canning grew pale before your terrible denunciation, and where even Peel still remembers your awful reply ? Is this indeed the lord of sarcasm, the mighty master of invective ? Is this indeed the identical man who took the offer of the Attorney-Generalship, and held it up to the scorn of the assembled Commons of England, and tore it, and trampled upon it, and spat upon it in their sympathising sight, and lived to offer the cold-blooded aristocrat, who had dared to insult genius, the consoling compensation of the Privy Seal?[1]

For your Lordship has a genius; good or bad, it marks you out from the slaves who crouch to an O'Connell and insult a Brougham. Napoleon marched from Elba. You, too, may have your hundred days. What though they think you are dying—what though your health is quaffed in ironical bumpers in the craven secrecy of their political orgies—what if, after all, throwing Brodie on one side and your Teutonic studies on the other, your spectre appear in the House of Lords on the fourth of February ! Conceive the confusion ! I can see the unaccustomed robes tremble on the dignified form of the lordly Cottenham, and his spick and span coronet fall from the obstetric brow of the baronial Bickersteth,[2] Lansdowne taking refuge in philosophical silence, and Melbourne gulping courage in the goblets of Sion !

January 23, 1836.

---

[1] " The Chancellor and the Hollands urged Lord Grey to take the Privy Seal. Lord Grey . . . rather smiled at the proposition, but he did not repress the pious resentment of his children. The Grey women would murder the Chancellor if they could. It certainly was a curious suggestion. . . . It is not always easy to discover the Chancellor's motives, but . . . he perhaps took this opportunity of revenging himself for the old offer of the Attorney-Generalship, which he has never forgiven " (Greville's "Memoirs," July 21, 1834).

[2] Henry Bickersteth (Lord Langdale) was first educated for the medical profession, but his health broke down through over-study.

LETTER V

To Sir Robert Peel

SIR,—Before you receive this letter you will, in all probability, have quitted the halls and bowers of Drayton; those gardens and that library where you have realised the romance of Verulam and where you enjoy "the lettered leisure" that Temple loved. Your present progress to the metropolis may not be as picturesque as that which you experienced twelve months back, when the confidence of your sovereign and the hopes of your country summoned you from the galleries of the Vatican and the city of the Cæsars.[1] It may not be as picturesque, but it is not less proud—it will be more triumphant. You are summoned now, like the Knight of Rhodes in Schiller's heroic ballad, as the only hope of a suffering island. The mighty dragon is again abroad, depopulating our fields, wasting our pleasant places, poisoning our fountains, menacing our civilisation. To-day he gorges on Liverpool, to-morrow he riots at Birmingham: as he advances nearer the metropolis, terror and disgust proportionately increase. Already we hear his bellow, more awful than hyænas; already our atmosphere is tainted with the venomous expirations of his malignant lungs; yet a little while and his incendiary crest will flame on our horizon, and we shall mark the horrors of his insatiable jaws and the scaly volume of his atrocious tail!

In your chivalry alone is our hope. Clad in the panoply of your splendid talents and your spotless character, we feel assured that you will subdue this unnatural and unnational monster; and that we may yet see sedition, and treason, and rapine, rampant as they may have of late figured, quail before your power and prowess.

[1] Sir Robert Peel was in Italy when summoned by the King to form an administration in 1834.

You are about to renew the combat under the most favourable auspices. When, a year ago, with that devotion to your country which is your great characteristic, scorning all those refined delights of fortune which are your inheritance, and which no one is more capable of appreciating, and resigning all those pure charms of social and domestic life to which no one is naturally more attached, you threw yourself in the breach of the battered and beleaguered citadel of the constitution, you undertook the heroic enterprise with every disadvantage. The national party were as little prepared for the summons of their eminent leader by their sovereign as you yourself could have been when gazing on the frescoes of Michelangelo. They had little organisation, less system; their hopes weak, their chieftains scattered; no communication, no correspondence. Yet they made a gallant rally; and if their numerical force in the House of Commons were not equal, Sir, to your moral energy, the return of Lord Melbourne, at the best, was but a Pyrrhic triumph; nor perhaps were your powers ever sufficiently appreciated by your countrymen until you were defeated. Your abandonment of office was worthy of the motives which induced you originally to accept power. It was not petty pique; it was not a miserable sentiment of personal mortification that led you to decide upon that step. You retained your post until you found you were endangering the King's prerogative, to support which you had alone accepted His Majesty's confidence. What a contrast does your administration as Prime Minister afford to that of one of your recent predecessors ! No selfish views, no family aggrandisement, no family jobs, no nepotism. It cannot be said that during your administration the public service was surfeited with the incapable offspring of the Premier; nor, after having nearly brought about a revolution for power which he has degraded, and lucre which degraded him, can it be said that you slunk into an undignified retirement with a whimpering Jeremiad over " the pressure from without." Contrast the

serene retirement of Drayton and the repentant solitude
of Howick; contrast the statesman, cheered after his
factious defeat by the sympathy of a nation, with the
coroneted Necker, the worn-out Machiavel, wringing his
helpless hands over his hearth in remorseful despair and
looking up with a sigh at his scowling ancestors !

But affairs are in a very different position now from
what they were in November, 1835.[1] You have an addition to the scutcheon of your fame in the emblazoned
memory of your brief but masterly premiership: they
cannot taunt you now with your vague promises of
amelioration: you can appeal to the deeds of your Cabinet,
and the plans which the applause of a nation sanctioned,
and the execution of which the intrigues of a faction alone
postponed. Never, too, since the peace of Paris, has the
great national party of this realm been so united as at
the present moment. It is no exaggeration to say that
among its leaders not the slightest difference of opinion
exists upon any portion of their intended policy. Pitt
himself, in the plenitude of his power, never enjoyed more
cordial confidence than that which is now extended to you
by every alleged section of the Conservative ranks; all
private opinions, all particular theories, have merged in
the resolute determination to maintain the English constitution in spite of Irish rebels, and to support, without
cavil and criticism, its eminent champion in that great
course of conduct which you have expounded to them.

That this admirable concord, a just subject of congratulation to the suffering people of this realm, has been in
some degree the result of salutary conferences and frank
explanations, I pretend not to deny; nor do I wish to
conceal a circumstance in which I rejoice, that at no
period have you displayed talents more calculated for the
successful conduct of a great party than at the present;
but, above all, this admirable concord is to be attributed
to the reason that, however individuals of the Conservative party may have occasionally differed as to the means,

[1] An obvious misprint for 1834.

they have at all times invariably agreed as to the end of
their system, and that end is the glory of the empire and
the prosperity of the people.

But it is not only among the leaders in the two Houses
of Parliament that this spirit of union flourishes; it
pervades the country. England has at length been completely organised; the battle which you told us must be
fought in the registry courts has been fought, and in
spite of the fanfaronade of the enemy, we know it has
been won. Every parliamentary election that has of
late occurred, in country or in town, has proved the disciplined power of the national party. It is not that they
have merely exceeded their opponents on the poll, and
often by vast majorities; but they have hastened to that
poll with an enthusiasm which shows that they are animated with a very different spirit to that which impels
their shamefaced rivals. Contrast these important
triumphs with the guerilla warfare of the Government
party on town-clerks and aldermen, and be convinced
how important have been our efforts in the registry
courts, by their feeble yet feverish attempts at what they
style Reform Associations.

If we contrast also this faithful picture of the state and
spirit of the party of which you are the leader with the
situation of your opponents, the difference will be striking.
Between the Opposition and the Government party there
is this difference; that, however certain sections of the
Opposition may occasionally have differed as to measures,
their end has always been the same; whereas the several
sections of the Ministerial party, while for obvious reasons
they agree as to measures, avowedly adopt them because
they tend to different ends. The oligarchical Whigs, the
English Radicals, the Irish Repealers—the patrons of rich
livings, the enemies of Church and State, hereditary
magistrates, professors of county reform—the sons of the
nobles, the enemies of the peerage—the landed proprietors,
the advocates of free corn, can only be united in a perverted sense. Their union then is this: to a certain point

they all wish to destroy; but the Whigs only wish to destroy the Tories, the Radicals the constitution, and the Repealers the empire. The seeds of constant jealousy and inevitable separation are here then prodigally sown.

What are to be the tactics of this heterogeneous band time will soon develop. Dark rumours are about which intimate conduct too infamous, some would fain think, even for the Whigs. But as for myself, history and personal observation have long convinced me that there is no public crime of which the Whigs are not capable, and no public shame which for a sufficient consideration their oligarchical nerves would not endure. But whether they are going to betray their anti-national adherents, or only to bribe them, do you, Sir, proceed in your great course, free and undaunted. At the head of the most powerful and the most united Opposition that ever mustered on the benches opposite a trembling Minister, conscious that by returning you to your constituents he can only increase and consolidate your strength, what have you to apprehend ? We look to you, therefore, with hope and with confidence. You have a noble duty to fulfil—let it be nobly done. You have a great task to execute—achieve it with a great spirit. Rescue your sovereign from an unconstitutional thraldom, rescue an august Senate which has already fought the battle of the people, rescue our National Church, which your opponents hate, our venerable constitution at which they scoff; but above all rescue that mighty body of which all these great classes and institutions are but some of the constituent and essential parts—rescue *The Nation*.

January 26, 1836.

LETTER VI

To the Chancellor of the Exchequer

SIR,—I really think that your celebrated compatriot, Daniel O'Rourke,[1] when, soaring on the back of an eagle, he entered into a conversation with the man in the moon, could scarcely be more amazed than Mr. Spring Rice must be when he finds himself, as Chancellor of the Exchequer, holding a conference with the First Lord of the Treasury.   Your colleagues, who, to do them justice, are perpetually apologising for your rapid promotion, account for your rocket-like rise by the unanswerable reason of your being " a man of business "!   I doubt not this is a capital recommendation to those who are not men of business; and indeed, shrewd without being sagacious, bustling without method, loquacious without eloquence, ever prompt though always superficial, and ever active though always blundering, you are exactly the sort of fussy busybody who would impose upon and render himself indispensable to indolent and ill-informed men of strong ambition and weak minds.   Cumberland,[2] who, in spite of the courtly compliments of his polished Memoirs, could be racy and significant enough in his conversation, once characterised in my presence a countryman of yours as " a talking potato."   The race of talking potatoes is not extinct.

Your recent harangue at Cambridge was quite worthy

---

[1] Croker's "Fairy Legends," published by Mr. John Murray on Disraeli's recommendation.   After the publication of the first volume, Croker wrote to a friend concerning his tour in the South of Ireland "for the purpose of gleaning, in the course of six weeks, the remainder of the fairy legends and traditions which Mr. Murray of Albemarle Street suspected were still to be found lurking among its glens, having satisfied himself as to the value of dealing in the publication of such fanciful articles, and the correctness of my friend Ben. Disraeli's estimate thereof."

[2] Richard Cumberland, author and dramatist, died in 1811, when Disraeli was seven years old !

of your reputation, and of those to whom it was addressed. Full of popular commonplaces and ministerial propriety, alike the devoted delegate of " the people " and the trusty servant of the Crown, glorying in your pledges, but reminding your audience that they were voluntary, chuckling in your " political triumph," but impressing on your friends that their " new power " must not be used for party purposes, I can see you with Irish humour winking your eye on one side of your face as you hazard a sneer at " the Lords," and eulogising with solemn hypocrisy with the other half of your countenance our " blessed constitution."[1] How choice was the style in which you propounded the future measures of the Cabinet ! What heartfelt ejaculations of " Good God, sir !" mingled with rare jargon about " hoping and trusting !" You even ventured upon a tawdry simile, borrowed for the occasion from Mr. Sheil,[2] who, compared with his bolder and more lawless colleague, always reminds me of the fustian lieutenant, Jack Bunce, in Sir Walter's tale of the " Pirate " contrasted with his master, the bloody buccaneer, Captain Cleveland.

You commenced your address with a due recollection of the advice of the great Athenian orator, for your action was quite striking. You clasped the horny hand of the astonished Mayor, and, full of your punch-bowl orgies, aptly alluded to your " elevated feelings." As for the exquisite raillery in which your graceful fancy indulged about Tory port and Whig sherry, you might perhaps have recollected that if " old Tory port affects to be a new mixture, is ashamed of its colours, and calls itself Conservative," that the Whig sherry has disappeared altogether, and that its place has been deleteriously supplied by Irish whisky from an illicit still, and English blue ruin. Your profound metaphysics, however, may amply compensate for this infelicitous flash of jocularity. A Senator, and a Minister, and a Cabinet Minister, who

[1] Compare " A Character " in Political Satires in Verse, p. 400.
[2] Richard Lalor Sheil.

gravely informs us that " the political history of our
times has shown us that there is something in human
motive that pervades and extends itself to human
action," must have an eye, I suspect, to the representation of the University. This is, indeed, " a learned
Theban." That human motives have some slight connection with human conduct is a principle which will,
no doubt, figure as an era in metaphysical discovery.
The continental imputations of our shallowness in
psychological investigation must certainly now be removed for ever. Neither Kant nor Helvetius can enter
the arena with our rare Chancellor of the Exchequer.
The fall of an apple was sufficient to reveal the secret
of celestial mechanics to the musing eye of Newton, but
Mr. Spring Rice for his more abstruse revelations requires
a revolution or a Reform Bill. It is " the political
history of our times " that has proved the connection
between motives and actions. The Chancellor of the
Exchequer must have arrived at this discovery by the
recollection of the very dignified and honourable conduct
to which the motives of power and place have recently
impelled himself and his friends. I cannot help fancying
that this display of yours at Cambridge may hereafter
be adduced as irrefutable evidence that there is at least
one portion of the Irish Protestant population which has
not received " adequate instruction."

It seems that you and your Katterfelto[1] crew are
going to introduce some very wonderful measures to
the notice of the impending Parliament. And, first of
all, you are about to " remedy the still existing grievances
to which the great dissenting bodies are subject." " Good
God ! sir," as you would say, are you driven to this ?
The still existing grievances of the Dissenters ! Do you
and your beggarly Cabinet yet live upon these sores ?

---

[1] Gustavus Katterfelto, conjurer and quack doctor.

> " Katterfelto, with his hair on end
> At his own wonders, wondering for his bread."
>   COWPER: *The Task.*

Dissenting grievances are like Stilton cheeses and Damascus sabres, never found in the places themselves, though there is always some bustling huckster or other who will insure you a supply. "The still existing grievances of the Dissenters," if they exist at all, exist only because, after four years of incapacity, you and your clumsy coadjutors could not contrive to remove and remedy what Sir Robert Peel could have achieved, but for your faction, in four days.

Then we are to proceed in "our great work of the reform of the Courts of Equity." I "hope and trust" not. What! after creating the Court of Review, the laughing-stock of the profession; after having at length succeeded in obtaining a second-rate Lord Chancellor at the expense of four coronets,[1] whose services might have been secured without the waste of one; after having caused more delay, more expense, more mortification and ruin in eight months of reform than the annals of the Court can offer in a similar period in the worst days of its management—still must you amend! Spare us, good sir; be content with your last achievements of law reform; be content with having, by your corporation magistrates, made for the first time in England since the days of Charles the Second, the administration of justice a matter of party. Will not even this satisfy the Whig lechery for mischief ?

Then, "Ireland must be tranquillised." So I think. Feed the poor ; hang the agitators. That will do it. But that's not your way. It is the destruction of the English and Protestant interest that is the Whig specific for Irish tranquillity. And do you really flatter yourself, because an eccentric course of circumstances has metamorphosed an Irish adventurer into the Chancellor of the English Exchequer, that the spirited people of this island will allow you to proceed with impunity in your projected machinations ? Rest assured, sir, your career draws rapidly to a close. Providence, that for our sins and the

[1] See note 1, p. 241.

arrogance of our flush prosperity has visited this once great and glorious empire with five years of Whig government, is not implacable. Our God is a God of mercy as well as justice. We may have erred, but we have been chastened. And Athens, when ruled by a Disdar Aga, who was the deputy of the chief of the eunuchs at Constantinople, was not so contemptible as England governed by a Limerick lawyer—the deputy of an Irish rebel !

Prepare, then, for your speedy and merited dismissal. It is amusing to fancy what may be the resources of your Cabinet in their permanent retirement. The First Lord of the Treasury, in all probability, will betake himself to Brocket, and compose an epilogue for the drama just closed. Your Lord Chancellor may retire to his native village, like a returned cheese. Lord John, perhaps, will take down his dusty lyre, and console us for having starved Coleridge by pouring forth a monody to his memory. As for the polished Palmerston and the pious Grant,[1] and the other trading statesmen of easy virtue— for them it would be advisable, I think, at once to erect a political Magdalen Hospital. Solitude and spare diet, and some salutary treatises of the English constitution, may, after a considerable interval, capacitate them for re-entering public life, and even filling with an approximation to obscure respectability some of the lower offices of the State. But, Sir, for yourself, with your " businesslike talents," which must not be hid under a bushel, it appears to me that it would be both the wisest and the kindest course to entrust to your charge and instruction a class of beings who, in their accomplishments and indefatigableness, alike in their physical and moral qualities, not a little resemble you—the INDUSTRIOUS FLEAS.

January 28, 1836.

---

[1] Lord Glenelg.

LETTER VII

To Lord John Russell [1]

My Lord,—Your name will descend to posterity—you have burnt your Ephesian temple. But great deeds are not always achieved by great men. Your character is a curious one; events have proved that it has been imperfectly comprehended, even by your own party. Long and, for a period, intimate opportunities of observing you will enable me, if I mistake not, to enter into its just analysis.

You were born with a strong ambition and a feeble intellect. It is an union not uncommon, and in the majority of cases only tends to convert an aspiring youth into a querulous and discontented manhood. But under some circumstances—when combined, for instance, with great station, and consequent opportunities of action— it is an union which often leads to the development of a peculiar talent—the talent of political mischief.

When you returned from Spain, the solitary life of travel and the inspiration of a romantic country acting upon your ambition had persuaded you that you were a great poet; your intellect, in consequence, produced the feeblest tragedy in our language. The reception of " Don Carlos " only convinced your ambition that your imaginative powers had been improperly directed. [2] Your ambition sought from prose-fiction the fame which had been denied to your lyre; and your intellect in consequence produced the feeblest romance in our literature. [3] Not deterred by the unhappy catastrophe of the fair maid

---

[1] In "Coningsby," Book V., Chapter IV., the estimate of Lord John Russell is very different indeed from that contained in this Letter.

[2] Yet "Don Carlos" ran through five editions in twelve months.

[3] "The Nun of Arrouca," which appeared in 1822, was founded on an incident of Lord John's travels in the Peninsula.

of Arrouca, your ambitions sought consolation in the
notoriety of political literature, and your intellect in
due time produced the feeblest political essay on record.[1]
Your defence of close boroughs, however, made this
volume somewhat popular with the Whigs, and flushed
with the compliments of Holland House, where hitherto
you had been treated with more affection than respect,
your ambition resolved on rivalling the fame of Hume
and Gibbon. Your " Memoirs of the Affairs of Europe,"[2]
published with pompous parade in successive quarto
volumes, retailed in frigid sentences a feeble compilation
from the gossip of those pocket tomes of small talk
which abound in French literature. Busied with the
tattle of valets and waiting-maids, you accidentally
omitted in your " Memoirs of the Affairs of Europe " all
notice of its most vast and most rising empire. This
luckless production closed your literary career; you flung
down your futile pen in incapable despair; and your
feeble intellect having failed in literature, your strong
ambition took refuge in politics.

You had entered the House of Commons with every
adventitious advantage—an illustrious birth, and the
support of an ancient and haughty party. I was one
of the audience who assisted at your first appearance,[3]
and I remember the cheering attention that was extended
to you. Cold, inanimate, with a weak voice and a
mincing manner, the failure of your intellect was complete; but your ambition wrestled for a time with the
indifference of your opponents and the ill-concealed
contempt of your friends.

Having, then, failed alike in both these careers which
in this still free country are open to genius, you subsided
for some years into a state of listless moroseness which
was even pitiable. Hitherto your political opinions had

[1] " An Essay on the History of the English Government and
Constitution," 1821.
[2] " Memoirs of the Affairs of Europe from the Peace of
Utrecht," 1824-1829.
[3] 1814. Disraeli was then barely ten years old !

been mild and moderate, and, if partial, at least constitutional; but, as is ever the case with persons of your temperament, despairing of yourself, you began to despair of your country. This was the period when among your intimates you talked of retiring from that public life in which you had not succeeded in making yourself public, when you paced, like a feeble Catiline, the avenues of Holland House; and when the most brilliant poet of the day, flattered by your friendship, addressed you a remonstrance in which your pique figured as patriotism and your ambition was elevated into genius.[1]

Your friends—I speak of the circle in which you lived—superficial judges of human character as well as of everything else, always treated you with a species of contempt, which doubtless originated in their remembrance of your failure and their conviction of your feebleness. Lord Grey, only five years ago, would not even condescend to offer you a seat in the Cabinet, and affected to state that, in according you a respectable office, he had been as much influenced by the state of your finances as of your capacity. Virtual Prime Minister of England at this moment, you have repaid Lord Grey for his flattering estimate and his friendly services, and have afforded him, in your present career, some curious meditations for his uneasy solitude, where he wanders, like the dethroned Caliph in the halls of Eblis, with his quivering hand pressed upon his aching heart.

A finer observer of human nature than that forlorn statesman might have recognised at this crisis in a noble with an historic name and no fortune, a vast ambition and a balked career, and soured, not to say malignant, from disappointment, some prime materials for the leader of a revolutionary faction. Those materials have worked well. You have already banished your great leader; you

[1] " Thus gifted, thou never canst sleep in the shade
    If the stirring of genius, the music of fame,
  And the charm of thy cause, have not power to persuade
    Yet think how to freedom thou'rt pledged by thy name."
                              MOORE'S *Remonstrance.*

have struck down the solemn idol which you yourself
assisted in setting up for the worship of a deluded people;
you have exiled from the Cabinet, by your dark and dis-
honourable intrigues, every man of talent who could have
held you in check; and, placing in the seat of nominal
leadership an indolent epicurean, you rule this country
by a coalition with an Irish rebel, and with a council of
colleagues in which you have united the most inefficient
members of your own party with the Palmerstons and
Grants, the Swiss statesmen, the *condottieri* of the political
world, the " British legion " of public life.

A miniature Mokanna,[1] you are now exhaling upon the
constitution of your country which you once eulogised,
and its great fortunes of which you once were proud, all
that long - hoarded venom and all those distempered
humours that have for years accumulated in your petty
heart and tainted the current of your mortified life—
your aim is to reduce everything to your own mean level,
to degrade everything to your malignant standard.
Partially you have succeeded. You have revenged
yourself upon the House of Lords, the only obstacle to
your degenerating schemes, by denouncing with a frigid
conceit worthy of " Don Carlos," its solemn suffrage as
" the whisper of a faction,"[2] and hallooing on, in a flimsy
treble, your Scotch and Irish desperadoes to assail its
august independence. You have revenged yourself upon
the sovereign who recoiled from your touch, by kissing,

---

[1] The Veiled Prophet of Khorassan, an impostor who, being
terribly disfigured, wore a veil under pretence of shading the
dazzling light of his countenance.
　　　　　　　　　　" The prophet-chief,
The Great Mokanna.　O'er his features hung
The Veil, the Silver Veil, which he had flung
In mercy there, to hide from mortal sight
His dazzling brow, till man could bear its light."
　　　　　　　　　　　　　　　　　MOORE.

Maclise exhibited in 1833 " Mokanna unveiling his Features to
Zelica."
[2] " It is impossible that the whisper of a faction should prevail
against the voice of the nation " (Lord John Russell's message to
the Birmingham Political Union).

in spite of his royal soul, his outraged hand. Notwithstanding your base powers and your father's fagot votes, the gentlemen of England inflicted upon you an indelible brand, and expelled you from your own county; and you have revenged yourself upon their indignant patriotism by depriving them of their noblest and most useful privileges, and making, for the first time since the reign of Charles the Second, the administration of justice the business of faction. In all your conduct it is not difficult to detect the workings of a mean and long-mortified spirit suddenly invested with power—the struggles of a strong ambition attempting, by a wanton exercise of authority, to revenge the disgrace of a feeble intellect.

But, my Lord, rest assured that yours is a mind which, if it succeeded in originating, is not destined to direct, a revolution. Whatever may be the issue of the great struggle now carrying on in this country, whether we may be permitted to be again great, glorious, and free, or whether we be doomed to sink beneath the ignoble tyranny which your machinations are preparing for us, your part in the mighty drama must soon close. To suppose that, with all your efforts and all your desperation, to suppose that, with all the struggles of your ambition to supply the deficiency of your intellect, your Lordship, in those heroic hours when empires are destroyed or saved, is fated to be anything else than an instrument, is to suppose that which contradicts all the records of history and all our experience of human nature.

I think it is Macrobius who tells a story of a young Greek, who, having heard much of the wealth and wisdom of Egypt, determined on visiting that celebrated land. When he beheld the pyramids of Memphis and the gates of Thebes, he exclaimed: " O wonderful men ! what must be your gods !" Full of the memory of the glorious divinities of his own poetic land, the blooming Apollo and the bright Diana, the awful beauty of the Olympian

Jove and the sublime grace of the blue-eyed Athena, he entered the temples of the Pharaohs. But what was his mingled astonishment and disgust when he found a nation prostrate before the most contemptible and the most odious of created beings ! The gods of Egypt are the Ministers of England.

I can picture to myself an intelligent foreigner, attracted by the fame of our country, and visiting it for the first time. I can picture to myself his admiration when he beholds our great public works; our roads, our docks, our canals; our unrivalled manufactories, our matchless agriculture. That admiration would not be diminished when he learnt that we were free; when he became acquainted with our social comfort and our still equal laws. " O wonderful men !" he would exclaim, " what must be your governors !" But conceive him now, entered into our political temple; conceive his appalled astonishment as he gazes on the ox-like form of the Lansdowne Apis. On one side he beholds an altar raised to an ape, on the other incense is burned before a cat-like colleague. Here, placed in the shapes of Palmerston and Grant, the worship of two sleek and long-tailed rats; and then learns, with amazement, that the Lord Chancellor of this great land is an onion or a cheese. Towering above all, and resting on a lurid shrine bedewed with blood and encircled with flame, with distended jaws and colossal tail, is the grim figure of the O'Connell crocodile. But, my Lord, how thunderstruck must be our visitor when he is told to recognise a Secretary of State in an infinitely small scarabæus;—yes, my Lord, when he learns that you are the leader of the English House of Commons, our traveller may begin to comprehend how the Egyptians worshipped—AN INSECT.

January 30, 1836.

LETTER VIII

To the People

This is the first direct address that has ever been made to the real people of England. For the last few years, a gang of scribblers, in the pay of a desperate faction, have cloaked every incendiary appeal that they have vomited forth to any section of your numbers, however slight, or however opposed to the honour and happiness of the nation, by elevating the object of their solicitude into that imposing aggregate, the people. Thus have they played, for their ulterior purposes, dissenting sects against the National Church, manufacturing towns against agricultural districts, the House of Commons against the House of Lords, new burgesses against ancient freemen, and finally, the Papists against the Protestants. With scarcely an exception, you may invariably observe that in advocating the cause of "the people" these writers have ever stimulated the anti-national passions of the minority. But, in addressing you now, I address myself in very truth to the English people—to all orders and conditions of men that form that vast society, from the merchant to the mechanic, and from the peer to the peasant.

You are still a great people. You are still in the possession and enjoyment of the great results of civilisation, in spite of those who would destroy your internal prosperity. Your flag still floats triumphant in every division of the globe, in spite of the menaces of dismemberment that threaten your empire from every quarter. Neither domestic nor foreign agitation has yet succeeded in uprooting your supremacy. But how long this imperial integrity may subsist, when it is the object of a faction in your own land to array great classes of your population in hostile collision, and when, from the Castle of Dublin to the Castle of Quebec, your honour is tampered with by the deputies of your sovereign, is a question which well deserves your quick and earnest consideration.

In the mesh of unparalleled difficulties in which your affairs are now entangled, who are your guides ? Are they men in whose wisdom and experience, in whose virtue and talents, principle and resolution, in whose acknowledged authority and unblemished honour and deserved celebrity, you are justified in reposing your hopes and entrusting your confidence ? Lucian once amused the ancients with an auction of their gods. Let us see what Mr. George Robins[1] might think of an auction of your Ministers. The catalogue may soon be run over.

A Prime Minister in an easy-chair, reading a French novel. What think you of that lot ? Three Secretaries of State, one odious, another contemptible, the third both. They have their price, yet I would not be their purchaser. A new Lord Chancellor, like a new cheese, crude and flavourless: second-rate as a lawyer, as a statesman a nonentity, bought in by his own party from sheer necessity. A President of the India Board,[2] recovering from the silence of years imposed upon him by Canning, by the inspiration of that eloquent man's chair which he now fills. As we are still a naval nation, our First Lord of the Admiralty should be worth something; but, unfortunately, nobody knows his name.[3] The President of the Council[4] has always indicated a tendency to join any Government, and therefore should be a marketable article enough. In Egypt, where their favourite food are pumpkins that have run to seed, such a solid and mature intelligence might be worth exporting to the Divan. The Chancellor of the Exchequer, being " a man of business," would doubtless fetch " a long figure "; refer for character to the mercantile deputations who leave the Treasury after an interview, bursting

[1] G. H. Robins (1778–1847), the great auctioneer.
[2] Sir John Cam Hobhouse.
[3] The Earl of Minto.   [4] The Marquis of Lansdowne.

with laughter from sheer admiration of his knowledge and capacity. Lord Howick, who is a Minister on the same principle that the son of an old partner is retained in the firm to keep together the connection, might command a price on this score, were it not notorious that his parent has withdrawn with his person, his capital, and confidence. The remainder may be thrown into one lot, and the auction concluded with the item on the Dutch system.

Were the destinies of a great people ever yet entrusted to such a grotesque and Hudibrastic crew? Why, we want no candid confessions or triumphant revelations from Mr. Sheil; we want no audacious apostacy of a whole party to teach us how such a truckling rout governs England. They govern England as the mock dynasties governed Europe in the time of the Revolution, by a process as sure and as simple, as desperate and as degrading—by being the delegates of an anti-national power. And what is this power beneath whose sirocco breath the fame of England is fast withering? Were it the dominion of another conqueror, another bold bastard with his belted sword, we might gnaw the fetter which we could not burst; were it the genius of Napoleon with which we were again struggling, we might trust the issue to the god of battles with a sainted confidence in our good cause and our national energies: but we are sinking beneath a power before which the proudest conquerors have grown pale, and by which the nations most devoted to freedom have become enslaved—the power of a foreign priesthood.

The Pope may be an old man, or an old woman, once the case, but the Papacy is independent of the Pope. The insignificance of the Pope is adduced by your enemies as evidence of the insignificance of the Papacy. 'Tis the fatal fallacy by which they mean to ride roughshod over England. Is the Pope less regarded now than when Bourbon sacked Rome? Yet that exploit preceded the massacre of St. Bartholomew and the revocation of the

Edict of Nantes.   The Constable of Bourbon lived before
Sir Phelim O'Neale.   The Papacy is as rampant now in
Ireland as it was in Europe in the time of Gregory; and
all its energies *are* directed to your humiliation.

Who is this man whose name is ever on your lips ?
Who is this O'Connell ?   He is the feed advocate of the
Irish priesthood; he is the hired instrument of the Papacy.
That is his precise position.   Your enemies, that wretched
anti-national faction who wish to retain power, or creep
into place, by clinging to the skirts of this foreign rebel,
taunt those who would expose his destructive arts and
unmask the purpose of his desperate principals with the
wretched scoff that we make him of importance by our
notice.   He cannot be of more importance than he is.
Demoralised in character, desperate in fortunes, infinitely
over-estimated in talents, he is the most powerful individual in the world because he is entrusted with the delegated influence of the greatest power in existence.   But
because an individual exercises a great power, it does not
follow that he is a great man.   O'Connell is not as yet as
great as Robespierre, although he resembles that terrific
agitator in everything except his disinterestedness.
Robespierre presided over public safety as O'Connell over
Reform.   A precious foster-dam !   Would it have been
any answer to those who would have struggled against
the great insurer of public security, that his intended
victims made him of importance by their notice ?   Would
it have been endured that these deprecators of resistance
should have urged, " He is not a Cæsar, he is not an
Alexander, he has no amplitude of mind, he is not
a great genius; let him go on murdering, you make
him of importance by noticing his career of blood and
havoc !"

This man, O'Connell, is the hired instrument of the
Papacy; as such, his mission is to destroy your Protestant
society, and, as such, he is a more terrible enemy to
England than Napoleon, with all his inspiration.   Your
empire and your liberties are in more danger at this

moment than when the army of invasion was encamped at Boulogne.

Now we have a precise idea of the political character of O'Connell. And I have often marvelled when I have listened to those who have denounced his hypocrisy or admired his skill, when they have read of the triumphant demagogue humbling himself in the mud before a simple priest. There was no hypocrisy in this, no craft. The agent recognised his principal, the slave bowed before his lord; and when he pressed to his lips those sacred robes, reeking with whisky and redolent of incense, I doubt not that his soul was filled at the same time with unaffected awe and devout gratitude.

If we have correctly fixed his political character, let us see whether we can as accurately estimate his intellectual capacity and his moral qualities. The hired writers would persuade you that he is a great man. He has not a single quality of a great man. In proportion as he was so gifted, he would be less fitted for the part which he has to perform. There is a sublime sentiment in genius, even when uncontrolled by principle, that would make it recoil with nausea from what this man has to undergo. He is shrewd, vigorous, versatile; with great knowledge of character, little of human nature; with that reckless dexterity which confounds weak minds, and that superficial readiness that masters vulgar passions; energetic from the certainty of his own desperate means, and from the strong stimulus of his provisional remuneration; inexhaustible in unprincipled expedients, and audacious in irresponsible power; a *nisi prius* lawyer, with the soul of a demagogue. That is the man. He is as little a great orator as a great man. He has not a single quality of a great orator except a good voice. I defy his creatures to produce a single passage from any speech he ever delivered illumined by a single flash of genius, or tinctured with the slightest evidence of taste, or thought, or study. Learning he has none; little reading. His style in speaking, as in writing, is ragged, bald, halting, disjointed. He has

no wit, though he may claim his fair portion of that Milesian humour which everyone inherits who bears a hod.
His pathos is the stage sentiment of a barn; his invective
is slang.   When he aspires to the higher style of rhetoric,
he is even ludicrous.   He snatches up a bit of tinsel, a
tawdry riband, or an artificial flower, and mixes it with
his sinewy commonplace and his habitual soot like a
chimney-sweeper on May-day.

Of his moral character it might be enough to say that
he is a systematic liar and a beggarly cheat, a swindler
and a poltroon.   But of O'Connell you can even say more.
His public and his private life are equally profligate; he
has committed every crime that does not require courage:
the man who plunders the peasant can also starve his
child.   He has denounced your national character and
insulted your national honour.   He has said that all your
men are cowards and all your women wantons.   He has
reviled your illustrious princes—he has sneered at your
pure religion—he has assailed your National Church.   He
has endeavoured to stir up rebellion against your august
Senate, and has described your House of Commons, even
when reformed, as an assembly of "six hundred scoun-
drels."   Everything which is established comes under his
ban, because everything which is established is an obstacle to the purpose for which he is paid—the destruction
of everything which is ENGLISH.

February 2, 1836.

LETTER IX

To LORD STANLEY

MY LORD,—The classical historian of our country said
of your great ancestor that " the Countess of Derby had
the glory of being the *last* person in the three kingdoms,
and in all their dependent dominions, who submitted to
the victorious rebels."   Charlotte de la Trémoille was a
woman who might have shamed the degenerate men of

the present day; but your Lordship may claim, with a slight though significant alteration, the eulogium of that illustrious princess. The rebels are again victorious, and, to your Lordship's lasting honour, you have been the *first* to resist their treasonable authority.

Never has a statesman yet been placed in a position so difficult and so trying as the present heir of the house of Derby; never has a statesman under similar circumstances yet conducted himself with more discretion and more courage. When the acerbities of faction have passed away, posterity will do justice to your disinterestedness and devotion, and the future historian of England will record with sympathising admiration the greatness of your sacrifice.

If the gratification of your ambition had been your only object, your course was clear. Less than three years ago the Whigs, and loudest among them my Lord Melbourne, announced you as the future Prime Minister of England. Young, of high lineage, of illustrious station, and of immaculate character, and unquestionably their ablest orator—among your own party you had no rival. They looked upon you as the only man who could at the same time maintain their power and effectually resist the machinations of those who would equally destroy the constitution and dismember the empire. With what enthusiastic cheers did they not greet the winged words with which you assailed the anti-national enemy when you rose in the House like a young eagle, and dashed back his treason in the baffled countenance of the priestly delegate!

Who could believe that the same men who cheered you in the House, and chuckled over your triumphs in their coteries, should now be the truckling slaves of the sacer-dotal power from whose dark influence they then shrank with disgust and terror? Who could believe that the projected treason of these very men should have driven you and your high-minded colleagues from the contagion of their councils? Who could believe that the famous

" Reform Ministry," that packed a Parliament by bellowing " gratitude to Lord Grey " throughout the empire, should finally have expelled that same Lord Grey from his seat, under circumstances of revolting insult;[1] that the very Lord Melbourne who had always indicated yourself as Lord Grey's successor should himself have slid into that now sullied seat, where he maintains himself in indolent dependence by a foul alliance with the very man whom he had previously denounced as a traitor ? Can the records of public life, can the secret archives of private profligacy, afford a parallel instance of conduct so base, so completely degrading, so thoroughly demoralised?

You, my Lord, preferred your honour to your interest, the prosperity of your native land to the gratification of your ambition. You sacrificed without a pang the proudest station in your country, to prove to your countrymen that public principle was not yet a jest. You did well. The pulse of our national character was beating low. We required some great example to rebrace the energies of our honour. From the moment that you denounced this disgusting thraldom and the base expedients of your chicaning colleagues, a better feeling pervaded England and animated Englishmen. In this sharp exigency you did not forget your duty to yourself as well as to your country. Yours was no Coriolanus part; neither the taunts of the recent supporters who had betrayed you, nor the ready compliments of your former adversaries, tempted you to swerve for a moment from the onward path of a severe and peremptory principle. When Sir Robert Peel was summoned to the helm, in the autumn of 1834, your position was indeed most painful. Your honour and your duty seemed at conflict. You reconciled them. You supported the policy while you declined the power.

These, my Lord, are great deeds. They will live. The defence of Lathom[2] was not more heroic. They will live

---

[1] The Littleton intrigue with O'Connell, July, 1834.
[2] By Charlotte de la Trémoille, Countess of Derby, in 1644–45.

in the admiration and the gratitude of an ancient and honourable nation, ever ready to sympathise with the pure and noble, and prompt to recognise a natural leader in blood that is mingled with all the traditionary glories of their race.

You had now placed your character above suspicion. The most virulent of the hired writers of the faction did not dare to impugn the purity of your motives. You had satisfied the most morbid claims of an honour which the worldly only might deem too chivalrous. When, therefore, I find you at length avowedly united with that eminent man, on whom the hopes of his country rest with a deserving and discerning confidence, and who, in his parliamentary talents, his proud station, and his unsullied fame, is worthy of your alliance, I was rejoiced, but not surprised. It is a fit season to "stand together in your chivalry." The time is ripe for union and fair for concord. When, some days back, in my letter to Sir Robert Peel— a letter, let me observe in passing, written by one whose name, in spite of the audacious licence of frantic conjecture, has never yet been even intimated, can never be discovered, and will never be revealed—I announced the fact that the great Conservative party was at length completely united, it was a declaration equivalent to England being saved. The debates upon the address have proved the accuracy of my information. The hired writers and the place-hunting dependents of the priestly junta triumph over the division in the Commons; they might have read their knell in the voice of the tellers. They assure us, with solemn or with sparkling countenance, that they did not reckon upon a moiety of such a majority. And do they indeed think that the people of England care one jot whether there be ten or twenty traitors more or less in the House of Commons ? It is not a miserable majority in that assembly, either way, that will destroy or preserve the empire. That very debate, my Lord, over the result of which these short-sighted desperadoes affect to triumph, sealed the doom

of the faction and announced the salvation of the country.
It will fill every loyal and discerning heart throughout
England with more than hope. Whatever the hired
writers and the expectant runners may bawl or scribble,
that division numbered the days of the present Cabinet.
And they know it. The sacerdotal delegates know full
well that the moment the Conservatives are united, the
priestly plot is baffled.

When the First Lord of the Treasury was reinstalled in
the office which he won by so patriotic a process, and
which he fills with such diligent ability, shrinking from
the contamination of O'Connell, the very mention of
whose name in his private circle makes him even now
tremble with compunctious rage, he declared that affairs
might be carried on without "the victorious rebels,"
from the mere disunion of the Conservative camp. No
one was more completely aware than his Lordship that
the moment that disunion ceased, his authority must
tremble. To perpetuate distrust, and to excite division
among the different sections of the Conservative party,
all the energies of the anti-English cabal have of late been
directed. The Municipal Bill filled them with a fluttering
hope; a severance between the Duke of Wellington and
Sir Robert Peel was announced as inevitable. To-day a
great commoner and a learned lord no longer meet; to-
morrow the appropriation clause is to be got rid of by
some new juggle, and your Lordship and your fellow-
leaders are to return to the tainted benches of the Treasury. Now the conferences at Drayton hang fire; then
midnight visits from illustrious Princes bode splits and
schisms. We have scarcely recovered from the effect of
a suspicious dinner, when our attention is promptly
directed to a mysterious call. The debates on the address
have laid for ever these restless spectres of the disordered
imagination of a daunted yet desperate faction. In a
Peel, a Stanley, a Wellington, and a Lyndhurst, the people
of England recognised their fitting leaders. Let the
priestly party oppose to these the acrid feebleness of a

19

Russell and the puerile commonplace of a Howick, Melbourne's experienced energy, and Lansdowne's lucid perception !

February 6, 1836

LETTER X

To Lord William Bentinck [1]

My Lord,—I have just read your Lordship's Address to the Electors of the City of Glasgow; and, when I remember that the author of this production has been entrusted for no inconsiderable period with the government of 100,000,000 of human beings, I tremble. I say not this with reference to the measures of which you have there announced yourself the advocate, but to the manner in which that announcement is expressed. It implies, in my opinion, at the same time, a want of honesty and a want of sense.

This Address to the Electors of the City of Glasgow is made by an individual who has been employed for more than a quarter of a century by his sovereign in foreign service of the utmost importance, ascending, at last, even to the Viceregal throne of India; he is a member of a family of the highest rank and consideration; and some very persevering paragraphs in the Government journals have of late sedulously indicated him as a fit and future member of Lord Melbourne's Cabinet. Your Lordship, therefore, is a very considerable personage; the public are familiar with your name, if not with your career; they are instructed to believe you an individual of great mark and likelihood, of great promise as well as of great performance; as one who is not unwilling to devote to

[1] Lord William Bentinck (1774–1839), second son of the third Duke of Portland, was appointed Governor-General of Bengal in 1827, and on the passing of the East India Company's Charter Act in 1833 became the first Governor-General of India. He resigned in 1835, was elected Liberal Member for Glasgow in Feburary, 1836, and retained the seat until a few days before his death, June 17, 1839.

their interests at home all those talents which have been
so long exercised, and all that experience which has been
so laboriously obtained in their service in other and distant lands.   'Tis distance lends enchantment to the view,
sings a bard of that city which your Lordship is to represent: 'tis distance which has invested your Lordship with
the haze of celebrity; but I doubt whether the shadowy
illusion will be long proof against that nearer inspection
and more familiar experience of your judgment and capacity which your Lordship has favoured us with in your
Address to the Electors of the City of Glasgow.[1]

---

[1] The following is the address alluded to:

To the Electors of the City of Glasgow.

GENTLEMEN,—It is only in consequence of the very numerous
requisition which I have had the honour to receive that I could
have ventured to aspire to the high distinction of representing
you in Parliament. Encouraged by this invitation, I shall at
once proceed to state, frankly and explicitly, my opinion upon
the various topics and measures that are likely to be brought
before Parliament in the ensuing session, with a confident hope
that in this exposition nothing will be found at variance with
those principles which for many years of my life I have professed and practised; and upon which alone, and to no particular competency of my own, I can found a claim to your
suffrages.

Permit me then, in the outset, to give my adherence to the
now happily established conviction among all reformers, that by
firm union, by the abandonment of all separate and minor views,
and by a steady support of Lord Melbourne's Ministry, the
present and future cause of reform can alone be supported.

With respect to expected measures, I should decidedly support the ministerial plan of Irish Church Reform, imperfect and
insufficient as I must consider that measure to be.

I, of course, am a decided friend to a complete reform of the
Irish Municipal Corporations.

I am favourable to the shortening of the duration of Parliaments; but without having had occasion seriously to consider
this subject, I should prefer, as a present measure, the quin-
quennial to the triennial term.

With respect to the extension of the suffrage, into the details
of which I have never entered, I can only generally state my
firm belief that the broader the admission of all the intelligent
classes to the government of the country, the greater will be the
security of our existing institutions.

I am opposed to the vote by ballot; I consider it a complete
illusion. It will not destroy the exercise of undue influence,

There are some, indeed, who affirm—and those, too, persons of no mean authority—that this address may even be considered a manifesto of the least constitutional portion of the Cabinet to whom your Lordship and my Lord Durham are speedily to afford all the weight of your influence and all the advantage of your wisdom. How this may be, events will prove; the effusion is certainly sufficiently marked by the great characteristic of the Whig-Radical school; a reckless readiness to adopt measures of the details and consequences of which they are obviously and often avowedly ignorant.

The address itself consists of fourteen paragraphs. In the first your Lordship informs us that you come forward in consequence of " a very numerous requisition." What " a very numerous requisition," by-the-bye, may be, I pretend not to decipher. It may be Hindostanee; it may be Sanscrit; it is not English. With a modesty natural to an Oriental Viceroy, the late Master of the Great Mogul, you then make your salaam to the electors,

---

but it will give rise to another influence still more pernicious—that of money and corruption, against which there is no security but in publicity. At the same time, as the vote by ballot affects no existing right, I should willingly acquiesce in the general wishes of my constituents to vote for it as an experimental and temporary measure.

I am profoundly penetrated with the indispensable necessity that the two branches of the Legislature should be brought into harmony with each other; and I am of opinion that the result may be advantageously accomplished through the constitutional exercise of the prerogative of the Crown without any organic change.

I need not promise my support to all measures regarding freedom of trade, and economy and retrenchment in every department of the State, consistently, of course, with efficiency and safety.

The Corn Laws are a difficult question. I am for their abolition. If railways, as I believe, may become necessary in the race of competition that we have to run with other countries, the prices of subsistence must in a still greater degree contribute to success. I should hope that an equitable compromise between the agricultural and manufacturing interests might not be found impracticable.

I shall advert, in the last place, to the application for a grant of £10,000 towards the endowment of additional chapels and places of worship for the Established Church of Scotland. I

assuring them that but for this very numerous requisition you " could not have ventured to aspire to the high
distinction of representing Glasgow in Parliament "—of
representing Glasgow after having ruled Calcutta !

Your Lordship then proceeds to state, "frankly and
explicitly," your political creed, " with a confident hope,"
which seems, however, but a somewhat hesitating and
trembling trust, that "nothing will be found at variance
with those principles which for many years of your life
you have professed and practised." How many years,
my Lord William ?

After eulogising " union among all Reformers," but of
course in favour of Lord Melbourne's Government, and
the abandonment of " all separate and minor views," you
immediately declare, with admirable consistency, that
the Ministerial plan of Irish Church Reform does not go
far enough, but is " imperfect and insufficient." This is
certainly a very felicitous method of maintaining union
among all Reformers. There is no doubt with what

---

am entirely averse to this grant. The event, of all others, that
in my humble judgment would best establish peace and good-
will and concord among all classes of men, would be a perfect
equality of civil and religious rights.

But as this cannot at present be, at least let us be careful
not to aggravate an obnoxious distinction. Let the Established
Churches retain what they possess, but let nothing more be
taken from the public funds. The same religious zeal which
exclusively maintains all the places of worship and the ministers
of Dissenters, cannot fail to supply those additional aids of which
the Established Churches of England and Scotland may stand in
need.

I will now conclude with the expression of my very deep
regret that the effects of the very long and severe illness which
drove me from India will not allow me without positive risk,
to appear at the election. But if I am so fortunate as to obtain
the honour to which I aspire, I shall take the earliest opportunity, after the session, of visiting Glasgow; and should it
then be the opinion of the majority of my constituents that the
generous confidence which they have been pleased to place in
me has been in any degree disappointed, I shall be most ready
to resign the trust confided in me.

I have the honour to be, Gentlemen,
Your most obedient servant,
W. BENTINCK.

LONDON,
February 4, 1836.

section of that rebellious camp your Lordship will herd,
you who are, " of course, a decided friend to a complete
reform in the Irish municipal corporations."

Your Lordship, it appears, is also "favourable to the
shortening of the duration of Parliaments," although you
ingenuously allow that you " have had no occasion
seriously to consider the subject "; and that you are
partial to the " extension of the suffrage," into the details
of which, however, you candidly admit you " have never
entered "! Admirable specimen of the cautious pro-
fundity of Whig Radicalism! Inimitable statesman,
who, busied with concocting constitutions for Sicily, and
destroying empires in India, can naturally spare but few
hours to the consideration of the unimportant topics of
domestic policy.

Your decisive judgment, however, on the subject of the
ballot will clear your Lordship in a moment from any
silly suspicion of superficiality. This paragraph is so
rich and rare that it merits the dangerous honour of a
quotation:

"I am opposed to the vote by ballot; I consider it a
complete illusion. It will not destroy the exercise of undue
influence, but it will give rise to another influence still more
pernicious, that of money and corruption, against which there
is no security but in publicity. At the same time, as the
vote by ballot affects no existing right, I should willingly
acquiesce in the general wishes of my constituents to vote
for it as an experimental and temporary measure."

Without stopping to admire your refined distinction
between an influence which is undue and " another influence " which is pernicious, one cannot too ardently
applaud the breathless rapidity with which your Lordship hurries to assure your future constituents that you
will willingly support an illusion and a pest.

The ninth paragraph of this memorable production
informs us that your Lordship is " profoundly penetrated " with an idea. Pardon my scepticism, my Lord;
whatever other claims you may have to the epithet, I
doubt whether your Lordship's *ideas* are radical. I am

indeed mistaken if their roots have ever "profoundly penetrated" your cultured intellect. Was it this "profound penetration" that prompted the brother of the Duke of Portland to declare his conviction of "the indispensable necessity of bringing the two branches of the legislature into harmony with each other by the constitutional exercise of the prerogative of the Crown"? Your Lordship may settle this point with His Grace.

The tenth paragraph is only remarkable for the felicity of its diction. The honourable member for Middlesex has at length found in the future member for Glasgow a rival in the elegance of his language and the precision of his ideas.

But now for your masterpiece! "The Corn Laws are a difficult question; I am for their abolition." How exquisitely does this sentence paint your weak and puzzled mind and your base and grovelling spirit! Confessing at the same time your inability to form an opinion, yet gulping down the measure to gain the seat. Space alone prevents me from following the noble candidate for Glasgow through the remainder of his address, admirably characteristic as it is of the same mixture of a perplexed intellect and a profligate ambition.

My Lord, I have not the honour of your acquaintance; I bear you no personal ill-will. I stop not here to inquire into the proceedings of your former life—of your Sicilian freaks or of your Spanish exploits, or of your once impending catastrophe in India. I form my opinion of your character from your last public act, and, believing as I do, that there is a conspiracy on foot to palm you off on the nation as a great man, in order that your less hackneyed name may prolong the degrading rule of a desperate faction, I was resolved to chalk your character on your back before you entered the House where you are doomed to be silent or absurd. There are some of your acquaintances who would represent you as by no means an ill-intentioned man; they speak of you as a sort of dull Quixote. For myself, I believe you to be without any political principle, but that you are unprincipled from the weakness of your head, not from the badness of your heart. Your great connections have thrust you into great places. You have been haunted with a restless conviction that you ought not to be a nonentity, and, like bustling men without talents, you have always committed great blunders. To avoid the Scylla of passive impotence, you have sailed into the Charybdis of active incapacity.

But you are, or you will be, member for Glasgow. The author of such an address meets, of course, with "no opposition." Discriminating electors of Glasgow! Send up your noble member to the House, where the Government newspapers assure us he will soon be a Minister. His difference with the present Cabinet is trifling. He only deems the Irish Church reform "imperfect and insufficient." He is, "of course," for a complete reform of the Irish corporations. He is for short Parliaments, he is for the ballot, he is for extension of the suffrage, he is for the abolition of the Corn Laws, the virtual annihilation of the House of Lords, and the gradual destruction of all alliance between the Church and the State. What more can you require? His Sicilian constitution?

It would, however, be disingenuous to conceal that there is at the conclusion of your Lordship's address a sentence which almost leads one to impute its production to other causes than the impulse of a party or the original weakness of your character. It appears that "a long and severe illness drove you from India," and even now incapacitates you from personally soliciting the suffrages of your choice constituents. Have, then, the republican electors of Glasgow, eager to be represented by a Lord, selected for their champion in the Senate one of those mere lees of debilitated humanity and exhausted nature which the winds of India and the waves of the Atlantic periodically waft to the hopeless breezes of their native cliffs? The address is ominous; and perhaps, ere the

excitement of a session may have passed, congenial
Cheltenham will receive from now glorious Glasgow the
antiquated Governor and the drivelling Nabob !

February 11, 1836.

LETTER XI

To Viscount Palmerston

My Lord,—The Minister who maintains himself in
power in spite of the contempt of a whole nation must
be gifted with no ordinary capacity. Your Lordship's
talents have never had justice done to them. Permit me
to approach you in the spirit of eulogy; if novelty have
charms, this encomium must gratify you. Our language
commands no expression of scorn which has not been
exhausted in the celebration of your character; there is
no conceivable idea of degradation which has not been,
at some period or another, associated with your career.
Yet the seven Prime Ministers,[1] all of whom you have
served with equal fidelity, might suffice, one would think,
with their united certificates, to vamp up the first; and
as for your conduct, so distinguished an orator as your
Lordship has recently turned out can never want a
medium for its triumphant vindication, even if it were
denied the columns of that favoured journal where we
occasionally trace the finished flippancy of your Lordship's
airy pen.

[1] Portland, Perceval, Liverpool, Canning, Goderich, Grey, and
Melbourne. He also served for a few months under the Duke of
Wellington. On March 8, 1842, in the House of Commons, Disraeli sharpened the point of this dart against Lord Palmerston,
who had sarcastically expressed a hope that Disraeli would
obtain promotion from Sir Robert Peel, who had neglected him
on forming his administration. Disraeli replied to the following
effect: " The noble Viscount is a consummate master of the subject, and if to assist my advancement he will only impart to me
the secret of his own unprecedented rise, and by what means he
has contrived to enjoy power under seven successive administrations, I shall at least have gained a valuable result by this discussion."

The bigoted Tories under whose auspices your Lordship entered public life had always, if I mistake not, some narrow-minded misgiving of your honesty as well as your talents, and with characteristic illiberality doomed you to official insignificance. It was generally understood that under no circumstances was your Lordship ever to be permitted to enter the Cabinet. Had you been an anticipated Aislabie,[1] you could not have been more rigidly excluded from that select society; you were rapidly advanced to a position which, though eminent, was also impassable; and having attained this acme of second-rate statesmanship, you remained fixed on your pedestal for years, the Great Apollo of aspiring under-strappers.

When the ambition of Mr. Canning deprived him of the ablest of his colleagues, your Lordship, with that dexterity which has never deserted you, and which seems a happy compound of the smartness of an attorney's clerk and the intrigue of a Greek of the Lower Empire, wriggled yourself into the vacant Cabinet. The Minister who was forced to solicit the co-operation of a Lansdowne might be pardoned for accepting the proffer of a Palmerston; but even in his extreme distress Mr. Canning was careful not to promote you from your subordinate office; nor can I conceive a countenance of more blank dismay, if that brilliant rhetorician, while wandering in the Elysian fields, were to learn that his favourite portfolio was now in your Lordship's protocolic custody.

A member of Mr. Canning's Cabinet by necessity, you became a member of the Duke of Wellington's by sufferance. You were expelled from your office for playing a third-rate part in a third-rate intrigue. Your Lordship was piqued, and revenged yourself on your country by becoming a Whig. I remember when, in old days, you

---

[1] John Aislabie (1670–1742), who, for his connection with the South Sea Bubble, was compelled to resign his position as Chancellor of the Exchequer, being adjudged by the House of Commons guilty of "most notorious, dangerous, and infamous corruption."

addressed the Speaker on our side of the House, your
oratorical displays were accompanied not only by the
blushes, but even the hesitation, of youth. These might
have been esteemed the not unpleasing characteristics
of an ingenuous modesty, had they not been associated
with a callous confidence of tone and an offensive flippancy
of language, which proved that they were rather the
consequence of a want of breeding than of a deficiency
of self-esteem. The leader of the Whig Opposition was
wont to say, in return perhaps for some of those pasquinades with which you were then in the habit of
squibbing your present friends, that your Lordship reminded him of a favourite footman on easy terms with
his mistress. But no sooner had you changed your
party than all Brooks's announced you as an orator.
You made a speech about windmills and Don Quixote,
and your initiation into Liberalism was hailed complete.
Your Lordship, indeed, was quite steeped in the spirit
of the age. You were a new-born babe of that political
millennium which gave England at the same time a
Reform Bill and your Lordship for a Secretary of State.
I can fancy Mr. Charles Grant assisting at your adult
baptism, and witnessing your regeneration in pious
ecstasy.

The intellectual poverty of that ancient faction who
headed a revolution with which they did not sympathise
in order to possess themselves of a power which they
cannot wield, was never more singularly manifested than
when they delivered the seals of the most important
office in the State to a Tory underling. You owe the
Whigs great gratitude, my Lord, and therefore I think
you will betray them. Their imbecility in offering you
those seals was only equalled by your audacity in accepting them. Yet that acceptance was rather impudent
than rash. You were justly conscious that the Cabinet
of which you formed so ludicrous a member was about
to serve out measures of such absorbing interest in our
domestic policy, that little time could be spared by the

nation to a criticism of your Lordship's labours. During
the agitation of Parliamentary Reform your career re-
sembled the last American war in the midst of the
revolutions of Europe: it was very disgraceful, but never
heard of. Occasionally, indeed, rumours reached the
ear of the nation of the Russians being at Constantinople,
or the French in Italy and Flanders. Sometimes we
were favoured with a report of the effective blockade of
our ancient allies, the Dutch; occasionally of the civil
wars you had successfully excited in the Peninsula,
which we once delivered from a foreign enemy. But
when life and property were both at stake, when the
Trades Unions were marching through the streets of the
metropolis in battle array, and Bristol was burning,
your countrymen might be excused for generally believing
that your Lordship's career was as insignificant as your
intellect.

But your saturnalia of undetected scrapes and un-
punished blunders is now over. The affairs of the
Continent obtrude themselves upon our consideration
like an importunate creditor who will no longer be denied.
There is no party cry at home to screen your foreign
exploits from critical attention. The author of the
New Whig Guide[1] may scribble silly articles in newspapers about justice to Ireland, but he will not succeed
in diverting public notice from the painful consequences
of his injustice in Europe.   To-night, as we are informed,
some results of your Lordship's system of non-interference
in the affairs of Spain are to be brought under the consideration of the House of Commons.   I am not in the
confidence of the Hon. Gentleman who will introduce
that subject to the notice of the assembly of which, in
spite of the electors of Hampshire, your Lordship has
somehow or other contrived to become a member.   But
I speak of circumstances with which I am well acquainted,
and for the accuracy of which I stake my credit as a

[1] See Disraeli's note to his "Heroic Epistle to Lord Visct.
Mel——e."

public writer, when I declare that of the 10,000 or
12,000 of your fellow-countrymen whom your crimping
Lordship inveigled into a participation in the civil wars
of Spain[1] for no other purpose than to extricate yourself
from the consequences of your blundering policy, not
3,000 effective men are now in the field; such have been
the fatal results of the climate and the cat-o'-nine-tails,
of ignoble slaughter and of fruitless hardship. Your
Lordship may affect to smile, and settle your cravat as
if you were arranging your conscience; you may even
prompt the most ill-informed man in His Majesty's
dominions—I mean, of course, the First Lord of His
Majesty's Treasury—to announce in the Upper House
that the career of the British Legion has been a progress
of triumph, and that its present situation is a state of
comparative comfort; but I repeat my statement, and
I declare most solemnly, before God and my country,
that I am prepared to substantiate it.   When the most
impudent and the vilest of your Lordship's supporters
next amuses the House with his clap-trap appeals to the
tears of the widow and the sighs of the orphan, your
Lordship may perhaps remember the responsibility you
have yourself incurred, and, sick as the nation may be of
this inglorious destruction, there is one silly head, I
believe, that it would grieve no one to see added to the
heap.   It would atone for the havoc, it would extenuate
the slaughter, and the member for Westminster, who is
a patriot in two countries, would be hailed on his return
as the means of having rid both England and Spain of
an intolerable nuisance.

For the last five years a mysterious dimness seems to
have been stealing over the gems of our imperial diadem.
The standard of England droops fitfully upon its staff.
He must indeed be an inexperienced mariner who does
not mark the ground swell of the coming tempest.   If
there be a war in Europe to-morrow, it will be a war
against English supremacy, and we have no allies.

[1] General de Lacy Evans's British Legion.

None but your Lordship can suppose that the Cabinet of the Tuileries is not acting in concert with the Court of the Kremlin.   Austria, our natural friend on the Continent of Europe, shrinks from the contamination of our political propagandism.   If there be a European war, it will be one of those contests wherein a great State requires for its guidance all the resources of a master mind; it would be a crisis which would justify the presence of a Richelieu, a Pombal, or a Pitt.   O my country! fortunate, thrice fortunate England! with your destinies at such a moment entrusted to the Lord Fanny[1] of diplomacy!   Methinks I can see your Lordship, the Sporus of politics, cajoling France with an airy compliment, and menacing Russia with a perfumed cane!

February 22, 1836.

LETTER XII

To Sir John Hobhouse

Sir,—Your metamorphosis into a Whig and a Cabinet Minister has always appeared to me even less marvellous than your transformation into a wit and a leader, after having passed the most impetuous years of life in what might have appeared to the inexperienced the less ambitious capacity of a dull dependent.   In literature and in politics, until within a very short period, you have always shone with the doubtful lustre of reflected light. You have gained notoriety by associating yourself with another's fame.   The commentator of Byron, you naturally became in due season "Sir Francis Burdett's man," as Mr. Canning styled you, to your confusion, in the

---

[1] A nickname originally given by Pope to John, Lord Hervey, author of the "Memoirs of the Reign of George the Second"; also called by Pope "Sporus":

"What, that thing of silk?
Sporus, that mere white curd of ass's milk?
Satire or sense, alas! can Sporus feel?
Who breaks a butterfly upon a wheel?"

House of Commons; and to which sneer, after having taken a week to arrange your impromptu, you replied in an elaborate imitation of Chatham, admitted by your friends to be the greatest failure in parliamentary memory. At college your dignified respect for the peerage scarcely prepared us for your subsequent sneers at the order. Your readiness to bear the burden of the scrapes of those you honoured by your intimacy announced the amiability of your temper. Yet, whether you were sacrificing yourself on the altar of friendship, or concocting notes upon the pasquinades which others scribbled, there was always " something too ponderous about your genius for a joke "; and when these words fell from your lips on Friday night,[1] to me they seemed to flow with all the practised grace of a *tu quoque*, and to be not so much the inspiration of the moment as the reminiscence of some of those quips and cranks of Mathews and Scrope Davies [2] of which you were the constant, and often the unconscious, victim.

It may be the prejudice of party, perhaps the force of old associations, but to me your new character seems but thinly to veil your ancient reputation. There is a massy poise even in your airiest flights, that reminds one rather of the vulture than the eagle; and your lightest movements are pervaded with a sort of elephantine grace which forces us to admire rather the painful tutorage of art than nature's happier impulse. Bustling at the University, blustering on the hustings, dangling the seals of office—a humble friend, a demagogue, or a placeman— your idiosyncrasy still prevails, and in your case. " piddling Theobalds " has, at the best, but turned into " slashing Bentley."[3]

Allow me to congratulate you on your plaintive confession, amid the roars of the House, that " circumstances

[1] In the debate on Spain.
[2] Scrope Berdmore Davies, a " scholar-dandy," the friend of Byron.
[3] " From slashing Bentley down to pidling Tibalds."—Pope's " Epistle to Dr. Arbuthnot."

have brought you and your noble friend, the Secretary of State for Foreign Affairs, together on the same bench." The honour of sharing the same seat with an individual might, in another's estimation, have sufficed, without the additional disgrace of calling attention to the stigma. There is something so contaminating in a connection with that man that, when you voluntarily avowed it, we might be excused for admiring your valour rather than your discretion. It is, in truth, a rare conjunction; and Circumstance, "that unspiritual god," as your illustrious companion, Lord Byron, has happily styled that commonplace divinity, has seldom had to answer for a more degrading combination. You have met, indeed, like the puritan and the prostitute on the banks of Lethe in Garrick's farce, with an equally convenient oblivion of the characteristic incidents of your previous careers; you giving up your annual parliaments and universal suffrage, he casting to the winds his close corporations and borough nominees; you whispering Conservatism on the hustings, once braying with your revolutionary uproar, he spouting reform in the still recesses of the dust of Downing Street; the one reeking from a Newgate cell, the other redolent of the boudoirs of Mayfair; yet both of them, alike the Tory underling and the Radical demagogue, closing the ludicrous contrast with one grand diapason of harmonious inconsistency—both merging in the Whig Minister.

That a politician may at different periods of his life, and under very different aspects of public affairs, conscientiously entertain varying opinions upon the same measure, is a principle which no member of the present House of Commons is entitled to question. I would not deny you, Sir, the benefit of the charity of society; but when every change of opinion in a man's career is invariably attended by a corresponding and advantageous change in his position, his motives are not merely open to suspicion— his conduct is liable to conviction. Yet there is one revolution in your sentiments on which I may be permitted particularly to congratulate you and that country which you assist in misgoverning. Your sympathy on Friday night with the success of the British arms came with a consoling grace and a compensatory retribution from the man who has recorded in a solemn quarto [1] his bitter regret that his countrymen were victorious at Waterloo. I always admired the Whig felicity of your appointment as Secretary at War.

Pardon, Sir, the freedom with which I venture to address you. My candour may at least be as salutary as the cabbage-stalks of your late constituents.[2] There are some, indeed, who, as I am informed, have murmured at this method of communicating to them my opinion of their characters and careers. Yet I can conceive an individual so circumstanced that he would scarcely be entitled to indulge in such querulous sensitiveness. He should be one who had himself published letters without the ratification of his name, and then suppressed them; he should be one who had sat in trembling silence in the House when he was dared to repeat the statement which he had circulated by the press; he should be one to whom it had been asserted in his teeth that he was " a liar and a scoundrel, and only wanted courage to be an assassin." It does not appear to me that such an individual could complain with any justice of the frankness of " Runnymede."

February 27, 1836.

LETTER XIII

To Lord Glenelg

My Lord,—Let me not disturb your slumbers too rudely: I will address you in a whisper, and on tiptoe. At length I have succeeded in penetrating the recesses

---

[1] " The Substance of Some Letters written by an English Gentleman resident at Paris during the Last Reign of the Emperor Napoleon."

[2] The electors of Westminster.

of your enchanted abode. The knight who roused the Sleeping Beauty could not have witnessed stranger marvels in his progress than he who has at last contrived to obtain an interview with the sleeping Secretary.

The moment that I had passed the Foreign Office an air of profound repose seemed to pervade Downing Street, and as I approached the portal of your department, it was with difficulty I could resist the narcotic influence of the atmosphere. Your porter is no Argus. "His calm, broad, thoughtless aspect breathed repose," and when he "slow from his bench arose, and swollen with sleep," I almost imagined that, like his celebrated predecessor in the Castle of Indolence, he was about to furnish me with a nightcap, slippers, and a *robe de chambre*. I found your clerks yawning, and your under-secretaries just waking from a dream. A dozy, drowsy, drony hum, the faint rustling of some papers like the leaves of autumn, and a few noiseless apparitions gliding like ghosts, just assured me that the business of the nation was not neglected. Every personage and every incident gradually prepared me for the quiescent presence of the master mind, until, adroitly stepping over your private secretary, nodding and recumbent at your threshold, I found myself before your Lordship, the guardian of our colonial empire, stretched on an easy couch in luxurious listlessness, with all the prim voluptuousness of a puritanical Sardanapalus.

I forget who was the wild theorist who enunciated the absurd doctrine that "ships, colonies, and commerce," were the surest foundation of the empire. What an infinitely ridiculous idea ! But the march of intellect and the spirit of the age have cleansed our brains of this perilous stuff. Had it not been for the invention of ships, the great malady of sea-sickness, so distressing to an indolent Minister, would be unknown; colonies, like country-houses, we have long recognised to be sources only of continual expense, and to be kept up merely from a puerile love of show; as for commerce, it is a vulgarism, and fit only for low people. What have such dainty nobles as yourself and Lord Palmerston to do with cottons and indigoes ? Such coarse details you fitly leave to Mr. Poulett Thomson, whose practical acquaintance with tallow is the only blot on the scutcheon of your refined and aristocratic Cabinet.

Although a grateful nation has seized every opportunity of expressing their confidence in your Lordship and your colleagues, and although myself, among more distinguished writers, have omitted no occasion of celebrating your inexhaustible panegyric, it appears to me, I confess, that scant justice has hitherto been done to the grand system of our present administration, and which they are putting in practice with felicitous rapidity and their habitual success. This grand system, it would seem, consists of a plan to govern the country without having anything to do.

The meritorious and unceasing labours of the noble Secretary for Foreign Affairs for the destruction of English influence on the Continent will soon permit his Lordship to receive his salary without any necessary attendance at his office. Lord Morpeth [1] has nearly got rid of Ireland. The selection of your Lordship to regulate the destinies of our colonies insures the speediest and the most favourable results in effecting their emancipation from what one of your principal supporters styles "the unjust domination of the mother country "; and we are already promised a Lord Chancellor who is not to preside over the Chancery. The recent government of Lord William Bentinck will, I fear, rob Sir John Hobhouse of half the glory of losing India, and the municipal corporations, if they work as well as you anticipate, may in due season permit Lord John Russell to resume his relinquished lyre. Freed of our colonies, Ireland, and India, the affairs of the Continent consigned to their own insignificance, Westminster Hall delivered over to the cheap lawyers, and our domestic polity regulated by

[1] Chief Secretary for Ireland.

vestries and town councils, there is a fair probability
that the First Lord of the Treasury, who envies you your
congenial repose, may be relieved from any very onerous
burden of public duty, and that the Treasury may establish the aptness of its title on the *non lucendo* character
of its once shining coffers.

Vive la bagatelle! His Majesty's Ministers may then
hold Cabinet Councils to arrange a whitebait dinner at
Blackwall, or prick for an excursion to Richmond or
Beulah Spa. Such may be the gay consequences of a
Reform Ministry and a reformed Parliament! No true
patriot will grudge them these slight recreations, or
hazard even a murmur at their sinecure salaries. For to
say the truth, my Lord, if you must remain in office, I
for one would willingly consent to an inactivity on your
part almost as complete as could be devised by the
united genius for sauntering of yourself and that energetic
and laborious nobleman who summoned you to a worthy
participation in his councils.

Affairs, therefore, my dear Lord Glenelg, are far from
disheartening, especially in that department under your
own circumspect supervision. What if the Mauritius be
restive—let the inhabitants cut each others' throats : that
will ultimately produce peace. What if Jamaica be in
flames—we have still East India sugar; and by the time
we have lost that, the manufacture of beetroot will be
perfect. What if Colonel Torrens, perched on the
Pisgah height of a joint-stock company, be transporting
our fellow-countrymen to the milk and honey of Australia, without even the preparatory ceremony of a trial
by jury—let the exiles settle this great constitutional
question with the kangaroos. What if Canada be in
rebellion—let not the menacing spectre of Papineau[1] or
the suppliant shade of the liberal Gosford[2] scare your
Lordship's dreams. Slumber on without a pang, most

[1] The French leader of the rebellion in Canada.
[2] Lord Gosford, Governor of Canada.

vigilant of Secretaries. I will stuff you a fresh pillow with your unanswered letters, and insure you a certain lullaby by reading to you one of your own despatches.

March 12, 1836.

LETTER XIV

To the Right Hon. Edward Ellice[1]

Sir,—In this age of faction, it is delightful to turn to one public character whom writers of all parties must unite in addressing in terms of unqualified panegyric. From " a man discreditably known in the City," you have become a statesman creditably known at Court. Such is the triumph of perseverance in a good cause, undaunted by calumny and undeterred by the narrow-minded scruples of petty intellects. That influence which, in spite of prejudice, you have gained by the uniform straightforwardness of your conduct, you have confirmed by that agreeable and captivating demeanour which secures you the hearts of men as well as their confidence. Uninfluenced by personal motives, always ready to sacrifice self, and recoiling from intrigue with the antipathy native to a noble mind, you stand out in bold and favourable relief to the leaders of that party whose destinies, from a purely patriotic motive, you occasionally condescend to regulate.

I ought, perhaps, before this to have congratulated you on your return to that country whose interests are never absent from your thoughts; but I was unwilling to disturb, even with my compliments, a gentleman who, I am aware, has been labouring of late so zealously for the commonweal as the Right Hon. Mr. Ellice. Your devotion in your recent volunteer visit to Constantinople has not been lost on the minds of your countrymen.

---

[1] "Bear" Ellice was a business man connected with the northwest fur trade. Secretary for War in Lord Grey's Government, he went out with Melbourne in 1834, and never again took office.

They readily recognise your pre-eminent fitness to wrestle with the Russian bear; and they who have witnessed in a northern forest a duel between those polished animals, must feel convinced that you are the only English statesman duly qualified to mingle in a combat which is at the same time so dexterous and so desperate. Happy England, whose fortunes are supervised by such an unsalaried steward as the member for Coventry! Thrice fortunate Telemachus of Lambton Castle, guided by such a Mentor!

After the turmoil of party politics, you must have found travel delightful! I can fancy you gazing upon the blue Symplegades, or roaming amid the tumuli of Troy. The first glance at the Ægean must have filled you with classic rapture. Your cultured and accomplished mind must have revelled in the recollections of the heroic past. How different from the associations of those jobbing politicians, who, when they sail upon Salamis, are only reminded of Greek bonds, and whose thoughts, when they mingle amid the imaginary tumult of the Pnyx at Athens, only recur to the broils of a settling day at the Stock Exchange of London!

In your political career you have emulated the fame, and rivalled, if not surpassed, the exploits of the great Earl of Warwick. He was only a King-maker, but Mr. Ellice is a maker of Ministers. How deeply was Lord Grey indebted to your disinterested services! Amid the musings of the Liternum[1] of Howick, while moralising on the gratitude of a party, how fondly must he congratulate himself on his fortune in such a relative. It is said that his successor is not so prompt to indicate his sense of your services as would be but just. But the ingratitude of men, and especially of Ministers, is proverbial. Lord Melbourne, however, may yet live to be sensible of your amiable exercise of the prerogative of the Crown. In the meantime the unbounded confidence of Lord Palmerston in your good intentions may in some degree console

[1] The town to which Scipio Africanus retired.

you for the suspicions of the Prime Minister, to say nothing of the illimitable trust of the noble Secretary for the Colonies, who sleeps on in unbroken security as long as you are the guardian angel of his slumbers.

Distinguished as you are by the inflexible integrity of your conduct, both in public and private life, by your bland manners and your polite carriage, your total absence of all low ambition and your contempt for all intrigue and subterranean practices, you are, if possible, still more eminent for your philosophical exemption from antiquated prejudice. The people of England can never forget that it was your emancipated mind that first soared superior to the mischievous institution of a National Church, and that, with the characteristic liberality of your nature, yours was the intellect that first devised the ingenious plan of appeasing Ireland by the sacrifice of England. Had you been influenced in your conduct by any factious object of establishing your friends in the enjoyment of a power to exercise which they had previously proved themselves incapable, it might in some degree have deteriorated from the single-ness of your purpose; but no one can suppose, for an instant, that in forming a close alliance one year with a man whom twelve months before they had denounced as a rebel, or in decreeing the destruction of an institu-tion which they had just recently pledged themselves to uphold, your pupils of the present administration were actuated by any other motives but the most just, the most disinterested, and the most honourable.

You have recently been gratified by witnessing the proud and predominant influence of your country in the distant and distracted regions of the East. The compli-ments which were lavished on yourself and your com-panion by the Czar must have been as flattering to the envoy as they were to the confiding sovereign with whose dignity you were entrusted. It must be some time before the salutes of Odessa cease ringing in your ear, and it cannot be supposed that your excited imagination can speedily disembarrass itself of your splendid progress in a steamer over the triumphant waters of the Euxine. Yet, when you have in some degree recovered from the intoxication of success and the inebriating influence of Royal and Imperial condescension, let us hope that you may deign to extend your practised attention to our domestic situation. The country is very prosperous; the Stock Exchange has not been so active since 1825. They certainly have missed you a little in Spanish, but the railways, I understand, have been looking up since your return, especially the shares of those companies which have no hope or intention of prosecuting their designs. In the meantime, perhaps, for you may be destined the glory of inducing Lord Melbourne to tolerate the presence of Mr. O'Connell at an official banquet. That would be an achievement worthy of your great mind. The new Liberal Club, too, which, like Eldorado, is to supply

" Shirts for the shirtless, suppers for the starved,"

may merit your organising patronage. For the rest, the unbounded confidence which subsists between our gracious Sovereign and his Ministers, the complete harmony at length established between the two Houses of Parliament, the perfect tranquillity of Ireland, vouched by the *de facto* member for Dublin, and guaranteed by Lord Plunket, and the agreeable circumstance that the people of England are arrayed in two hostile and determined parties, all combine to assure us of a long, a tranquil, and a prosperous administration of our affairs by the last Cabinet which was constructed under your auspices.

March 20, 1836.

LETTER XV

TO VISCOUNT MELBOURNE

MY LORD,—I always experience peculiar gratification in addressing your Lordship—your Lordship is such a general favourite. I have read somewhere of " the best-natured man with the worst-natured muse." I have always deemed your Lordship the best-natured Minister with the worst-natured party. And really, if you have sometimes so lost your temper—if for those Epicurean shrugs of the shoulder, and *nil admirari* smiles, which were once your winning characteristics, you have occasionally of late substituted a little of the Cambyses' vein, and demeaned yourself as if you were practising " Pistol " for the next private theatricals at Panshanger—very extenuating circumstances may, I think, be found in the heterogeneous and Hudibrastic elements of that party which Fate, in a freak of fun, has called upon your Lordship to regulate. What a crew! I can compare them to nothing but the Swalbach swine in the Brunnen Bubbles,[1] guzzling and grunting in a bed of mire, fouling themselves, and bedaubing every luckless passenger with their contaminating filth.

We are all now going into the country, and you and your colleagues are about to escape for a season from what your Lordship delicately terms the " badgering " of Parliament. I trust you will find the relaxation renovating. How you will recreate yourselves, we shall be anxious to learn. I think the Cabinet might take to cricket—they are a choice eleven. With their peculiarly patriotic temperaments and highly national feelings, they might venture, I think, to play against " all England." Lord Palmerston and Lord Glenelg, with their talent for

[1] Sir Francis Bond Head's "Bubbles from the Brunnens of Nassau " (1834).

keeping in, would assuredly secure a good score. Lord
John, indeed, with all his flourishing, will probably end
in knocking down his own wicket; and as for Sir Cam,
the chances certainly are that he will be "caught out,"
experiencing the same fate in play as in politics. If you
could only engage Lord Durham to fling sticks at the seals
of the Foreign Office, and the agile Mr. Ellice to climb a
greasy pole for the Colonial portfolio, I think you will
have provided a very entertaining programme of Easter
sports.

My Lord, they say, you know, when things are at
the worst, they generally mend. On this principle our
affairs may really be considered highly promising. The
state of Spain demonstrates the sagacity of our Foreign
Secretary. The country is divided into two great parties;
we have contrived to interfere without supporting either,
but have lavished our treasure and our blood in upholding
a Camarilla. This is so bad that really the happiest
results may speedily be anticipated. Canada is in a state
of rebellion, and therefore after Easter we may perhaps find
loyalty and peace predominant, especially when we recall
to our recollection the profound intellect your Lordship
has selected for the settlement of that distracted colony.
The Whigs, my Lord, seem indeed to have a happy knack
in the choice of Governors, and almost to rival in their
appointments the Duke in "Don Quixote." To them we
are indebted alike for the prescient firmness of a Gosford
and the substantial judgment of a Sligo.[1] The spring-
like promise of the experienced Elphinstone will explain
the genial seed so deftly sown by the noble member for
Glasgow,[2] and complete the trio. Three wise and learned
rulers! To whomsoever of the leash my Lord Glenelg
may award the golden palm, I doubt not it will prove an
apple of sufficient discord.

"But all our praises why should Lords engross?"

---

[1] Formerly Governor of Jamaica.
[2] Lord William Bentinck, ex-Governor-General of India.

particularly when the appointments of Lord Auckland and Lord Nugent[1] are duly mentioned.

" Rise, honest muse, and sing Sir Francis Head!" [2]

The convenient candour of that celebrated functionary will at least afford one solacing reminiscence for your Easter holidays.

But what is Spanish anarchy or Canadian rebellion, the broils of Jamaica or the impending catastrophe of Hindostan, when Ireland is tranquil ? And who can doubt the tranquillity of Ireland ? Has not your Lordship the bond of the trustworthy Mr. O'Connell, whose private praises you celebrate with such curious felicity, and the choice collateral security of the veracious Lord Plunket. With such a muniment in the strong box of your Cabinet securities, what care you for the charges of Baron Smith and the calendar of Tipperary ? And yet, my Lord, though Ireland is tranquil, and though the Papists, in their attempts on the lives of their rivals, seem of late charitably to have substituted perjury for massacre, I fancy I mark a cloud upon your triumphant brow at my incidental mention of that fortunate land. Be of good cheer, my Lord; and if you cannot be bold, at least be reckless. In spite of the elaborate misrepresentations of party, the state of Irish affairs is very simple. The point lies in a nutshell, and may be expressed in a single sentence. Your Lordship's accommodation bills with Mr. O'Connell are becoming due, and unless you can contrive to get them renewed, the chances are your Lordship's firm will become bankrupt.

It seems, my Lord, that the hon. member for Finsbury[3] is about to move a petition to our gracious sovereign to intercede with the King of the French in favour of the State-victims of the three glorious days, persecuted like other great men for anticipating their age, and attempting to do that in 1830 the consummation of which was re-

[1] High Commissioner of the Ionian Islands.
[2] Lieutenant-Governor of Upper Canada.
[3] Mr. Thomas Slingsby Duncombe.

served for 1835. My Lord, buffoonery after a while wearies; put an end, I beseech you, to the farce of your government, and, to save time, consent at once that you and your colleagues should be substituted in their stead. Nay, I wish not to be harsh; my nature is not vindictive. I would condemn you to no severer solitude than the gardens of Hampton Court, where you might saunter away the remaining years of your now ludicrous existence, sipping the last novel of *Paul de Kock*, while lounging over a sundial.

March 30, 1836.

LETTER XVI

To the House of Lords

My Lords,—If there be one legislative quality more valuable than another, it is the power of discriminating between the Cause and the Pretext.[1] For two sessions of Parliament an attempt has been made to force upon your Lordships' adoption a peculiar scheme of policy under the pretext of doing " justice to Ireland." A majority of the members of the House of Commons, no matter how obtained, have not felt competent, or inclined, to penetrate beneath the surface of this plausible plea. They have accepted the pretext as a sound and genuine principle of conduct, and have called for your Lordships' co-operation in measures which you have declined to sanction, because you believe you have distinguished the concealed from the ostensible motive of their proposition. Your Lordships believe, that under the pretext of doing " justice to Ireland," you are called upon to do " injustice to England," and to assist the cause of Irish independence and papal supremacy.

[1] " A very good pretext may be the delusive cloak of a very bad cause " (Disraeli in the *Morning Post*, August 21, 1835). " It is an important principle in morals and in politics not to mistake the cause for the pretext, nor the pretext for the cause, and by this means to distinguish between the concealed and the ostensible motive " (Isaac D'Israeli: " Curiosities of Literature ").

My Lords, the English nation agrees with you. The experience of the last few years has not been lost upon your reflective countrymen. Under the pretext of emancipating the Irish people, they have witnessed the establishment of the dominion of a foreign priesthood—under the pretext of Parliamentary Reform, they have witnessed the delusive substitution of Whig Government—under the pretext of Municipal Reform in England, they have seen a sectarian oligarchy invested with a monopoly of power, tainting the very fountains of justice, and introducing into the privacy of domestic life all the acerbities of public faction—and under the pretext of "justice to Ireland," they have already beheld the destruction of Protestant ascendancy, and the Papacy, if not supreme, at least rampant. The English nation are reaping the bitter fruits of not sufficiently discriminating between the ostensible and concealed purposes of legislation. Had they been aware some years back, as they now keenly feel, that they were only extending power and privileges to a priesthood when they thought they were emancipating a people, the miserable dilemma of modern politics would never have occurred. They would not have witnessed the gentlemen of Ireland driven from its parliamentary representation, and deprived of their local influence; they would not have witnessed a fierce and bloody war waged against the property of the Protestant Church and the lives of its ministers; they would not have witnessed the Imperial Parliament occupied in a solemn debate on the propriety of maintaining the legislative union. Political revolutions are always effected by virtue of abstract pleas. "Justice to Ireland" is about as definite as "the Rights of Man." If the Irish have an equal right with ourselves to popular corporations, have they less a right to a domestic Legislature or a native Sovereign? My Lords, are you prepared to go this length? Are you prepared to dismiss circumstances from your consideration, and legislate solely upon principles? Is the British Senate an assembly of dreaming schoolmen that they are resolved to deal with words in preference to facts ?   Is a great empire to be dissolved by an idle logomachy ?   If Dublin have an equal right with Westminster to the presence of a Parliament, is the right of York less valid ?   Be consistent, my Lords, in the development of the new system of politics. Repeal the Union, and revive the Heptarchy.

When the Irish papists were admitted to the Imperial Parliament, we were told that they would consist of a few gentlemen of ancient family and fortune.   That class is already banished from our councils.   When the Protestant Establishment in Ireland was reformed by the Whigs, we were told that the Church in Ireland would then be as safe as the Church in Yorkshire.   That Establishment is now an eleemosynary one.   When the repeal of the union was discussed in the English Parliament, we were told that it was only supported by a feeble section.   That section now decides the fate of the British Government and the policy of the British Empire.   Because much has been conceded, we are told that all must be given up; because the Irish papists have shown themselves unworthy of a political franchise, we are told that it necessarily follows that they should be entrusted with a municipal one; because   *   *   *

        *   *   *   *   *
        *   *   *   *   *
        *   *   *   *   *
        *   *   *   *   *

This new system of inductive reasoning may pass current with some bankrupt noble, panting to nestle in the bowers of Downing Street; this topsy-turvy logic may flash conviction on the mind of some penniless expectant of the broken victuals of the official banquet; but the people of England recoil with disgust from the dangerous balderdash, and look up to your Lordships as their hereditary leaders, to stand between the ark of the constitution and the unhallowed hands that are thrust forward to soil its splendour and violate its sanctity. The people of England are not so far divorced from their ancient valour. that, after having withstood Napoleon and the whole world in arms, they are to sink before a horde of their manumitted serfs and the *nisi prius* demagogue whom a foreign priesthood have hired to talk treason on their blasphemous behalf. After having routed the lion, we will not be preyed upon by the wolf. If we are to fall, if this great empire, raised by the heroic energies of the English nation—that nation of which your fathers formed a part—is indeed to be dissolved, let us hope that the last moments of our career may prove at least an euthanasia: let no pestilent blight, after our meridian glory, sully the splendour of our setting; and whether we fall before the foreign foe we have so often baffled, or whether, by some mysterious combination of irresistible circumstances, our empire sinks, like the Queen of the Adriatic, beneath the waves that we still rule, let not the records of our future annalist preserve a fact which, after all our greatness, might well break the spirit of the coming generations of our species. Let it not be said that we truckled to one, the unparalleled and unconstitutional scope of whose power is only equalled by the sordid meanness of his rapacious soul. Let it not be said that the English constitution sank before a rebel without dignity and a demagogue without courage. This grand pensionary of bigotry and sedition presumes to stir up the people of England against your high estate. Will the Peers of England quail to this brawling mercenary— this man who has even degraded crime, who has deprived treason of its grandeur and sedition of its sentiment; who is paid for his patriotism, and whose philanthropy is hired by the job—audacious, yet a poltroon—agitating a people, yet picking their pockets; in mind a Catiline, in action a Cleon ?

This disturber is in himself nothing. He has neither learning, wit, eloquence, nor refined taste, nor elevated feeling, nor a passionate and creative soul. What ragged ribaldry are his public addresses, whether they emanate from his brazen mouth or from his leaden pen! His pathos might shame the maudlin Romeo of a barn; his invective is the reckless abandonment of the fish-market. Were he a man of genius, he would be unsuited to the career for which he is engaged; for, after all, he is but a slave. But it is the awful character of his master that invests this creature with his terrible consideration. However we may detest or despise the *nisi prius* lawyer hired to insult and injure the realm of England, we know that he is the delegate of the most ancient and powerful priesthood in Europe. It is as the great papal nominee that this O'Connell, with all his vileness, becomes a power to control which requires no common interference.

My Lords, the English nation believes that that interference can be efficiently exercised by your august assembly. In you are reposed their hopes; you will not disappoint them. In a few hours, in obedience to the mandate of the papal priesthood, that shallow voluptuary who is still Prime Minister of England, will call upon your Lordships with cuckoo note, to do " justice to Ireland." Do it. Justice to Ireland will best be secured by doing justice to England. The people of England created the empire. At the time when we were engaged in that great strife which will rank in the estimation of posterity with the Punic wars and the struggles of the Greeks against Asia, the very men who are now menacing your illustrious order, and stirring up war against our national institutions, were in communication with our most inveterate foe, and soliciting invasion. My Lords, you will not forget this; you will not forget to distinguish their pretext from their cause. These men cannot be conciliated. They are your foes because they are the foes of England. They hate our free and fertile isle. They hate our order, our civilisation, our enterprising industry, our sustained courage, our decorous liberty, our pure religion. This wild, reckless, indolent, uncertain, and superstitious race have no sympathy with the English character. Their fair ideal of human felicity is an alternation of clannish broils and coarse idolatry. Their history describes an unbroken circle of bigotry and blood. And now, forsooth, the cry is raised that they have been misgoverned ! How many who sound this party shibboleth have studied the history of Ireland ? A savage population, under the influence of the Papacy, has, nevertheless, been so regulated, that they have contributed to the creation of a highly-civilised and Protestant empire. Why, is not that the paragon of political science ? Could Machiavel teach more ? My Lords, shall the delegates of these tribes, under the direction of the Roman priesthood, ride roughshod over our country—over England—haughty and still imperial England ? Forbid it all the memory of your ancestors ! Rest assured that if you perform your high and august office as becomes you, rest assured that in this agony of the Protestant cause and the British empire, the English nation will not desert you. All parties and all sects of Englishmen, in this fierce and yet degrading struggle, must ultimately rally round your House. My Lords, be bold, be resolute, be still " the pillars of the State."

April 18, 1836.

LETTER XVII

To the House of Lords

My Lords,—You have unfurled the national standard. Its patriotic and hearty motto is, " Justice for England." The English nation will support you in your high endeavours. Fear not that they will be backward. They recognise your Lordships as their natural leaders who have advanced, according to your hereditary duty, to assist them in the extremity of their degraded fortunes. The time is come for bold and vigorous conduct; the time is come to rid ourselves of that base tyranny, offensive to the pride of every Englishman, no matter what his religious sect or class of political opinions. The English

21

nation will not be ruled by the Irish priesthood. Five years of Whig government have not yet so completely broken our once proud spirit that we can submit without a murmur or a struggle to such a yoke. If Athens, even in her lower fortunes, could free herself of her thirty tyrants, let us hope that England, in spite of all the jobs of our corrupt and corrupting Government, may yet chase away those gentlemen who, fresh from the unction of M'Hale and the mild injunctions of the apostolic Kehoe,[1] have undertaken to guard over the rights and liberties, the property and the religion, of Protestant England. We have not reformed the third estate of the realm in order that England should be governed by the nominees of the Papacy. There is not a man in Britain, Tory or Radical, Episcopalian or Presbyterian, who can stand this long; there is not a man in Britain who at the bottom of his heart is not proud of our empire, and who does not despise the inferior race who dare to menace its integrity. However faction may corrupt and machinate, the people of England will never long submit to a Milesian master; and when they reflect upon their present degradation, and are conscious that they have experienced it only to secure in power the dull and desperate remains of a once haughty oligarchy, long baffled in their anti-national attempts upon the free realm of England, the nation will rise in its wrath, and execute vengeance upon the cabal which has thus trifled with this great country's immemorial honour.

The English nation requires justice; and it is not content to receive that justice by instalments—a process that may suit their lately manumitted serfs, but which will not accord with their stern and determined spirits, habituated to the ennobling exercise and the proud enjoyment of an ancient liberty. They require justice, and they will have that justice full and free. It must be meted

[1] John M'Hale (1791–1881), appointed Archbishop of Tuam in 1834; and possibly John Keogh (1740–1817), the Irish Catholic leader, to whose efforts the passing of the Relief Act of 1793 was mainly due.

out speedily and not scantily. They require this justice, with the Peers of England at their head, and the result will prove whether the Milesian peasantry, led on by the papist priesthood, can cope with this proud and powerful society. It is not just to England that the Sovereign should be deprived of his undoubted prerogative; it is not just to England that M'Hale and Kehoe should dictate to our King the servants whom our Royal master should employ; it is not just to England that the King of England should by any such an anti-national process be surrounded by the Ministers, not of his choice, but of his necessity; it is not just to England that a knot of papist legislators should deal with the polity and property of our Protestant Church; it is not just to England that no English blood in Ireland should be secure from plunder or assassination; it is not just to England that a hired disturber, paid by the Roman priesthood, should ramble over our country to stir up rebellion against your Lordships' august estate; that his ribald tongue should soil and outrage all that we have been taught to love, honour, and obey—our women, our princes, and our laws; and lastly, it is not just to England that its constitution should be attacked, its empire menaced, and its religion scoffed at.

My Lords, the same party that demands justice for Ireland is not less clamorous in its requisition of justice for Canada. Will you grant it ? Justice for Botany Bay, too, is, I have heard, in the market, and the cry is said to be worth some good £2,000 per annum. The noble member for Glasgow, the vigorous writer of that lucid address which I had the honour of transferring from its original Sanscrit and first introducing to the notice of the British public, has, I believe, already done justice to India. My Lords ! when and where is this dangerous nonsense to terminate ? How compatible is the prevalence of such windy words with the subsistence of an empire ? It may be as well for your Lordships to ponder on the consequences. The English nation formed the empire. Ours is the imperial isle. England is the Metro-

politan country, and we might as well tear out the living
heart from the human form, and bid the heaving corpse
still survive, as suppose that a great empire can endure
without some concentration of power and vitality.

My Lords, the season is ripe for action. In spite of all
the machinations of the anti-English faction, never was
your great assembly more elevated in the esteem and
affection of your countrymen than at this perilous hour.
The English are a reflecting and observant people; they
ponder even amid tumult; they can draw a shrewd moral
even from the play of their own passions; and they cannot
but feel that—after all the revolutionary rhetoric which
has been dinned into their ears of late in panegyric of
a Reform Ministry and a Reformed Parliament, and in
simultaneous depreciation of your Lordships' power and
usefulness—not only in eloquence and knowledge, in
elevation of thought and feeling, and even in practical
conduct, your Lordships need fear no comparison with
that assembly which, from a confusion of ideas, is in
general supposed to be more popular in its elements and
character, but that on all occasions when the dignity of
the empire and the rights of the subject have been threatened and assailed, the national cause has invariably found
in your Lordships' House that support and sympathy
which have been denied to it by the other Chamber.

Your Lordships, therefore, commence the conflict with
the anti-English party under great advantages. Not only
is your cause a just one, and your resolution to maintain
its justice unshakable, but there happens in your instance
that which unfortunately cannot always be depended on
in those great conjunctures which decide the fate of crowns
and nations. The sympathy of the nation is arrayed
under your banner. And inasmuch as the popularity
which you now enjoy is to be distinguished from that
volatile effusion which is the hurry-skurry offspring of
ignorance and guile, but is founded on the surer basis of
returning reason and mellowed passions and sharp experience, you may rest assured that the support of your

countrymen will not be withdrawn from you in the hour
of trial.

But, my Lords, do not undervalue the enemy which, at
the head of the English nation, you are about to combat.
If you imagine that you are going to engage only an
ignorant and savage population, led on by a loose-tongued
poltroon, you will indeed deceive yourselves, and the
truth will not be in you. My Lords, you are about to
struggle with a foe worthy even of the Peers of England,
for he is a foe that has placed his foot upon the neck of
Emperors. My Lords, you are about to struggle with the
Papacy, and in its favourite and devoted land. Whether
the conspiracy of the Irish priests be more successful than
the fleets of Spain, and more fatal to the freedom and the
faith of England, time can alone prove, and Providence
can alone decide. But let us not forget that Heaven aids
those who aid themselves, and, firm in the faith that
nerved the arms of our triumphant fathers, let us meet
without fear that dark and awful power that strikes at
once at the purity of our domestic hearths and the
splendour of our imperial sway.

April 23, 1836.

LETTER XVIII

To the Lord Chancellor [1]

MY LORD,—The gay liver, who, terrified by the consequences of his excesses, takes to water and a temperance
society, is in about the same condition as the Whig
Ministers in their appointment of a Lord Chancellor,
when, still smarting under the eccentric vagaries of a
Brougham, they sought refuge in the calm reaction of
your sober Lordship. This change from Master Shallow
to Master Silence was for a moment amusing; but your
Lordship has at length found the faculty of speech. and
your astonished countrymen begin to suspect that they

[1] Lord Cottenham.

may not be altogether the gainers in the great transition
from Humbug to Humdrum. We have escaped from the
eagle to be preyed upon by the owl. For your Lordship is
also a Reformer, a true Reformer; you are to proceed in
the grand course of social amelioration and party jobbing,
and the only substantial difference, it seems, that a
harassed nation is to recognise, is that which consists
between the devastation of the locust and the destruction
of the slug.

Your Lordship has figured during the last week in the
double capacity of a statesman and a legislator. With
what transcendent success let the blank dismay that
stamped the countenance of the Prime Minister bear
flattering witness ; as he hung with an air of awkward
astonishment on the accents of your flowing eloquence,
and listened with breathless surprise, if not admiration,
to the development of those sage devices which, by a
curious felicity of fortune, have succeeded in arraying
agianst them the superficial prejudices of all parties.
Yet one advantage, it cannot be denied, has resulted
from your Lordship's last triumphant exhibition. The
public at length become acquainted with the object of
Lord Langdale's surprising elevation, and the agreeable
office which it appears the noble Master of the Rolls is to
fulfil in the Senate of Great Britain. We have heard
before of a Lord Chancellor's devil; but my Lord Cottenham is the first guardian of the Great Seal whom his
considerate colleagues have supplied not only with a
coronet, but a critic.

That your Lordship should be an advocate for " justice
to Ireland," might reasonably have been expected from
your eminent situation. Your party may share with you
the odium or the glory of your political projects, but the
laurels which you have recently acquired by your luminous
eloquence and your profound legal knowledge are all your
Lordship's own, and I doubt whether any of your friends
or your opponents will be aspiring enough to envy you
their rich fruition.

And here, as it is the fashion to do " justice to Whig-gism," I cannot but pause to notice the contrast, so flattering to the judgment and high principle of your Lordship's party, which their legal appointments afford when compared with those of the annihilated Tories, and especially of the late Government. The administration of justice is still a matter of some importance, and we naturally shrink from the party who have entrusted its conduct to men so notoriously incompetent as a Sugden or a Scarlett, or placed upon the judgment seat such mere political adventurers as an Alderson and a Park, a Patteson and a Coleridge, a Taunton and a Tindal ! How refreshing it is, after such a prostitution of patronage and power, to turn to a Lord Chief Justice like a Denman, raised to his lofty post by the sheer influence of his un-equalled learning and his unrivalled practice, or to recog-nise the homage which has been paid to professional devotion in the profound person of Mr. Baron Williams !

I say nothing of your Lord Chancellors; one you have discarded, and the other you are about to deprive of his functions. And, indeed, it cannot be denied, that the appointment of your Lordship to the custody of the Great Seal, as a preliminary step to the abolition of the office of Lord Chancellor itself, displayed a depth of statecraft in your party for which the nation has hitherto given them scarcely sufficient credit. Had it been en-trusted to a Hardwicke, an Eldon, or a Lyndhurst, to some great functionary to whom the public had been accustomed to look up with confidence, and the pro-fession with respect, some murmurs might naturally have arisen at the menaced disturbance of an ancient order which had long contributed to that pure and learned administration of justice which was once the boast of Britons. But if the Whigs, as their organs daily assure us, are indeed to be our perpetual masters, we may be excused for viewing with indifference, if not with com-placency, that promised arrangement by which the most important duties of the State are no longer assigned at the caprice of a party, which, with a singularly sound judgment, has periodically selected for their performance an Erskine, a Brougham, and finally your learned Lordship. The still haughty Venetians sometimes console themselves with the belief that their State would not have fallen if the last of their Doges had not unfortunately been a plebeian; the Bar of England, that illustrious body which has contributed to our fame and our felicity not less than the most celebrated of our political institutions, may perhaps, in a sympathetic strain of feeling, some day be of opinion that they would not have been expelled from their high and just position in our society if the last of the Lord Chancellors had been worthy of being their chief; and posterity may perhaps class together, in the same scale of unsuitable elevation, the ignoble Manini[1] and the feeble Cottenham.

My Lord, the same spirit that would expel the heads of our Church from the Senate, would banish the head of our law from the King's Council. Under pretext of reform and popular government, your party, as usual, are assailing all the democratic elements of our constitution. The slang distinction of the day between the political and legal duties of a Lord Chancellor tends, like all the other measures of the party which has elevated your Lordship to the peerage, and is now about to lower you to a clerkship, to the substitution of an oligarchical government. We may yet live to regret that abrogated custom which, by giving the head of the law a precedence over the haughtiest peers, and securing his constant presence in the Cabinet of the sovereign, paid a glorious homage to the majesty of jurisprudence, announced to the world that our political constitution was eminently legal, guaranteed that there should be at least one individual in the realm who was not made a Minister because he was a noble, insured the satisfactory administration of domestic justice, and infused into our transactions with foreign Courts and Cabinets that high and severe spirit

[1] Ludovico Manini, the last Doge of Venice.

of public rectitude which obtained our own rights by acknowledging those of others.

Will the hybrid thing which, under Lord Cottenham's scheme of legal reform, is to be baptised in mockery a Lord Chancellor, afford these great advantages in the Cabinet or the Senate ? He is to be a lawyer without a court, and a lawyer without a court will soon be a lawyer without law. The Lord High Chancellor of England will speedily subside into a political nonentity like the President of the Council; that office which is the fitting appanage of pompous imbecility. Lord Cottenham may be excused for believing that to make a Lord Chancellor it is enough to plant a man upon a woolsack, and thrust a wig upon his head and a gold-embroidered robe upon his back; but the people of England have been accustomed to recognise in a Lord Chancellor, a man who has won his way to a great position by the exercise of great qualities—a man of singular acuteness and profound learning, and vast experience, and patient study, and unwearied industry—a man who has obtained the confidence of his profession before he challenges the confidence of his country, and who has secured eminence in the House of Commons before he has aspired to superiority in the House of Lords—a man who has expanded from a great lawyer into a great statesman, and who brings to the woolsack the commanding reputation which has been gained in the long and laborious years of an admired career.

My Lord, this is not your portrait. You are the child of reform, the chance offspring of political agitation and factious intrigue. The Whigs have stirred up and made muddy even the fountain of justice; for a moment an airy bubble, glittering in the sunshine, floated on the excited surface; but that brilliant bubble soon burst and vanished, and a scum, thick and obscure, now crests the once pure and tranquil waters.

April 30, 1836.

LETTER XIX

To Viscount Melbourne

My Lord,—I had the honour of addressing you on the eve of your last holidays; the delightful hour of relaxation again approaches: I wish you again to retire to the bowers of Brocket with my congratulations. The campaign about to close has been brief, but certainly not uneventful; I will not say disastrous, because I wish to soothe, rather than irritate, your tortured feelings. The incidents have been crowded, as in the last act of one of those dramas to which it was formerly your ambition to supply an epilogue. Why did that ambition ever become so unnaturally elevated ? Why was your Lordship not content to remain agreeable ? Why did you aspire to be great ? A more philosophical moderation would have saved you much annoyance and your country much evil; yourself some disgraceful situations, perhaps some ludicrous ones. When I last addressed you, your position was only mischievous; it is now ridiculous. Your dark master, the Milesian Eblis, has at length been vanquished by that justice for which he is so clamorous, and which he has so long outraged. The poisoned chalice of revolutionary venom which your creatures prepared for our august Senate, august although you are a member of it, has been returned to their own lips.[1] The House of Lords, decried for its ignorance and inefficiency by adventurers without talents and without education, has vindicated its claims to the respect of the country for its ability and its knowledge. Held up to public scorn by your hirelings as the irresponsible tyrants of the land, a

---

[1] *Cf.* "The reformed House of Commons, proud of its new-fangled existence . . . permitted a Minister of State to stigmatise a vote of the House of Lords as ' the whisper of a faction '; but now the poisoned chalice is returned to their own lips" (Disraeli in the House of Commons, May 27. 1841)

grateful nation recognises in the Peers of England the hereditary trustees of their rights and liberties, the guardians of their greatness, and the eloquent and undaunted champions of the integrity of their empire. The greater portion of the nation has penetrated the superficial characteristics of Whig Machiavelism. Your hollow pretences all evaporated, your disgraceful manœuvres all detected, your reckless expedients all exhausted, we recognise only a desperate and long-baffled oligarchy, ready to sacrifice, for the possession of a power to which they are incompetent, the laws, the empire, and the religion of England.

My Lord, it requires no prophet to announce that the commencement of the end is at length at hand. The reign of delusion is about to close. The man who obtains property by false pretences is sent to Botany Bay. Is the party that obtains power by the same means to be saved harmless ? You have established a new colony in Australia; it wants settlers. Let the Cabinet emigrate. My Lord Glenelg, with all his Canadian experience, will make an excellent colonial governor. And there your Lordship may hide your public discomfiture and your private mortification. And, indeed, a country where nature regulates herself on an exactly contrary system to the scheme she adopts in the older and more favoured world, has some pretensions, it would seem, to the beneficial presence of your faction. The land where the rivers are salt, where the quadrupeds have fins and the fish feet, where everything is confused, discordant, and irregular, is indicated by Providence as the fitting scene of Whig government.

The Whigs came into office under auspices so favourable, that they never could have been dislodged from their long-coveted posts except by their own incompetence and dishonesty. From circumstances which it would not be difficult to explain, they were at once sanctioned by the King and supported by the people. In the course of five years they have at once deceived the

sovereign and deluded the nation. After having recon-
tructed the third estate for their own purposes, in the
course of five years a majority of the English representatives is arrayed against them; wafted into power on the
wings of the public press, dusty from the march of intellect, and hoarse with clamouring about the spirit of the
age, in the course of five years they are obliged to declare
war against the journals, the faithful mirrors of the public
mind. With peace, reform, and retrenchment for their
motto, in the course of five years they have involved us in
a series of ignoble wars, deluged the country with jobs and
placemen, and have even contrived to increase the
amount of the public debt.

What rashness and what cowardice, what petty
prudence and what vast recklessness, what arrogance
and what truckling, are comprised in the brief annals of
this last assault of your faction upon the constitutional
monarchy of England ! Now hinting at organic changes,
now whimpering about the pressure from without;
dragged through the mud on the questions of military
discipline and the pension list, yet ready at the next
moment to plunder the Church or taint the very fountain of justice; threatening the Peers of England on one
day, and crouching on the next before the Irish priests !
A few months back you astounded the public by announcing that you had purchased a Lord Chancellor at
the price of three coronets.[1] The cost has been considered not only exorbitant, but unconstitutional: but
the nation, wearied by your vexatious delay of justice,
was content to be silent, and awaited the anticipated
presence of a Minos. You produced Cottenham. Moses
and his green spectacles was not in a more ludicrous
position than your Lordship with your precious purchase.
Yet this impotent conclusion was announced in January
as a *coup d'état*, and the people of England were daily
congratulated on an arrangement now universally acknowledged as the most ridiculous act even of your ad-

[1] The four coronets have now decreased to three (see note, p. 241).

ministration. Moralists have contrasted the respective
careers of the knave and the fool, and have consoled
humanity by the conviction that the scoundrel in the
long-run is not more fortunate than the simpleton.   I
leave this controverted question to the fabler and the
essayist; the man of the world, however, will not be surprised at the fate of a political party, the enormity of
whose career is only equalled by the feebleness of their
conduct.

My Lord, the Whigs a century back or so were at least
no fools. When the Dukes of Somerset and Argyle
attended a Privy Council without being summoned,[1] and
forced a dying Queen to appoint the Duke of Shrewsbury
Prime Minister, they did not perpetrate a greater outrage than the Whig leader, who, by virtue of a papist
conspiracy, returned to the post from which he had
been properly expelled, and became the Minister, not of
the King's choice, but of the King's necessity. These
same Whig leaders, when thus unconstitutionally established in power, introduced the Peerage Bill, which if
passed into a law would have deprived the sovereign
of his prerogative of creating further Peers, and they
remodelled the House of Commons by the Septennial Act.
The Whigs in 1718 sought to govern the country by
" swamping " the House of Commons; in 1836 it is the
House of Lords that is to be "swamped"! In 1718
the *coup d'état* was to prevent any further increase of the
Lords; in 1836 the Lords are to be outnumbered : different
tactics to obtain the same purpose—the establishment of
an oligarchical government by virtue of a Republican cry.
Where Argyle and Walpole failed, is it probable that
Lord Melbourne and Lord John Russell will succeed ?
The Whigs, a century back, were men of great station,
great talents, great eloquence, supported by two-thirds
of the nobles of the land; by the Dissenters, because they
attacked the Church, inasmuch as the Establishment,
like every other national institution, is an obstacle to

---

[1] July 3, 1714.

oligarchical power; and by the commercial and "monied interest" of the country, now, like every other interest of property, arrayed against them. And what are you? Is it your eloquence, your knowledge, your high descent, and vast property, or the following of your order, that introduce you into the King's Cabinet? No, you are the slave of a slave, the delegate of a deputy, the second-hand nominee of a power the most odious and anti-national in existence, foreign to all the principles and alien to all the feelings of Britons. My Lord, the popular and boisterous gale that originally drove your party into power has long since died away, and though some occasional and fitful gusts may have deceived you into be- lieving that your sails were to be ever set and your streamers ever flying, the more experienced navigators have long detected the rising of the calm yet steady breeze fatal to your course. It is a wind which may be depended on—a great monsoon of national spirit, which will clear the seas of those political pirates who have too long plundered us under false colours.

And yet, my Lord, let us not part in anger. Yours is still a gratifying, even a great position. Notwithstand- ing all your public degradation and all your private annoy- ances, that man is surely to be envied who has it in his power to confer an obligation on every true-hearted Englishman. And this your Lordship still can do; you can yet perform an act which will command the gratitude of every lover of his country; you can—RESIGN.

May 15, 1836.

THE SPIRIT OF WHIGGISM

["THE SPIRIT OF WHIGGISM" was published as an addendum to the book containing the Letters of Runnymede. It is the "Vindication" in little—a popular summary that Disraeli hoped might be easily read and easily remembered. It is perhaps freer from extravagances of style than any other of his writings of the period. Of its genesis little is known. It may be that it represents the original form of the Letter to Lord Lyndhurst, when, as he says, he found that the subject gave rise to so many reflections that what was originally intended for a pamphlet expanded almost into a volume. Published anonymously within a few months of the appearance of the "Vindication" which bore his name, it could not have failed, by similarity of views and of method of expression, to carry conviction that the writer of "Runnymede" was identical with Disraeli the Younger.]

CHAPTER I

HISTORICAL

ENGLAND has become great by her institutions. Her hereditary Crown has in a great degree insured us from the distracting evils of a contested succession ; her Peerage, interested, from the vast property and the national honours of its members, in the good government of the country, has offered a compact bulwark against the temporary violence of popular passion ; her House of Commons, representing the conflicting sentiments of an estate of the realm not less privileged than that of the Peers, though far more numerous, has enlisted the great mass of the lesser proprietors of the country in favour of a political system which offers them a constitutional means of defence and a legitimate method of redress; her ecclesiastical establishment, preseved by its munificent endowment from the fatal necessity of pandering to the erratic fancies of its communicants, has maintained the sacred cause of learning and religion, and preserved orthodoxy while it has secured toleration; her law of primogeniture has supplied the country with a band of natural and independent leaders, trustees of those legal institutions which pervade the land, and which are the origin of our political constitution.

That great body corporate, styled a nation—a vast assemblage of human beings knit together by laws and arts and customs, by the necessities of the present and the memory of the past—offers in this country, through these its vigorous and enduring members, a more substantial and healthy framework than falls to the lot of other nations. Our stout-built constitution throws off with more facility and safety those crude and dangerous humours which must at times arise in all human communities. The march of revolution must here at least be orderly. We are preserved from those reckless and tempestuous sallies that in other countries, like a whirlwind, topple down in an instant an ancient crown, or sweep away an illustrious aristocracy. This constitution, which has secured order, has consequently promoted civilisation; and the almost unbroken tide of progressive amelioration has made us the freest, the wealthiest, and the most refined society of modern ages. Our commerce is unrivalled, our manufacturers supply the world, our agriculture is the most skilful in Christendom. So national are our institutions, so completely have they arisen from the temper and adapted themselves to the character of the people, that when for a season they were apparently annihilated, the people of England voluntarily returned to them, and established them with renewed strength and renovated vigour.

The constitution of England is again threatened, and at a moment when the nation is more prosperous, more free, and more famous than at any period of its momentous and memorable career. Why is this? What has occasioned these distempered times, which make the loyal tremble and the traitor smile? Why has this dark cloud suddenly gathered in a sky so serene and so splendid? Is there any analogy between this age and that of the first Charles? Are the same causes at work, or is the apparent similarity produced only by designing men, who make use of the perverted past as a passport to present mischief? These are great questions which it may be profitable to discuss and wise to study.

Rapin, a foreigner who wrote our history,[1] in the course of his frigid yet accurate pages, indulged in one philosophical observation. Struck at the same time by our greatness and by the fury of our factions, the Huguenot exclaimed, " It appears to me that this great society can only be dissolved by the violence of its political parties."

What are these parties? Why are they violent? Why should they exist? In resolving these questions, we may obtain an accurate idea of our present political position, and by pondering over the past we may make that past not a prophecy, as the disaffected intend, but a salutary lesson by which the loyal may profit.

The two great parties in which England has during the last century and a half been divided originated in the ancient struggle between the Crown and the aristocracy. As long as the Crown possessed or aspired to despotic power, the feeling of the nation supported the aristocracy in their struggles to establish a free government. The aristocracy of England formed the constitution of the Plantagenets; the wars of the Roses destroyed that aristocracy, and the despotism of the Tudors suc-

[1] Paul de Rapin de Thoyras, whose " Histoire d'Angleterre," in eight volumes, appeared in 1724.

ceeded. Renovated by more than a century of peace and the spoils of the Papacy, the aristocracy of England attacked the first Stuarts, who succeeded to a despotism which they did not create. When Charles the First, after a series of great concessions which ultimately obtained for him the support of the most illustrious of his early opponents, raised the royal standard, the constitution of the Plantagenets, and more than the constitution of the Plantagenets, had been restored and secured. But a portion of the able party which had succeeded in effecting such a vast and beneficial revolution was not content to part with the extraordinary powers which they had obtained in this memorable struggle. This section of the aristocracy were the origin of the English Whigs, though that title was not invented until the next reign. The primitive Whigs—" Parliament-men," as they liked to call themselves, " Roundheads," as they were in time dubbed—aspired to an oligarchy ; for a moment they obtained one; but unable to maintain themselves in power against the returning sense and rising spirit of a generous and indignant people, they called to their aid that domestic revolutionary party which exists in all countries, and an anti-national enemy in addition. These were the English Radicals, or Root-and-Branch men, and the Scotch Covenanters. To conciliate the first they sacrificed the Crown; to secure the second they abolished the Church. The constitution of England in Church and State was destroyed, and the Whig oligarchy, in spite of their machinations, were soon merged in the common ruin.

The ignoble tyranny to which this great nation was consequently subject produced that reaction which is in the nature of human affairs. The ancient constitution was in time restored, and the Church and the Crown were invested with greater powers than they had enjoyed previously to their overthrow. So hateful had been the consequences of Whig rule that the people were inclined rather to trust the talons of arbitrary power than to take refuge under the wing of these pretended advocates of popular rights. A worthless monarch and a corrupted Court availed themselves of the offered opportunity; and when James the Second ascended the throne, the nation was again prepared to second the aristocracy in a struggle for their liberties. But the Whigs had profited by their previous experiment: they resolved upon a revolution, but they determined that that revolution should be brought about by as slight an appeal to popular sympathies as possible. They studiously confined that appeal to the religious feelings of the nation. They hired a foreign prince and enlisted a foreign army in their service. They dethroned James, they established themselves in power without the aid of the mass; and had William the Third been a man of ordinary capacity, the constitution of Venice would have been established in England in 1688. William the Third told the Whigs that he would never consent to be a Doge. Resembling Louis Philippe in his character as well as in his position, that extraordinary Prince baffled the Whigs by his skilful balance of parties; and had Providence accorded him an heir, it is probable that the oligarchical faction would never have revived in England.

The Whigs have ever been opposed to the national institutions because they are adverse to the establishment of an oligarchy. Local institutions, supported by a landed gentry, check them; hence their love of centralisation and their hatred of unpaid magistrates. An independent hierarchy checks them; hence their affected advocacy of toleration and their patronage of the Dissenters. The power of the Crown checks them; therefore they always labour to reduce the sovereign to a nonentity, and by the establishment of the Cabinet they have virtually banished the King from his own councils. But, above all, the Parliament of England checks them, and therefore it may be observed that the Whigs at all times are quarrelling with some portion of those august estates. They despair of destroying the Parliament; by it. and by it alone, can they succeed in their objects. Corruption for one part, force for the other, then, is their motto. In 1640 they attempted to govern the country by the House of Commons, because the aristocracy was then more powerful in the House of Commons than in the House of Lords, where a Peerage, exhausted by civil wars, had been too liberally recruited from the courtiers of the Tudors and the Stuarts. At the next revolution which the Whigs occasioned, they attempted to govern the country by the House of Lords, in which they were predominant; and, in order to guarantee their power for ever, they introduced a Bill to deprive the King of his prerogative of making further Peers. The revolution of 1640 led to the abolition of the House of Lords because the Lords opposed the oligarchy; the revolution of 1688 led to the remodelling of the House of Commons by the Septennial Act, because the House of Commons then were influenced by the same feelings as the Lords during the great rebellion.

The accession of the House of Hanover revived the hopes of the Whigs, baffled by the subtle policy of William, and by the Tory triumphs of Anne. The new dynasty was unpopular with the mass of the nation, and proportionately dependent on the Whig oligarchy. Having a majority in the House of Lords, the Whigs introduced the Peerage Bill, by which the House of Lords would have been rendered independent of the sovereign ; unpopular with the country, the Whigs attacked the influence of popular election, and the moment that, by the aid of the most infamous corruption, they had obtained a temporary majority in the Lower House, they passed the Septennial Act. The Whigs of the eighteenth century "swamped" the House of Commons; the Whigs of the nineteenth would "swamp" the House of Lords. The Whigs of the eighteenth century would have rendered the House of Lords unchangeable; the Whigs of the nineteenth re-model the House of Commons.

I conclude here the first chapter of the "Spirit of

Whiggism "—a little book which I hope may be easily read and easily remembered. The Whig party have always adopted popular cries. In one age it is Liberty, in another Reform; at one period they sound the tocsin against popery, in another they ally themselves with papists. They have many cries, and various modes of conduct; but they have only one object—the establishment of an oligarchy in this free and equal land. I do not wish this country to be governed by a small knot of great families, and therefore I oppose the Whigs.

CHAPTER II

AT WAR WITH THE CONSTITUTION

WHEN the Whigs and their public organs favour us with their mysterious hints that the constitution has provided the sovereign with a means to re-establish at all times a legislative sympathy between the two Houses of Parliament, it may be as well to remind them that we are not indebted for this salutary prerogative to the forbearance of their party. Suppose their Peerage Bill had passed into an Act, how would they have carried the Reform Bill of 1832 ? The Whigs may reply, that if the Peerage Bill had become a law, the Reform Bill would never have been introduced; and I believe them. In that case, the British House of Lords would have been transformed into a Venetian Senate, and the old walls of St. James's might have witnessed scenes of as degrading mortification as the famous ducal palace of the Adriatic.

George the Third routed the Whigs, consolidated by half a century of power; but an ordinary monarch would have sunk beneath the Coalition and the India Bill. This scheme was the last desperate effort of the oligarchical party previous to 1830. Not that they were inactive during the great interval that elapsed between the advent of Mr. Pitt and the resurrection of Lord Grey: but, ever on the watch for a cry to carry them into power, they mistook the yell of Jacobinism for the chorus of an emancipated people, and fancied, in order to take the throne by storm, that nothing was wanting but to hoist the tricolour and to cover their haughty brows with a red cap. This fatal blunder clipped the wings of Whiggism; nor is it possible to conceive a party that had effected so many revolutions and governed a great country for so long a period, more broken, sunk, and shattered, more desolate and disheartened, than these same Whigs at the Peace of Paris. From that period till 1830, the tactics of the Whigs consisted in gently and gradually extricating themselves from their false position as the disciples of Jacobinism, and assuming their ancient post as the hereditary guardians of an hereditary monarchy. To make the transition less difficult than it threatened, they invented Liberalism, a bridge by which they were to regain the lost mainland, and daintily recross on tiptoe the chasm over which they had originally sprung with so much precipitation. A dozen years of "liberal principles" broke up the national party of England, cemented by half a century of prosperity and glory, compared with which all the annals of the realm are dim and lacklustre. Yet so weak intrinsically was the oligarchical faction that their chief, despairing to obtain a monopoly of power for his party, elaborately announced himself as the champion of his patrician order, and attempted to coalesce with the liberalised leader of the Tories. Had that negotiation led to the result which was originally intended by those interested, the Riots of Paris would not have occasioned the Reform of London.

It is a great delusion to believe that revolutions are ever effected by a nation. It is a faction, and generally a small one, that overthrows a dynasty or remodels a constitution. A small party, stung by a long exile from power, and desperate of success except by desperate means, invariably has recourse to a *coup d'état*. An oligarchical party is necessarily not numerous. Its members in general attempt, by noble lineage or vast possessions, to compensate for their poverty of numbers. The Whigs, in 1830, found themselves by accident in place, but under very peculiar circumstances. They were in place but not in power. In each estate of the realm a majority was arrayed against them. An appeal to the Commons of England, that constituency which, in its elements, had undergone no alteration since the time of Elizabeth, either by the influence of the legislature or the action of time—that constituency which had elected Pym, and Selden, and Hampden, as well as Somers, Walpole, and Pulteney—an appeal to this constituency, it was generally acknowledged, would be fatal to the Whigs, and therefore they determined to reconstruct it. This is the origin of the recent parliamentary reform : the Whigs, in place without being in power, resolved as usual upon a *coup d'état*, and looked about for a stalking-horse. In general the difficult task had devolved upon them of having to accomplish their concealed purpose while apparently achieving some public object. Thus they had carried the Septennial Act on the plea of pre-serving England from popery, though their real object was to prolong the existence of the first House of Commons in which they could command a majority.

But in the present instance they became sincerely parliamentary reformers, for by parliamentary reform they could alone subsist; and all their art was dedicated so to contrive, that in this reformation their own interest should secure an irresistible predominance.

But how was an oligarchical party to predominate in popular elections ? Here was the difficulty. The Whigs had no resources from their own limited ranks to feed the muster of the popular levies. They were obliged to look about for allies wherewith to form their new popular estate. Any estate of the Commons modelled on any equitable principle, either of property or popu-lation, must have been fatal to the Whigs; they, therefore, very dexterously adopted a small minority of the nation,

consisting of the sectarians, and, inaugurating them as
the people with a vast and bewildering train of hocus-
pocus ceremonies, invested the Dissenters with political
power. By this *coup d'état* they managed the House of
Commons, and having at length obtained a position, they
have from that moment laid siege to the House of Lords,
with the intention of reducing that great institution and
making it surrender at discretion. This is the exact
state of English politics during the last five years. The
Whigs have been at war with the English constitution.
First of all they captured the King; then they vanquished
the House of Commons; now they have laid siege to the
House of Lords. But here the fallacy of their grand
scheme of political mystification begins to develop itself.
Had, indeed, their new constituency, as they have long
impudently pretended, indeed been " the people," a
struggle between such a body and the House of Lords
would have been brief but final. The absurdity of supposing that a chamber of two or three hundred individuals
could set up their absolute will and pleasure against
the decrees of a legislative assembly chosen by a whole
nation, is so glaring that the Whigs and their scribes
might reasonably suspect that in making such allegations
they were assuredly proving too much. But as " the
people " of the Whigs is in fact a number of Englishmen
not exceeding in amount the population of a third-rate
city, the English nation is not of opinion that this arrogant and vaunting moiety of a class privileged for the
common good, swollen though it may be by some jobbing
Scots and rebel Irish, shall pass off their petty and selfish
schemes of personal aggrandisement as the will of a great
people, as mindful of its duty to its posterity as it is
grateful for the labours of its ancestors. The English
nation, therefore, rallies for rescue from the degrading
plots of a profligate oligarchy, a barbarising sectarianism,
and a boroughmongering Papacy round their hereditary
leaders—the Peers. The House of Lords, therefore, at
this moment represents everything in the realm except

the Whig oligarchs, their tools—the Dissenters, and their masters—the Irish priests. In the meantime the Whigs bawl aloud that there is a " collision " ! It is true there is a collision; but it is not a collision between the Lords and the People, but between the Ministers and the Constitution.

CHAPTER III

THE REPUBLIC OF THE WHIGS

It may be as well to remind the English nation that a revolutionary party is not necessarily a liberal one, and that a republic is not indispensably a democracy. Such is the disposition of property in England that, were a republic to be established here to-morrow, it would partake rather of the oligarchical than of the aristocratic character. We should be surprised to find in how few families the power of the State was concentrated. And although the framers of the new commonwealth would be too crafty to base it on any avowed and ostensible principle of exclusion, but on the contrary would in all probability ostentatiously inaugurate the novel constitution by virtue of some abstract plea about as definite and as prodigal of practical effects as the Rights of Man or the Sovereignty of the People ; nevertheless I should be astonished were we not to find that the great mass of the nation, as far as any share in the conduct of public affairs was concerned, were as completely shut out from the fruition and exercise of power as under that Venetian polity which has ever been the secret object of Whig envy and Whig admiration. The Church, under such circumstances, would probably have again been plundered, and therefore the discharge of ecclesiastical duties might be spared to the nation; but the people would assuredly be practically excluded from its services, which would swarm with the relations and connections of the senatorial class; for, whether this country be governed

only by the House of Commons, or only by the House
of Lords, the elements of the single chamber will not
materially differ; and although in the event of the
triumph of the Commons, the ceremony of periodical
election may be retained (and we should not forget that
the Long Parliament soon spared us that unnecessary
form), the selected members will form a Senate as irresponsible as any House of Parliament whose anomalous
constitution may now be the object of Whig sneers or
Radical anathemas.

The rights and liberties of a nation can only be preserved by institutions. It is not the spread of knowledge
or the march of intellect that will be found sufficient
sureties for the public welfare in the crisis of a country's
freedom. Our interest taints our intelligence, our passions paralyse our reason. Knowledge and capacity are
too often the willing tools of a powerful faction or a dexterous adventurer. Life is short, man is imaginative; our
means are limited, our passions high.

In seasons of great popular excitement, gold and glory
offer strong temptations to needy ability. The demagogues throughout a country, the orators of town-councils
and vestries, and the lecturers of mechanics' institutes,
present, doubtless in most cases unconsciously, the ready
and fit machinery for the party or the individual that
aspires to establish a tyranny. Duly graduating in corruption, the leaders of the mob become the oppressors
of the people. Cultivation of intellect and diffusion of
knowledge may make the English nation more sensible
of the benefits of their social system, and better qualified
to discharge the duties with which their institutions
have invested them, but they will never render them
competent to preserve their liberties without the aid of
those institutions. Let us for a moment endeavour to
fancy Whiggism in a state of rampant predominance; let
us try to contemplate England enjoying all those advantages which our present rulers have not yet granted
us, and some of which they have as yet only ventured

to promise by innuendo. Let us suppose our ancient monarchy abolished, our independent hierarchy reduced to a stipendiary sect, the gentlemen of England deprived of their magisterial functions, and metropolitan prefects and sub-prefects established in the counties and principal towns, commanding a vigorous and vigilant police, and backed by an army under the immediate orders of a single House of Parliament. Why, these are threatened changes—ay, and not one of them that may not be brought about to-morrow, under the plea of the " spirit of the age " or " county reform " or " cheap government." But where then will be the liberties of England ? Who will dare disobey London ? the enlightened and reformed metropolis ! And can we think, if any bold Squire, in whom some of the old blood might still chance to linger, were to dare to murmur against this grinding tyranny, or appeal to the spirit of those neighbours whose predecessors his ancestors had protected, can we flatter ourselves that there would not be judges in Westminster Hall prepared and prompt to inflict on him all the pains and penalties, the dungeon, the fine, the sequestration, which such a troublesome Anti-Reformer would clearly deserve ? Can we flatter ourselves that a Parliamentary Star Chamber and a Parliamentary High Commission Court would not be in the background to supply all the deficiencies of the laws of England ? When these merry times arrive—the times of extraordinary tribunals and extraordinary taxes—and, if we proceed in our present course, they are much nearer than we imagine—the phrase " Anti-Reformer " will serve as well as that of " Malignant," and be as valid a plea as the former title for harassing and plundering all those who venture to wince under the crowning mercies of centralisation.

Behold the Republic of the Whigs ! Behold the only Republic that can be established in England except by force ! And who can doubt the swift and stern termination of institutions introduced by so unnatural and irrational a process. I would address myself to the

English Radicals. I do not mean those fine gentlemen
or those vulgar adventurers, who, in this age of quackery,
may sail into Parliament by hoisting for the nonce the
false colours of the Movement; but I mean that honest
and considerable party, too considerable, I fear, for their
happiness and the safety of the State—who have a definite
object which they distinctly avow—I mean those thoughtful and enthusiastic men who study their unstamped
press, and ponder over a millennium of operative amelioration. Not merely that which is just, but that which
is also practicable, should be the aim of a sagacious politician. Let the Radicals well consider whether, in
attempting to achieve their avowed object, they are not,
in fact, only assisting the secret views of a party whose
scheme is infinitely more adverse to their own than the
existing system, whose genius I believe they entirely
misapprehend. The Monarchy of the Tories is more
democratic than the Republic of the Whigs. It appeals
with a keener sympathy to the passions of the millions;
it studies their interests with a more comprehensive
solicitude. Admitting for a moment that I have mistaken the genius of the English constitution, what chance,
if our institutions be overthrown, is there of substituting
in their stead a more popular polity ? This hazard, both
for their own happiness and the honour of their country,
the English Radicals are bound to calculate nicely. If
they do not, they will find themselves, too late, the tools
of a selfish faction or the slaves of a stern usurper.

CHAPTER IV

THE ESTATES OF THE REALM

A chapter on the English constitution is a natural
episode in the spirit of Whiggism. There is this connection between the subjects—that the spirit of Whiggism is
hostile to the English constitution. No political institu-

tions ever yet flourished which have been more the topic
of discussion among writers of all countries and all parties
than our famous establishment of " King, Lords, and
Commons "; and no institutions ever yet flourished, of
which the character has been more misrepresented and
more misconceived. One fact alone will illustrate the
profound ignorance and the perplexed ideas subsisting on
this point. The present Whig leader of the House of
Commons, a member of a family who pique themselves on
their constitutional reputation, an author who has even
written an elaborate treatise on our polity, in one of his
speeches, delivered only so late as the last session of Parliament, declared his desire and determination to uphold the
present settlement of the " three estates of the realm,
viz.—King, Lords, and Commons." Now, His Gracious
Majesty is no more an estate of the realm than Lord John
Russell himself. The three estates of the realm are the
estate of the Lords Spiritual, the estate of the Lords Temporal, and the estate of the Commons. An estate is a popular class established into a political order. It is a section
of the nation invested for the public and common good
with certain powers and privileges. Lord John Russell
first writes upon the English constitution, and then
reforms it, and yet, even at this moment, is absolutely
ignorant of what it consists. A political estate is a complete and independent body. Now, all power that is
independent is necessarily irresponsible. The sovereign
is responsible because he is not an estate; he is responsible
through his Ministers; he is responsible to the estates
and to them alone.

When the Whigs obtained power in 1830, they found
the three estates of the realm opposed to them, and the
Government, therefore, could not proceed. They resolved,
therefore, to remodel them. They declared that the
House of Commons was the House of the people, and
that the people were not properly represented. They
consequently enlarged the estate of the Commons; they
increased the number of that privileged order who appear

by their representatives in the Lower House of Parliament. They rendered the estate of the Commons more powerful by this proceeding, because they rendered them more numerous; but they did not render their representatives one jot more the representatives of the people. Throwing the Commons of Ireland out of the question, for we cannot speculate upon a political order so unsettled that it has been thrice remodelled during the present century, some 300,000 individuals sent up, at the last general election, their representatives to Westminster. Well, are these 300,000 persons the people of England ? Grant that they are; grant that these members are divided into two equal portions. Well, then, the people of England consist of 150,000 persons. I know that there are well-disposed persons that tremble at this reasoning, because, although they admit its justice, they allege it leads to universal suffrage. We must not show, they assert, that the House of the people is not elected by the people. I admit it; we must not show that the House of the people is not elected by the people, but we must show that the House of Commons is not the House of the people, that it never was intended to be the House of the people, and that, if it be admitted to be so by courtesy, or become so in fact, it is all over with the English constitution.

It is quite impossible that a whole people can be a branch of a legislature. If a whole people have the power of making laws, it is folly to suppose that they will allow an assembly of 300 or 400 individuals, or a solitary being on a throne, to thwart their sovereign will and pleasure. But I deny that a people can govern itself. Self-government is a contradiction in terms. Whatever form a government may assume, power must be exercised by a minority of numbers. I shall, perhaps, be reminded of the ancient republics. I answer, that the ancient republics were as aristocratic communities as any that flourished in the Middle Ages. The Demos of Athens was an oligarchy living upon slaves. There is a great

slave population even in the United States, if a society
of yesterday is to illustrate an argument on our ancient
civilisation.

But it is useless to argue the question abstractedly.
The phrase " the people " is sheer nonsense. It is not
a political term. It is a phrase of natural history. A
people is a species; a civilised community is a nation.
Now, a nation is a work of art and a work of time. A
nation is gradually created by a variety of influences—
the influence of original organisation, of climate, soil,
religion, laws, customs, manners, extraordinary accidents
and incidents in their history, and the individual character
of their illustrious citizens. These influences create the
nation—these form the national mind, and produce in
the course of centuries a high degree of civilisation. If
you destroy the political institutions which these influences have called into force, and which are the machinery by which they constantly act, you destroy the nation.
The nation, in a state of anarchy and dissolution, then
becomes a people; and after experiencing all the consequent misery, like a company of bees spoiled of their
queen and rifled of their hive, they set to again and
establish themselves into a society.

Although all society is artificial, the most artificial
society in the world is unquestionably the English nation.
Our insular situation and our foreign empire, our immense
accumulated wealth and our industrious character, our
peculiar religious state, which secures alike orthodoxy
and toleration, our church and our sects, our agriculture
and our manufactures, our military services, our statute
law and supplementary equity, our adventurous commerce, landed tenure, and unprecedented system of credit,
form, among many others, such a variety of interests,
and apparently so conflicting, that I do not think even the
Abbé Sieyès himself could devise a scheme by which this
nation could be absolutely and definitely represented.

The framers of the English constitution were fortunately not of the school of Abbé Sieyès. Their first object

was to make us free; their next to keep us so. While, therefore, they selected equality as the basis of their social order, they took care to blend every man's ambition with the perpetuity of the State. Unlike the levelling and destructive equality of modern days, the ancient equality of England elevates and creates. Learned in human nature, the English constitution holds out privilege to every subject as the inducement to do his duty. As it has secured freedom, justice, and even property to the humblest of the commonwealth, so, pursuing the same system of privileges, it has confided the legislature of the realm to two orders of the subjects—orders, however, in which every English citizen may be constitutionally enrolled—the Lords and the Commons. The two estates of the Peers are personally summoned to meet in their chamber: the more extensive and single estate of the Commons meets by its representatives. Both are political orders, complete in their character, independent in their authority, legally irresponsible for the exercise of their power. But they are the trustees of the nation, not its masters; and there is a High Court of Chancery in the public opinion of the nation at large, which exercises a vigilant control over these privileged classes of the community, and to which they are equitably and morally amenable. Estimating, therefore, the moral responsibility of our political estates, it may fairly be maintained that, instead of being irresponsible, the responsiblity of the Lords exceeds that of the Commons. The House of Commons itself not being an estate of the realm, but only the representatives of an estate, owes to the nation a responsibility neither legal nor moral. The House of Commons is responsible only to that privileged order who are its constituents. Between the Lords and the Commons themselves there is this prime difference—that the Lords are known, and seen, and marked; the Commons are unknown, invisible, and unobserved. The Lords meet in a particular spot; the Commons are scattered over the kingdom. The eye of the nation rests upon the Lords, few in number, and notable in position; the eye of the nation wanders in vain for the Commons, far more numerous, but far less remarkable. As a substitute the nation appeals to the House of Commons, but sometimes appeals in vain; for if the majority of the Commons choose to support their representatives in a course of conduct adverse to the opinion of the nation, the House of Commons will set the nation at defiance. They have done so once; may they never repeat that destructive career! Such are our two Houses of Parliament—the most illustrious assemblies since the Roman Senate and Grecian Areopagus; neither of them is the " House of the People," but both alike represent the " Nation."[1]

CHAPTER V

A DEMOCRATIC CONSTITUTION

THERE are two propositions, which, however at the first glance they may appear to contradict the popular opinions of the day, are nevertheless, as I believe, just and true. And they are these:—

First. That there is no probability of ever establishing a more democratic form of government than the present English constitution.

Second. That the recent political changes of the Whigs are, in fact, a departure from the democratic spirit of that constitution.

Whatever form a government may assume, its spirit must be determined by the laws which regulate the property of the country. You may have a Senate and Consuls, you may have no hereditary titles, and you may dub each householder or inhabitant a citizen; but if the spirit of your laws preserves masses of property in a particular class, the government of the country will

---

[1] The argument of this chapter, and indeed the language, may be found in the *Morning Post* articles (Chapters V., VI., XII.), and in the " Vindication " (Chapter XXIII.).

follow the disposition of the property. So also you may have an apparent despotism without any formal popular control, and with no aristocracy, either natural or artificial, and the spirit of the government may nevertheless be republican. Thus the ancient polity of Rome, in its best days, was an aristocracy, and the government of Constantinople is the nearest approach to a democracy on a great scale, and maintained during a great period, that history offers. The constitution of France during the last half century has been fast approaching that of the Turks. The barbarous Jacobins blended modern equality with the refined civilisation of ancient France; the barbarous Ottomans blended their equality with the refined civilisation of ancient Rome. Paris secured to the Jacobins those luxuries that their system never could have produced: Byzantium served the same purpose to the Turks. Both the French and their turbaned prototypes commenced their system with popular enthusiasm, and terminated it with general subjection. Napoleon and Louis Philippe are playing the same part as the Soleimans and the Mahmouds. The Chambers are but a second-rate Divan; the Prefects but inferior Pachas: a solitary being rules alike in the Seraglio and the Tuileries, and the whole nation bows to his despotism on condition that they have no other master save himself.

The disposition of property in England throws the government of the country into the hands of its natural aristocracy. I do not believe that any scheme of the suffrage, or any method of election, could divert that power into other quarters. It is the necessary consequence of our present social state. I believe, the wider the popular suffrage, the more powerful would be the natural aristocracy. This seems to me an inevitable consequence; but I admit this proposition on the clear understanding that such an extension should be established on a fair, and not a factious, basis. Here then, arises the question of the ballot, into the merits of which I shall take another opportunity of entering, recording only now my opinion that, in the present arrangement of the constituencies, even the ballot would favour the power of the natural aristocracy, and that, if the ballot were simultaneously introduced with a fair and not a factious extension of the suffrage, it would produce no difference whatever in the ultimate result.

Quitting, then, these considerations, let us arrive at the important point. Is there any probability of a different disposition of property in England—a disposition of property which, by producing a very general similarity of condition, would throw the government of the country into the hands of any individuals whom the popular esteem or fancy might select ?

It appears to me that this question can only be decided by ascertaining the genius of the English nation. What is the prime characteristic of the English mind ? I apprehend I may safely decide upon its being industry. Taking a general but not a superficial survey of the English character since the Reformation, a thousand circumstances convince me that the salient point in our national psychology is the passion for accumulating wealth, of which industry is the instrument. We value our freedom principally because it leaves us unrestricted in our pursuits; and that reverence for law and all that is established, which also eminently distinguishes the English nation, is occasioned by the conviction that, next to liberty, order is the most efficacious assistant of industry.

And thus we see that those great revolutions which must occur in the history of all nations, when they happen here produce no permanent effects upon our social state. Our revolutions are brought about by the passions of creative minds taking advantage, for their own aggrandisement, of peculiar circumstances in our national progress. They are never called for by the great body of the nation. Churches are plundered, long rebellions maintained, dynasties changed, parliaments abolished; but when the storm is passed, the features of the social landscape remain unimpaired ; there are no traces of the hurricane, the earthquake, or the volcano; it has been but a tumult of the atmosphere, that has neither toppled down our old spires and palaces nor swallowed up our cities and seats of learning, nor blasted our ancient woods, nor swept away our ports and harbours. The English nation ever recurs to its ancient institutions—the institutions that have alike secured freedom and order; and after all their ebullitions, we find them, when the sky is clear, again at work, and toiling on at their eternal task of accumulation.

There is this difference between the revolutions of England and the revolutions of the Continent—the European revolution is a struggle against privilege; an English revolution is a struggle for it. If a new class rises in the State, it becomes uneasy to take its place in the natural aristocracy of the land: a desperate faction or a wily leader takes advantage of this desire, and a revolution is the consequence. Thus the Whigs in the present day have risen to power on the shoulders of the manufacturing interest. To secure themselves in their posts, the Whigs have given the new interest an undue preponderance; but the new interest, having obtained its object, is content. The manufacturer, like every other Englishman, is as aristocratic as the landlord. The manufacturer begins to lack in movement. Under Walpole the Whigs played the same game with the commercial interest; a century has passed, and the commercial interest are all as devoted to the constitution as the manufacturers soon will be. Having no genuine party, the Whigs seek for succour from the Irish papists; Lord John Russell, however, is only imitating Pym under the same circumstances. In 1640, when the English movement was satisfied, and the constitutional party, headed by such men as Falkland and Hyde, were about to attain power, Pym and his friends, in despair at their declining influence and the close divisions in their once unanimous Parliament, fled to the Scotch Covenanters, and entered into " a close compact " for the destruction of the Church of England as the price of their assistance. So events repeat themselves; but if the study of history is really to profit us, the nation at the present day will take care that the same results do not always occur from the same events.

When passions have a little subsided, the industrious ten-pounder, who has struggled into the privileged order of the Commons, proud of having obtained the first step of aristocracy, will be the last man to assist in destroying the other gradations of the scale which he or his posterity may yet ascend; the new member of a manufacturing district has his eye already upon a neighbouring park, avails himself of his political position to become a county magistrate, meditates upon a baronetcy, and dreams of a coroneted descendant.

The nation that esteems wealth as the great object of existence will submit to no laws that do not secure the enjoyment of wealth. Now, we deprive wealth of its greatest source of enjoyment, as well as of its best security, if we deprive it of power. The English nation, therefore, insists that property shall be the qualification for power, and the whole scope of its laws and customs is to promote and favour the accumulation of wealth and the perpetuation of property. We cannot alter, therefore, the disposition of property in this country without we change the national character. Far from the present age being hostile to the supremacy of property, there has been no period of our history where property has been more esteemed, because there has been no period when the nation has been so industrious.

Believing, therefore, that no change will occur in the disposition of property in this country, I cannot comprehend how our government can become more democratic. The consequence of our wealth is an aristocratic constitution; the consequence of our love of liberty is an aristocratic constitution founded on an equality of civil rights. And who can deny that an aristocratic constitution resting on such a basis, where the legislative, and even the executive office may be obtained by every subject of the realm, is, in fact, a noble democracy ? The

English constitution, faithfully representing the national character, secures to all the enjoyment of property and the delights of freedom.   Its honours are a perpetual reward of industry; every Englishman is toiling to obtain them; and this is the constitution to which every Englishman will always be devoted, except he is a Whig.

In the next chapter I shall discuss the second proposition.

CHAPTER VI

RECENT POLITICAL CHANGES

THE Tories assert that the whole property of the country is on their side; and the Whigs, wringing their hands over lost elections and bellowing about "intimidation," seem to confess the soft impeachment. Their prime organ also assures us that every man with £500 per annum is opposed to them. Yet the Whig-Radical writers have recently published, by way of consolation to their penniless proselytes, a list of some twenty Dukes and Marquises, who, they assure us, are devoted to "Liberal" principles, and whose revenues, in a paroxysm of economical rhodomontade, they assert, could buy up the whole income of the rest of the hereditary Peerage. The Whig-Radical writers seem puzzled to reconcile this anomalous circumstance with the indisputably forlorn finances of their faction in general. Now, this little tract on the "Spirit of Whiggism" may perhaps throw some light upon this perplexing state of affairs. For myself, I see in it only a fresh illustration of the principles which I have demonstrated, from the whole current of our history, to form the basis of Whig policy. This union of oligarchical wealth and mob poverty is the very essence of the "Spirit of Whiggism."

The English constitution, which, from the tithing-man to the Peer of Parliament, has thrown the whole government of the country into the hands of those who are qualified by property to perform the duties of their respective offices, has secured that diffused and general freedom, without which the national industry would neither have its fair play nor its just reward, by a variety of institutions, which, while they prevent those who have no property from invading the social commonwealth, in whose classes every industrious citizen has a right to register himself, offer also an equally powerful check to the ambitious fancies of those great families, over whose liberal principles and huge incomes the Whig-Radical writers gloat with the self-complacency of lackeys at the equipages and establishments of their masters. There is ever an union in a perverted sense between those who are beneath power and those who wish to be above it; and oligarchies and despotisms are usually established by the agency of a deluded multitude. The Crown, with its constitutional influence over the military services; a Parliament of two houses, watching each other's proceedings with constitutional jealousy; an independent hierarchy, and, not least, an independent magistracy, are serious obstacles in the progressive establishment of that scheme of government which a small knot of great families, these Dukes and Marquises, whose revenues, according to the Government organ, could buy up the income of the whole peerage, naturally wish to introduce. We find, therefore, throughout the whole period of our more modern history, a powerful section of the great nobles ever at war with the national institutions; checking the Crown; attacking the independence of that House of Parliament in which they happen to be in a minority, no matter which; patronising sects to reduce the influence of the Church; and playing town against country to overcome the authority of the gentry.

It is evident that these aspiring oligarchs, as a party, can have little essential strength; they can count upon nothing but their mere retainers. To secure the triumph of their cause, therefore, they are forced to manœuvre with a pretext, and while they aim at oligarchical rule, they apparently advocate popular rights. They hold out, consequently, an inducement to all the uneasy portion of the nation to enlist under their standard; they play their discontented minority against the prosperous majority, and, dubbing their partisans " the people," they flatter themselves that their projects are irresistible. The attack is unexpected, brisk, and dashing, well matured, dexterously mystified. Before the nation is roused to its danger, the oligarchical object is often obtained; and then the oligarchy, entrenched in power, count upon the nation to defend them from their original and revolutionary allies. If they succeed, a dynasty is changed, or a Parliament reformed, and the movement is stopped; if the Tories or the Conservatives cannot arrest the fatal career which the Whigs have originally impelled, then away go the national institutions; the crown falls from the King's brow; the crosier is snapped in twain; one House of Parliament is sure to disappear, and the gentlemen of England, dexterously dubbed Malignants, or Anti-Reformers, or any other phrase in fashion, the dregs of the nation, sequester their estates and install themselves in their halls; and " liberal principles " having thus gloriously triumphed, after a due course of plunder, bloodshed, imprisonment, and ignoble tryanny, the people of England, sighing once more to be the English nation, secure order by submitting to a despot, and in time, when they have got rid of their despot, combine their ancient freedom with their newly-regained security by re-establishing the English constitution.

The Whigs of the present day have made their assault upon the nation with their usual spirit. They have already succeeded in controlling the sovereign and in remodelling the House of Commons. They have menaced the House of Lords, violently assailed the Church, and reconstructed the Corporations. I shall take the two most comprehensive measures which they have succeeded in carrying, and which at the time certainly were popular, and apparently of a very democratic character—their reform of the House of Commons, and their reconstruction of the municipal corporations. Let us see whether these great measures have, in fact, increased the democratic character of our constitution or not— whether they veil an oligarchical project, or are, in fact, popular concessions inevitably offered by the Whigs in their oligarchical career.

The result of the Whig remodelling of the order of the Commons has been this—that it has placed the nomination of the Government in the hands of the popish priesthood. Is that a great advance of public intelligence and popular liberty ? Are the parliamentary nominees of M'Hale and Keogh more germane to the feelings of the English nation, more adapted to represent their interests, than the parliamentary nominees of a Howard or a Percy ? This papist majority, again, is the superstructure of a basis formed by some Scotch Presbyterians and some English Dissenters, in general returned by the small constituencies of small towns—classes whose number and influence, intelligence and wealth, have been grossly exaggerated for factious purposes, but classes avowedly opposed to the maintenance of the English constitution. I do not see that the cause of popular power has much risen, even with the addition of this leaven. If the suffrages of the Commons of England were polled together, the hustings-books of the last general election will prove that a very considerable majority of their numbers is opposed to the present Government, and that therefore, under this new democratic scheme, this great body of the nation are, by some hocus-pocus tactics or other, obliged to submit to the minority. The truth is, that the new constituency has been so arranged that an unnatural preponderance has been given to a small class, and one hostile to the interests of the great body. Is this more democratic ? The apparent majority in the House of Commons is produced by a minority of the Commons themselves ; so that a small and favoured class command a majority in the House of Commons, and the sway of the administration, as far as that House is concerned, is regulated by a smaller number of individuals than those who governed it previous to its reform.

But this is not the whole evil: this new class, with its unnatural preponderance, is a class hostile to the institutions of the country, hostile to the union of Church and State, hostile to the House of Lords, to the constitutional power of the Crown, to the existing system of provincial judicature. It is, therefore, a class fit and willing to support the Whigs in their favourite scheme of centralisation, without which the Whigs can never long maintain themselves in power. Now, centralisation is the death-blow of public freedom; it is the citadel of the oligarchs from which, if once erected, it will be impossible to dislodge them.

But can that party be aiming at centralised government which has reformed the municipal corporations? We will see. The reform of the municipal corporations of England is a covert attack on the authority of the English gentry—that great body which perhaps forms the most substantial existing obstacle to the perpetuation of Whiggism in power. By this apparently democratic Act the county magistrate is driven from the towns where he before exercised a just influence, while an elective magistrate from the towns jostles him on the bench at quarter sessions, and presents in his peculiar position an anomaly in the constitution of the bench, flattering to the passions, however fatal to the interests, of the giddy million. Here is a lever to raise the question of county reform whenever an obstinate shire may venture to elect a representative in Parliament hostile to the liberal oligarchs. Let us admit, for the moment, that the Whigs ultimately succeed in subverting the ancient and hereditary power of the English gentry. Will the municipal corporations substitute themselves as an equivalent check on a centralising Government? Whence springs their influence? From property? Not half a dozen have estates. Their influence springs from the factitious power with which the reforming Government has invested them, and of which the same Government will deprive them in a session, the moment they cease to be corresponding committees of the reforming majority in the House of Commons. They will either be swept away altogether, or their functions will be limited to raising the local taxes which will discharge their expenses of the detachment of the metropolitan police, or the local judge or governor, whom Downing Street may send down to preside over their constituents. With one or two exceptions, the English corporations do not possess more substantial and durable elements of power than the municipalities of France. What check are they on Paris ? These corporations have neither prescription in their favour, nor property. Their influence is maintained neither by tradition nor substance. They have no indirect authority over the minds of their townsmen; they have only their modish charters to appeal to, and the newly engrossed letter of the law. They have no great endowments of whose public benefits they are the official distributors; they do not stand on the vantage-ground on which we recognise the trustees of the public interests; they neither administer to the soul nor the body; they neither feed the poor nor educate the young; they have no hold on the national mind; they have not sprung from the national character; they were born by faction, and they will live by faction. Such bodies must speedily become corrupt; they will ultimately be found dangerous instruments in the hands of a faction. The members of the country corporations will play the game of a London party, to secure their factitious local importance and obtain the consequent results of their opportune services.

I think I have now established the two propositions with which I commenced my last chapter : and I will close this concluding one of the " Spirit of Whiggism " with their recapitulation, and the inferences which I draw from them. If there be slight probability of ever establishing in this country a more democratic govern-

ment than the English constitution, it will be as well,
I conceive, for those who love their rights to maintain that constitution; and if the recent measures of
the Whigs, however plausible their first aspect, have, in
fact, been a departure from the democratic character
of that constitution, it will be as well for the English
nation to oppose, with all their heart, and all their soul,
and all their strength, the machinations of the Whigs
and the " Spirit of Whiggism."

OPEN LETTERS

[THE OPEN LETTERS represent a selection from Disraeli's fugitive contributions to the *Times*. Among them are two Runnymede Letters, written after the publication of the others in book form, and never since reprinted. The Letters signed "Lælius" are in similar vein. Probably most interest attaches to that " To the Queen," written at Lord Lyndhurst's request, in support of Sir Robert Peel in his contention with Queen Victoria over the Ladies of the Bedchamber. It is a curious fact that sixty years later the Queen said, " I was very young then, and perhaps I should act differently if it was all to be done again ;" while Disraeli, on the other hand, veered round to the view that Sir Robert had made an error in his treatment of the young Sovereign. The " Letter to the Queen " caused a stir at the time, and was in some quarters attributed to Brougham. Thus Disraeli, writing to his sister :[1]

> " B. denies the letter to the Queen. Croker, ostensibly writing to him on some literary point, but really to extract some opinion from him on the subject of the letter, put in a postscript:
> " *Have you seen the Letter to the Queen ? They give it to you.*
> " Brougham answered, in a postscript also:
> " *I have seen the Letter to the Queen. It was lent to me.*"

The Atticus Letter to the Duke of Wellington has also a value of its own. In 1852 it fell to Disraeli, in his first period of office, to deliver as a funeral oration in the House of Commons a fuller estimate of the Great Duke. The manuscript from which the oration was delivered was handed to the Press, and is now to be seen in the Manuscript Room of the British Museum.]

[1] Additional Manuscripts, British Museum.

To His Excellency the Lord Lieutenant of Ireland [1]

My Lord,—Allow me to congratulate your Excellency, to use the revolutionary jargon of the day, " on carrying out " by so unforeseen a method the great measure of Roman Catholic Emancipation. It was a bright idea, that of emptying the gaols of the Barataria [2] over whose destinies your Excellency so shrewdly presides; and it is interesting to witness the philosophical civilisation of the nineteenth century, in triumphant defiance of ancient prejudice, communicating with so much effect the rude yet prophetic conceptions of a Jack Cade. Fortunate island, that an O'Connell supplies with justice, and a Mulgrave with mercy; the severer quality typified by a murdered Protestant, the gentler attribute only by the release of a Papist convict.

Your Excellency has by this time doubtless digested the Parliamentary bulletin of the grand encounter of last week. The annals of political warfare do not record an instance of a more arrogant attack, or of a defeat more disastrous.

The recent debates are valuable for weightier reasons than the illustrations they richly afford of your Lordship's character, in itself, however, no uninteresting topic when its spirit may affect the destinies of an empire. Vain, volatile, and flimsy, headstrong without being courageous, imperious rather than dignified, and restless rather than energetic, but always theatrical, with a morbid love of mob popularity and a maudlin flux of claptrap sensibility, his anger a stage scowl, his courtesy a simper; every glance directed to the lamps, every movement arranged into an attitude; now frowning on an Orange functionary,

[1] Constantine Henry Phipps, Earl of Mulgrave, and afterwards Marquis of Normanby, was appointed Lord Lieutenant of Ireland in 1835, and held the position until 1839. His administration was much criticised on account of his leniency to political prisoners.   [2] Sancho Panza's island city.

now releasing a criminal with a sympathetic sigh: behold
the fluttering and tinsel thing of shreds and patches,
the tawdry-property man, whom the discrimination of the
Whigs has selected at this crisis to wrestle with the
genius of the Papacy in its favourite stronghold.

It is not, however, because the recent debates have
furnished me with the traits with which I sketched your
Excellency's portrait, and the English nation with experience to appreciate its resemblance, that they are
principally valuable; these debates, my Lord, have
demonstrated to the satisfaction of every clear-headed
Briton the identity of the Irish Government and the
" National Association." In that case the Irish Government cannot be in worse hands, nor Ireland under a sway
at the same time more disastrous and more dishonest;
and I much mistake the character of the English nation
if they will for a moment submit with humiliating patience
to a system which enables an impudent assembly of self-
delegated adventurers, pledged to the eradication of
every English institution and every English feeling, to
meet under the shadow of the Viceregal castle, and,
arrogating to themselves a title so comprehensive and
corporate, launch their destructive decrees with the
avowed or implied ratification of the King's representative.

Well said the eloquent and patriotic Member for
Cumberland,[1] on passing in review the terrible array of
your fatal folly, that the question of this mischievous
identity might be decided by a single instance—the
appointment of Mr. Pigot![2] It is in the bosom of the
rebel Association that the loyal Lord Lieutenant seeks
his confidential adviser. I also would observe that your
connection with a single individual is conclusive as to
this disgraceful union of the power of the Crown and
the plots of those who are conspiring against its dignity—

[1] Sir James Graham.
[2] David Richard Pigot, law adviser to the Lord Lieutenant
and subsequently Chief Baron of Exchequer in Ireland.

this monstrous partnership of authority and insurrection. I take the case of a man who is the avowed and acknowledged founder of the " National Association." I listen to him in that assembly venting the most revolutionary doctrines and seditious menaces; I trace him afterwards on a provincial tour of treason, fresh from these halls of initiative outrage, stirring up the multitude even to massacre in language unparalleled for its spirit of profligate persecution. I hear of this man, at a blasphemous banquet of his followers still calling for blood, announced by a Bishop of his Church with sacerdotal unction as the messenger of the Divinity; I am informed that the gentry of the county where he made these terrific appeals assembled together to invoke your protection, as the King's representative, against the consequence of his sanguinary machinations. And what do you do ? By what means does your Excellency testify your disapprobation of his career of infamous tumult ? By an invitation to dinner. Notwithstanding all that had occurred, and the strongly expressed disapprobation of your Sovereign of this man ever appearing at your table, he is nevertheless your cherished guest.[1] Why, courtesy to this man is no longer a question of party politics; it is a question of civilisation. After such conduct on your part, who can doubt your sanction of the system he had been pursuing ? I, for one, cannot hesitate as to the perfect identity of your government and the will of this man, even if I had not witnessed him the other night in the House of Commons, at the conclusion of your delegated defiance, grasp the trembling palm of your noble champion with that subtle and savage paw that can alike rifle the pocket of a Raphael[2] or hurl a dead dog into the grave of a Kavanagh.

Observe the gradations of official sympathy with Irish treason. The Association, repudiated by Lord Melbourne,

[1] The King, in a letter to Lord Melbourne, had protested against O'Connell being received at the table of the Lord Lieutenant.
[2] A charge of misappropriation made against O'Connell by Mr. Raphael, M.P. for Carlow, and disproved.

is apologised for by Lord John Russell and justified by
Lord Morpeth. What, then, remains ? The Viceregal
panegyric. Lord Grey retired from the helm because he
detected that some of his colleagues had secretly carried
on a disgraceful intrigue with your Excellency's guest.
How will Lord Melbourne act now that he discovers that
the very association he denounced is, in fact, the government of Ireland ? His Lordship is at least a man of
spirit. There is nothing base in his composition, though
much that is reckless. He might be induced to become
a desperate leader, but he will never submit to being made
the cat's-paw of his own followers. I believe that Lord
Melbourne will follow the example of Lord Grey; the lion
stalked off with majestic grandeur; the wolf may yet
effect his retreat with sullen dignity. The rapacious
band of modern Whigs must seek for a new leader in a
more ignoble beast of prey. But they need not despair,
my Lord. The Government need not break up. It has
at least my ardent aspirations for its continuance. After
all its transmutations, I wish it to assume its last phasis
of contempt. Your Excellency is now skilled in government. Come, then, my Lord, and rule us ! Come and
insult our gentry and open our prisons ! Be the last
leader of the Reformed Parliament and the Reform
Ministry. Come, my Lord, and make revolution at length
ridiculous.

RUNNYMEDE.

February 11, 1837.

To Lord Viscount Melbourne

My Lord,—It has sometimes been my humble but
salutary office to attend your triumph, and remind you
in a whisper that you are mortal. Amid the blaze of
glory that at present surrounds you, it may be advisable
for me to resume this wholesome function, lest in the
intoxication of success your Lordship may for a moment

24

forget that, although still a Minister, you are yet only a man.[1] I willingly admit, however, that the qualities both of your Lordship and your colleagues are far from being identical with those of ordinary mortals. If I cannot venture to acknowledge them as supernatural, I make your Lordship a present of a new word, the introduction of which into our language the fact of your admonition will amply authorise with our future lexicographers. No one can deny that the abilities of yourself and of your colleagues are subterhuman.

You and your partners appear to me at present to be very much in the situation of a firm of speculative country bankers who have been generously stimulating the prosperity of their neighbourhood by a frank issue of their peculiar currency. Whether Ireland required justice, or Spain only freedom—whether the sectarists were anxious to subvert the Establishment, or the Papists merely to plunder it—they were sure of being accommodated at your counter. But your notes are now returned, and it seems you lack bullion; and ere long it may be expected that you will figure in the *Gazette,* resigning your seals and your salaries, as a bankrupt delivers up to his creditors his watch and his purse.

When the Right Hon. Baronet the Member for Tamworth,[2] who in all probability will be the official assignee of your abortive projects and your disastrous schemes, recently seized the happy opportunity of criticising your balance-sheet, it appears that his comments called a smile to the serene visage of the noble Secretary for Foreign Affairs. Our intimate relations with France, the triumph of our countrymen in the Peninsula, and the profound consideration which Russia seizes every occasion of testifying for our flag, might justify the complacent ebullition of this fortunate functionary. But why

[1] "A Minister, but still a Man" (Pope's "Epistle to James Craggs, Esq., Secretary of State").
[2] Sir Robert Peel.

should smiles be confined to my Lord Palmerston ?
Why should

> " Quips and cranks, and wanton wiles,
> Nods and becks, and wreathed smiles,"[1]

deck merely that debonair countenance ? Could not the
successful consciousness of his hereditary hostility to a
Church summon one simper to the pensive cheek of Lord
John ? Could not Mr. Rice screw his features into
hilarity ? He might have remembered the deputation
from Liverpool. Was the state of Manchester forgotten
by Mr. Thomson that he was so grave ? Or was the
reminiscence of his Indian majority by Sir John Hobhouse " too ponderous for a joke "? I think, my Lord,
if this scene had been performed in the Upper House,
your Colonial Secretary, the sleeping partner, by-the-by,
of your confederacy, might have laughed outright at
some Canadian vision. And you, my Lord, you were
wont once to be a hearty and jocose man enough: I
really think the merriment of Lord Melbourne at this
moment might rank with the fiddling of Nero.

The state of the realm is indeed unparalleled. Each
division of the national interests is in like disorder.
Commerce, manufactures, public credit, our colonial and
Continental relations—the same confusion pervades every
section of our policy. There is not a department that is
not in a condition of feeble tumult. You cannot rally,
you have nothing to fall back upon. Like your famous
General, you have no reserve. You are all in a state of
distraction, and all running away at the same time. We
have before this had unpopular, and feeble, and mischievous Cabinets. One Minister has been accused of
sacrificing our foreign influence to our domestic repose,
another of preferring distant fame to internal prosperity.
One has been said to mismanage the colonies, another
suspected of unconstitutional designs upon India. A
successful expedition has been counterbalanced by an
improvident loan, or social order has been maintained

---

[1] " L'Allegro."

at the cost of despotic enactments. Some department, perhaps, of every Ministry has supplied the people with a safety-valve of grumbling ; but your administration, my Lord, is the first that has failed in every department of the State, and covered every member of the Cabinet with equal odium. It has failed in everything, both at home and abroad. Beneath its malevolent genius our glory has been sullied and our purses thinned; our colonies have rebelled, and our allies have deserted us; our soldiers are runagates, and our merchants bankrupts.

Those who know you cannot easily be persuaded that you have a serious design on the existence of the empire, and some may even question whether you have a serious design of any kind. You began in a careless vein, and you will terminate in a tragical one. The country was swinging itself very prosperously in its easy-chair, when, half in mirth and half in mischief, you kicked over the unconscious victim, and now, frightened out of your wits, in a paroxysm of nervous desperation you are going to hack and hew in detail, and add mutilation to murder.

But never mind, my Lord; Bobadil, though beaten, was still a captain, and Lord Melbourne, in spite of all his blunders, is still a Reformer. What though Russia captures our ships, and Englishmen are saved from Spanish bayonets only by their heels, no one can deny that the seals of the Foreign Office are entrusted to a sincere Reformer. What though Ireland be ruled by the Romish priesthood, is not our Home Secretary as ardent a Reformer as M'Hale and Cantwell ? Let Canada boast her Papineau, we have as tried a Reformer in our Glenelg. And though we may be on the verge of national bankruptcy, 'tis some consolation that a most trustworthy Reformer presides over our Exchequer. For six years the talismanic cry of reform has reconciled the English nation to every vicissitude that can annoy or mortify the fortunes and spirit of a people. Soothed by its lullaby, we have endured domestic convulsion and foreign disgrace. Your Lordship therefore is safe; for who for a moment can suppose that the nation will so stultify itself as to suspect, at the tenth hour, that there may be an indissoluble connection between Reform and ruin ?

RUNNYMEDE.

April 15, 1837.

TO LORD JOHN RUSSELL

MY LORD,—I have read your letter to your constituents.[1] I like it. It lacks, perhaps, something of the racy and epigrammatic vigour which characterised the memorable epistle in defence of the corn laws. It is somewhat too prodigal, perhaps, of images which are not very novel and which are occasionally rather confused; but it is thoughtful and determined, and worthy of one who, from his lineage, ambition, and career, will occupy no mean space in the future history of our country.

Your Lordship in this document, which will not easily be forgotten, figures in a new, a strange, and an important character. You appear as the great Conservative Precursor, heralding the advent of a Tory Administration, and expounding the *rationale* of reaction.

Little more than eight years have elapsed since the project of the Reform Act, but they are eight years replete with events. Wise men compute time, not by the almanacks, but their impressions;[2] and with reference to political instruction the experience of eight such years is worth the results of half a century of undisturbed prescription.

It is only by this mode of estimating the progress of time that I can philosophically account for the changes in your Lordship's opinions, and for the revolution of your political temper. The former champion of representation instead of nomination in the House of Commons has

[1] "Letter to the electors of Stroud on the Principles of the Reform Act." The letter ran through seven editions.
[2] "Count them by sensation, and not by calendars," wrote Disraeli in "Sybil" of the race for the Derby in 1837, "and each moment is a day, and the race a life."

at length discovered that we may have election without
representation; and the denouncer of the constitutional
decision of the House of Lords as "the whisper of a
faction" now delicately intimates to his astonished
followers that "the moral influence" of that assembly is
alike indisputable and irresistible, and that its members
are in general superior to the Reformed House in every
statesmanlike quality.

The necessity which compels the father of the Reform
Act to enter, only six years after its passing, into a defence
of that measure, leads me to reflect upon the nature of
parties under the new Parliamentary scheme, which is
threatened never to become old.

It is, perhaps, a fanciful theory of the physicians who
hold that man is born with the seeds of the disease which
terminates his life.   Undoubtedly, however, these are the
exact circumstances which must inevitably attend the
birth of every "Movement" Administration.   The causes
of their dissolution accompany their nativity.   They have
attained power by agitation.   Their success is at the same
time a precedent and an encouragement for continued
disturbance.   The original innovators, having no inclination for further progress, take refuge in "finality."
Three parties then appear in the State—their original
opponents, who are conservative of institutions; themselves, who are administrative of institutions; and their
new adversaries, who are aggressive against institutions.
The first party may count the nation in their ranks; the
last may appeal successfully to the mob; but for the
middle party only remain the population of the offices—
those who enjoy and those who expect.

The result, as far as the Government is concerned, cannot be doubtful.   After having protracted the catastrophe
by every expedient consistent with their determination not
to make any substantial concession, they take refuge in
those conservative opinions of which your Lordship has
just developed the philosophy; and, retiring from public
life with the consolation they have enjoyed their fair share

of official power, or, to use language sentimental, that
" they have had their dream," they gratify their spleen as
well as exemplify their patriotism by crushing the nascent
efforts of the party that has outbid them in popular
overtures, and surpassed them in popular favour.

The fate of the Whig party has indeed been hurried.
Truly the elements of the famous Reform Ministry seem
never to have been settled.　After two years of initiatory
tumult, your first session of affairs was distinguished by
the sullen, yet significant, retirement of Lord Durham.
Twelve months more, and a Secretary of State, a First
Lord of the Admiralty, and two of their colleagues
abruptly quit your councils; and before the public mind
has recovered from the uneasiness which such events
naturally occasion, a conspiracy explodes, and we are
startled by the overthrow of Lord Grey and the resignation of Lord Althorp.　In a few months the vamped-up
Cabinet quits and returns to power.　You throw over your
Lord Chancellor—you affect to justify the catastrophe.
But was Lord Glenelg an intriguer and traitor ?　The
Whigs are said to be bitter opponents; for my part, I
should shrink from their friendship.

Eight members of the Reform Ministry betrayed by
their own party in eight years !—on an average a victim for
every session.　Yet, with all these violent alteratives, the
original disease has worked its irresistible course, and
after having immolated your Constitutional colleagues,
the picture is completed by your Lordship publishing, on
the same day, a loyal proclamation against the Chartists,[1]
and a Conservative manifesto against the Radicals.　The
history of reform should be written in epigrams.

The march of events has indeed been rapid.　It is only
five years ago since the staple subject of Whig journalism
was a jest against reaction.　In another year the jest
became a controversy; and now, only six years after the
passing of the Reform Act, the wealth and the irresistible

---

[1] A proclamation in the *London Gazette* forbidding unlawful
assemblies for the purpose of drilling persons to the use of arms.

power, the numbers and the high character, of the Tory party are sketched by an individual no less celebrated and no less free from any imputation of partiality than the nobleman who commenced his literary career by defending close boroughs, and his political one by destroying them.

Your Lordship will retire from public life with dignity, for you have prepared the way for your great rival. He has deserved this service, for he has been a generous antagonist; and if you adorn your solitude by writing the memoirs of your administration—a task which you would perform admirably—I have such confidence in that nobility of sentiment which is inseparable from genius that I do not doubt you will do justice to his consummate abilities.

Far, however, is it from my desire that you should relinquish the power which you are prepared to exercise so much to the satisfaction of every lover of our institutions. You really seem to me to be the fair ideal of a Conservative statesman. They tell me that you are in somewhat of a scrape at present about Jamaica. Trust to your natural allies, the Tories, to extricate you from it. Although not your friend, I am so much your admirer that I will present you with a specific for this colonial embroilment. 'Tis simple—take it. Let Lord Normanby return to the first scene of his administrative talents. With his peculiar practice of policy I should hardly think there would be the present want of accommodation in the Jamaica prisons.

LÆLIUS.

May 4, 1839.

To the Queen [1]

MADAM,—That freedom happily secured to us by the settlement of your Royal race on the throne of this island permits me to address your Majesty on an occasion inter-

[1] This letter was written by Disraeli at Lord Lyndhurst's request (see "Life of Disraeli," by W. F. Monypenny, vol. ii., p. 58). In "Sybil" (1845) Disraeli gave his more matured

esting to your personal happiness, important to the fortunes of your realm.

The week that is now closing embraces the most critical events in the life of the Queen of England. At its commencement, your Majesty's Minister publicly and formally announced that he no longer possessed the confidence of your Parliament, and that he was unable to carry measures which he believed to be indispensable to the service of the State. Your Majesty accepted his tendered resignation, and entrusted to the leader of the party opposed to him the formation of another Ministry. It was well known that your Majesty honoured your retiring Minister as much by your personal regard as by your political confidence; but your Majesty, with a dignified intelligence worthy of your station, encouraged your new adviser by a gracious and voluntary expression of the unlimited confidence and the unrestricted authority which you extended to him.

Thus auspiciously Sir Robert Peel proceeded to form a Government, and in twenty-four hours after receiving your Majesty's commands to that effect he waited on your Majesty with the announcement that he had achieved your object. Then it was learned for the first time that your Majesty would permit no change in the female offices of the Royal Household, and, though your Majesty's late Ministers had quitted your service, and were in all probability about to oppose the policy of your new councillors, that it was indispensable that their wives, sisters, or daughters, should still be the constant companions of the Sovereign. Under these circumstances Sir Robert Peel felt himself bound to resign the task

---

opinion as follows: "One may be permitted to think that, under all the circumstances, he" (Sir Robert Peel) "should have taken office in 1839. His withdrawal seems to have been a mistake. . . . It was unfortunate that one who, if any, should have occupied the proud and national position of the leader of the Tory party, the chief of the people and the champion of the Throne, should have commenced his career as Minister under Victoria by an unseemly contrariety to the personal wishes of the Queen."

which he had been invited to accomplish; and your kingdom is, consequently, still governed by a Ministry which its leader in the House of Lords describes as not possessing the confidence of the country—a confidence which its leader in the House of Commons has just written a pamphlet to prove it never can obtain.

Unquestionably, Madam, the most painful office of a British Minister is the necessity imposed on him of partially controlling the society of his Sovereign. But there are certain combinations of courtly intimacy which, it is obvious, cannot be tolerated without great public inconvenience and embarrassment. The nation may be in error, but it will with difficulty be convinced that a Minister possesses the confidence of his Sovereign if the family of his predecessor be retained in the Royal Household, and are seen and heard of as the constant companions of the Royal person. The public, unaware that a Royal mind is schooled from infancy in habits of severe self-control, will not be apt to comprehend how the secret of the Cabinet can be constantly concealed from the companion of the closet; and will be indignant, rather than astonished, if occasionally the tactics of Opposition be felicitously adapted to the concealed weaknesses of the Government. Under such circumstances, the Minister, if popular, is looked upon, not as the Minister of the Crown, but as the Minister of the Parliament; and the throne that had been hitherto esteemed as a high political institution assumes the unfortunate aspect of a mere courtly pageant.

I can easily conceive how a young and ingenuous mind, full of innocence, and giving others credit for the same singleness of purpose as animates herself, can, without difficulty, reconcile the fulfilment of the duties of even a royal station with the indulgence of the affections of the heart. Your Majesty looks upon the female relatives of your Ministers as the mere companions of the pleasures of your life, and doubtless these ladies compliment your Majesty upon your just and discriminating appreciation of their pursuits and motives. I will even myself at present give them credit for sincerity, and, while their husbands and their fathers are sitting at your council table, they perhaps are not aspiring enough to conceive that they are formed for severer duties than to glitter at the banquet and glide in the saloon.

But even Mistresses of the Robes and Ladies of the Bedchamber, though angelic, are human. Let their relatives quit office and be nightly arrayed in attempts to destroy your Majesty's Government; let success to some of these relatives in their party conflicts be a matter of imperious necessity. Is the courtly child to repudiate the faction of her father ? Is the wife in waiting expected to feel no sympathy with the Parliamentary assault that may bear its plunder to the exhausted coffers of a desperate husband ?

But your Majesty has confidence in the strength of your own character. You are convinced that the line of demarcation between public duty and private affection is broad and deep. On all that concerns the State, you are assured that your lips and your heart will be for ever closed to the circle in which you pass your life. Be it so. I humbly presume to give your Majesty credit for all the exalted virtues which become a throne. But where, then, are the joys of companionship ? The Royal brow is clouded, but the Royal lip must never explain its care. The Queen is anxious, but the Lady in Waiting must not share her restlessness or soothe her disquietude.

Madam, it cannot be. You are a Queen; but you are a human being and a woman. The irrepressible sigh will burst forth some day, and you will meet a glance more interesting because there is a captivating struggle to suppress its sympathy. Wearied with public cares, crossed, as necessarily you must sometimes be, the peevish exclamation will have its way, and you yourself will be startled at its ready echo. The line once passed, progress is quick; fascinating sympathy, long suppressed indignation, promised succour; the tear, the tattle, the innuendo, the direct falsehood; in a moment they will convince you you are a victim, and that they have heroes in wait to rescue their Sovereign. Then come the Palace conspiracy and the backstairs intrigue. You will find yourself with the rapidity of enchantment the centre and the puppet of a Camarilla, and Victoria, in the eyes of that Europe which once bowed to her, and in the hearts of those Englishmen who once yielded to her their devotion, will be reduced to the level of Madrid and Lisbon.

And shall this be the destiny of that "fair virgin throned in the west," who was to have been our second Elizabeth ? —the mistress of an Empire more vast than that mighty monarchy that attempted to crush Elizabeth with its baffled Armadas ? Ah ! Madam, pause. Let not this crisis of your reign be recorded by the historian with a tear or a blush. The system which you are advised to establish is one degrading to the Minister, one which must be painful to the Monarch, one which may prove fatal to the monarchy.[1]

LÆLIUS.

May 11, 1839.

To Lord Melbourne

My Lord,—The world is perplexed about your purposes; perhaps you share their embarrassment and anxiety. For my own part, I cannot forget that in politics, as well as in everything else, "no-meaning puzzles more than wit," and while some are giving you credit for an impending Machiavelian stroke of state, I should not be surprised if, after all, you have only turned a fresh page in the chapter of accidents.

Yet are there rumours of great changes. Your followers bruit about a " programme of liberal measures." Your temporary secession from power, they insinuate, produced the most salutary effects upon your intellect and your temper. A momentary relief from the toils of State per-

[1] Lord Morley records that Mr. Gladstone also composed on the same subject a letter which has not been published.

mitted profound reflection on the spirit of the age. You
returned to Downing Street as Napoleon from Elba, ready
to concede a Constitution adapted to the necessities of
the times. The rapacious appetite of the Republican
for innovation is to be satiated by paying only a penny
for his letters; the more moderate Radical professors
satisfied by not paying a shilling for the registration of
their votes. A penny and a shilling! Whig ways and
means to prevent revolutions and arrest the fall of
monarchies! But even this is not all. The Reform Act
is still to be final, but it is not to be conclusive. Nice
distinction! There are to be considerable alterations,
but then they are to be made in its spirit. More of the
precious metal, indeed, is not to be introduced into circu-
lation, but, then, the currency is to be considerably increased by its debasement. Add to this the strong yet
not astounding conviction of your colleagues of the necessity of education, and the "programme" is complete.
Imaginary resources of beggared gamesters!

It will not do, my Lord. These scrapings and cheese-
parings of your famished larder will never serve a banquet.
The primary and restless cause of all the embarrassment
of your party, past and present, can never be removed
or eradicated. I have traced its fatal birth, its indefatigable activity, and its inevitable consequences, in the
letter which I addressed to the most distinguished of your
colleagues.[1] A "progressive" party is a party that must
dash over the precipice.

But your Lordship is again in power. Your bankruptcy is superseded, though your credit is not restored.
I admired the characteristic naïveté, from one whom his
experience should have made so close and callous, not
without charm, with which you assured the House of
Lords that had your Lordship been in the situation of
Sir Robert Peel, when recently summoned by his Sovereign, you would have acted very differently. I believe
you. Enjoying such an opportunity, the leader of a party

[1] The letter to Lord John Russell, p. 365.

such as your Lordship heads would have seen only within his grasp power to which neither the essential strength of that party nor his own reputation legitimately entitled him. The temptation would have been too strong for nerves less flexible than those of the former Irish Secretary of the Duke of Wellington; and however brief the lease of office, however degrading the terms by which it was secured, sinister the means by which it was maintained, and mischievous the results which it entailed on the Crown and the country, it could bear no damage to a party in whose expiring condition even defeat might figure as an achievement, as proving their vitality. In the most ignominious discomfiture they must reap some profit—as bands of fugitive marauders can still sack villages and plunder peasants.

But, my Lord, there may be statesmen and parties differently circumstanced. Let me consider the character and position of a political leader whom, to use only the admissions of his adversaries, I may describe as a man unrivalled for Parliamentary talents, of unimpeached integrity, of unsullied personal conduct, of considerable knowledge, both scholastic and civil, and of an estate ample and unencumbered—one of long official practice, of greater political experience; of that happy age when the vigour of manhood is not impaired, and when men have attained as much experience as, without over-refining action, is compatible with practical wisdom; when an elevated and thoughtful ambition is not eager, yet prepared, for power, free from both the restlessness of youth and the discontent of declining age—epochs that alike deem life too short for delay. Add to this a temperament essentially national, and a habit of life pleasing to the manners and prejudices of his countrymen, with many of the virtues of the English character, and some of its peculiarities; confident rather than sanguine; guided by principles, yet not despising expedients; fearful to commit himself, yet never shrinking from responsibility; proud, yet free from vanity, and reserved rather from disposition than from an ungenerous prudence; most courageous when in peril; most cautious in prosperity.

It is difficult to estimate the characters of our contemporaries, but this I believe, though a slight, to be not an incorrect sketch of that of Sir Robert Peel—a statesman who is at the head of the most powerful party that ever flourished in this country—that in opposition commands a large majority in one House of Parliament, equals the united factions in the other, and, by general consent, needs only a recurrence to the sense of the nation to overwhelm them. But, moreover, and above all, a statesman who has watched and witnessed this mighty party congregate and expand under his advice and guidance, in an ill-favoured season of trial, turbulence, and trouble, with small beginnings, forlorn hopes, extreme difficulties, struggling at the same time against popular prejudice and courtly alienation.

My Lord, such a man, and the leader of such men, must never obtain an entrance to the councils of his Sovereign—I will not say by artifice or intrigue, but in any other style or spirit than become an elevated character and a commanding position. His administration must never be one existing on sufferance by any branch of the Legislature. He forfeits too great a station to accept power grudged and hampered by any estate of the realm. The essential strength of his party, the permanent character of the constitutional principles and material interests that bind them together, his own vigorous time of life, authorise on his part patience and justify delay. He of all men must never deign to be a seeker. Time is one of his partisans. For two years Lord Melbourne submitted to be the Minister of his late Sovereign's necessity, not of his choice. Sir Robert Peel never will. There is the difference between you.

A quarrel about a Lady of the Bedchamber! Pah! Your Lordship remembers the contemptuous exclamation of Mr. Burke when, at the commencement of the great revolutionary struggle, the war was described by some

superficial rhetorician as a war about the opening of the
Scheldt. The scornful image which in that instance
flashed from his indignant and irritated imagination
would not be altogether out of keeping with that scene
and sanctuary into which you have at length pursued the
jaded destinies of your country. But I will not profane
the mysteries of the Bona Dea.

It is not want of ability, or lack of knowledge, or even
deficiency of patriotism, that disqualifies a Lord Melbourne
or a Lord John Russell from being Ministers of their
country. Their difficulties, and they are insuperable, are
inherent in the Whig party. It is a party that now is only
a name. It has no principle of action, no essential quality
of cohesion, no bond of union except traditionary exploits
and hereditary connections, both fast fleeting and fading
away before the course of time and the stern and urgent
pressure of reality. It was once a great and high-spirited
aristocratic confederacy; it has its place, and will keep it,
in our history, for its annals are illustrious, but the chapter
of its fate is about to close; and with your Lordship and
your colleague it rests whether its end shall be a revolutionary catastrophe or a patriotic euthanasia.

                                                    LÆLIUS.
      May 25, 1839.

THE STATE OF THE CASE

["ATTICUS is an immense hit," wrote Disraeli in the
postscript of a letter to his sister, of which two pages
are reproduced on p. 377, by permission of Messrs.
Maggs Brothers, from the original in their possession.
The text of the letter is as follows:

                                CARLTON CLUB,
                                      March 16 [1841].
MY DEAREST SA,
      A most agreeable party at Bulwer's—Morpeth, Hanley
of the Treasury, Mr. Charrington, an Irish ruffian, D'Orsay,
Col. Maberly, Quin. Much *Attic* badinage and serious

appreciation; at last Morpeth recited a whole passage of
Runnymede. Yesterday I dined at the Carlton with Lyndhurst, walking up together past the House. He was most
amiable and delightful. Rd. Plantagenet, de Lisle, and

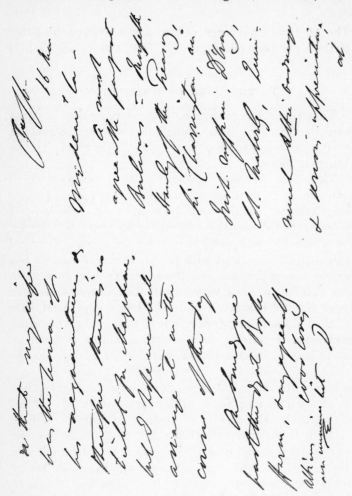

Canterbury came and dined at the next table, and there was
a feast of reason and a flow of grumbling (on the part of P.
and C.)—very amusing. Esterhazy has sent me an invitation
for his assembly to-morrow, but he doesn't know that I am

married, or that my wife has the honour of his acquaintance, and therefore there is no ticket for Mary Anne, but I hope we shall arrange it in the course of the day. On Sunday we past the day at Boyle Farm, and very agreeably. 1000 loves.

D.

The "Atticus" reference, of course, was to Disraeli's letter to the Duke of Wellington on "The State of the Case."]

To the Duke of Wellington.

Your Grace has performed a greater number of great exploits than any living man; but you never achieved a deed more remarkable or more difficult than keeping the Whigs in office.

Various reasons are circulated for the permission which you accord them to serve their Sovereign and to receive their salaries. Some would insinuate that, satisfied—not to say satiated—by the celebrity of an unrivalled career, your Grace is indisposed to re-enter the arena of political responsibility, content with the possession of passive but unquestioned power. But these are speculators who, in my opinion, are not very apt in their discrimination of your Grace's character, and take but a superficial view of the bent and temper of minds of your stamp and order. This idea of retiring on a certain quantity of fame, as some men retire on a certain quantity of money, has the twang of mediocrity. It is generally the refuge of those whose distinction has been more owing to chance than their own conceptions. They are perplexed, almost alarmed, by the results of their good fortune, and in retiring from enterprise they think they realise success.

But original and creative spirits are true to the law of their organisation. An octogenarian Doge of Venice scaled the walls of Constantinople; Marius had completed his seventieth year when he defeated the elder Pompey and quelled the most powerful of aristocracies; white hairs shaded the bold brain of Julius the Second when he planned the expulsion of the barbarians from Italy; and the great King of Prussia had approached his grand climacteric when he partitioned Poland.[1] In surveying your Grace's career of half a century, I cannot perceive any very obtrusive indications of moderation in your purposes, though abundant evidence of forbearance in your conduct. Celebrated for caution, I should rather select as your characteristic a happy audacity. No one has performed bolder deeds in a more scrupulous manner; and plans which, in their initial notion, have assumed even the features of rashness have always succeeded from the wariness of your details. I speak chiefly of your civil life; but I am inclined to believe that your more illustrious, though not perhaps your more eminent, services will not contradict this inference. Your physical aspect is in complete harmony with your spiritual constitution. In the classic contour of your countenance at the first glance, we recognise only deep thoughtfulness and serene repose; but the moment it lights up into active expression, command breathes in every feature; each glance, each tone, indicates the intuitive mind impervious to argument, and we trace without difficulty the aquiline supremacy of the Cæsars.[2]

[1] Contrast the famous passage in "Coningsby" in which Disraeli extols the power of young men: "The history of heroes is the history of youth."

[2] The following lines written by Disraeli are quoted from the *Morning Post* by Sir Herbert Maxwell in his "Life of the Duke of Wellington":

To THE DUKE OF WELLINGTON.

Not only that thy puissant arm could bind
The tyrant of a world, and, conquering fate,
Enfranchise Europe, do I deem thee great;
But that in all thy actions do I find
Exact propriety; no gusts of mind
Fitful and wild, but that continuous state
Of ordered impulse mariners await
In some benignant and enriching wind,
The breath ordained by Nature. Thy calm mien
Recalls old Rome, as much as thy high deed;
Duty thine only idol, and serene
When all are troubled; in the utmost need
Prescient; thy country's servant ever seen,
Yet sovereign of thyself whate'er may speed.
                                    B. DISRAELI.

I dismiss, then, at once the idea that your Grace shrinks from action. The sublime vanity of a mind like yours will not suffer that any great transactions shall be conducted in your lifetime without your special interference. Is it then, as others suggest, from a subtle regard for the ultimate interest of your party that you have more than once thrown your ægis over the trembling Treasury Bench ? Is it, in short, your Grace's opinion that the hour has not yet arrived ? That the triumph of old English principles will be not only insured, but confirmed, by the prolonged feebleness of that administration, which is still representative of the new doctrines, however mean and spiritless ? If you looked only to the personal interests of your political friends, such consideration might be influential, for the duration of the Government that some deem impending might probably bear some relation to the incapacity of its predecessor. But I know well that your mind soars far above such limited calculations, and I believe that you are only reconciled to the continuance in office of the present administration from an opinion that, checked by your power, they can do no harm, and in the enjoyment of place they will not care to project it.

Before we can form a correct judgment on this head, it is necessary that we should possess a precise idea of the present situation of the Government in the House of Commons. It is not only curious, it is unprecedented.

Her Majesty's Ministers carry on the government of the country by two methods : first, practically, by a Conservative majority, and secondly, theoretically, by a revolutionary majority. As long as public credit is to be maintained or the national honour vindicated, a tax to be raised or an armament equipped—in a word, as long as anything is to be done, a successful appeal is made to the loyal support of the Conservative party ; but the moment that party evinces any ambition to possess itself of the forms as well as the spirit of power, and because it fills the Treasury would sit upon the Treasury Bench, and because it mans the fleet would counsel at the Admiralty Board—then the theoretical method is forthwith recurred to by the alarmed administration. Some abstract declaration as to the nature of ecclesiastical property, or the exercise of the political franchise, is pompously announced; the capacity of an administrative body is made to depend upon the Parliamentary assertion of some unfeasible principle; and by the assistance of the revolutionary majority it is demonstrated that the Conservative party are disqualified for the conduct of public business, because at the beginning of a session they vainly declare the impracticability of a measure the impossibility of which is not acknowledged by the Government until the close of that session. These ingenious manœuvres are described in Ministerial rhetoric as the assertion of a great principle.

This, then, is the Parliamentary position which great authorities are not anxious to disturb—as one, if not productive of benefit, at least inefficient for injury; and, on the whole, a political arrangement adapted to a country fast rallying from a recent revolutionary convulsion.

Let us reconnoitre the position a little more closely.

There may be some, perhaps, who may find no mean constitutional objections to the government of a country being habitually carried on by an Opposition, even if that Opposition be headed by such men as the Duke of Wellington and Sir Robert Peel. These objections may claim our future consideration. Here only we may observe that it is difficult to foresee how the consequence of such a conjecture can ultimately be other than a struggle for supremacy between the Crown and the Parliament. For the nation it matters little in what form the inevitable despotism may develop itself—in that of a Select Committee or in that of a Privy Council; in the decision of a Parliamentary vote or the decree of a Royal proclamation.

There may be others who may view with apprehension a state of affairs which accustoms the great body of the people to associate the idea of regular government with that of revolutionary doctrines. Your Grace and your party have for years inculcated on this nation that the doctrines of the persons in power menaced the institutions of the country and the existence of the empire. They have not changed those doctrines, and their indispensable supporters, the theoretical majority, have aggravated them. Yet the public observe that the affairs of State are conducted with sobriety and order; they have not time for refined speculation on the condition of parties; they cannot comprehend that the order and sobriety are in contradiction to the doctrines of the Ministry, and in spite of the support of their adherents; and thus they may cease to connect the idea of revolutionary government with that of revolutionary principles. Hitherto they have rallied round you with eager sympathy, and readily responded to your call for constitutional succour. It may be necessary to appeal to them again. Circumstances may change. The present administration, for instance, may cross the floor of the House. What if they then consistently spout the sedition which in office they have never recanted ? What if they are prepared to re-enter office to practise as well as to preach it ? And in all probability they would not be able to re-enter office on any other terms. Will your cry of the Constitution in danger avail you again ? May not the people of England fairly rejoin, The cry of the Constitution in danger means only the return of the Whigs to power; and why should they not return to that power which, when they possessed it before, they exercised exactly as yourselves ? Thus, Sir, you perceive that refined political tactics may mystify the practical simplicity of the popular mind. A nation perplexed, like a puzzled man, will act weakly, inefficiently, erroneously — in a word, blunder. But the blunder of a people may prove the catastrophe of an empire.

I present you, Sir, yet with another great public consideration which results from your Parliamentary policy. It is exactly ten years since the author of the " Essay on the English Constitution "[1] introduced into the House of Commons his measure for the reconstruction of the third estate of the realm commonly called the Parliamentary Reform Bill. That violent proposition was temperately rejected by the House of Commons; and the House of Commons was instantly dissolved—in the then state of affairs, I might say destroyed. The reintroduced proposition was opposed by the Lords Spiritual, another Parliamentary estate of the realm, and the Bishops were burnt in effigy, their persons assailed, and their palaces plundered. It was opposed by the Lords Temporal, and the present Minister of England denounced the constitutional expression of their judgment " as the whisper of a faction." For four years the Whigs hallooed on the popular blood against your Grace and your peers; and your House tottered. At length, baffled by the returning sense of the country, the arrogant hostility that would have destroyed the House of Lords was succeeded by the sullen vengeance that would rule the country in defiance of it. The character and office of the House of Commons were systematically exaggerated and misrepresented. But by degrees even this reorganised and all-sufficient House of Commons began to slip their moorings from the Whig sandbank. The Ministers even formally acknowledged and announced that they had forfeited its confidence. But they are still Ministers. These constitutional denouncers of " the whisper of a faction " now chuckle in their orgies over the consolatory conviction that " one is enough," but after the Supplies it seems that even a minority of ten will do no harm. And thus the great Reform struggle, that has now lasted as long as the siege of Troy, terminates by the Reform Ministry governing the country independent of the Reformed Parliament.

[1] Lord John Russell.

To me there is nothing in this conduct of the Whigs at all inconsistent with their whole management since their accession to power. To me our domestic history for the last ten years is a visible and violent attempt by an oligarchy to govern this country in spite of its Parliament. The policy of the Whigs has been a continued assault upon some portion or other of our Parliamentary institutions. They destroyed the old House of Commons because it was intractable; they menaced the House of Lords because it was unmanageable; and, for the new House of Commons, they will bully it as long as it is submissive, and attempt to reconstruct it the moment it is mutinous.

But is it the Duke of Wellington—is it that statesman, so impressed with the importance of popular responsibility that he declared that after the Reform Act no Prime Minister ought to sit in the Upper House—is it you, Sir, who will countenance an administration of whom it may be said that they are dependent upon everything and everybody except Parliament ?

With the means at the command of the Ministry, it is possible that the present state of affairs may be continued for three more sessions. But at the inevitable close of the existing Parliament are we certain of redress ? What if this be the last House of Commons that is elected by the present constituency ? What if a Royal proclamation issues a Commission to inquire into the best means of obtaining a full and fair representation of the people, and in the meantime provides that no portion of them shall be represented to the detriment of the others by not summoning a Parliament on the old scheme ? With a skilful adaptation of means, and a dexterous agitation of the popular spirit, the Supplies, under such circumstances, might perhaps be obtained by an Order in Council. At least we have the satisfaction of feeling that in all probability our Sovereign would not be destitute, and that a Parliament holden in Dublin in 1844, full of " affectionate loyalty," could scarcely refuse a civil list.

We start at such portents. They are grave probabilities. The Whigs for two centuries have been great dealers in *coups d'état*. They are the natural consequences of the Parliamentary policy that permits the Whigs simultaneously to carry on the Government by a Conservative majority, and to carry on the Revolution by a Radical one.

And this, my Lord Duke, is the state of the case.

ATTICUS.

March 10, 1841.

DISRAELI OR MAGINN ?

[IN the Introduction it is suggested that three of
the biographical sketches which appeared in *Fraser's
Magazine* in 1835–36, and which have hitherto been
attributed to Maginn, were in fact by Disraeli. The
grounds for this belief are to be found in the articles
themselves; so far as is known there is nothing in Disraeli's private papers either to confirm or to disprove the
assumption.   In the first eight years of *Fraser's* existence
there appeared the famous Gallery of Illustrious Literary
Characters.   The drawings, some eighty in number, were
by Maclise, and the accompanying biographical sketches,
concise and witty, were by Maginn.   There were some
known exceptions; five of the articles have been traced to
the pens of Carlyle, Lockhart, and Father Prout (the Rev.
Francis Mahony).   All were republished in 1873 by Professor Bates as the " Maclise Portrait Gallery," and dedicated to Disraeli, whose familiar portrait by Maclise forms
No. 36 of the Gallery.   The original drawing, with many
others of the series, was purchased by Forster at the
Maclise sale, and is now in the Forster collection at South
Kensington.

When the stock of Illustrious Literary Characters
showed signs of exhaustion, the net was spread a little
wider, and a few persons who were of political rather than
literary repute were admitted to the company of the elect.
Among them were the Earl of Mulgrave, afterwards
Marquis of Normanby (No. 64), November, 1835; Sir John
Cam Hobhouse (No. 72), May, 1836; and Lord Lyndhurst
(No. 77), October, 1836.   These three politicians figure
frequently in Disraeli's writings, and his mental attitude
towards them is known.   The view of the writer of the

sketches in *Fraser* is precisely that of Disraeli in his published writings of the period. Not only so, but characteristic phrases which occur in articles now republished for
the first time as his reappear in the *Fraser* contributions,
and are allotted impartially to one or other of the charac-
acters. Now Disraeli, as has been pointed out, was a
confirmed self-plagiarist. The main evidence is therefore
contained in the parallel passages; add to them the fact
that Disraeli was in friendly relations with the Fraserians,
and especially with Maclise and Count D'Orsay; note the
casual allusions to visits paid to Athens and Florence, both
of which cities had been included in his recent itinerary;
contrast the Disraelian acerbity of treatment of Cam Hobhouse and Mulgrave with the humorous badinage meted
out to other illustrious characters in the Gallery; compare
the panegyric of Lord Lyndhurst, his patron, with the
sentiments in the *Times* article by Disraeli—one of " four
bolts of veritable Olympian thunder," concerning which
he wrote to his sister on August 20, 1836; and there will be
found, surely, an accumulation of evidence sufficient to
justify the inclusion in this volume of the three sketches
as Disraeli's.

Below are set out in adjoining columns the more striking
parallel passages :

It was a bright idea, that of
emptying the gaols of the Barataria over whose destinies your
Excellency so shrewdly presides, and it is interesting to
witness the philosophical civilisation of the nineteenth century, in triumphant defiance of
ancient prejudice, communicating with so much effect the rude
yet prophetic conceptions of a
Jack Cade. Fortunate island
that an O'Connell supplies with
justice, and a Mulgrave with
mercy !—*Open Letters : Runnymede to Mulgrave, February* 11,
1837.

Perhaps His Excellency may
have stumbled on the second
part of " Henry the Sixth," in
which Jack Cade made his appearance . . . but do we compare
the undaunted "Mortimer, Lord
of the City," to O'Connell ?—
*Mulgrave: Frazer's Magazine,
November,* 1835.

The time has come when, in the
queer revolution of things which
we are doomed to witness, our
Sancho has got the government
of an island, and rules India
with a degree of wisdom which
would excite envy in the Cabinet of Bataria.—*Hobhouse :
Fraser's Magazine, May,* 1836.

My candour may, at least, be as salutary as the cabbage-stalks of your late constituents. There are some indeed who, as I am informed, have murmured at this method of communicating to them my opinion of their characters and careers. Yet I can conceive an individual so circumstanced that he would scarcely be entitled to indulge in such querulous sensitiveness. He should be one . . . to whom it had been asserted in his teeth that he was a liar and a scoundrel, and only wanted courage to be an assassin.—*Runnymede Letter to Hobhouse, February 27, 1836.*

The Rienzi of Westminster smiles with marvellous complacency at the strange chapter of accidents which has converted a man whose friends pelted George Lamb with a cabbage-stalk into a main prop of William Lamb's Cabinet.—*Runnymede Letter to Melbourne, January 18, 1836.*

The Commentator of Byron, you naturally became in due season " Sir Francis Burdett's man," as Mr. Canning styled you, to your confusion, in the House of Commons.—*Runnymede Letter to Hobhouse, February 27, 1836.*

A demagogue or a placeman. —*Idem.*

That " first tragedy man," the Lord of Mulgrave.—*Runnymede Letter to Melbourne, January 18, 1836.*
Vain, volatile, and flimsy, headstrong without being courageous . . . always theatrical, with a morbid love of popularity and a maudlin flux of claptrap sensibility, his anger a stage scowl, his courtesy a simper; every glance directed to

This Right Hon. Baronet is now a member of the Cabinet presided over, at least nominally, by the brother of the gentleman whom he so unmercifully exposed in Covent Garden to the cabbages and turnip-tops of its Liberal electors. . . . When he makes a gathering of the writings attributed to him, we trust that he . . . may append to it, as a fitting note, Canning's complimentary billet that the author of a certain pamphlet was a liar and a scoundrel, who only wanted courage to be an assassin.—*Hobhouse : Fraser's Magazine, May, 1836.*

He began life as a butt of Lord Byron's. Cobbett styled him Sancho, from his obsequious servility to Sir Francis Burdett, to whom he bore the same relation as the greasy clown did to his mistaken but chivalrous master.—*Hobhouse : Fraser's Magazine, May, 1836.*

The brawling patriot has been transformed into the lickspittle placeman.—*Idem.*

Among fashionable people he is distinguished as an amateur actor, who is equally meritorious in his performance of " Hamlet " and the " Cock." . . . When duly curled, oiled, painted, and lighted up, he does look passably well, and might be trusted in a third-rate walking gentleman cast. — *Mulgrave : Fraser's Magazine, November, 1835.*

the lamps, every movement arranged into an attitude.— *Open Letters : Runnymede to Mulgrave, February* 11, 1837.

Lord Lyndhurst terminated last night his splendid career for this session by an oration which ought to be printed at every press and posted under every roof in old England. . . . For luminous arrangement and perspicuous statement, combined with the most polished sarcasm and irresistible irony, we know no effusion of the noble lord, distinguished as they ever are by these striking qualities of accomplished eloquence, superior to this well-timed and well-executed address. Its effect upon the House is only the herald of its effect upon the country. . . . No words can describe the outrageous irritability of Lord Melbourne or the blank rage of Lord Holland. One found words in his wrath, and the other lost them in his perplexity. — *In the " Times," August* 18, 1836.

His profound legal knowledge, his calm yet courageous bearing, his statesmanlike comprehension of a subject, and his humorous eloquence, have fairly won him the post of leader of the Conservative party in the House of Lords.—*In the " Morning Post," August* 21, 1835.

The celebrated speech which closed the last session . . . demolished the reputation of the unfortunate Government, or rather shadow of a Government, stridden over by O'Connell. All parties agree that it had the most withering effect. The Whigs were silent, in breathless rage or fear; the Tories entranced in admiration and mute wonder, as the eloquent periods flowed from the lips of the stately speaker. — *Lyndhurst : Fraser's Magazine, October,* 1836.

He is the recognised leader of the most honourable party in what, considered on public grounds as a whole, and without reference to the factious fraction which he opposes, is the noblest body in the world, and he owes this lofty station to his own overwhelming talents. — *Lyndhurst : Fraser's Magazine, October,* 1836.]

THE EARL OF MULGRAVE

(*Fraser's Magazine, November,* 1835.)

WE present to our readers the ex-Governor-General of Jamaica, the President of the Garrick, and the Lord Lieutenant of Ireland. Among literary men he is known or heard of as the author of several novels which have not materially contributed to swell his repute; among fashionable people he is distinguished as an amateur actor, who is equally meritorious in the performance of "Hamlet" and the "Cock." We recollect him when he used to perform in Florence all manners of characters to all manners of audiences; and we never failed to appreciate the discriminating civility with which, after having crowded his rooms with a miscellaneous collection of all the English who could be found tolerant enough to listen to him, he used to go through the weary mob, inviting a select few, in the hearing of the whole company, to remain to supper (a *little* supper he used to call it, and in that particular he amply kept his word), to the exclusion of the indignant multitude, who thought that, in common justice, they should have had something to wash down his Lordship's dose of histrionism.

Our artist is rather too favourable to Mulgrave. Thanks to Delcroix, or some other artist of that profession, the locks look exuberant still; but woe worth the day! crow's-feet tell about the temples, and deep wrinkles beseam the well-rouged face. But still, when duly curled, oiled, painted, and lighted up, he does look passably well, and might be trusted in a third-rate walking gentleman cast. He is at present showing off in a part for which he is just as much fitted as he is for enacting "Romeo," but one in which he can do more mischief than could attend the most vigorously hissed performance that ever disgraced a theatre.

Perhaps His Excellency may have stumbled on the Second Part of "Henry the Sixth," in which Jack Cade makes his appearance. This great reformer declared that the laws of England should come out of his mouth (which even his own partisans allowed to be fœtid and disgusting); that that mouth should be the Parliament of England; that he would leave no lord or gentleman in the land; that a universal destruction should take place, so that all men should be arrayed in one livery, and worship him

their lord. In these particulars we have now a revived
Jack Cade; but do we compare the undaunted "Mortimer,
Lord of the City," to O'Connell? They both may be
designated beggars ; but the beggary of Cade was
valiant. *He* had no vow in heaven to protect him
from the consequence of his outrages; nor, on the other
hand, could he, after he had doomed "the nobility
to go in leathern aprons," have found a representative of the King to allow him to play the part of
"protector over him." *That* was reserved for our own
times.

Mulgrave is poor, and is glad to escape from the eleemosynary hospitality of the Duke of Devonshire on any
terms. He is vain, and the title of Viceroy must tickle
his fancy. We are told that he is annoyed at the marked
absence of the Irish gentry from his parties or levees; but
the shouting in the upper gallery compensates in his ear
for the hissing of the boxes; and we recommend him to
exhibit at Donnybrook grinning through a horse-collar,
which would at once show his features in their most
appropriate expression, and afford the most congenial
gratification to the friends on whom he relies. In the
short list of his ancestors, we find that one invented a
diving-bell—typical of sinking and mud-seeking propensities; that another was that Lord Chancellor of Ireland
who was made the victim of Curran's bitterness more than
a half-century after his death, and about another half-
century before his descendant grovelled at the hoofs of
those who adhere to all the sedition, without a tithe of
the talent, of Curran; that another (Commodore Phipps)
was, like his nephew, sent upon an experimental voyage,
in which he had no great success; and that formerly
His Excellency's father enjoyed, for good reason (*vide*
Cobbett), the title of Lord Lonsdale's boots. The
noble son plays the part of boots to a very different
person.

To conclude. Mulgrave is about forty years old,
desperately hard up, a most industrious scribbler, a

capital led-captain, a passable buffoon; but when we see
him sent to govern Ireland just now, we are irresistibly
reminded of one of his own novels, and must say:

" By *Yes* and *No*, but it is very strange." [1]

SIR JOHN CAM HOBHOUSE

(Fraser's Magazine, May, 1836.)

THIS right honourable Baronet is now a member of the
Cabinet presided over, at least nominally, by the brother
of the gentleman whom he once so unmercifully exposed
in Covent Garden to the cabbages and turnip-tops of its
Liberal electors, and the unsparing raillery of Mr. Canning,
poured in with so much effect upon the " mud-bespattered
Whigs taking refuge from the oppression of their popularity under the bayonets of the Horse Guards."   Times
are changed since.   Hobhouse no longer writes letters to
Lord Erskine or Lord Erskine's friends, sneering at green
ribands, and laughing at the pretensions to political
purity in the holders of place and pension.   We are no
longer told to " Ask him, gentlemen," when any of the
Whigocracy forgets to advocate in power those doctrines
which he had maintained to be indispensable to the very
existence of the country while out of office.   No ! the
usual change has taken place: the brawling patriot has
been transformed into the lickspittle placeman.

He began life as a butt of Lord Byron's, who made
many most unsavoury rhymes on his name.   In fact, we
do not remember any person of note among us who has
had the fortune of being saluted with titles less redolent
of grace than Cam Hobhouse.   Hook, by an error of
the press, saluted him with an appellation which, it must
be admitted, his personal appearance perpetually tends
to suggest.   Galt, in his notice of the Pot and Kettle
controversy, bestowed upon him the title of the former

---

[1] Mulgrave was the author of a book entitled " Yes and No."

utensil. Lord Palmerston (we believe) eulogised him in
an ode in the *John Bull*, the first distich of which was:

"I care not a —— (very familiar beast)
For John Cam Hobhouse."

Cobbett styled him Sancho, from his obsequious servility
to Sir Francis Burdett, to whom he bore the same relation as the greasy clown did to his mistaken but chivalrous master. The time has come when, in the queer
revolution of things which we are doomed to witness, our
Sancho has got the government of an island, and rules
India with a degree of wisdom which would excite envy
in the Cabinet of Barataria.

We remember him—we regret to say, a good many years
ago—in Athens, where he distinguished himself by wear-
ing a pair of green baize breeches, which produced an
epigram hardly fit to be repeated to ears polite; but
which, nevertheless, has appeared in print. The collection of such compliments paid to Hobhouse would be
large. It is a pleasant reflection for any man that he
should have been so particularly distinguished by his
contemporaries. When he makes a gathering of works
attributed to him, we trust that he will not forget the
famous letter in which he boasted that three hundred
Muciuses had sworn to murder Canning. He may append
to it, as a fitting note, Canning's complimentary billet—
that the author of a certain pamphlet was a liar and a
scoundrel, who only wanted courage to be an assassin.
It would also be an agreeable literary curiosity if he
were to publish at the same time Lord Byron's confidential note, in which his Lordship recommended certain
folks not to trouble themselves by making vain efforts to
appear in the alien character of men of honour.

He is, perhaps, the best exemplification of Lord Mansfield's saying, that popularity is gained without a merit,
and lost without a fault. He had no claim whatever,
except impudence and servility, on Westminster, when
he was elected; and these qualities he possessed when he
was turned out. One of the main pretences for his ejection

26

was his devotion to the cat-o'-nine-tails. His successor
has made that much-abused instrument the principal
engine of discipline in his well-whipped and ill-fed army.
Of Hobhouse's political career the records are short. The
man has done nothing, because nothing is in him. *Ex
nihilo nil fit*—there is no getting blood from a turnip; and
it is one of our misfortunes that we should be compelled
to write about such people at all. But the amber of
office embalms them for their day. Shrined for a while in
that, we are doomed to observe the forms of creeping
things, our wonder at which—a small one under existing
circumstances—secures the tribute of a page even to " my
boy, Hobbio." We have added to his name the title of
his first performance—the *Miscellany ;* or, as his friend
Lord Byron (Murray's edition, vol. i., p. 185) too truly
called it, the *Miss-sell-any.* The names of his other
literary performances we have forgotten.

LORD LYNDHURST

(*Fraser's Magazine, October,* 1836.)

IT is hardly possible to conceive a prouder situation than
that which is now occupied by Lord Lyndhurst. He is
the recognised leader of the most honourable party in
what, considered on public grounds as a whole, and without reference to the factious fraction which he opposes,
is the noblest body in the world; and he owes this lofty
station to his own overwhelming talents. In an assembly
which comprises men who have filled the greatest offices,
governed vast provinces, led victorious armies, conducted
important missions, presided over courts of justice, represented large constituencies—who have, in short, fulfilled
with distinction the highest functions of public life in
every department—in an assembly where we find princes
and marshals, viceroys and ambassadors, chancellors
and judges, orators and statesmen, knights and nobles,
the presence of any one of whom, with a few disgraceful

Lord Lyndhurst

LORD LYNDHURST.

From a drawing by Daniel Maclise, R.A.

exceptions, would be considered to be an ornament in any company in the world; in this assembly, illustrious as it is by high birth, ancient descent, polished breeding, and not more so than by great talent, knowledge, and eloquence, its most illustrious portion has, without a dissenting voice, chosen Lord Lyndhurst as its organ and its chief. It is a distinction of which any man might justly be proud; and that just pride must be enhanced by the consciousness that he executes the duty entrusted to him so as to excite the admiration of his noble allies, and, what is a tribute no less decisive, the bitter fury of his ignoble antagonists.

It is quite unnecessary that we should attempt the slightest sketch of the life of a man so long before the public. The bawling demagogue of the day has threatened to expose his private history, and he may indulge his slanderous propensities with impunity, for all people duly appreciate the reason which dictates the lies he may publish in some obscure journals. They feel that in his sinking estate—for sinking he is, in spite of his swagger and bluster—he attributes his fall to the eloquence of that eminent orator whom we have enrolled in our Gallery. The celebrated speech which closed the last session,[1] and which gives us the title to place his portrait on the opposite page, demolished the reputation of the unfortunate Government, or rather shadow of a Government, stridden over by O'Connell. All parties agree that it had the most withering effect. The Whigs were silent, in breathless rage or fear; the Tories, entranced in admiration and mute wonder, as the eloquent periods flowed from the lips of the stately speaker. It is generally reported that O'Connell was present under the gallery while Lord Lyndhurst addressed to him, in one of his speeches, the passage directed by Cicero against Catiline, and that the triple-bronzed beggar-man shrank away in abashment. Yet that passage pleased us not. It was not fair to Catiline to compare him, who, as Sallust tells, was "*nobili loco*

---

[1] Republished as the "Summary of the Session."

natus," who never shrank from danger of any kind in the midst of the stirring period of human history, whose hands are free from the stain of money, and who died gallantly fighting, at last, amid his brave companions—

> " Each stepping where his comrade stood
> The instant that he fell "

—with one whose name is unconnected with any honourable action, whose whole life has been one scene of skulking from dangers into which he had drawn others, and who is occupied from one end of the year to the other in devising plans of drawing enormous fortunes from squalid beggary.[1]

What Lord Lyndhurst is as a politician and lawyer is known to all.   In both characters he is pre-eminent. We shall invade his private life no further than to say that the orator of the Senate is the wit of the dinner-table—the profound lawyer of the Bench or Woolsack, the gayest of the gay in drawing-room and boudoir.   Our artist has been happy in catching his likeness at a moment when, the robes of office or nobility being thrown aside, he aims at no other character than one in which he is so well qualified to shine—a gentleman.   A pleasanter fellow does not exist; and in his case, at least, the fair author was mistaken when she said that " the judge and the peer is a world-weary man."

It is rarely that a man of genius leaves behind him a son also a man of genius.   It has been so, however, in the present case.   But little could Copley have contemplated, when he was painting his celebrated picture of the death of Chatham, that his own son was destined to equal the fame of Chatham in such an assembly as that on which he was employing his pencil.

[1] " I am not one of those public beggars that we see swarming with their obtrusive boxes in the chapels of your creed, nor am I in possession of a princely revenue arising from a starving race of fanatical slaves " (Disraeli's Letter to O'Connell, May 5, 1835).

THE SUMMARY OF THE SESSION[1]

LORD LYNDHURST terminated last night his splendid
career for this session of Parliament by an oration which
ought to be printed at every press and posted under every
roof in old England. It was a summary of the session—of
this session, so memorable in the annals of our country, and
in which his Lordship has acquired laurels that even his
most ardent admirers had not anticipated. For luminous arrangement and perspicuous statement, combined
with the most polished sarcasm and irresistible irony, we
know no effusion of the noble Lord, distinguished as they
ever are by these striking qualities of accomplished eloquence, superior to this well-timed and well-executed
address. Its effect upon the House is only the herald of
its effect upon the country. It fell upon the ranks of the
Government like a Congreve rocket. Two Cabinet
Minsters, one the Prime Minister, rose to answer it. They
spoke one immediately after the other, as if they felt
conscious that two of their number at least were wanting
to combat such an antagonist. No words can describe
the outrageous irritability of Lord Melbourne or the blank
rage of Lord Holland. One found words in his wrath,
and the other lost them in his perplexity. Yet the First
Lord of the Treasury, though he raged, and the Chancellor
of the Exchequer, though he whimpered, must yield in
the effect that they produced to the solemn testiness of the
Lord Chancellor. Lord Melbourne writhed like a scotched
snake, Lord Holland gambolled like an excited elephant,
but the present keeper of the Great Seal, the successor of
Lord Lyndhurst, was the crowning glory of this grand
scene of Ministerial propriety and administrative justifi-
cation, and to the satisfaction of all present assuredly
" wrote himself down " a most grave and reverend,
though not most potent Signior.

Will these men go on ? We hope so. Lord Viscount

[1] Leading article by Disraeli in the *Times* of August 19, 1836.

Melbourne assured us last night that he was Minister, and Minister he would remain, come what might.[1] His Lordship condescended to say nothing in favour of the Crown, not even of the confidence of the nation. We are wearied of experiments and restless change. What this country requires is a firm and vigorous and able administration, supported by the property and intelligence of the country, not by a pennyless and ignorant faction. The Duke of Wellington last night well described the character of the British Empire, its vast and various interests, its diversified population, and its complicated wealth. Can a Ministry, tied to the hackney-chariot wheels of a contemptible crew of political adventurers, the spawn of a malignant class of our society, generated in an ill-seasoned and distempered time, rise to the height of this elevated office ? Say what the jobbing levellers like, England must still be governed by men whose wealth creates a natural anxiety for the stability of all property, and whose education and intelligence enable them to appreciate, and induce them to cling to, those institutions which form the strength and essence of constitutional freedom.

The able and seasonable speech of Lord Lyndhurst may be considered as the manifesto of the Conservative party. Will its delivery assist the Government in their machinations as to the King's Speech ? What have they heard from Windsor to-day ? Will the paragraph be admitted ?[2] What says the worthy Chancellor of the Exchequer ? Lord Lansdowne was dumb last night. This motion of the great Conservative leader, this powerful vindication of the legislative career of the House of Lords by its ablest member, chimes in opportunely with the well-

[1] "I conscientiously believe," said Lord Melbourne in the debate, "that the well-being of the country requires that I should hold my present office—and hold it I will till I am constitutionally removed from it."

[2] The Tories had spread a report that the Ministers wanted to thrust into the Speech some allusions to the conduct of the House of Lords, but no such thing was ever contemplated (Greville's "Memoirs").

digested scheme of the baffled Whigs to cast contumely
upon the Upper House of Parliament for their constitutional opposition to an incapable and unprincipled
Ministry. This Ministry, vanquished, as Lord Lyndhurst well observes, in one House by an irresistible
majority, and maintained in the other by abandoning
their prime measures at the sudden dictation of " a
mutinous and sullen section "—such a Ministry are exactly
the men to hold the Government in *duresse* and outrage
the Constitution ! We tell them once for all, the people
of England scorns them; we know our countrymen. It
is our pride to advocate on all occasions their interests,
maintain their rights, and consult their feelings. It is not
Lord Viscount Melbourne, with all his loose-tongued and
ill-conditioned ribaldry, that will persuade us he knows
more than ourselves of the heart and soul of the English
nation. We tell him the core of his political body is
rotten, its foundation sand, and its days numbered.

POLITICAL SATIRES IN VERSE

A CHARACTER

WITH smile complacent, and with candid air,
Each gesture frank, and every sentence fair;
Skilful alike each party to appease,
And ready from each side each hint to seize;
Fixed to defend the Crown, uphold the Church,
And meaning but to leave them in the lurch;
Firm in his faith, and in his tenets strong,
Yet open to conviction if he's wrong;
Ready to die, and yet prepared to live,
Eager to grasp, yet half resolved to give;
Convinced no government is like a King,
Yet deems republics still may be the thing;
Abhorring spoliation, hinting plunder,
And joining Church and State quite well asunder;
See *Blarney*[1] rise; the House attentive listens,
And quite persuaded all is gold that glistens;
Beneath his fostering care exchequers thrive,
Bright sage, who proves that two and two make five!

SKELTON, JUN.

March 7, 1837.

---

[1] Mr. T. Spring Rice, afterwards Lord Monteagle, an Irishman, whose Bill for the abolition of Church rates had been introduced in Parliament. The *Times* declared of the Chancellor's measure that " a more despicable compound of tricky assumption, political trimming, party inconsistency, false reasoning, perverted quotation, unconstitutional principle, and odious pretence, consummated by a proposal equally insulting to Dissenters and treacherous to the Church, has never yet been produced within the walls of a deliberative assembly."

OPEN QUESTIONS : A POLITICAL ECLOGUE

" Formosum pastor Corydon ardebat Alexin." [1]

FOR charming place the patriot B—l—r[2] sighed,
And through the Mall with mournful footsteps hied,
To where its classic front the Treasury rears,
The solemn temple of his hopes and fears;
Or down that street now traced his anxious way,
Sacred to statesmen and to quarter-day:
There to the sullen windows plaintive sings,
And with his cries the official welkin rings :

" Oh, cruel Johnny, are my votes then nought ? (a)
And must I ever then remain unbought ?
Will pity never touch that haughty breast,
Nor nightly labours lead to daily rest ?
Are all my efforts, then, to save the nation
To end in nothing but in sharp starvation ?
Better with Peel on adverse bench to sit,
And share at least the triumph of his wit : (b)
Doomed still to see each Lordling seize the prize
By me secured with unproductive ' ayes.'

" Was it for this I voted black was white, (c)
And proved in patriot strains that wrong was right ?
Ah ! haughty youth, we yet may break the spell,
Trust not thy vast majorities too well;
To-morrow's night may prove that white is black,
To-morrow's night may send thee baffled back
To those lorn benches where thy youth was spent
In barren opposition's discontent,
Mourning in vain thy ineffectual lot,
A would-be Catiline without a plot.

[1] Virgil's Second Eclogue.
[2] Charles Buller, the clever young Member for Liskeard, whom
Carlyle described as " the genialest Radical I have ever met."

" You slight me, Johnny ! think, I have some claim—(d)
M.P. for Lis——d; not unknown to fame;
Nor am I such a fool as some men say, (e)
As lately proved on that memorial day,
When our good E—l—e[1] Tories caught at fault,
And true Reform seemed nearly at a halt,
While in his private pouch the public money,
Perversely found, made prospects somewhat funny;
I bore the brunt, and, mingling in the fray,
I proved the second Scipio pure as day ! (f)

" Nor pass unnoticed that accomplished pen
To *columns* known, if not to gods and men;
That can with equal ease, and like applause,
Remodel Senates, or reform our laws,
A code contribute, or a Peer disrobe,
And sway the fortunes of the mighty (g) *Globe !*

" Come, haughty youth, (h) I yet will gain thy heart;
List to the tale my trembling lips impart;
Two Rads I lately found in wicked play,
Young, mischievous, malignant, wild, and gay,
And ready quite to vote the other way; (j)
'Tis I will gain these Rads to thee once more,
And clip the wings with which they sought to soar;
Yes, lead our M——th[2] once more to his traces,
And tempt e'en Ro——k[3] with a choice of places.

" Fool that I am !   He scorns my tempting bribe, (k)
And turns a deaf ear to our restless tribe;
What various tastes divide his fickle crew ! (l)
L——[4] likes a trull, and H——d[5] loves a shrew.

---

[1] Edward Ellice, Member for Coventry, was charged with having used public funds for election purposes in 1832, but the charge was refuted.
[2] Sir William Molesworth, Liberal Member for East Cornwall.
[3] J. A. Roebuck, Liberal Member for Sheffield.
[4] William Lamb, Viscount Melbourne.
[5] Lord Holland.

In easy-chairs their limbs the G—ts[1] intrench.
While Palmy loves a protocol in French.
H——e[2] they say, before a speech a brimmer,
And Blarney's[3] ever partial to a trimmer.
Repentant Rads methought might Johnny please,
And place a Whigling once more at his ease."

He ceased, then to the House dejected hies,
And yields a sullen vote to Whig Supplies.

                                        SKELTON, JUN.
March 9, 1837.

ORIGINAL FOOTNOTES.

(*a*) " O crudelis Alexi ! nihil mea carmina curas;
    Nil nostri miserere; mori me denique coges ?"
(*b*) " Nonne fuit melius tristes Amaryllidis iras "
(*c*) "   . . . . nonne Menalcan,
    Quamvis ille niger, quamvis tu candidus esses,
    O ! formose puer, nimium ne crede colori !
    Alba ligustra cadunt, vaccinia nigra leguntur."
(*d*) " Sum tibi despectus; nec qui sim quæris, Alexi."
(*e*) " Nec sum adeo informis; nuper," etc.
(*f*) The hon. member's parallel between the Right Hon. Mr.
Ell—e and Scipio Africanus will never be forgotten, and is not
surpassed by anything in Plutarch.
(*g*) Q. Mity.
(*h*) " Huc ades, O formose puer."
(*j*) " —duo nec tuta mihi valle reperti
    Capreoli," etc.
(*k*) " Rusticus es, Corydon; nec munera curat Alexis."
(*l*) " —trahit sua quemque voluptas."

AN HEROIC EPISTLE TO LORD VISCOUNT MEL——E

O THOU, who, lolling in an easy-chair,
Rulest a realm, with far-niente air;
Viewing alike with philosophic pride
An empire threatened, or a law defied;
Statesman supreme, who by a secret paction
Insults a nation, just to gain a faction;
Scholar refined, whose taste sublime, or bland,
Now soars to Hooker, and now sinks to Sand; (*a*)

[1] Lord Glenelg and his brother.
[2] Sir J. Cam Hobhouse.
[3] T. Spring Rice.

Chivalric knight, whose all-considerate love
The records of thy Master's Bench may prove;
To laud thy triple fame this verse shall flow,
Deep Sage, great Minister, successful Beau !

For all thy praises why should Whigs supply ?
Rise, Tory Muse, and wave thy wings, and try !
Still must I hear, shall *Globes* and *Couriers* pour
Their pensioned paragraphs from door to door ? [1]
Or some dark Papist, in a patriot guise,
By *Chronny's* aid, throw dust in English eyes ?
Shall to thy fame all strain their loudest pitch,
From flippant F—nb—que [2] down to priggish R——; [3, 4]
And I my modest muse with trembling hide,
Nor write like Pal——n a " New Whig Guide." (*b*)

Yet dread not, Sir, this friendly pen shall trace
Aught that may bring the blushes to your face.
Unnoticed let me pass, oh ! graceless truth !
Your boyish promise and your loyal youth;
When, foremost struggling in a hallowed cause,
Your voice upheld a country's outraged laws;
Or, mid the tumult of sedition's storm,
With zeal denounced the juggle of Reform.
Not mine the pen the struggle to relate
Of your ambition and your better fate,
Your half-resolves of good, and desperate deeds of hate,
Reckless and yet remorseful, rash yet wise,
The conscious tool of traitors you despise;
True to the Crown your faction would alloy;
Sighing to save the country you destroy !

[1] *Cf.* " Still must I hear ?   Shall hoarse Fitzgerald bawl
    His creaking couplets in a tavern hall ?"
            BYRON: *English Bards and Scotch Reviewers.*

[2] Albany Fonblanque, the brilliant journalist.
[3] Probably Henry Rich, Liberal Member for Knaresborough,
and afterwards for Richmond; Lord of the Treasury, 1846 ; author
of several political pamphlets ; created a Baronet, 1863.

[4] *Cf.* " From Soaring Southey down to Grovelling Stott."
            BYRON: *English Bards and Scotch Reviewers.*

Survey the Imperial realm and haughty State,
To thee entrusted by some freak of fate !
Once in each land that meets the solar beam
The standard of St. George might wave supreme,
And greet on every shore beneath the sky
A faithful subject or a fond ally.
Now panting couriers to thy trembling gate
But bear the tokens of our falling fate,
And with a gloomy whisper, quaking, tell,
How this rejects us, and how these rebel:
The mournful records of thy rule, comprised
Of treaties broken and of sway despised.

Is't not enough from Lisbon to the Hague
Thy word is shunn'd, as shuns a Turk the plague:
That in those lands which Wellesley fought to save,
Where every victim found a hero's grave,
By Whiggish skill our British host appears
To Europe's scorn a band of bucaniers;
While the proud flag, that o'er a hundred seas
Has dared alike the battle and the breeze,[1]
Skulks like a smuggler with a muffled oar,
Or steals a pirate by Trafalgar's shore ?

Is't not enough, on Europe's scoffing stage,
The wars of luckless Pantaloon to wage,
The jeer of feigning friend and open foe,
And bustling ever but to gain a blow:
A smile from Talleyrand, an Austrian leer,
A scowl from Berlin, from the Russ a sneer ?

Is't not enough, that H——e[2] to break their vow
May counsel colonies with brazen brow;
Or from his penny trump a R—b—k[3] blow
The dread defiance of his Papineau ?

[1] *Cf.* "Whose flag has braved a thousand years
		The battle and the breeze."
				CAMPBELL : *Ye Mariners of England.*
	[2] Hume.			[3] Roebuck.

The proverb says, two differ of a trade,
Yet these are patriots both, and both are paid.
Is't not enough that e'en Calypso's rock
Swells with its tiny cry sedition's stock; (c)
That, not content with foreign broils and fears,
You e'en must set the country at its ears,
Domestic trouble blend with distant shame,
And blast at once our comfort and our fame ?

Well for the man who now may hold the helm,
And guide the groaning fortunes of the realm,
If faithful messmates and a skilful crew
Rise to his signal vigilant and true.
Pipe all your hands, and let old England learn
Who trims her ballast, and who guides her stern;
While swift before the wind the vessel flies
To meet the gathering menace of the skies !
With brooding bosom and with sullen mien,
Pacing the dangerous deck Lord John is seen—
Your first lieutenant; yet, if truth appear,
Trusted perforce, and half a mutineer.
Beside him lounging, voluble and pert,
And greatly glorying in a gay check shirt,
Behold the "New Whig Guide !"   Prophetic name !
The youthful volume suits his present shame,
For a most novel Whig, him all decide,
And everyone must own he needs a guide.

Meanwhile, with jabber brisk, and bustling air,
Blarney, the purser, mounts the gangway stair,
Deals out his junk as if a feast he spread,
And shares his mouldy biscuit like fresh bread.
Past midshipmen a type in P—tty[1] find,
That solemn emblem of a seedy mind;
While on the maintop Gr—nt[2] discreetly snores,
And keeps a sure look-out for hostile shores.

[1] Henry Petty, third Marquis of Lansdowne.
[2] Lord Glenelg.

His quadrant then Dun—n—n[1] quick prepares, (d)
And beckons H—b—e,[2] who the duty shares;
H—b—e, though Indian realms his sway confess,
A man of science once, and F.R.S.
While H—w—k,[3] young Ascanius of the Whigs,
Sneers at strange shrouds, and lauds his father's rigs,
And whispers Th—m—n,[4] much renowned for figs.
Speed on, bold mariners ! with careless brow,
Place at your helm, and pension at your prow ;[5]
Say, shall my little bark attendant sail,
Pursue your triumph and partake the gale ?
Prompt in bright verse to celebrate your force,
And keep the log-book of your blundering course !

SKELTON, JUN.

March 20, 1837.

ORIGINAL FOOTNOTES.

(a) The favourite reading of his Lordship consists of old divinity and new French novels. From the first he acquires his profound knowledge of all details of the Church question, and from the last the conviction of the total inutility of ecclesiastical establishment at all.

(b) "The New Whig Guide," a collection of Tory lampoons ridiculing the principal leaders and members of the Reform party, and chiefly written by the present noble and consistent Secretary of State for Foreign Affairs.

(c) Under the Whigs even Malta has rebelled, but the rebellion is to be quelled in the true Whig style—by a Commission.

(d) His Lordship, it is said, is in the habit of taking an *observation* weekly, and with a very old-fashioned and rusty instrument.

---

[1] Lord Duncannon.
[2] Hobhouse.
[3] Viscount Howick.
[4] Poulett Thomson.
[5] " Youth on the prow, and Pleasure at the helm."

GRAY: *The Bard.*

OLD ENGLAND

By CŒUR-DE-LION

[THE OLD ENGLAND series of articles appeared in the
Times of January, 1838, just before the opening of the new
session of the Parliament in which Disraeli had taken his
seat for the first time as the Member for Maidstone. It is
cast in quite a different mould from his other writings; but
the phraseology of Carlyle does not altogether obscure the
sentiments of Disraeli. Home, foreign, and colonial
affairs were troublesome; his party were in Opposition;
full of enthusiasm and excitement, it was his cue for the
moment to represent that a Crisis—not the sham " Crisis "
of 1834 and 1835, or the daily " Crisis " from Ireland, but
a real Crisis due to a prolonged deadlock in the workings
of government—had been reached. The nation was de-
manding to know how the Queen's Empire was to be
maintained. The key to the deadlock was duty; whoever
could find that key, and could reinvest the Government
with the moral power of which it had been stripped by
the Whigs, was fit to be the Prime Minister of England.]

CHAPTER I

ASLEEP

ARE you asleep, John Bull ? Could I but hear you snore
I should not care. They might catch you napping, as
they have done before this; but what then ? A vigorous
shake of your drowsy shoulders, and who so alive as you ?
More lively from a sweet, wholesome slumber, more
vigorous.

But now it seems you have fallen into a trance, you do not even nod. There is no health in this repose. What if you have thrown yourself on your couch only to forget sorrows, woes with which you cannot struggle, fate inevitable—as an insolvent of vast credit, who knows to-morrow must see his name in the *Gazette?* That would be a vile, cowardly rest, if rest such a feeble, nerveless swoon deserves to be counted. Have you no dreams? Come, come, John, you must wake. There are many messengers waiting in your hall; many letters to answer; much business to transact; and, lo! a new year to transact it in.

Remember what the great Prussian said, old iron-hearted Frederick, when affairs were very desperate, though his salvation was nearer at hand than he deemed it : "After seven years of struggle, all parties began to know their own position." You, too, have had your seven years' war, John. Let us see whether all parties in your case do not begin to know their position also. And, for the first, what may be yours? 'Tis seven years and more since old William the Fourth, who also had a lion heart in his way, did *not* dine in the city;[1] and the great question has not yet been answered, "How is the King's Government to be carried on?" Great question of a great man![2] True hero-question, prescient, far-seeing, not easily answered by common men.

And now other questions arise, not less great, not more easily responded to, and not asked by heroes, but by common people. When a nation asks questions, it will be replied to. And, first, how is the empire to be maintained? There is a question. The seven years' war of *agitation* has brought us to that. In 1831 question how King's Government is to be carried on: in 1838 question how Queen's Empire is to be maintained. Here is philosophy; the nation has become Socratic; one question answered by another question. Will the same solution serve for both? Here be Christmas riddles and new year

---

[1] November, 1830.   [2] The Duke of Wellington.

27

charades, and if we cannot untwist them we must pay forfeit.   Reformed Parliament has not answered them; Reform Ministry has not answered them; town councils have not answered them; New Poor Law has not answered them; justice to Ireland has not answered them; colonial conciliation has not answered them; new allies and old allies have not answered them; St. Stephen's is dumb, and Downing Street is dumb; and Castle of Dublin and Castle of Quebec, both are dumb; and new Mayors are dumb, though their brains be no longer offuscated by Aldermen; and board of guardians are dumb, notwithstanding their well-regulated dietaries: no answer from the Euxine; no answer from the Caspian; no answer from Barbary, or Spain, or Portugal, or Constantinople.   Strange to say, no answer from St. Cloud or the Tuileries.

Yet answers must be found to both—to hero question and national question.

You see, John, you must really wake.

January 3, 1838.

CHAPTER II

A CONVERSATION BETWEEN OLD ENGLAND AND YOUNG FRANCE

Questions : How King's Government to be carried on ?   How Queen's Empire to be maintained ?—John Bull has received no answers; but here is a sharp note of a conversation between two eminent personages, which came to hand in a manner wonderful but nameless, but is nevertheless as authentic as many State papers.

YOUNG FRANCE. How do you do, old foe ?

OLD ENGLAND. The compliments of the Season to you, new ally.

YOUNG FRANCE. Your Reform Bill, does it please you as much as ever ?

OLD ENGLAND. As much as the three glorious days do you.

YOUNG FRANCE. We have a new dynasty, that is something.

OLD ENGLAND. If we have not yet come to that, our Prime Minister, after seven years of reflection, has just given in his adhesion to our old monarchy. That is something.

YOUNG FRANCE. Extraordinary reaction!

OLD ENGLAND. Undoubtedly, a very great demonstration.

YOUNG FRANCE. We have at least conquered Barbary.

OLD ENGLAND. And we have not yet lost Canada.

YOUNG FRANCE. How is your old favourite, Lord Grey?

OLD ENGLAND. He is quite as well as Mr. Laffitte.[1]

YOUNG FRANCE. And my Lord Russell?

OLD ENGLAND. Is as tall as M. Thiers.[2]

YOUNG FRANCE. We live in droll times. That affair of the Vixen?[3]

OLD ENGLAND. Was purely commercial; at least, they tell us so.

YOUNG FRANCE. And the Prussian league?

OLD ENGLAND. Not in the least political; we are well assured.

YOUNG FRANCE. And the Russian tariff?

OLD ENGLAND. Entirely an affair of finance, according to our Ministers, who ought to know, for they are paid for it.

YOUNG FRANCE. And Mr. Van Buren,[4] is he quite well?

OLD ENGLAND. What is Mr. Van Buren to me?

YOUNG FRANCE. Some half-century back the same as M. Papineau.[5] Do not lose your temper.

[1] The French financier and politician.
[2] Premier and Foreign Minister of France, afterwards President of the Republic.
[3] In February, 1837, trouble arose with Russia over the capture of the *Vixen*, a British vessel owned by Mr. George Bell, the Russian admiral giving as his reason for the act that the *Vixen* was attempting to break a blockade, and that the Circassians were at war with Russia.
[4] President of the United States.
[5] Leader of the Canadian revolt

OLD ENGLAND. I assure you I am quite calm.

YOUNG FRANCE. I see it. Did you give up your sovereignty of the seas with your rotten boroughs ?

OLD ENGLAND. That is a question with which at least you have nothing to do.

YOUNG FRANCE. *Nous verrons.* At Paris it is asked, Is the sovereignty of the seas in schedule A or schedule B?

OLD ENGLAND. I have heard it is your habit there to ask idle questions.

YOUNG FRANCE. My Lord Palmerston, it is a great man ?

OLD ENGLAND. He has at least preserved peace.

YOUNG FRANCE. By the aid of Marshal Evans.[1]

OLD ENGLAND. That was a private business.

YOUNG FRANCE. Precisely; a speculation, purely commercial, like Mr. Bell to the Circassians.

OLD ENGLAND. You seem very lively; you forget our intimate alliance.

YOUNG FRANCE. Not at all; it allows me to take the liberty of a close friendship, and to ask you a question.

OLD ENGLAND. Well, what is it ?

YOUNG FRANCE. In case of a war with Mr. Van Buren, do you count upon Russia ?

OLD ENGLAND. Perhaps not.

YOUNG FRANCE. Austria will of course be neutral ?

OLD ENGLAND. It may be so.

YOUNG FRANCE. And attend to the carrying trade of the Levant. Very wise !

OLD ENGLAND. If it were not for these troubles in the Atlantic, we should soon settle that question.

YOUNG FRANCE. Ay, ay, my dear hereditary foe and new ally, we shall take care that you have not in future to deal with one question at a time.

OLD ENGLAND. How, this language from you ! Have you forgotten our intimate alliance ?

YOUNG FRANCE. Not on New Year's Day. 'Tis the season of mirth. But tell me, how did you get Canada ?

[1] De Lacy Evans, commander of the British Legion in Spain.

OLD ENGLAND. You should know.

YOUNG FRANCE. From old France, I think ?

OLD ENGLAND. Well ?

YOUNG FRANCE. And we have gone through two revolutions to erase the memory of the *bêtises* of old France.

OLD ENGLAND. That is your affair.

YOUNG FRANCE. Not so quick. Do you believe that young France will assist you in maintaining an empire wrested by you from old France ? That would be to make both our revolutions ridiculous.

OLD ENGLAND. For my part, I begin to think all revolutions are so.

YOUNG FRANCE. Ha ! ha ! That is very well for you, who ever had everything your own way. The use of revolutions is to destroy monopolies, ancient comrade.

OLD ENGLAND. Monopolies ?

YOUNG FRANCE. Verily. You begin to suspect, like the Emperor Joseph, that revolution is not your *métier*. There is nothing like experience. Adieu ! We part the most intimate friends in the world, but as for our alliance, this is the 1st of January; this day three months I will send you *un poisson d'Avril*.

January 4, 1838.

CHAPTER III

THE DUKE'S QUESTION

I THINK one eye is open, John. Nay, it is even said one foot is in the stocking. Come, the other ! What, shall life consist of putting on one's stockings and pulling them off again ? Even that better than nothing. Oh ! Arthur Wellesley, great man, great have been thy deeds. Rightly art thou a Duke, a true Dux, a leader. Great was thine Indian career, greater thine European. Great was Assaye, Talavera, Torres Vedras, Salamanca, Vittoria, above all Waterloo ! Very great thine entrance into

Madrid, into Paris; very great when thou didst hold
Cabinet Councils without colleagues, and the seals of
three secretaries dangled at thy side, to say naught of the
keys of the Exchequer. But greater than all thine exploits, is this thy "Question." Truly a Sphinx question
which has perplexed a nation for seven years, and which
they seem to be further off from answering than ever.
Yet answered it must be. The query puzzling, yet the
response inevitable—or ruin. Is not that great? To
puzzle a whole nation for seven years. To puzzle all
Britain, and nineteenth century, and march of intellect,
and spread of knowledge. Rightly art thou Chancellor
of Universities. What is Duns Scotus to thee, or Aquinas,
or Erigena? Doctors seraphic, irrefragable, invincible?
Have not thy fellow-men essayed to answer? Verily to
their utmost, to their wit's end. Great question that has
caused four dissolutions of Parliament, yet, lo! no reply.
The chattering of multitudinous hustings, infinite gabble
of brawling debates, yet all dark—dark now as ever—
darker. Great question—that has written more pamphlets, set up more newspapers, established more reviews,
quarterly, monthly, bimensal, than all the causes and
parties and "great interests" since Fourth Estate was
recognised. Let my Lord Vaux, with his wrigglings and
windings and infinite eel-motions, educate us as he will in
true reverence and adoration of Broughamocracy; thou
alone hast set us athinking—and with nine words. Spartan! Lycurgus-Leonidas!

And now the nation, worthily imitating thee, whom it
cannot answer, has asked its question also—"How is the
Queen's Empire to be maintained?" What if this
question be only thine own in another guise? But nation
will be answered; nation is omnipotent; will be omniscient; will go to everyone; will clutch them in the street.
in House of Lords, House of Commons, quarter-sessions,
town-councils, mechanics' institutes, will come, among
others, to thee, and wait for response beneath the far-
spreading branches, old oak of the forest! Nation will

go to Brocket, to Woburn, to Drayton, to Knowsley, ay !
even to Lambeth and Finsbury, but answer it will have.
If not from palace, from cellar ; if not from common man,
from man inspired, from prophet; if no prophet, will
make one, will believe in one.

This is Tekel Upharsin work; gold chains and fine linen,
and robes of purple, honour for whomsoever will expound,
but answer there must be.   Notable the difference between moral and material questions: King's Government,
a spiritual essence; Queen's Empire, form substantial;
one asked by a far-seeing statesman, no reply; the other
asked by a whole nation, by all, even by the mob, and
must be answered.

January 5, 1838.

CHAPTER IV

NATION-CRIES

NOTE ever, John, the difference between a true nation-cry
and a sham nation-cry.   Reform House of Commons,
wise or unwise, true nation-cry; Reform House of Lords,
sham nation-cry.   Respecting the voice of the nation
there can be no mistake; it sounds everywhere, in town
and in country, streets and fields, lordly mansion, ten-
pound tenement, unglazed hovel.   Great chorus wherein
all join, prince and peasant, farmer and factor, literate and
illiterate, merchant and artisan, mariner and landlubber.
The same thought stamped on the brain of everyone,
from him who wears a coronet to him who drives a coster-
monger's cart; same thought on the brain, same word on
the tongue.

But a sham cry, however loud, no one knows whence it
comes.   Truly, we are told it is heard everywhere, except
in the circle wherein we live.   Very sham, ultimately
discovered to be but the roaring of " the public," " the
people," and the like.   Many names has the impostor,

numerous as the firms of Coster and Co., or the Sieur Minter Hart, but all worth nothing, living on the rascality of mutual reference and the scoundrelism of mutual accommodation. By-and-by the swindlers are found out, and fail to gull even the silliest. Then come a new cry and a new name like a new quack medicine. Dr. Eady is worn out, then try Dr. Morison. "Public Opinion" is discovered to be a hoax, then try "The People." If "People," with all their irresistible powers, turn out, after all, to be but a very drastic dose of gamboge, then heigh! for animal magnetism and "The Masses."

Public opinion, discovered to be party opinion, is laid on the shelf; the people detected to be a little coterie dressed up for the occasion, very generally avoided as suspicious, with a cry of "Swell mob," and "Take care of your pockets." Being analysed, and found consisting of a disreputable minority, heard of no more, and the Masses introduced; name portentous! Now, forsooth, the Masses are to have it, and all their own way; for who can resist the Masses? Mighty Masses, mighty mysterious! Papineau orators in the House of Commons quote Masses, condescend to represent no other, laugh at all constituencies, because they are known, palpable, inscribed on the registry, mere flesh and blood, go for nothing; Papineau writers out of Parliament concoct articles in reviews, specially in Sunday journals, about the Masses; would have no tax on pen, ink, or paper, or be supplied by the Government gratis, that Masses may read and believe their lucubrations, which all others do most heartily resist. Glory to the Masses; choice, generous phrase! By no means inert or cloddish; specially complimentary. What if said Papineau orators and writers, by some mischance of a *lapsus linguæ*, or damnable error of the press, do but omit the initial letter of that name, wherewith they have defined, and in a manner baptised, their countrymen? And may not the next stage come even to this?—

First ..	..	..	.. Public.
Second..	..	..	.. People.
Third ..	..	..	.. Masses.
Fourth..	..	..	.. Asses.

" O Richard ! *O mon Roi !*" O England ! O my
country ! Shall I live even to see this ? Shall I live to
see thee even governed by the Asses ? Arise Aristoph-
anes, rise from thine Attic sepulchre, here is theme fit
only for thee ! Our long-eared Government, braying in
all quarters, filling Downing Street with their melodious
song; not condescending, indeed, to stretch out their
resounding necks in House of Lords or at Quarter
Sessions, cashiered institutions, not fit indeed for donkeys;
but in House of Commons triumphant, as indeed there
they have had some practice, in town-councils very much,
and in mechanic lectureshops potent. And by St.
George, I believe, it will even end in this, unless the old
Duke's question be not speedily answered.

January 6, 1838.

CHAPTER V

A CONVERSATION BETWEEN MR. TOMKINS, M.P., AND
MR. JENKINS

TOMKINS. Jenkins ! or my eyes deceive me.

JENKINS. The same; you are surprised to find me again
so unexpectedly in England.   I have arrived within these
ten days from New York.

TOMKINS. A bearer of good news from Canada, I hope ?

JENKINS. Quite the contrary; the truth is, our Papineau is too perfect an imitation of O'Connell.

TOMKINS. I would he were a bolder copy.

JENKINS. Liberalism has gained no laurels there; it
does not shine apparently as much in practice as in theory.
And, to speak my mind, our affairs do not appear to
flourish here much more vigorously.   I can scarcely be-

lieve this is the country I left four years ago so ripe. You have had a succession of frosts, I think.

TOMKINS. Things have certainly changed somewhat; we must consider 'tis a bigoted land, encumbered with the prejudices of centuries; nevertheless, our progress has not been entirely arrested.

JENKINS. No; I have heard of your promotion, and beg to congratulate you upon it; an unquestioned M.P., I believe?

TOMKINS. Not even petitioned against. Can I do anything for you in the franking way?

JENKINS. I may avail myself of your kindness. But tell me, my dear Tomkins, how can you explain this vexatious Conservative rally?

TOMKINS. The causes are numerous; in the first place, want of education.

JENKINS. Indeed! Why, when I was here last our success seemed mainly to depend upon the all-acknowledged diffusion of intelligence and knowledge.

TOMKINS. We were too sanguine; the enlightened classes who possess power wish to make a monoply of their intelligence, and therefore are against us.

JENKINS. The enlightened classes against us!

TOMKINS. It is useless to conceal the difficulties of our position, though, of course, as I took occasion to mention last night in the House, our ultimate triumph is certain. But we must remember that public opinion is a great force to struggle against.

JENKINS. Public opinion! What, is that against us, too?

TOMKINS. The public opinion of this country is founded on wrong principles, and therefore opposed to us; but, still, it is public opinion all the same.

JENKINS. How are we to change it?

TOMKINS. We must change its elements.

JENKINS. Ah! our old friend "the People." I see it, we must call them in; that will do the business. I will answer for the people; the people has not changed.

TOMKINS. My dear Jenkins, it is unnecessary for you to remind me you have been absent for several years. "The People" is a phrase we now never use—a body of whom we never speak.

JENKINS. What, our old friend, the People! Has the people turned against us too?

TOMKINS. It is not a philosophical term; it served its purpose for the time, but it led at length to awkward Conservative analyses of the constituent elements of a nation, and it began to be turned against us. We never mention it now.

JENKINS. I am afraid affairs are very flat indeed.

TOMKINS. Oh no! As I said in the House yesterday, "Hon. gentlemen opposite may cheer, and the noble Lord, the Secretary for the Home Department, may feel proud of his new allies, but the eternal principles of democracy, like——"

JENKINS. Miss the metaphor; I see we are at a discount. I confess I thought the People was an inexhaustible fund.

TOMKINS. We overdrew it. We attacked and abused so many elections of the population, that at last our adversaries began to count up and to prove that even the majority was against us—an infamous Tory fallacy, of course, but still it began to tell. So it was thought prudent to drop the subject.

JENKINS. Have we come to prudence?

TOMKINS. You are impatient. Even the triumph of democracy requires time. Is it nothing that even in the House of Commons, as at present constituted, with all the unphilosophical antagonism of bigotry and property, we still have the good fortune of counting a few who are not the mere nominees of the aristocracy?

JENKINS. A very few indeed! Why, where is our Radical party? I was glad, however, to see your name in the minority on Wakley's motion.

TOMKINS. Ah! my dear Jenkins, you know not what temptations assail a Radical M.P. The moment he is returned to Parliament there comes a most corrupt and insidious invitation to dine with a Minister. A Government should not be permitted to entertain a most profligate and unconstitutional method of spending the public money. The aristocratic attrition of these official banquets is fatal to all the racy roughness of Radicalism. Few have sufficient strength of mind to vote against a Minister with whom they are in the habit of taking wine. Then, sir, it leads to a very disgusting refinement in dress. You would be surprised at the number of fine waistcoats that gradually steal, as the session advances, among men pledged on the hustings against the aristocratic corruption of which these fine waistcoats are the symbol. 'Tis a trying life. You will find many of your old acquaintances, friends of the people five years ago, and all that, very much altered.

JENKINS. My eyes begin to open.

TOMKINS. They will stare soon.

JENKINS. Our cause seems hopeless.

TOMKINS. By no means.

JENKINS. We have no party.

TOMKINS. Oh yes !

JENKINS. Why, Crown, Lords, and Commons, were always against us; Church, of course; all learned professions and unlearned too; every landholder in the kingdom; every man who has £500 per annum, as we ourselves long ago confessed; the whole agricultural population are slaves; all the small towns rotten boroughs, and half the great ones to be purchased by the highest bidder; landholder, fundholder, merchant, manufacturer, every solvent tradesman, all are aristocrats. I hear even of Operative Conservative Associations; and as for sympathy with revolted colonies, 'tis out of the question. The fact is, this country is devoted to capital, and every capitalist is our enemy. We succeed ! Why, even the Whigs can only retain power through the Irish, the Irish whom we thought our tools, and whose instruments we have become!

TOMKINS. A little too fast, friend Jenkins. You forget we have on our side the Masses.

JENKINS. The Masses ! Who are they ?

TOMKINS. A body so numerous that it is really impossible to tell you who they may be. But the Masses, my dear fellow, will carry us through yet. Never mind who they are or where they may be. It is a party; it is *our* party. The Whigs may intrigue, the Irish may blarney, the Tories may egg on Lord John and laugh at our minorities, but after all the English Radical leaders are backed by the Masses. As long as we have a party, never mind. Revolutions are never effected by large parties; ever by small ones. We have an excellent small party with an excellent large name. The Masses for ever ! They brought me into Parliament, and they shall bring you. Come into the Reform Club, and I will give you your frank.

January 8, 1838.

CHAPTER VI

CRICIS AT LAST

JOHN BULL is now fairly awake. He will bestir himself. He will know what has been going on in his household. There have been strangers and unauthorised visitors; he has heard of them. Who is this Masses who has been caught more than once sneaking down the area ? A scurvy knave who, it is rumoured, has been round the neighbourhood to John's tradesmen, and obtained goods under false pretences. John rings the bell for his breakfast; substantial meal—the roast beef of old England; nor shall it be cooked *à la Papineau*. It shall be still dressed in the old way, shall appear still as stately sirloin; nor will John's keen appetite be satisfied even by a slice from the rump, Whig fashion.

And now he must learn the news. While napping, it would seem, colonies have revolted, but they tell him are now appeased. Be it so; but why revolt ? This must be explained.

Will explanation come on the 18th of this month at Westminster ?

What if Canada even be quiet, the *rationale* of revolt must now be dissected. Is cause of revolt peculiar to Canada ? May not some cause occasion revolt in other places ? This must be seen to. Is reason of revolt reason why Queen's Empire cannot be maintained ? Is it reason why King's Government cannot be carried on ? All the same reason ? Here is business. For the great Duke's great question mixes with all other questions, and lies at the bottom of every well where truth must be inquired after.

So, then, it would seem, if the reason of Canadian revolt be discovered, peradventure at length may be discovered answer to the Duke's question. Yet it has taken seven years to arrive at this. In seven years the difficulties in carrying on King's Government, foreseen by a sage, have become embodied in a shape palpable and intelligible to all. This, then, is a Crisis.

A Crisis ? What is this same Crisis ? Often have we heard of him these last seven years. Now, indeed, it would appear he has really come. Who is he ? Who is Crisis ? Is he any relation to Masses ? Do we know as little about him ? We must have his paternity, his pedigree.

Advance heralds !

We live in an age of change. True; but what have been all ages but ages of change ? But of rapid change. Ay, there it is ! Why rapid ?

The progress of society is gradual, not to say slow. When it makes these sudden starts, forward or sideways, as it may be, ending ever in as sudden stops and stand-stills, has the progress been gradual ? Has not party intrigue, for special purpose, mixed itself up with national progress, accelerated the movement by temporary stimu-lants, say burning draughts, instead of good wholesome nutriment, and so national movement, pushed on before its time, finds no post-horses ready, and so a dead stop, a standstill, a Crisis !

In 1830, remodelling of third estate, commonly called Reform of Parliament, was required. National progress required it, had long summoned it. Remodelling was advancing but slowly, gradually, yet its shadow was already recognised. A party, shut out from power, by an accident possess themselves of power. How to retain it ? There is the difficulty All estates of the realm arrayed against them; majority against them in House of Lords; majority against them in House of Commons. The natural changes of national progress will not avail them, are too slow for them; change, therefore, must become more rapid.

Whereupon the cork is drawn, and the nation drinks the burning draught of agitation. All now is progress; the nation is galloping. But at the end of the stage, no relays, no horses ready, nothing prepared. Is it a Crisis ?

No; for they will post on another stage with the same horses. Nevertheless, not quite at the same pace.

Is there reaction, then ?

So some say. Those who approve of slower travelling are better pleased, while the others curse the drivers, who have disappointed them, and who, they say, are to their fancy no better than slugs.

But lo ! another stage; again no post-horses, and the old ones, jaded to death, fairly jib and move no more. A dead stop, a Crisis at last !

January 9, 1838.

CHAPTER VII

A CONVERSATION BETWEEN JOHN BULL AND CRISIS

JOHN BULL. So you have come at last ?

CRISIS. I have indeed that honour.

JOHN BULL. Honour be hanged; I have heard a great deal of you, and nothing to your credit. They tell me you have been long expected here.

CRISIS. I am much flattered.

JOHN BULL. Fiddle-faddle ! And where do you come from last ?

CRISIS. Straight from Canada.

JOHN BULL. And you have been very active there, they say.

CRISIS. I seldom interfere without producing a result.

JOHN BULL. Well, take care of what you are about in England. I give you fair notice; I will have no revolutions here.

CRISIS. You mistake me; I am connected with no party; I am perfectly independent.

JOHN BULL. Why, I took you for a regular Jacobin!

CRISIS. Quite an error; I never interfere until affairs are at a standstill, and then I invariably side with the strongest party.

JOHN BULL. Hem ! Well, I think there is no doubt which is the strongest party here.

CRISIS. We shall see ; the strength of a party does not depend upon its numbers, or its property but upon the tactics of its leaders.

JOHN BULL. That sounds very Jesuitical. I am afraid you are a Papist.

CRISIS. My religious opinions are like my political— they depend upon the circumstances of the moment.

JOHN BULL. A very dangerous character, I fear.

CRISIS. On the contrary, a most useful one. I never interfere until my interference is a matter of necessity.

JOHN BULL. Is this your first visit to England ?

CRISIS. By no means; I was here in 1640, and again in 1688. Had I not been very much engaged at Paris, I should have paid you a visit in 1830; but some of my retinue were here.

JOHN BULL. I have heard of them, and for the last seven years I have almost daily expected yourself.

CRISIS. In all my visits to this country, I have invariably found the strong and successful party a very small one. It was the same in Paris in 1830. Everybody was

surprised at the triumph of Louis Philippe, except myself.
He owes his crown entirely to my management.

JOHN BULL. Well, I hope the present instance will
form an exception to your usual experience, for I think
the strongest party here is both the most numerous and
the most wealthy.

CRISIS. It may be so; it will soon be decided.

JOHN BULL. Egad, I shall not be sorry if it be, for, to
speak the truth, I am heartily wearied of the present
unfruitful state of affairs.

CRISIS. Ay! ay! There is no doubt I am wanted.
However, here I am. They have sent for me continually
of late years; but I know my time better than those who
apply to me. They wanted me to come over with Sir
Robert Peel in 1834, but I knew better; they urged me
very much in 1835 to meet Lord Lyndhurst, but they
were quite mistaken; there was not the least necessity.
As for my invitations to Ireland, I have received one
almost daily for the last twenty years. Whigs, Tories,
Radicals, Papists, Protestants, Reformers, Orangemen,
Conservatives, Repealers, have all in turn sent for me,
but I have no intention of going.

JOHN BULL. Well, I am glad of that.

CRISIS. I am generally found where least expected. I
have been busy at Canada for the last five years, and
even gave the Whigs warning of it, but nobody attended
to me.

JOHN BULL. And, pray, why are you here now?

CRISIS. You are frank in your questions. In reply, let
me ask you one. How does your Government work?

JOHN BULL. Work! Why, not at all! There has
been a dead-lock for the last three years.

CRISIS. And suppose the dead-lock remains, what then?

JOHN BULL. What then! Why, then everything will
fall into confusion, which indeed it is fast doing. What
an odd question!

CRISIS. And why do you not remedy this inconvenience? For is not a Government that cannot govern the

28

greatest practical grievance that a nation can labour under ?

JOHN BULL. It is very fine talking, but how am I to do it ? I have tried everything and everybody. No party can carry on affairs. I have tried Lord Grey and the Whigs, and did all for him I possibly could; he promised everything, but he broke down. Then I tried Peel, much against his will: he made a gallant effort, but he broke down. Then I tried a Whig-Radical Cabinet, and they will not even break down; they stand stockstill. I would try the Radicals if they could do anything, but they honestly confess the affair is totally beyond their capacity.

CRISIS. You have answered your own question. When all parties are confessedly inoperative, I make it a rule invariably to appear.

January 10, 1838.

CHAPTER VIII

DEADLOCK

CRISIS has spoken out; his conversation with John Bull yesterday was frank. This visitor, whom all talk of, many fear, has told John Bull the truth. He has at length come to our shores. He had given us seven years to answer the Duke's great question—" How is the King's Government to be carried on ?" We have not answered it, and now Crisis has arrived. Was it not time ? Colonies revolting without practical grievances and without power or capability of independence; plainly because they were not governed; colonies revolting, not because they were misgoverned or could govern themselves, but because they were not governed at all. It is time for Crisis to appear.

Is Canada the only portion of the realm that is not governed ?—that rebels, in short, because it is not con-

trolled ? Are there any others ? Why has the power
of government of the British Empire in so many quarters
degenerated into mere administration ? As a nation, are
we less brave, less rich, less powerful, than heretofore ?
We have fleets and armies; we have a great revenue.
Why, in the words of the great Duke—why, then, cannot
the government be carried on, when all the visible means
of government are at hand ? It must be answered; it
cannot longer be delayed. The whole nation cries out:
" Question, question."

January 11, 1838.

CHAPTER IX

FORMAL POWER AND MORAL POWER

IN every part of the kingdom and the empire, authority
has dwindled into a mere affair of administration. Government has lost its moral power; it has degenerated into
a mere formula, obeyed in Britain from habit and the love
of order peculiar to the nation, the necessary quality of a
people devoted to industry; obeyed in all other places
according to circumstances, and of these the principal
is, whether there be a sufficient physical force to uphold
it. As long as there be a sufficient force, agitation only;
if not a sufficient force, then revolt.

Let us endeavour to ascertain the cause of this unprecedented and perilous state of affairs.

And first we must distinguish between the formal and
the moral power of the Government.

The formal power of Government is its authority by
law, and the modes by which the law has directed such
authority to be exercised.

The moral power of Government is the known and
universally recognised support which it receives from the
powerful institutions and classes of the State.

But when a Government accepts formal power on the

condition that it shall attack the sources of its moral power, the necessary consequence must be that its authority will rest mainly, not to say merely, on its official position, and the physical force with which that position invests it.

A powerful peerage, a powerful Church, a powerful gentry, a powerful colonial system, involving the interests of the merchant, the manufacturer, and the ship-owner, a powerful military system, a learned bar, a literary press—these were formerly some of the great interests on whose support the moral power of a British Government was founded. During the last seven years we have seen every one of these great interests in turn attacked. And by whom ? By the Ministers of the Crown.

They have denounced the peerage; they have attempted to degrade the Church; they have held up the gentlemen of England to public reprobation as bigoted oppressors; they have maintained themselves in power by means of a party who have declared the dominion of the metropolis over her colonies to be baneful; they have disbanded the militia; they have menaced the bar; and they have vainly attempted to annihilate the intelligence of the press. They have themselves set an example to the mob to attack everything that is established.

Can they be surprised that they themselves are at last attacked ? Under the term " agitation " they have encouraged the questioning of all authority except their own. Is it wonderful that their own, ever the weakest, should be at length assailed ? Threatened themselves, they exercise their formal power, and it fails, and must fail. What resource remains ? None for the Whigs. They cannot call for the support of those institutions and classes whom they have taught the mob to hate and despise—the institutions and classes that formed the empire, and by whom alone the empire can be maintained. The Whigs have destroyed the moral influence of Government.

January 13, 1838:

CHAPTER X

THE KEY

It may perhaps be deemed that we yesterday advanced a step in the solution of the great Duke's great question. When His Grace asked, " How the King's Government was to be carried on ?" he felt that that Government had been rudely and suddenly stripped of its sources of moral power.

Invest the Royal Government once more with that moral influence, and we shall be able to put an end to what may be truly termed our present immoral state; for such is the epithet applicable to a condition of public society of which the principal characteristic is a total absence of *duty*.

Here, then, is a key to open the dead-lock—could we but find it. Here is a word to put the whole machine in motion—did we but know how to pronounce it. A magical word ! But whisper it in the ear of Crisis, and he would vanish in an instant.

Whoever can find this key is fit to be Prime Minister of England; and without it, the wisdom of assuming power by any existing party in the State would be questionable.

Where is the key ?

We know where it is not. It is not at present in Downing Street. Is it at Lambton Castle ? It can scarcely be at Petersham. Is it at Strathfieldsaye ? Is it at Drayton Manor ?

Oh ! look sharp, look sharp, noble seigneurs, right honourable gentlemen; there are but a few days more, and you will all meet at Westminster. Proud will be his position who enters either House of Parliament with the key to the dead-lock.

Is not Parliament stuffed full of questions ? Why is this great question always forgotten ? All the rest mere mockery ! Yet there are leading questions and second-rate questions, and interesting questions and uninteresting questions, and important questions and unimportant questions, and questions which call hon. members up to town and questions which invariably send hon. gentlemen out of town. What are Irish questions—forms of Protean blarney; what military flogging, public walks, and Mr. Spottiswoode[1]; what even Corn Law question, or even Poor Law question, compared with this all-absorbing query, which, if it be not answered, all questions will alike become dumb ?

Gentle Mr. Stanley, active Mr. Holmes, is it not worth a whip ?

January 15, 1838.

---

[1] Mr. Spottiswoode, the Queen's Printer, had set on foot a subscription list to provide Protestant candidates for Irish constituencies and to finance petitions against Roman Catholic members. Disraeli dealt with the matter in his maiden speech on December 7, 1837.

A LATER DISRAELIAN CHAPTER

[The LETTERS TO THE WHIGS were written in 1853. Disraeli was by that time a statesman of assured position; he had succeeded to the leadership of the Tory party in the House of Commons on the overthrow of Peel, and he had been Chancellor of the Exchequer in Lord Derby's Ministry in the previous year.   When, the Budget having been defeated, the Coalition Government under Lord Aberdeen took office, with Gladstone as Chancellor, Disraeli founded the *Press*, a clever weekly political organ, to further his views.   He probably inspired more than he wrote; and until the private papers of the period have been examined, it would be unsafe positively to identify as his the brilliant political essays which marked the earlier years of that periodical's existence.   But that his influence and inspiration were over all there can be no doubt.   "Coalition" was the first leading article published in the organ, and the first issue also contained the opening chapter of the caustic Letters to the Whigs by Manilius, which are now reprinted here for the first time.]

COALITION

THE state of political parties in England at the present moment is very peculiar, and, with a prosperous and tranquil surface, not without considerable danger.   The administration of our affairs is carried on by a Coalition of individuals, who have avowedly no opinions in common, except upon a subject which is no longer a matter of public controversy, the principles of our commercial system.   There are members of the Ministry who are in favour of vote by ballot; there are members of the Ministry who, having been in favour of vote by ballot, have formally renounced that conviction within the last two years; there are members of the Ministry who are, and have been, always decidedly hostile to vote by ballot. If we take any of the other great constitutional questions, either in Church or State, we shall find among Her Majesty's principal advisers equal discrepancies of opinion and sentiment. The Coalition is carried on not even by a compromise, but by a mere suspension of principle. There is no similar instance on record. The Administration, therefore, is not morally, but literally, a Government without principles. They administer affairs, but they represent no opinion.

The excellence of representative government, however, is that it should represent opinion. It is this quality which compensates for its inevitable and innate deficiencies. As a mere instrument of legislation nothing can be more clumsy or cumbrous than a process which requires the sanction and receives the suggestions of between five and six hundred individuals. It is as a means which allows the predominant opinion of a community to stimulate or control that a representative government becomes powerful and beneficial. But the representative form is not merely a clumsy machine; it has a tendency to be a corrupt one. Five or six hundred individuals invested with legislative functions, and subject to the influences of a powerful executive, are capable of any misconduct. Their very numbers divide the responsibility, and their assumed popular origin diverts and dissipates the odium.

Our ancestors discovered in party, or political connection, a remedy for these injurious consequences, and a means of combining efficient and comparatively pure government with popular authority and control. Bodies of men acting in concert, advocating particular tenets, and recognising particular leaders, were animated by the principle of honour as well as by a sense of duty. The reputation of the party kept up the high tone of the individual who was a member of it, and, deferring to the superior judgment of the most eminent of the association, union of opinion and of action were found compatible with a multitude of counsellors and agents. Notwithstanding some passages in the course of two centuries touched by the infirmity of human passion, the annals of English party form one of the noblest chapters in the history of man.

It is not in a moment that you can dissolve the ancient political connections of this Parliamentary country, but the first dilapidation of the structure of our free government has taken place when our affairs are administered by a Cabinet of suspended opinions. Tradition, the sense of honour, the social influences which still prevail among the representatives of the landed constituencies, may for a while avert or mitigate the consequences of this state of affairs; but these consequences are sure, and will be ultimately found in a multitude without cohesion, without consistency or even decorum of conduct, in individual scandals, in aggregate humiliation, in a general loss of weight, authority, and character, which will lower the once proud, aristocratic, free Parliament of England to the level of those Continental assemblies whose brief and tumultuous careers have been alike the terror and the ridicule of the world.

The most singular characteristic of this strange conjecture is the apologetical reason that is given for its occurrence. It is conveniently maintained that, in consequence of the abrogation of the protective principle in commerce, the distinctive characters of the two great parties in the country no longer exist. The persons who circulate this tenet are the very individuals who deprecated the uncompromising opposition of Lord George Bentinck, on the ground that the question which then divided the Conservative party was only one of tariffs, and that the great principles of the Conservative connection were in nowise in controversy.

It would not, at the first glance, appear that the repeal of the Corn Laws or the reduction of the sugar duties had solved the momentous problem what classes should be the principal depositary of power in this country. The nature of the franchise, and its extent, which depends on a right appreciation of its nature; whether the royal supremacy in matters ecclesiastical should be maintained; whether our Upper House should be a territorial or an elective senate; whether, as an element of strength and duration, a preponderance should be given in our polity to the landed franchise, or whether, on the contrary, the municipal ingredient should predominate; the rights of inheritance and the laws of tenure—these are the vast questions of permanent interest which will occupy at intervals the mind of the nation, and on which they will receive no solution or guidance from a Cabinet consisting of members who are diametrically at variance on all these important heads.

It will not do to gloss over their inconsistent and incoherent position by announcing themselves the disciples of progress. We want to know of what progress they are the votaries. Is it English progress? Or is it French, or American, or German progress? A centralised administration, a tyrant majority, or a Pantheistic religion? There is no progress for a country except in the spirit of its national character, or which runs counter to the principle of its institutions. If the national character be exhausted, the nation is worn out, notwithstanding the price of Consols may be at par. If the principle of its institutions no longer animates and inspires, a new race, like the Goths in Italy, may establish new institutions; but an old race will find that what it deems progress is only change, and that change is only the epilepsy of decay.

For our part we have confidence in the enduring character of this country, and believe that there is yet an inspiring force in the principle of its free aristocracy which may secure the continuance of our power and the improvement of our society. These ends, however, can be most surely obtained by the Parliamentary government of this country being carried on by two parties with distinctive principles, eliciting in their discussions the conclusions of political truth, and giving, by their arguments and appeals, a tone to the public mind. And what prevents all this ? Why has the constitutional habit of the realm been disturbed and discontinued ? Why is the country governed neither by the Liberal nor by the Conservative party ? From personal and petty causes only. The Chancellor of the Exchequer, professing high Conservative opinions, will not, from a personal feeling, combine with the leader of the Conservative party in the House of Commons. The morbid vanity of Woburn Abbey must be represented without an interval in the royal councils. The Whigs may perish, but the Duke of Bedford must be satisfied. To accomplish these noble ends, to gratify a prejudice, and to pander to an oligarch, an austere intriguer, without any following in the country and without any lustre of career, is installed in the high place. Around him are clustered a motley crew of statesmen, who, magnanimously forgetting careers of recrimination, and veiling their mutual aversion with sinister frankness and affected cordiality, devote their heterogeneous energies to the service of a perplexed Sovereign and an amazed country.

May 7, 1853.

TO THE WHIGS

CHAPTER I

GENTLEMEN,—Whatever praise or whatever censure attach to the name it was once your boast to assume, the name itself is so identified with the History of England that we have a right to ask why it has disappeared from our records. Hitherto you have been an essential element in that collision of opinion from which flash all the political truths that enlighten statesmen and save nations. Even at the period in which your numbers were reduced to the lowest—exiled from the Court and alienated from the People—the genius of your leaders sustained the enthusiasm of Party. It is enthusiasm alone that gives flesh and blood to the skeletons of abstract opinion, and the devotion of the genial patricians who gloried to call themselves the friends of Fox carried on that hereditary affection of clanship which bound you together, and which ultimately enabled you, in the enactment of the Reform Bill, to obtain the renown and reap the rewards which belong to the successful arbiters between rival classes and conflicting passions. It was this close and firm connection, however justly it exposed you to the charge of exclusiveness, that atoned in discipline and compactness for your want of numercial force.

The enthusiasm is vanished—the connection is broken —the discipline is gone. What and where are the Whigs now ? Your history itself seems to cease; you are merged into a section of your former opponents; you are subordinates in a Cabinet from which the name of Whig is excluded; your ancient badge is exchanged for a shred from the mantle of the dead chief who in life most derided your pretensions, most damaged your reputation, and who, even when accepting your opinions, shrunk pointedly from all thought of your alliance. Twice did Sir Robert Peel pass into your camp a deserter from his own forces, but in neither case an associate with yours. He did but seize upon your weapons to pile them up as trophies for himself. And perhaps all his hostilities never so injured the Whigs as when he appropriated, to enlarge, the measures he had before resisted, and showed the practical people of England that he alone could perform what you, the Whigs, had in vain attempted to do. Nay, even when on the abolition of the Corn Laws he assigned to each associate in his victory the due proportion of merit, so eager was his desire to disparage your earnestness, and cast a slur on your own claims to popular gratitude, that, with all his habitual abhorrence to extra-forensic agitation, he gave the lion's share of conceded praise to the Orator of the League.

And yet it is to the special followers of your most illustrious enemy that you now postpone all your claims of two centuries, not participating on equal terms in the *spolia opima*,[1] and consenting to erase the very name of Whig from the cornerstone of the Government, to cement the foundation of which you fritter your own masonry into splints and rubble. And what do you gain by an alliance in which you figure, not as confederate potentates, but as dependent auxiliaries ? It is in vain to boast of the sacrifices of patriotism—of the necessities of carrying on the Queen's Government—Government in which your two most distinguished leaders actually hold no official appointment ! From the list which includes each scattered subaltern of Peel are cashiered the men who had formed the first ranks of your phalanx. The thoughtful mind of Lord Grey ; the ready vigour and force of his cousin, Sir George ;[2] the financial reputation of

[1] The Cabinet was composed of six Peelites, six Whigs, and a Radical.

[2] Sir George Grey, Home Secretary for nearly twenty years. He joined the Coalition Ministry later.

Baring;[1] the earnest intelligence of Labouchere;[2] the liberal accomplishments and exquisite temper of Carlisle;[3] the wit and the courage of Clanricarde;[4] the business-like abilities of Seymour;[5] the scholarship and moderation of Vernon Smith;[6] the immense erudition and dazzling eloquence of Macaulay,[7] are severed from the sides of those who serve as subordinates to Gladstone. True, Macaulay's abnegation is voluntary. Can you say the same of the rest ? Why these exclusions of your own natural officers, except that they have been too much identified with the memory of your past battles; and in the eyes of your new associates their scars are not the tokens of honour, but the excuse for dismissal from service ? But the Queen's Government must be carried on. True; but how and by whom ?

The nation is divided between two great parties—that of the Movement commonly called the Radical, and that composed of the supporters of the policy which characterised the short Government of Lord Derby. Between these two great divisions of the electoral body there are noble intermediators, I grant—men whose sublime duty it may be to grasp with firm hand the balance of opposing parties. But it is clear that no mere junction of petty sections can obtain what is the first requisite of a Government — a strength of numbers sufficient to carry its measures. But neither of these parties do you gain; neither of them do you conciliate in your fusion with politicians equally dissevered from both. You win the Conservative Gladstone, but not the Conservatives; you win the Radical Molesworth, but not the Radicals. You

[1] Sir Francis Thornhill Baring (Lord Northbrook), Chancellor of the Exchequer, 1839–1841.
[2] Henry Labouchere (Lord Taunton).
[3] George W. F. Howard, seventh Earl of Carlisle, who as Lord Morpeth took a leading part in the politics of the Reform period.
[4] Postmaster-General in Lord John Russell's administration.
[5] Edward Adolphus (Lord Seymour), Member for Totnes, and afterwards twelfth Duke of Somerset.
[6] Robert Vernon Smith, afterwards Lord Lyveden.
[7] T. B. Macaulay.

rally round you no popular sympathies when you invest all your political capital in the precarious speculation of a Peelite Cabinet. Look to the last General Election. What men less popular then than the Peelites, despite their unquestionable talents ? Peel himself was a name that carried with it the affection and trust of an immense proportion of the electoral class. I grant this most fully; but to his individual memory alone the popular attachment confines itself. How many men in the House of Commons can be called Peelites ? Are there forty ? So, then, is this fragment from the main Conservative body—without popular prestige, without electoral influence, without definite policy—you, the Whigs, to whom Lord Grey bequeathed the Government of England, while not one opposing litigant had resources sufficient to contest your title—you, the Whigs, at last sink your identity and vanish out of sight ! So thus do the organs of the Government which your leaders help to compose emphatically style it the Conservative—so thus the very title of Whig is ignored as a thing past and obsolete. And the highest compliment the Premier can pay to your veteran chief is to assure the startled public that My Lord John Russell is—Conservative !

Is this a position that can flatter the just pride of party? And is this the Be All and End All of the descendants of Somers and Walpole ? Is the position—if you grant it undignified—wholly the fault of the accomplished and practised chief to whom the conduct of your party was consigned in the Commons when Lord Althorp was lost amongst the Peers ? If his be the fault, it arises from no defect in the inherent qualities which command admiration and justify power. To a name to which history has given a blazon beyond all the *or* and *azur* of heralds, Lord John Russell united an intellect refined by letters and invigorated by practical life. Consummate in the usual tactics of party—courteous to opponents, if somewhat indifferent to friends—rising on legitimate occasions to an eloquence ennobled by generous sentiments and en-

riched by a various knowledge, Lord John's just pretensions to be the leader of gentlemen and the exponent of
party opinion were never denied, save by the mutinous
followers who sat at his rear, only with more effect to
assail him from behind.

Where, then, was his fault, when we ask, " What has
become of the mighty party that passed to his guidance?"
It seems to me simply this, that he never comprehended
the true ground he should occupy, nor the directions in
which he should advance. For the last twenty years one
choice has lain before the judgment of statesmen, viz.,
the maintenance of those institutions—nay, of those
habits of thought which preserve monarchy, or that
gradual change into absolute democracy to which Tocque-
ville somewhat rashly considered all the tendencies of our
age impel the destinies of Europe.

It was this choice that Lord John could never prevail
on himself to make with unequivocal and systematic
decision; it is by seeking to evade or to toy with it, and by
attempting to dignify vacillation into political prudence,
that, under the leadership of Lord John, you have year
after year thinned your ranks and damaged your influence.
And now the sole principle upon which you can defend
your coalition is based upon precisely the same error—
that of playing Conservatives against Radicals, and obtaining majorities that have no faith in your policy and
no heart in your cause.

Yet your true position was so directly in sympathy
with the views and wishes of the great middle class—of
which as Whigs you aspire to be the fittest representatives—that you had but to understand and maintain it
in order to render yourselves indispensable to the necessities of the State.

Let us pause and examine. The Parliamentary Reform
Bill was the great work of the Whigs. From that epoch
dates the influence they gained with Lord Grey, to lose at
last under Lord Aberdeen. You had thus created a new
constitution, amidst the loud hurrahs of the people.

What was your obvious and easy task ? Was it not to identify yourselves inseparably with your own work, and to be strictly the conservatives of the liberal constitution you had formed ? But you imperfectly understood that task when, through the mouth of Lord John, you declared yourselves for finality. A problem like the Reform Bill entails the task of solving its corollaries. To conserve this new constitution, you had first, it is true, to maintain its roots, but secondly to establish the value of its products; in other words, your task, as the authors of a fresh charter between the throne and the people, was to maintain the charter intact from democratic invasion, and to disarm democracy itself by proving that it sufficed for all those ends of practical government, the failure of which alone excuses his own creed to the democrat. Firmness to defend the reformed constitution, unrelaxing energy to work out its legitimate results—this should have been your twofold aim : this was Lord Grey's.

And had you proved yourselves equal to that position you would have carried off from Conservatives on one side, and Radicals on the other, a majority all your own. For you would have become the representatives of the real sense of the public, and rapidly have formed the Third Party amongst the electoral constituencies which withered away under your hesitating discouragements. For why did the Government of Lord John gradually die of exhaustion ? Because it unsettled much as to the new constitution, and settled nothing that was expected to be the result of it. And just towards the close, at the moment most inopportune, when insurgent populations and tottering thrones throughout the Continent, when quick successions of excess and despotic reaction rendered it most unwise to tamper with settled institutions at home, and disposed the public least to demand a change, my Lord John comes down to the House of Commons with his notable proposition—to undo the Reform Bill ! Six years of languid legislation, six years' subsistence on the legacy of Free Trade, six years and nothing done that

29

could show the innate vigour of the existent constitution
to remove all grievances and advance all progress, contrasted by a spasmodic violence against the Reform Bill
itself, and a classical dissertation by the very Premier who
had been most in collision with the democrats during all
his tenure of office—on the advantageous construction of
the word "democracy"! All this explains why the Whigs
had fallen at the commencement of the present Parliament into so great disrepute. They had not only thrown
away their right position; they had perversely taken up
the wrong one. They had done nothing to prove that
Reform works well; and their only pretence to what the
jargon of the day calls "Liberal opinion" was in the
abortive attempt to create agitation against the very
title-deeds of the possessions they had obtained from the
State. Could it be supposed, then, when thus thrown
out of power—meeting the present Parliament with
reduced numbers, internal divisions, popular discredit—
they would obstinately insist again on precisely the same
error? And yet is not that error the very basis of their
present coalition, or rather submersion? They form a
Government on the principle of a further Reform Bill
whenever Mr. Gladstone and Sir William Molesworth[1]
can concur in amalgamating the opinions of the Reform
Club with those of the Carlton. Every attempt to vindicate the constitution is put off for some indefinite plot on
the constitution itself, on which, if it be possible to form
a rational conjecture, not two of the conspirators can
possibly agree together. It is true, meanwhile, that you
have assisted to swell the reputation which you, above
all men, are forbidden to share—the reputation that
Mr. Gladstone has procured from a Budget of which the
chief popular merit is in its signal contrast to all your
own financial principles, and its covert blow to the policy
by which you have hitherto supported Aristocracy as an
element necessary alike to the safety of freedom and the

---

[1] The representative of the Radicals in the Cabinet.

duration of monarchy. What in this be your gain shall
be considered later.

Here I pause for the present. In my next letter I shall
endeavour to show that the Government of Lord Derby
assumed precisely that position which you, the Whigs,
had thrown away; and I shall take leave to inquire if you
then took the best means to reunite your forces, regain
your ascendancy, and identify your natural leaders with
the cause they profess to cherish.

May 7, 1853.

CHAPTER II

GENTLEMEN,—The case at issue in the last General
Election had not been confined to the question whether
the Act that repealed the Corn Laws should or not be
modified. Even in the counties the general cry of the
farmers was, not that Free Trade should be abandoned,
but that Free Trade should be impartially carried out.
The paramount question everywhere was " Ay " or " No "
to a fair trial of Lord Derby's Government. The question
was answered by the return of about three hundred
members more or less pledged to grant to the new Administration a support, whether provisional or permanent,
cordial or qualified. What were the other parties which
assembled in November last on the floor of the House of
Commons ? First in point of numbers were the Radicals
—viz., those who favoured a bold increase of the Democratic element in the constitution. Nor was the body
undistinguished by leaders remarkable for influence and
energy without the doors of Parliament, and for ability
and eloquence within its walls. It is impossible to affect
contempt for a party, whatever its defects, which comprises the ready intellect of Mr. Cobden, the inflexible
purpose of Mr. Bright, and the perseverance and acumen
of Mr. Villiers, sharpened into passion by his avowed
hostility to the aristocracy, to which by birth he belonged.

Sir William Molesworth lent his austere philosophy, and Mr. Bernal Osborne contributed his caustic wit to the intellectual resources of a host thus formidable to any Government from its numbers, and still more formidable to our mixed constitution from the principles which sought to remove the aristocratic medium placed by Time between those two contending powers that never yet in the history of the world have been long left nakedly confronting each other—viz., Monarchy and Popular Suffrage.

That all this party, whatever its subdivisions or its jealousies, would be actuated and combined for the time in one sentiment of hostility to Lord Derby's Government was clear. Free Trade was safe, but so was the Constitution; and the common object of this party was not only to preserve the one, but to change the other.

Below the gangway, in the ranks of this motley Opposition, assembled the special followers of the late Sir Robert Peel, determined not only to protect his policy, but to avenge his fall. These gentlemen could not but regard in Lord Derby and Mr. Disraeli the most illustrious victims they could dedicate to the Manes of their hero. With them, therefore, as with the Radicals, it was not enough that Free Trade should be recognised as the future principle of our financial system; it was not the future that engaged their fears; they had to efface a debt of resentment in the past.

Next came the Irish party, popularly termed the Brigade. Free Trade was no more to them than Hecuba to Hamlet. Whatever the financial measures of Lord Derby, to Lord Derby's Government they had pledged their opposition, on the simple ground that they had deemed it a duty incumbent on their patriotism and their conscience to oppose every conceivable Government whatsoever.

Now I turn to you, the Whigs, and I ask what could be your sympathy with any one of these three divisions, bent on the overthrow of that Government which had

succeeded to power on the inevitable expiration of your
own ? Could you sympathise with the ulterior objects
of the Radicals ? Was the " democracy " of Lord John
identical with the democracy—we will not say of Mr.
Bright, but of a single honest leader of the Movement ?
Could you sympathise with the followers of Sir Robert
Peel ? What to you was their desire of retribution
against those who had assailed his conversion on the
question of the Corn Laws ? You sympathise with *their*
resentment ! You were the last men to do so ; for none
were so bitter in all societies against the skilful adversary
who had contrived to *repique* you by a bold discard of the
suit you had counted on his retaining. Free Trade was
one thing ; *that* you were bound to defend : the supposed
wrong to a foe who, by destroying his own party, had
outwitted yours, was another thing ; and that wrong,
real or imaginary, you were not bound to avenge. Not
a sarcasm of Mr. Disraeli's in the most heated period of
old debate but what some of you had cheered in the
House of Commons, and nearly all of you cited in clubs
and drawing-rooms, with the acrimonious pleasure of
furtive enemies, when others say what themselves think,
but do not think it wise to be the first to utter.

Lastly, what had you in common with the Brigade ?
the author of the Durham letter[1] in common with Mr.
Duffy ?[2]

Thus, really remote from the three sections antagon-
istic to Lord Derby's Government, and unable to form
of yourselves an Administration, what was that position
which became you best ? Surely you had but to evince
neutrality in order to obtain the office of arbitrators.

Free Trade was secure. The first act of Lord Derby's
Government, on the assembling of the new Parliament,

[1] Lord John Russell's letter to the Bishop of Durham (November 4, 1850) on Roman Catholic pretensions. Disraeli had taken
a prominent part in the discussion on the letter.

[2] Mr. Gavan Duffy was prominent at the time on account of
a charge made by him (May 5, 1853) of Ministerial corruption of
Irish members.

was precisely that anticipated by every man of ordinary
sense. It was the recognition of that principle which
divides the rulers of a despotism from the Ministers of a
constitutional monarchy—viz., the submission of men,
made responsible to the Sovereign for the security of the
realm, to the power of public opinion when unequivocally expressed by a legitimate appeal to its verdict.
Here all taunts as to the inconsistency of politicians who,
in opposition, had opposed a law which in office they
ratified, were absurd on the lips of those who had studied
our history and comprehended our constitution. To
oppose a law, to represent the hardships it may inflict,
to argue on the consequences it may entail, to advise,
when it be passed, either congenial modifications or
supplementary amendments—all this belongs to the just
province of debate. But that law, confirmed in all its
integrity by fresh proofs of popular assent, and the
modifications or amendments advised rendered as impracticable as the repeal—nothing remains for those who
have passed from the freedom of opposition to the grave
responsibilities of office but to accept the law, and seek, by
means analogous to its spirit, remedies for whatever partial grievance it may inflict.

But if certain high and stubborn spirits, who, in the
severity peculiar to those Censors who cannot aspire to
be Consuls, refused to acknowledge that there could be
any virtue in necessity—if the Brights and the Bernal
Osbornes could not enlarge their comprehension of the
requisites of statesmen beyond quotations from Hansard,
there were surely some juster thinkers in the House of
Commons who must have trembled at the doctrine that
men in office are rigidly to carry out the opinions they
professed in opposition. Stand forth, my friends the
Whigs! Those juster thinkers must be you! Who in
opposition had been the most renowned supporter of
Roman Catholic emancipation? Was it not the very
archetype of Whiggery, Charles Fox? Charles Fox came
into office. What did he do? Honestly confess that, if

it be the noble duty of a member in opposition to advocate his own opinions, it is a stern necessity of a Minister of the Crown to defer to the opinions of the public and the Sovereign. Therefore Charles Fox requested the friends of Roman Catholic emancipation not to embarrass the Government; with too lively a remembrance of his former services to their cause, the ducal head of the house of Russell was commissioned by Mr. Fox to meet the more eminent strugglers for political franchise of their religious faith, and advise them not even to present their petition that session! The petition was accordingly suspended, and the fears of the Ministers relieved.

Who does not remember that, on the principle embodied in the Irish Appropriation Clause, Lord John Russell expelled the Government of Sir Robert Peel? And so keen in opposition was my Lord John's sense of the immediate and vital adoption of that principle, that he declared in Parliament that "he would rather have severed his political connection from those with whom he had so long allied, than continue any longer a system founded on bigotry and oppression!" Abjure his very party for a principle! Noble sacrifice!—not to be completed! Heaven had compassion on the Whigs: the party was not abjured, the principle was.

Lord John had only come into office, and bigotry and oppression obtained an instant reprieve. Lord Derby fought for his principle as long as there was a chance of a majority for its adoption. Lord John, having obtained a majority that brought himself into office, immolated the principle so intolerable in opposition to the austerer deities whom office intrudes into the creeds of men. Themis is the goddess of Opposition; Nemesis sits in Downing Street. Was it possible, then, that you, the Whigs, could have any just quarrel with Lord Derby's Government when it adopted your own peculiar policy of Free Trade in conformity with your own illustrious examples of political expediency? Or was it for you to insult the conscience of honourable men by coupling their public measures with a bill of indictment on their private opinions ?

I grant that if, when Lord Derby's Government at once accepted Free Trade as the principle henceforth incorporated in our commercial policy, and to be recognised in our financial system, that Government had nevertheless evinced, on all general measures, the tendencies to arbitrary rule, and resistance to the great law of progressive improvement, you, as Whigs, would have been justified in combining with all other sections for its downfall. But the whole spirit of Lord Derby's Government was to vindicate and to vivify your own Reform Bill—to preserve the constitution the Reform had created, but to put into action all its long-neglected machinery for the redress of grievances or the correction of abuse. This, in my next letter, I will endeavour to prove. Meanwhile I have thus far cleared the ground before us. First, the question between Free Trade and Protection no longer existed as an insuperable barrier between yourselves and any party with which, upon their general conduct upon State affairs, your hereditary sentiments might be more congenial than with other divisions of political opinion. Second, in reviewing those divisions we find banded against Lord Derby's Government, no matter what its merely commercial policy might be, the party of the Movement, regarding it as a barrier to those ulterior objects which you, as Whigs, had ever professed to oppose; the section of the Peelites, with whose desire for retribution it would be hypocrisy indeed, could you affect, to sympathise; the Irish Brigade—men, no doubt, very ardent in their patriotism and very zealous for their faith, but it is only to say that you were Protestants and Englishmen to prove that with those gentlemen you could have nothing in common, unless you could be prepared to destroy any Government whatsoever to which Protestants would trust their religion and Englishmen their rights. By the help of all these divisions you might destroy Lord Derby's Administration: by remaining aloof from them you might save it. You chose the former alternative. No Deluge has yet occurred, but it seems that you have foreseen its coming; for the Government you have helped to construct very much resembles the Ark, in which creatures of the most opposite species went in two by two.

May 14, 1853.

CHAPTER III

GENTLEMEN,—I have said that Lord Derby's Government took precisely that ground which the Whigs should have appropriated. Brief-lived as that Government was, never since the time of Lord Grey's Administration has any Cabinet evinced equal energy in the redress of popular grievances.

What was the loudest complaint throughout the kingdom ? The abuses of the Court of Chancery. And here the reform that had been put out to nurse, swathed and coddled by a Commission until it seemed to have lost all power of movement, at once assumed vitality and vigour; all that the Whigs, throughout six long years, had been proposing to do, was done by a Government that scarcely lasted six months; the spirit of Bentham united itself with the learning of Lord St. Leonards,[1] and became practical. What complaint, now so smothered (and why it is smothered we shall see later when examining Mr. Gladstone's Budget), was then loudest amongst all subdivisions of labour and skill ? The unequal assessment of the income tax. All Governments before had refused to deal with the injustice. A Whig Chancellor of the Exchequer had proposed to double it. The Government of Lord Derby founded its financial scheme on the remedy of this popular grievance. What had been for the last four years the urgent demand of the mercantile world ? The extension of our trade with China by the

---

[1] Lord Chancellor in the Derby Administration.

diminution of the tea duties. The demand was conceded. In a like spirit the complaints of the shipping interest, long neglected, were promptly heard. There remained the grievances urged by the colonial interest, and still more loudly by the agricultural. Here, Free Trade once established as a fixed principle, it was only in the power of the Government to give such redress as that principle permitted. It is true that the Government could not here restore immediate prosperity to diminished capital. But it could at least achieve one object of immense national importance—it could conciliate discontented classes.

To judge of the Budget produced by Mr. Disraeli in the dry spirit of a financier is to do signal injustice to the grand political principle that presided over the whole scheme, and should have won favour to a hundred petty errors in detail. That principle was the conciliation to an inevitable commercial policy of all whom the effects of the policy had, for the time, most alienated from the Legislature and the Constitution. That principle went farther still : it went to the foundation of our representative system; it animated the ancient liberty that exists in the Right of Petition; it connected the supply of subsidies with the redress of grievances.

Its merit here was precisely that which the Whig had ever affected to identify with the wisdom of Liberal legislation—the merit of recovering to the State the alienated affections of some large division of the people. Thus, the Derby Government having conceded Reform to all who appeal to law on behalf of property : having met the complaint which, day by day, the trading public and the press had united to utter against the iniquity of taxing precarious income at the same rate as that derived from realised capital; having taken into consideration the just assertion contained in the Report of the Committee on the Income Tax, that the whole of the burden was at present borne by about 350,000 persons, and that under such an assessment one person contributed not only his

own share to the expenditure, but the share justly charge-
able on three other capable persons; having given to the
merchant the boon he most demanded; having earned the
grateful acknowledgment of the representatives of the
shipping interest—it turned to the class most suffering
from the effects of Free Trade. It could not repeal Free
Trade for the sake of that class : was it, therefore, to
exclude that class from the benefits it was conferring on
those whom free trade had most enriched ? What was
its language to the agriculturists ? " We accept your
own cry at the hustings; we will seek to carry out Free
Trade fairly. You assert that the excise duty on malt
cripples your industry in the direction of your capital:
that assertion no political economist can deny. The
relief, in such reduction as we can effect, may be small;
but in dealing with the malt tax, and taking off one
moiety, we will at least try to do you this justice—we
will prosecute Free Trade for the enlargement of your own
energies, the freedom of your own capital." And something far more important than the reduction of a malt
tax is the conviction of English fair-play in the mind of
men in whose loyalty England recognises the best defence
for her domestic institutions, and the firmest guarantee
for that safety from a foreign foe for which, at this
moment, you are levying your militia and manning your
naval armaments. And yet, all that you, the Whig
gentlemen who aspire " to make democracy Conservative,"
could see in a measure framed with this obvious end was
the miserable question—whether the gain upon a pot of
beer would be a farthing or a penny !

Well, but the late Chancellor of the Exchequer proposed to bring the ten-pound householders within the
pale of taxation. Audacious man ! Regarded solely as
a question of political prudence, I grant candidly that
very reasonable doubts may be entertained whether the
same Budget should have contained an extension of the
tax on income, and an extension of the tax on houses.
But with respect to the last, the precise verge of exemption,

and the precise amount of the tax imposed, Mr. Disraeli
wisely and pointedly left as a detail.   The principle that
was asserted, you, the Whigs, were especially bound to
defend : you had created the class of the ten-pound householders; you had made those voters potent agents in the
decision of all fiscal burdens.   And was it for you to say
that the constituencies you had called into being were to
stand wholly exempt from the taxation their representatives were admitted to levy upon all householders save
themselves ?   Was that a doctrine agreeable to the theory
of representation ?   Was that your notion of a " Conservative Democracy "?   You inveigh against the bribery
practised in a borough election.   Small indeed is such
septennial corruption to that which you would perpetuate
in the doctrine that men who hold a suffrage in right of a
property qualification should keep sacred from fiscal
burdens the very property which qualifies them to tax
their neighbours ! And the danger becomes immeasurably
heightened when the only excuse you can make for their
exemption is that it might curtail their franchise (in other
words, diminish their political power) if you did not
annex to their right of thrusting their hands into the
pockets of others—the privilege of buttoning up their
own.

No, I repeat it, and I challenge you to disprove the
assertion, there was not a single *principle* in the Budget
on which Lord Derby's Government staked its existence
which you, the Whigs, were called upon to oppose—not
a principle which had not been recognised by all the
economical authorities you have received as guides—not
a principle which did not tend to consummate that policy
of which you were the legal inheritors, and to restore to
it the value it had lost by your neglect.   Had you, then,
refused to join all attempts to overthrow Lord Derby's
Government upon the introduction of its Budget, you
would have maintained the position you resigned to Mr.
Gladstone and his coterie; *you* would have been the party
to form a Cabinet whenever the fitting moment to regain

your ascendancy had arrived. I reinforce the proposition previously stated—present neutrality would have secured to you the power of future arbitration. And what then would have been your relative gain ? Clearly this: the Liberal tendencies of the late Government would have compelled you gradually to amalgamate with its chiefs. A Government reconstructed from Lord Derby's would have united all those who, instead of undoing your Reform Bill, would make the Reform Bill do its work. The old quarrels between Whigs and Tories would have passed away in the midst of the new combinations which, as Whigs, sooner or later you must resist, or they will sweep you wholly from the scene. Tories had already recognised the necessity of employing all the popular elements of the Constitution in support of its monarchical foundations; and you as Whigs would have recognised no less the necessity of preserving all that constitutes the life of monarchy from insidious attempts to remove from due influence in legislation that order of gentlemen which has hitherto given dignity to freedom, and maintained a constitutional throne apart from the dangerous hostility or the still more dangerous adulation of fickle numbers. Remove that order, and the republic of to-day is the despotism of to-morrow. Nor is there a country in the world in which the reaction from democracy to despotism would be so sudden and so complete as in England, because in no other country is there the same timidity of *Capital ;* and just in proportion as democratic progress, by levelling the influences of birth, elevates the influences of money, does it create a power that would at any time annihilate liberty—if liberty were brought into opposition with the Three per Cents.

But this post of neutrality you renounced. You preferred to become the tools of the section most embittered against Lord Derby's Government because most identified with the memory of your own inflexible opponent. Mr. Hayter[1] has conversations (unauthorised, of course—all

---

[1] Afterwards Sir W. G. Hayter, Liberal Whip.

such conversations are) with the chiefs of the Brigade. No income tax extends to Ireland, if Sir Charles Wood[1] be a consistent man and the member of a new Cabinet. You unite with the Radicals, who overthrew you before— whom, unless you also become Radicals, you can never conciliate. You unite with the Peelites, whose organs in the press had been, up to the last, treating your principles and your party with contumelious disdain. And you throw out the Government of which the Premier had been the most eloquent defender of your Reform Bill—of which the leader in the House of Commons had been accused of too warm a desire to reanimate that Toryism of Queen Anne's day which sought to identify itself with popular reforms—in order to make a Premier of my Lord Aberdeen, and a Chancellor of the Exchequer of Mr. Gladstone ! A Premier of the man who had treated your Lord John as a religious incendiary, and your Lord Palmerston as a meddling revolutionist ! A Chancellor of the Exchequer of the man who, in the very speech that preceded his elevation, styled himself " a Conservative," pathetically expressing his regret for the rupture of ancient ties and his hope of some future reunion. Amiable regret ! honourable hope ! reminding us of those inhabitants of the South Sea Islands who never devour their enemies—*that* would be paying them too great a compliment : they eat up only their own friends and relations, with an appetite proportioned to the love that they bear to them. And then they hasten to deck themselves in the feathers and trappings of those thus tenderly devoured, in memorial of their " regret at the rupture of ancient ties," and their "hope of some future reunion " ! Do you feel quite safe with your new ally ? Do you not dread that the same affectionate tooth will some day be fastened upon your own shoulders ?

May 21, 1853.

---

[1] Afterwards Viscount Halifax. " Sir Charles Wood in Cabinet (April 11, 1853) strongly disapproved of the extension of income tax to Ireland " (Morley's "Life of Gladstone ").

CHAPTER IV

GENTLEMEN,—Lord Derby's Government fell, not on a question of Free Trade, not on any principle opposed to Liberal opinion or to national progress. It fell because the Whigs resolved to abet the revenge of the Peelites and subserve the ambition of Mr. Gladstone; it fell because the party of the Movement desired at all hazards to destroy an Administration proving, by the spirit of its policy, that our mixed constitution suffices for the practical purposes of popular government. Not that Lord Derby's Government ever pronounced itself hostile to the principle of widening the existent franchise, or of securing the franchise we possess from whatever liabilities to corruption it is in the power of the law to control or counteract. Judging from the general tenor of its measures, such defects and anomalies in our representative system as are not inherent in all representative systems whatsoever would have received due care and correction. *This* only was the position Lord Derby's Government assumed: it refused to make its existence dependent upon a vague pledge to the Democratic party that it would introduce such reforms as the Democratic party might support. In a word, it was the guardian of those institutions which are essential to a tempered monarchy, and would therefore have been opposed to the innovations that insidiously prepare the way to the republic and the dictatorship. The true statesman regards individual measures less according to their merits, taken *per se*, than to their consequences as affecting the framework of the political system to which they are applied. States derive their vitality from elements too familiar to be discernible, as the air, the least visible of fluids, is yet the most necessary to existence. Aristocracy with us has no marked limit; the eye cannot track it to its vanishing point; it exists in every circle; you address a mob by the appella-

tion of "gentlemen "—a noble phrase, denoting a sentiment that elevates the whole tone of our national spirit.
But it is on this sentiment that the Democratic party
wage their way; Mr. Cobden defends the French for their
indifference to freedom on account of their love of equality.
Well, then, might the Democrats seek to destroy a
Government round which the bulk of the gentry had
rallied. But why the Whigs? Are the Whigs not
aristocrats?

And now, gentlemen, you have made your choice.
Half a dozen of you have got place; and the rest of you
are—where? and what? "Taciturna noctis signa!"
Contemplate the position to which you have reduced
yourselves after twenty years of political supremacy.
You have no leader in the Lords; you have scarcely a
voice of your own in that august assembly; and Lord
John only holds place in the Cabinet as your representative upon that single question on which he has hitherto
most notably failed, and on which all such perilous success
as belongs to a compact with democracy must destroy
irremediably whatever is substantial in Whig power—
remove from between the extremes of party the intermediate class of statesmen who, representing none of the
more vehement passions that sway the crowds below the
hustings, rely for their return to Parliament upon the
authority which birth, property, and education obtain
among the smaller or more rural constituencies brought
under the local influences of personal respect and hereditary affection.

Lord John holds a seat in the Cabinet solely as the
trustee for a new Reform Bill. But those who have consigned to him the trust imperatively demand the disfranchisement of small constituencies, and the introduction of fresh urban voters into the registration for counties. The disfranchisement of small constituencies is the
disfranchisement of the Whigs; and, if the territorial
interest is to be converted into a new supplement to the
electoral influence of urban householders, it is true that

you may weaken Conservatism, but you weaken yet more
every principle which can distinguish the Whig from the
Democrat. For, after all your endeavours to destroy
Conservatism, still the eternal and immutable tendencies
to conserve and to resist must remain. Even in the
largest mercantile or manufacturing towns there is
always at least a powerful and united minority in opposition to democratic opinion. In counties, swamp them
as you will with town voters, that opposition will be still
so vigorous, so sustained, that in the ordinary course of
events, when undisturbed by great popular excitement,
Conservatives will secure a large proportion of their
present strength. But you, who can neither accord with
the passions of the populace, nor win the favour of yeoman
and farmer through sympathy with their class and their
calling, will find that, just in proportion as you destroy
all the local influences which conciliate differences in
political opinion, you will vanish more and more from
the contests of public life. Here and there, as in the case
of Lord John, rare circumstances of name and past popular
service may sustain some individual in Parliament, and
secure to him the suffrages of voters proud of his repute,
though chafed against the moderation of his sentiments.
But, as a political party, the Whigs, both in name and in
thing, will be but as the fossils which speak of the race
before the flood. And observe, too, that, under the
peculiar circumstances of the position Lord John has
assumed, all the ordinary difficulties that attend the
recasting of the constitution, the remodelling of the
franchise, are gratuitously increased. For, by the dec-
larations, hints, and vague promises Lord John has made,
not only to his allies amongst the Movement, but to that
more moderate, though not more thoughtful, portion of
the public which imagines that for every ill legislation
can find a remedy, this bold statesman has committed
himself to a task much more difficult than that of commanding the Channel fleet—the task of bringing the law
written upon parchment to bear against the laws im-

30

pressed upon human nature. He undertakes to find, against the bribes which the rich candidate offers to the poor elector, remedies more effectual than those comprised in the rigorous severity with which Committees of the House now unseat every member to whom the practice of bribery is brought home—remedies that shall meet all of which the advocates for secret suffrage complain, yet dispense with secret suffrage itself. My Lord John, you are pledged to an impossibility ! Not that we need subscribe to the cynic code of Mr. Drummond, confound all men in one principle of corruption, and see no distinction between the sale of a vote for five pounds and the generous ambition that makes the soldier desire the token of honour, or the patriot labour for the power to accomplish noble schemes for his country. Narrow the view to the evil immediately before us—viz., the bribery or intimidation of voters; acknowledge the state and conditions of our civilisation, with all its disparities of wealth, all the passions of ambition and of greed that it engenders. See all those disparities brought to bear, all those passions let loose, at a contested election, and ask yourself if it be possible by any law to prevent wealth from the exercise of its power, or place avarice out of the reach of temptation ? Yes, there is one law, and but one—the law that would erase the theory of popular representation from our system; the law that would suspend the franchise or restrict it to an oligarchy; the law that would take wealth and poverty from juxtaposition; the law that would annihilate constitutional liberty in England, with all its virtues and with all its concomitant excesses. There is no other law, fill your statute book as you may. And the worst of it is that, when men enter into a war with human nature, they go on adding threat upon threat, penalty upon penalty, till the disproportion between the offence and the punishment makes justice itself disappear before the common-sense of the tribunal to which the verdict is referred. The advocates for the ballot have this at least in their favour—all your remedies will fail one after the other, and leave but the ballot-box alone untried. Manlier and wiser would have been the frank avowal: We must take civilisation and liberty as they exist, lamenting the temptations they offer, the excesses to which they are incident, seeing that the more civilisation and liberty are brought to bear upon the ferment of masses closely pressed together in towns, the more your evidence shows that the corruption of individuals is in ratio with the active principle that gives life to the State; and that thus the sparser population of agricultural districts is comparatively free from the vices which rage in the towns, whose electoral influence you desire us to increase. Nor is the large city more pure than the small borough. We can disfranchise St. Albans to please you. Would you have us disfranchise for the same offence Liverpool and London ? Or, if we are to adjust constituencies according to the evidences of bribery before our committees, would you have us accept those evidences, and say : Agricultural constituencies are so rarely condemned in comparison to urban that the facts call upon us to give to the rural population the very influence of which you would deprive them. No ! we cannot separate civilisation from all its consequences—the same causes that produce the vice call forth the virtue; you show us only the temptation to which men have yielded—show us also the magnanimity with which all threats have been defied and all bribes have been disdained. An election is but an epitome of human life. And it is to the glory of our commonwealth that, upon the whole, honesty is so prevalent; and that there never yet existed in the world a popular assembly in which the corruption of the representatives themselves was so rare as in the British House of Commons. Honour to us that, amidst all our hot feuds of faction, amidst all the changes of opinion and of party which our statesmen undergo, it never yet was suspected that one man to whose voice the English Parliament would listen for a second had accepted a pecuniary consideration for the change of an opinion and the record of a vote. Can you

say this even of the first statesmen of France, of America,
of the chiefs of the old republics ?   Individuals may be
corrupted in our boroughs—the National Assembly is
incorrupt.

Nor is this rash undertaking to accept civilisation, yet
reject its conditions, the only difficulty Lord John has
created for himself in becoming sponsor for a new Parliamentary Reform Bill.   He has undertaken what would
obviously require the most cordial unanimity as to the
ulterior objects which such reform, be it large or small,
should effect—in connection with men of opinions the
most opposite, and with whom the peculiarities of his own
mind can have the least of that sympathy which he might
have found amongst the Whigs cashiered from the Cabinet.
And thus, on the one hand a Gladstone, on the other a
Molesworth, he is to conciliate the University of Oxford
with the reforms that will satisfy the electors of Southwark !

This is his position, on this ground alone he holds
office, and to this, after scattering, subdividing, the party
that he led, does he commit all the chance of their
reunion !

But, Whigs and gentlemen, I have heard some of you
take this comfort to yourselves: " Rely on it," you say—
" rely on it that, with such colleagues as Lansdowne and
Aberdeen, Gladstone and Sidney Herbert, Lord John's
new Reform Bill will be so nominal that even Conservatives may support it."   Well, if that be so, why were
democrats enticed to destroy a Conservative Government ?   Have so many votes been purchased by a bill
at a year's date, which will then be dishonoured !   Possibly it may prove to be the fact.   It is easy for one party
to outbid another for popularity, when there is no intention to disburse the difference between the offers.   " What
salary do you give to your secretaries ?" asked a French
Prince of another *grand seigneur*.   " A hundred crowns,"
was the answer.   " A hundred crowns only !   How low !
What a trifle !   I give two hundred to mine—*but, to be
sure, I never pay them !*"

But in this case the secretaries will be Cobden and Bright, and I have a strong suspicion that they intend to be paid. Look to it.

May 28, 1853.

CHAPTER V

GENTLEMEN,—You have rallied round Mr. Gladstone's Budget as round a banner. The Budget is popular, I grant it. But why? Because of the political principle that lies concealed amongst its financial details. It is popular because it flatters all those whose passions are yet warmed by the remembrance of the long disputes on the Corn Laws. It revives the *ignes suppositos* by the *cineri doloso*.[1] It renews the triumph over the landed interest by a fresh attack upon the land. I have said in a former letter that we would consider why the complaint against the assessment of the income tax, once so loud, was now so silenced. I invite you to that consideration. You cannot deny that at the commencement of the present Parliament it was generally computed that not one hundred and fifty members could be found who would vote for the reassessment of the income tax, according to the principle upon which it has been imposed and continued. Now, Mr. Gladstone has obtained a willing majority not only to the renewal but to the extension of the tax, unmitigated in its stern principle—and how? By annexing to it the new duty on successions. Take from the Budget this tax, and where would be Mr. Gladstone's popularity—where the acquiescence in the renewal of the income tax, which, like that grim impartial visitor described by the poet,

"Æquo pulsat pede pauperum tabernas
Regumque turres "?[2]

---

[1] " Periculosæ plenum opus aleæ
Tractas; et incedis per ignes
Suppositos cineri doloso."
Horace, "Odes," II., i. 6.

[2] Horace, "Odes," I., iv. 13.

It may or may not be true that the new tax on successions is but a claptrap for popularity, that it will little injure the land, that only £400,000 will be raised from that description of property. Not so, at least, was the proposition regarded by the Movement who cheered the assault on aristocracy, and the shopkeeper who silenced as a Radical the complaints he had uttered as a tradesman. It became popular solely on the ground that it inflicted on the principle of hereditary aristocracy a something that had heretofore been resisted as detrimental to its existence. The popularity was increased because the attack was unaccompanied by one conciliatory measure towards the class it assailed—not even an attempt to mitigate the expenses of the sale or the mortgage which the tax might not unfrequently compel. Do the democrats pause to to think whether the gain from land will be less than half a million ? No ! To use the language of their own press, "They have inserted another wedge into the tree."

I say nothing on the general question as to whether real property should or should not be exposed to the legacy duty ; or whether it be a sound principle in political economy to relieve our own incomes by deductions from the capital of posterity. All that I say is that the time and the mode in which the duty is now imposed convert a question otherwise financial into a measure especially political.

The income tax was mainly defended as an instrument for the abolition of protective duties. And now the sole prospect of our release from that burden is made to rest upon the profits of a new tax on the very class which the abolition of those duties had most galled and most injured. You thus ultimately pay for Free Trade out of the pockets of those whom Free Trade had impoverished. You conclude your war, not by grace to the enemy who has retired from the field, but by an act that is meant to charge him with its expenses. You have cheered on your followers by the shout of "Væ victis !" and in the spirit of Eastern despots have made the proof of your victory consist in the fine you have levied on the vanquished. *Thus* it is that Mr. Gladstone purchased the popular consent to the inequalities of his income tax. And Lord John sate beside Mr. Gladstone, and Lord John subscribed to the impost, because it was a symbol of political insult—having during his whole career as a Whig opposed the impost as a measure of finance! And do you think that this fresh triumph to the Peelites is no fresh damage to the Whigs!

Mr. Gladstone's Budget itself, regarded purely as a financial measure, has some great merits; and amongst them that which is only second to originality—viz., felicitous imitation. Mr. Brodie's pamphlet supplies the conception of the new succession tax; to Mr. Disraeli's Budget we owe the mitigation of the tea duties, the relief of the shipping interest. There is one authority, indeed, to which Mr. Gladstone never turned his classical taste, whether for paraphrase or translation—viz., the Budgets of the Whigs.

But that which predistinguishes the scheme of Mr. Gladstone from the propositions of Mr. Disraeli is notable and significant. It is the utter absence of every desire to remove the irritation and to gain the affections of the vast class employed in the production of wealth, through its earliest and deepest source—the cultivation of the soil. When our Hannibal of the Exchequer has gained the summit of his Alps, and looks down on his Italy of Relief, a divine compassion seizes him for the sufferings of all—except the class which alone has suffered. He thinks the case of the posthorse-masters "very hard," he reserves a corner of his heart for the wrongs of attorneys, ponies and dogs come under benignant consideration; but the husbandman whose earnings had been seized to defray the cost of ascending the Alps is excluded from all the benefits showered down on the rest of Italy! The land is ignored for relief—it is only remembered for taxation. And therefore the old grudge still remains, and the golden opportunity of effecting conciliation between town and country upon easy terms is irrevocably cast away. Meanwhile the Parliament stands pledged for six years to the continuance of the income tax, with all the grievances which will again find voice when the hurrahs that cheered the new tax upon bloated landlords have passed away— remaining in full force, and extending to a wider range all the feelings that weaken respect for property, and all the temptations which can demoralise the honest. In the speech by which Mr. Disraeli introduced his Budget he contemplated the future extinction of the income tax, while redressing for the present its inequalities. But on what did he rely for aid to the resources obtained from the termination of the Long and other Annuities ? Upon the diminution of expenditure in the Public Works. The two millions which Mr. Gladstone is in six years to obtain from a tax that it now seems is to disappoint popular expectation, and fall rather upon humble house-owners than opulent landholders, Mr. Disraeli would have raised, perhaps, in three years, by drawing only on that *Magnum Vectigal Parsimonia*[1] which has no place in the calculation of Mr. Gladstone. "Retrenchment" was one of the three conditions of Lord Grey when he entered into office; Lord Derby's Government took up the long-dormant principle upon which the Whigs had based their pretensions to power; and the Whigs turned aside, to cry out, with Mr. Goulburn, "Dangerous and abominable principle ! to count on retrenchment for the future repeal of a tax."

And now, gentlemen, I close my appeal to you. You have united yourselves with men opposed to all your past policy, for the purpose of suspending your present existence as a party, and for the preparation of a measure which must either complete your unpopularity by its failure, or destroy all the elements of your future power by its success. Meanwhile you have the fullest opportunities to cultivate the virtue of patience under affront. My Lord John has had the presumption to speak for him-

[1] "Magnum vectigal est parsimonia" (Cicero, "Paradoxa Stoicorum," vi., 3, 49).

self on a question he might well be supposed to understand; my Lord Aberdeen disavows, on the part of himself "and many of his colleagues," the sentiments expressed by the nominal Leader of the Commons. Periods polished with literary care, and delivered with the frigid solemnity of elaborate preparation, are excused as expressions liable to be "misunderstood," indiscreet ebullitions from the "heat of debate"! The apology that would damage the raw tyro in politics is applied to the colleague grey with the experience and conflicts of forty years; and the services of Mr. Keogh[1] are repurchased by the marked humiliation of the *ci-devant* First Minister of the Crown. Your India Bill, purely Whig, is already exposed to contempt by the defenders of that part of the Cabinet which is purely Peelite; and the grave troubles in the East introduce into your councils every ancient subject of discord that can distinguish a Palmerston from an Aberdeen. But such differences of policy are insignificant compared to that which Lord John himself holds in reserve. Let the seeds of disunion lie interred through the present session—the crop will be richer for the repose of the fallow. Another year, and the old position of the Whigs will be gone for ever. You must then do as others have done before you—make your bold choice between abjuring your creed of moderation, and passing as Radicals to the expectant camp of Mr. Cobden, or carrying that creed into the forces that gather round the standard of Lord Derby. The brief Government which you overthrew lasted long enough to suffice for proof that a Ministry which never pledged itself to finality can comprehend the necessities of progress; that to redress grievances, conciliate classes, retrench expenditure, reform the laws, take into council Public Opinion, are not only within the power, but become the essential duty, of those who call themselves Conservatives—simply because they would preserve to their children the constitution once reverenced by the Whigs.

[1] Irish Solicitor-General.

I do not doubt the choice to which intelligence and patriotism will compel some amongst you, and those not the least eminent nor the least Liberal. And looking to your uneasy and undignified post in the present Administration, certain that all the motives which guide human conduct forbid you long to retain it—conscious that you cannot for years to come form an Administration solely from your own ranks—I foresee that fusion between the more thoughtful of the chiefs and supporters of the present Government and the leaders of the present Opposition which will terminate in the creation of such a Government as will bring all the forces of the constitution to bear upon the cure of its own diseases. With States, as with men, all that physicians can do is to assist Nature. To every political constitution is its own nature, its own idiosyncrasies. You cannot amend the abuses that have crept into an ancient monarchy by the remedies you would apply to the system of a young republic. Attempt it, and you do not cure the disease: you destroy the patient.

For myself, I stand somewhat distinct from the ordinary relations of party, and altogether remote from the interests of official ambition. The name I have assumed is so far appropriate that it is obscure to those who may yet well remember the more prominent disputants in the grand arena of old Roman politics; it is a name incidentally cited by Cicero as that of one among others who had studied the customs of his country, and might therefore be competent to suggest an occasional counsel to his fellow-citizens. I see before me a numerous and powerful party, animated by chiefs whose opinions in favour of all that can advance the cause of pure Democracy have been openly proclaimed. Amongst that party, no doubt there are some more moderate than others, some who march blindfold towards the goal which those of bolder vision see clear through the mists of faction. But all unite in the march of the caravan towards the heart of the desert; and if there be those who then discover that the fountain which allures them on is but the mirage, it will be too late to return, and it will be but destruction to pause. To that party the real sense of the country is nevertheless healthfully opposed. But what avails the sense of the country, when it is subdivided into sections who dispute on the straws which the wind will soon whirl away from their sight ? If England is to retain that empire which she owes to no natural resources, but to the various influences of a most complicated and artificial, but a most admirable and effective, social system, she must gather into one united phalanx all who hold the doctrine that England, to be safe, must be great—to continue free she must rest upon the intermediate institutions which fence round monarchy as the symbol of executive force from that suffrage of unalloyed democracy which represents the invading agencies of legislative change. Our system of policy must be opposed to all those who, by rules of arithmetic, would reduce the empire in which the sun never sets, to the isle of the Anglo-Saxon, and leave our shores without defence against a yet craftier Norman. Our measures of reform must be so framed as to gain all the purposes of good government, yet to admit under the name of reform no agency that tends by its own inevitable laws to the explosion of the machinery whose operations you pretend it will economise and quicken. By what plausible arguments were the dwellers in the Piræus admitted to vote in the Athenian Assembly ! They had fought at Salamis. What so just as that they should possess the franchise of the State they had assisted to save ? Regarded in itself, that extension of suffrage was reasonable enough; but as applied to the system of the Athenian commonwealth, all sound historians concur that it became the necessary destruction of Athens. A power was brought to play against the tendencies that preserved the good that was acquired from the greed of the fatal *something* that is yet to be obtained. In a word, those who had no stake in the soil swamped the votes of those who were its natural defenders. Hence, from that moment, arise the dictator and the demagogue—Pericles

and Cleon—the flatterer and the tyrant of mobs; hence
the rapid fluctuations, the greedy enterprises, the dominion
of the Have-nots, the ruin of the fleet, the loss of the
colonies, the Thirty Tyrants, the vain restoration of a
hollow freedom, the conquest of the Macedonian, the
adulation offered to Demetrius as to a god—licence—
corruption—servitude—dissolution.

Give the popular assembly of Great Britain up to the
controlling influence of the lowest voters in large towns,
and you have brought again a Piræus to destroy your
Athens.

But I see the sole hope for England in the union of those
men who will defend England as she is. History has
buried in the past all of the old feuds between Tories and
Whigs save that mere emulation for power which hunts
out pretexts for unsubstantial differences. Both have
now to protect from a common fate the constitution which
has been corrected and ennobled by their ancient collisions
of opinion. A manly alliance upon the broad understanding that reforms are to cement the foundation of monarchy, and not attempt the anomalous paradox of uniting
democratic institutions to a defenceless throne, would at
once give to the Whigs all that they require for the re-
sumption of their historical influence—electoral numbers
—and strengthen the liberal disposition of Lord Derby's
partisans by the accession of all that they need to make
the public fully comprehend their views—viz., colleagues
experienced in office and eloquent in debate. The
Whigs may lose that occasion; the stubborn prejudices
attached to obsolete feuds—not strong enough to resist
subordination to Aberdeen and Gladstone—may yet
induce them to reject association with men whom at
heart they more cordially approve. If so, the loss is to
themselves—their extinction will be doomed. It is the
Gladstones and the Aberdeens who will then ultimately
obtain all the ground that they forfeit. Meanwhile let
not the true Conservatives despond—let them be patient
till the storm which their opponents themselves have

invoked scatter the fleet which carries mutiny on board. All wrecks come to the shore—the shore does not go to the wrecks.

Not that I would have you suppose that Fortune is a goddess that favours the inert. They who think that it is sufficient to wait for the ripening season never reap the harvest. Sow first, and then wait. "Time," said Lord Plunket, in one of his great orations, "is represented with the hour-glass as well as with the scythe." By the one he mows down—by the other he reconstructs.

MANILIUS.

June 11, 1853.

INDEX

471

BILLING AND SONS, LIMITED, PRINTERS, GUILDFORD